THE OFFICIAL RED BOOK®

A Guide Book of

United States Paper Money

COMPLETE SOURCE FOR
HISTORY, GRADING, AND VALUES

THIRD EDITION

ARTHUR L. AND IRA S. FRIEDBERG

INTRODUCTION BY DAVID L. GANZ

Whitman
Publishing, LLC
PUBLISHING SINCE 1934

A Guide Book of

United States Paper Money

THIRD EDITION

www.whitman**books**.com

© 2011 Whitman Publishing, LLC
3101 Clairmont Road, Suite G, Atlanta, GA 30329
Material from *Paper Money of the United States,*
1st–19th ed. © 2010 Arthur L. Friedberg and Ira S. Friedberg

THE OFFICIAL RED BOOK is a trademark of Whitman Publishing, LLC.

Correspondence concerning this book may be directed to the publisher, at the address above.

ISBN: 0794832407
Printed in China

Disclaimer: Expert opinion should be sought in any significant numismatic purchase. This book is presented as a guide only. No warranty or representation of any kind is made concerning the completeness of the information presented. The authors, professional numismatists, regularly buy, sell, and sometimes hold certain of the items discussed in this book.

Caveat: The values given are subject to variation and differences of opinion. Before making decisions to buy or sell, consult the latest information. Past performance of the paper-money market or of any note or series within that market is not necessarily an indication of future performance, as the future is unknown. Such factors as changing demand, popularity, grading interpretations, strength of the overall market, and economic conditions will continue to be influences.

Advertisements within this book: Whitman Publishing, LLC, does not endorse, warrant, or guarantee any of the products or services of its advertisers. All warranties and guarantees are the sole responsibility of the advertiser.

About the front cover: The modern $100 bill is the denomination most frequently targeted by counterfeiters outside the United States. As a result, the new $100 Series of 2009 Federal Reserve Note has numerous security features, including color-shifting inks, microprinting, a 3-D security ribbon woven into the paper, a watermark portrait, an embedded security thread, and raised printing. The $2 "Lazy Deuce Note" (Series of 1875) and the $20 "Technicolor Note" (Series of 1905) are perennial favorites of collectors. *About the back cover:* The notes on the back cover are also collector favorites. Clockwise from top left: the $1,000 "Grand Watermelon Note" (Series of 1890); the $10 "Bison Note" (Series of 1901); the $5 "Silver Dollar Note" (Series of 1866); and the $5 "Indian Chief Note" (Series of 1899).

Other Whitman Publishing books on paper money include *100 Greatest American Currency Notes, A Guide Book of Southern States Currency, Modern Federal Reserve Notes,* the *Check List and Record Book of United States Paper Money,* the *Whitman Encyclopedia of U.S. Paper Money, United States Currency,* and *A Guide Book of Counterfeit Confederate Currency.*

For a complete catalog of numismatic reference books, supplies, and storage products, visit Whitman Publishing online at **www.whitmanbooks.com.**

CONTENTS

ABOUT THE AUTHORS

Arthur and Ira Friedberg have been professional numismatists for more than 30 years. Their firm, The Coin & Currency Institute, Inc., is a founding member of the elite International Association of Professional Numismatists (IAPN).

In June 2001, in Rome, Italy, Arthur Friedberg was elected president of the Association, marking the first time in the 50-year history of the organization that an American has occupied that office. He is also a life member of the American Numismatic Association and has been a member of the prestigious Professional Numismatists Guild since 1977.

Both brothers joined Coin & Currency (a family firm) after college. Arthur graduated in 1972 with a BA in history from The George Washington University in Washington, DC. He later earned an MBA from New York University, in 1976. Ira received his BS in journalism from Boston University in 1975. Within a short time they co-authored revisions of *Gold Coins of the World* (now in its eighth edition) and *Paper Money of the United States* (now in its 19th edition). They also wrote the new editions of *Appraising and Selling Your Coins*, the 24th edition of which was released in 1996, and which has more than a quarter of a million copies in print. They also published and edited the revisions to R.S. Yeoman's classics *Modern World Coins* and *Current Coins of the World*. Arthur is a contributor to the *Standard Catalog of World Coins* and has written numerous articles for *The Numismatist*, the journal of the American Numismatic Association.

Arthur Friedberg has been a consultant to the Money and Medal Programme of the Food and Agriculture Organization of the United Nations in Rome, Italy, and has testified as an expert on commemorative coin matters before the United States Senate Banking Committee. He has also been retained by advertising agencies, law firms, insurance companies, and others to provide advice on coins and on international and domestic numismatic marketing.

In 1993 the Friedbergs were awarded the Prix d'Honneur of the IAPN for *Gold Coins of the World* as the best book of the preceding year. They have also been presented the Medal of Merit of the American Numismatic Association (1992) for "distinguished service to the hobby." Arthur received the first place Heath Literary Award (1994) as author of the article judged best in *The Numismatist* during 1993, and the Swiss Vrenelli Prize (1999) for "outstanding contributions to numismatics."

David L. Ganz, the author of the introduction, is an attorney who practices with Ganz & Hollinger, PC, in New York City and with Ganz & Sivin, LLP, of Fair Lawn, New Jersey. He was the 48th president of the American Numismatic Association (1993–1995) and served as mayor of Fair Lawn from 1999 to 2005. Diverse experiences have given Ganz unique insight into our nation's paper money. As a member of the Board of Chosen Freeholders of Bergen County, New Jersey, he visited the Federal Reserve processing facility in Rutherford, New Jersey, and as a freelance writer for *Numismatic News* (weekly) he has covered the Bureau of Engraving & Printing since 1969. Ganz is the author of more than 14 books and thousands of articles since 1965, including *Smithsonian Guide to Coin Collecting*, *Profitable Coin Collecting*, and *The Official Guide to America's State Quarters* (second edition). He contributed an article to Whitman Publishing's award-winning book, *GOLD: Everything You Need to Know to Buy and Sell Today*.

CREDITS & ACKNOWLEDGMENTS

We express appreciation to the many collectors, dealers, and scholars in the field of paper money who helped in various ways with this and the first two editions:

Robert Azpiazu	David L. Ganz	Kevin Lafond	San Francisco Federal
Sandy Bashover	Martin Gengerke	Scott Lindquist	Reserve Bank
David Berg	Len Glazer	Jess Lipka	Museum
Ashley Billingsley	Stephen Goldsmith	Michael P. Marchioni	Sergio Sanchez
Q. David Bowers	Bruce R. Hagen	Marc Michaelsen	The Smithsonian
Jason Bradford	Warren S. Henderson	Allen Mincho	Institution
Lane Brunner	Peter Huntoon	Douglas Mudd	Harvey Stack
Jennifer Cangeme	Harry E. Jones	Doug Murray	Lawrence Stack
Murray Clark	Glen Jorde	Tom Nesser	Greg Stiles
Edward A. and	Donald H. Kagin	Susan Novak	David M. Sundman
Joanne Dauer	Judy Kagin	Louis Rasera	Peter Treglia
Jeff Fisher	Don C. Kelly	Fred Reed	Robin Wells

Lyn F. Knight provided notes for illustrations, including rarities. Various other contributors to the original Friedberg book are acknowledged in *Paper Money of the United States*, 19th edition.

Certain illustrations from the files of Littleton Coin Co. are used on a nonexclusive basis.

FOREWORD TO THE THIRD EDITION

Federal paper money offers a rich field for study, collecting, and enjoyment. While currency from the Civil War era to the present has been collected for a long time, in recent years the enthusiasm and interest have multiplied. This is due to a number of factors, including the presence of more useful information in print, activities of the Society of Paper Money Collectors (including *Paper Money* magazine) and the Professional Coin Dealers Association, the periodicals *Coin World's Paper Money Values* and *Bank Note Reporter*, the rise in popularity of certifying the grades of notes, increased auction activity, the annual Memphis paper money convention, and more. The publication of the first two editions of this book (in 2005 and 2008) and of *100 Greatest American Currency Notes* (Q. David Bowers and David M. Sundman), also published by Whitman, have contributed to the activity, as have the Internet and the new edition of *Paper Money of the United States* by Arthur and Ira Friedberg (Coin & Currency Institute, 2010).

Valuations in this third edition of *A Guide Book of United States Paper Money* have been compiled based on contributions from the nation's leading paper-money specialists and dealers. In general, the market for nearly all scarce and rare notes in high grades has risen since our first edition was prepared. New information has been added, and expanded coverage is given to several series. In all, this new edition should serve well both as an introduction to this fascinating field and as a useful resource.

· MICHAEL HILLEGAS ·
FIRST TREASURER OF THE U.S.

INTRODUCTION:
Collect U.S. Paper Money!
by David L. Ganz

If you aren't collecting American paper money, you should be.

Your library ought to have in it this essential book on American paper money. Encyclopedic in scope, it is lushly illustrated and filled with accurate valuations, and it contains the essential Friedberg numbering system that measures your collection's completeness and facilitates cataloging.

It also tells the fascinating story of our national monetary history from colonial times to the present, laying out in distinct format how the 12 original colonies produced their own paper currency and how a Continental Currency began and failed.

This book shows that, by the time of the adoption of the federal Constitution in 1789, there was a prohibition against anything other than gold or silver being legal tender, or money as we know it—a direct response to the hyper-inflation during the Revolutionary War.

America's experience using only gold and silver coin as money, with copper-change coinage rounding out the system, was disastrous—not least because from 1789 until the late 1840s the precious metal was always in small supply. (Indeed, all money was in short supply, with various early Mint officials unable to raise the requisite bonds to assume office.)

THE $2 BILL

The $2 denomination is an important part of American currency and its story enjoys a rich tradition in American history as a whole, dating back to the Continental Congress. The May 10, 1775, session of the Continental Congress records in its *Journals*, volume 2 (p. 103), the creation of the first federally issued money. The May 10 date of the commencement of the session is what is listed on the earliest currency notes, even though actual resolutions involved in creating the denomination were introduced June 22 and 23, 1775.

These provided that "a sum not exceeding two millions of Spanish milled dollars be emitted by the Congress in bills of Credit, for the defence [*sic*] of America," and further provided that the "number and denomination of the bills" include $1, $2, $3, $4, $5, $6, $7, $8, and $20. (Just 49,000 of the $2 notes were authorized, according to Eric P. Newman's *Early Paper Money of America*.)

The currency was not backed by anything other than the word of Congress, and it depreciated rapidly in value. "Not worth a Continental" became a catchphrase of the era, and soon paper money was eliminated, in large measure because the Constitution forbade its issuance (or so it appeared).

In the third volume of James Madison's papers (p. 1343), he though it advisable to leave in the Constitution that Congress might emit bills of credit but not have the right to make them legal tender. "Will it not be sufficient to prohibit making them a tender?" he queried.

Nearly a century later, in the midst of a civil war that had all but bankrupted the federal Treasury (which at one point had a mere three days' worth of money in all of its vaults), Treasury Secretary Salmon Chase, a staunch abolitionist, suggested issuance of Legal Tender Notes as an alternative for the cash-starved Union forces.

The measure was debated in Congress, where Representative Thaddeus Stevens of Pennsylvania was practical in his support on February 8, 1862, when he said: "I do not believe that such notes would circulate anywhere except at a ruinous discount. No notes not redeemable on demand and not made a legal tender have ever kept par. It will take the same amount of millions, with or without the legal tender, to carry on the war, except that the one would be below par and the other at par."

And so it was that the $2 Legal Tender Notes were first produced (Friedberg designs 8 and 9, F-41 and F-42), the very first one bearing the portrait of Alexander Hamilton, the second with the portrait of Thomas Jefferson engraved by James Smilie. Also on the bill: a rendering of the Capitol building in Washington. (As discussed later, the story has a constitutional dimension to it that went all the way to the U.S. Supreme Court.)

Use of the Jefferson portrait became commonplace, for it appeared as F-43 through F-60 between Series 1874 and Series 1917 on the Legal Tender Notes. It has also been used on all small-size $2 bills printed since 1928.

Throughout the 19th century, other versions of paper money utilized the $2 denomination. The Silver Certificates, backed by silver dollars deposited in the Treasury, included F-240, bearing the portrait of Civil War general Winfield Scott; while Treasury Notes of the 1890 series featured the portrait of General James B. McPherson. The Series of 1891 bore the portrait of William Windom, who served as secretary of the Treasury from 1881 to 1884 and again from 1889 to 1891.

Just after Windom's death in 1891, the Treasury Department issued what is widely referred to as the Educational Series of notes, among the most beautiful engraved currency designs ever printed. The $2 note was engraved by Charles Schlecht and G.F.C. Smillie after designs by Edwin Blashfield and Thomas Morris; the face shows allegorical figures of Science presenting Steam and Electricity to Commerce and Manufacture, while the reverse depicts portraits of inventors Robert Fulton (the steamboat) and Samuel F.B. Morse (the telegraph).

Some of these notes were no doubt utilized by Tammany Hall to purchase the votes of immigrants in the general elections. In a 1976 *COINage* interview, James Conlon, then director of the Bureau of Engraving and Printing, added, "There is the superstition associated with the bill, causing people to tear the corners—to dog-ear them."

All of this combined to give rise to the claim a generation later that the bill itself was distasteful. In no small measure, this may have contributed to the near-demise of the denomination.

In 1913, the Federal Reserve System was created under the aegis of President Woodrow Wilson, and the first Federal Reserve Bank Notes were issued with the Series of 1918, depicting (on the $2 bill) Jefferson on the face and an American battleship on the reverse. (Other Federal Reserve Notes had been issued earlier.)

Next of significance in the $2 bill's history was the 1928 size reduction—ending the era of the saddle-blanket currency and marking the use of the 2.61" by 6.14" standard dimension. Each bill is about 0.0043 inches thick.

By the start of the Kennedy administration, the bill had fallen into virtual disuse, with the 1963 and 1963A series last being printed in May 1965. The denomination was officially discontinued on August 10, 1966, because of low public demand. The cumulative total of printing was about 1.6 billion notes between 1862 and 1965. By 1966, BEP statistics suggested that about 67.6 million notes were still outstanding.

In 1969, James A. Conlon, director of the BEP, first suggested the reissue of the $2 bill as a cost-saving device. In an interview he expressed to me his belief that millions would be saved each year by a reduction of the number of $1 bills and substitution of the deuces for them.

Four years after the denomination's demise, the Coins and Medals Advisory Panel of the American Revolution Bicentennial Commission (later, Administration) made a formal recommendation on September 30, 1970, that a $2 bill be issued with a Bicentennial design.

In the early summer of 1974, Congressman Jerry Pettis (R-Cal.) introduced legislation to authorize and direct the secretary of the Treasury "to print Federal reserve notes in the denomination of $2 and bearing a design emblematic of the bicentennial of the American Revolution on the reverse and a design chosen by him [the secretary] on the obverse." In support of the move, he quoted from and reprinted in the *Congressional Record* an article that had appeared in the *Wall Street Journal*, and another that I had written in *Numismatic News Weekly*. By December of that year, the Federal Reserve commissioned a study by a group of Harvard Business School graduate students to evaluate the marketing feasibility of a newly reissued $2 bill. Completed by May 1975, the study concluded that there was no latent demand for the $2 bill but that, if it were reissued in substantial quantity, the public would use the note.

On November 3, 1975, Treasury Secretary William E. Simon announced the reissuance of the $2 bill, effective April 13, 1976—Thomas Jefferson's 233rd birthday. The obverse portrait was based on an engraving made after a contemporary Gilbert Stuart portrait; the back was based on the painting that now hangs in the Trumbull Gallery of Yale University. A larger mural version, also painted by Trumbull from the original painting, is in the Capitol rotunda.

The note differed from its predecessors in several different ways. First, it no longer promised that "The United States of America Will Pay to the Bearer on Demand Two Dollars," though it remained a legal tender for all debts, public and private.

The reverse contained a startling addition, utilizing a modification of Frederick Girsch's engraving of the Trumbull rendering of the signing of the Declaration of Independence at Philadelphia in July 1776.

Trumbull's work was first engraved more than a century ago by Girsch for use on the $100 National Bank Notes of the First Charter Period, issued between 1863 and 1875 (Friedberg 452–463). The original engraving included all 48 figures found in the original; the $2 bill contains just 42 of the patriots.

Security considerations were cited by the Treasury in 1976 when they decided to drop out six background figures, four on the left side of the engraving, two on the right side. The purpose was to leave a white area where the red- and blue-colored fibers that are found in paper money could clearly show.

"In addition," the Treasury said, "aesthetic considerations include the preference for 'fade out' treatment of subject matter in lieu of frame vignettes. Thus, a larger version of the Trumbull painting is utilized than appears on the earlier National Bank Note."

Missing on the $2 bill that had just been reissued were, from left to right, George Wythe of Virginia, William Whipple of New Hampshire, Josiah Bartlett of New Hampshire, Thomas Lynch of South Carolina, Thomas McKean of Delaware, and Philip Livingston of New York.

Of course, Trumbull's rendering was not historically accurate in the first place. There were 56 signers of the Declaration, yet only 48 appear in his representation of the scene. Of the 48, only 43 were actually signers. The others were closely tied to participation in the Second Continental Congress: George Clinton and Robert Livingston of New York; and Charles Thompson, Thomas Willing, and John Dickinson, all of Pennsylvania.

Thomas Jefferson continues to hold the distinction of being the first person to appear on both sides of a U.S. currency issue, for his portrait appears on the face, his full body on the back.

Interestingly, Jefferson was also responsible in part for Trumbull's painting. At Trumbull's request, Jefferson prepared the first rough sketch of the painting—a general blueprint of the set-up at the Philadelphia meeting hall.

THE CIVIL WAR YEARS

Absence of coin led to private bank-note issues—"broken bank notes" in today's parlance—which had as much success as the paper Continental Currency dollars. As with the latter, many banks lacked sufficient specie to back up the paper product; and despite the intricate designs and fine engraving, inevitably there were fictitious institutions as well as thinly capitalized ones.

By the time of the California gold rush, part of the precious-metal problem was solved; the remainder was resolved with Nevada silver strikes of Comstock Lode fame, but the money never flowed to the national government coffers because the coins contained their full measure of metal. A $20 gold piece contained $19.99 in gold, and a silver dollar contained $1 in its metal.

Enter the Civil War and the economic stranglehold that it created with insufficient precious coinage to finance the struggle, much less fuel the economy. Fractional pieces of paper money evolved in the interim. By 1863 the Union was nearly bankrupt, when Salmon P. Chase, secretary of the Treasury, conceived the scheme for the national government to issue paper money to finance the War Between the States.

Issuance of paper money had long been thought to be illegal by virtue of the provision in the Constitution that says—to this day—in article 1:

> Section 10. No State shall enter into any Treaty, Alliance, or Confederation; grant Letters of Marque and Reprisal; coin Money; emit Bills of Credit; make any Thing but gold and silver Coin a Tender in Payment of Debts; pass any Bill of Attainder, ex post facto Law, or Law impairing the Obligation of Contracts, or grant any Title of Nobility.

While there is no corresponding provision that prohibits Congress from making anything but gold or silver a legal tender, article 1, section 8 of the Constitution appears to limit congressional power to print paper money by virtue of a clause that gives Congress the power to "coin Money, regulate the Value thereof, and of foreign Coin, and fix the Standard of Weights and Measures," but not necessarily to "print" money, which phrase never appears in the Constitution.

Thomas Jefferson, in a famous letter to John Taylor dated November 26, 1798, wrote,

> I wish it were possible to obtain a single amendment to our Constitution. I would be willing to depend on that alone for the reduction of administration of our government to the genuine principles of its constitution; I mean an additional article, taking from the federal government the power of borrowing. I now deny their power of making money or anything else a legal tender. I know that to pay all proper expenses within the year would, in case of war, be hard on us. But not so hard as 10 wars instead of one.[1]

What the Union faced in 1862 was nothing short of financial ruin. If the records are accurate, the federal treasury held just 30 days' worth of funds and had no ready source of funds beyond customs duties and loans for which bonds were issued.

Chase's scheme worked, but no one was sure that the Supreme Court would sustain it. When Supreme Court chief justice Roger B. Taney died, President Lincoln's choice for his successor was motivated by two very real political considerations: Lincoln needed a justice who would sustain the Emancipation Proclamation, and he needed one who would approve of the legal-tender acts.

Lincoln nominated Chase—a noted abolitionist—as chief justice, but it was not until years later that the cases came to the Supreme Court. Imagine everyone's surprise when Chase wrote the majority (4-3) opinion declaring his own earlier actions as Treasury secretary unconstitutional and voiding Legal Tender Notes.

Of course, that's not the end of the story. Almost like something out of Dickens, various cases continued to be litigated. What is collectively today referred to as "the Legal Tender Cases" consists of these four:

1. *Hepburn v. Griswold*, 75 U.S. 603 (1870),[2] argued December 10, 1869, decided February 7, 1870, by vote of 4 to 3
2. *Knox v. Lee*
3. *Parker v. Davis*, 79 U.S. 457 (1871), argued February 23 and April 18, 1871, and decided May 1, 1871, by vote of 5 to 4
4. *Juilliard v. Greenman*, 110 U.S. 421 (1884)

During the time spanning these four cases, two justices of the Supreme Court retired and President Grant named their successors, and this time Chase was on the other side of a 5-4 decision whereby the nation's highest court sustained the Legal Tender Acts, paving the way for paper money to be used much as it is today.

THE BUREAU OF ENGRAVING AND PRINTING

Twenty-four hours a day, seven days per week, three hundred and fifty odd-days each year, one of the government's busiest entities that daily relates to each of us is hard at work in Washington and Fort Worth. It is not the Department of Defense, although this busy organization does occasional work for them; nor is it the White House, which often employs this agency's particularly unique talents. It isn't even the Post Office, which admittedly runs day and night, despite rain, snow, and sleet, but which would grind to a halt within days if this governmental organization were to halt work for a prolonged period of time. Neither is this mysterious agency the Federal Reserve, which works the year-round to circulate our national currency. Even the powerful Fed would be helpless without this agency.

The government agency is the Bureau of Engraving and Printing (BEP), and it functions for the executive branch of the American government in a multitude of ways.

The BEP produces all the Federal Reserve Notes in circulation, but it also manufactures more than 750 other products that include such collectible items as savings bonds, military payment certificates (used abroad by American troops in place of dollars), domestic postage stamps, food stamps, internal revenue stamps, engraved invitations used by the president for official functions, and citations used by the Department of Defense. It even produces special souvenir sheets printed on fine white stock for currency and stamp collectors (see the appendix for a discussion).

Created more than 145 years ago, the BEP began its history in the basement of the main Treasury building in Washington, D.C., with a single room and six employees. There, four women and two men separated the $1 and $2 United States notes that were, at that time, being printed for the government by private bank-note companies. For their work, each employee was paid the princely sum of $50 per month.

The BEP was destined to expand beyond one room and six employees, and by the middle of the 1870s it had expanded into the full attic and basement of the main Treasury building. A dumb-waiter was used to ferry paper to the attic, where the hand-operated printing presses were located.

These were hardly ideal conditions, and on July 1, 1880, the BEP moved to new headquarters built on the Washington Monument grounds. The new home of the BEP was large and fireproof, but it wasn't long before increased demands for currency forced additions to be built on to the structure. The dynamic American economy, constantly growing, proved to be the undoing of the red-brick building. Although expansions were added until the facility took up more than half a city block, the BEP was plainly cramped in its quarters. In 1906 the director of the BEP formally requested the Congress to consider authorizing the building of a new home for the Bureau of Engraving and Printing and related Treasury agencies.

After a good deal of argument as to the site of the new BEP, a plot of government land at 14th and C Streets, S.W., in Washington, D.C., was chosen. Work began on the building, and on February 24, 1914, the BEP began moving from the old brick building to the new headquarters, located just a few blocks away. On March 19, 1914, a flag-raising ceremony was held at the BEP, and the new building was open. It is still the preeminent building of the Bureau today.

Despite the large increase in space allotment in the new building, it was not long before the BEP was again feeling cramped. Additional currency held by the public, known as "high-powered money," rose from $3.2 billion in 1914 to $7.1 billion in 1920. Currency produced by the BEP, as ordered by the Federal Reserve, was used to meet this demand.

In the 1920s it was suggested that an annex be built for the BEP, but not until 1935 did Congress appropriate the necessary funds for work to begin. In August 1935, $2 million was initially appropriated to partially provide for the "site and construction of an additional building for the Bureau of Engraving and Printing." On May 17, 1938, the annex to the BEP, located just across the street from the main building, was opened. The buildings are connected by underground passageways.

About 30 years ago, the BEP once again outgrew its facilities and plans were initially made to construct another building to the south of the 1938 annex. It was later decided to build a satellite BEP plant in Fort Worth, the district of Congress represented by then-Speaker Jim Wright (D.-Tex.).

A posting from the Web site of the procurement division of the Bureau of Engraving and Printing announced that the BEP was conducting market research to ascertain the commercial availability of nine sheet-fed perfecting offset printing systems for both of its manufacturing facilities in the year 2000. As the government's largest contract printer, the BEP does a sizeable amount of work besides currency and postage-stamp production. So it was possible that this move was intended for other purposes. In deference to the procurement rules, inquiry was made to inquire whether it was "fair to characterize this as intended for currency production," to which the BEP responded yes.

Some 2,000 Bureau employees occupy 25 acres of floor space in two Washington, D.C., buildings flanking 14th and C Streets, S.W. Currency and stamps are designed, engraved, and printed 24 hours a day utilizing 23 high-speed presses. An additional 600 BEP employees are at the Western Currency Facility in Fort Worth, where currency is printed 24 hours a day, 5 days a week, on 12 high-speed presses.

THE BUCK STARTS HERE

Signs reading "The buck starts here," printed in green, are attached to each of the four machines that print between 8,000 and 10,000 sheets each hour containing the engraved portions of dollar bills at the multimillion-dollar Western Currency Facility of the BEP. Each sheet contains 32 notes. Twenty-four hours a day, in three shifts, the BEP's satellite plant in Fort Worth churns out dollar bills at the rate of almost a million notes an hour—nearly $24 million each day.

In fact, the BEP Fort Worth operations, which now account for about a quarter of American currency production, are gearing toward producing half the nation's paper-money needs. That will include the $1 bill—the only denomination it currently produces—and other denominations.

The presses churn out 2.3 billion notes each year, which are processed into $1.8 billion in currency that is distributed by four Federal Reserve districts: Dallas, San Francisco, Chicago, and Kansas City.

All of the BEP currency issues are produced for the Federal Reserve Board, whose member banks each pay the BEP about $30 per 1,000 notes—regardless of denomination.

Located on a 100-acre tract of former farmland, the facility is impressive in its size and scope and dwarfs the currency-printing facilities in Washington and other printing plants around the world.

In contrast to the Washington, D.C., building, which was erected when Woodrow Wilson was president and is located in the heart of the downtown, easily accessible to tourists, two fences of barbed wire ring the perimeter of Forth Worth's Western Currency Facility. A 20-yard strip between the two fences is designed to detect motion and unwanted intruders. Visitors are not sought, and the plant is not designed to accommodate them, despite the fact that the Washington printing factory is the second-most-visited attraction in the nation's capital.

Built in a modern style with extensive use of Texas pink granite and tan concrete, the style of the building is vaguely futuristic, using a triangular glass pyramid atop its entrance, similar to the Royal Canadian Mint's Winnipeg facility. Three flags fly on the flagpoles outside the building: the first for the United States, the second bearing a Lone Star for the State of Texas, and the third a green flag bearing the emblem of the Treasury Department and the year of Treasury's founding in 1789. Inside, the cool, polished marble of the lobby has set into it in metal the seal of the Treasury and the date of the BEP's birth. Even the interiors of the elevators contain pinkish Texas granite, which does not appear ostentatious but rather warm.

Above all, the BEP building is a factory, a production facility—one destined to grow in size. Its workers don't view the product as "money," but rather as high-quality paper. The views they express are similar to those held at other secure money factories. Doors to the facility opened in December 1990, production started in March 1991, and the official opening took place in April 1991. Yet, despite the finished look, at least part of the building initially consisted of unfinished dirt floors, and there is an as-yet-unbuilt factory area. When the interior renovation and expansion was completed in 1993, the facility contained 12 new presses, nine mechanical examination machines, and eight currency-overprinting processing equipment (COPE) devices. There were initially four printing presses, two mechanical examination machines, and two COPE units that take up the space equivalent to a large room in a person's home.

By 1993, some three billion notes a year were produced, each bearing the initials "FW" on the face, to the upper right of the signature of the secretary of the Treasury. After a first run that lays down the Washington engraving and the black-edge lettering, an overprinting is required for addition of the green Treasury seal and serial numbers. Signatures, which once were part of the overprinting operation, are engraved directly into printing plates that are composed of nickel and plated with chromium for longevity. The Fort Worth facility manufactures its own magnetic ink, engraves its own plates for printing, and even makes its own cleaner for inks with a solvent consisting of sulfuric acid, castor oil, and caustic soda. In fact, this largely self-contained facility is like a miniaturized city with its own water and heat sources, waste disposal, and internal police force. It has redundant systems: two separate power sources, its own cooling tower, compression pumps, and temperature control. The BEP's completely processed output (as opposed to pieces that have not been put into the COPE process) amounts to 500 million notes a year. The difference is a gap based on lack of equipment, not quality, since spoilage is only around 4.6 percent, compared with the 10 to 15 percent that is typical in a commercial operation.

Starting production of the notes in an area roughly 100 yards by 40 yards is a large, computerized intaglio press that initially produces the highly engraved black-and-white portion of the face of a dollar bill. The machine is a Delarue/Giori of America, and can spew out 8,000 to 10,000 sheets per hour. (By contrast, older equipment in Washington produces currency notes at a much slower rate, to a maximum of 8,000 notes per hour. Giori is the manufacturer of those presses.) Each sheet contains 32 notes that are positioned into four quadrants, each of which is numbered in a manner designed to make production secure, while simultaneously ensuring that errors can be traced to a particular plate. Each bill also has a unique serial number added in the COPE operations.

Plates for the currency, once produced only in Washington across the street from the BEP in the Annex Building, are now being made in Texas. Each plate lasts from 700,000 to one million impressions, and has 32 separate images on it. Since printing plates are good for up to one million passes through the currency press, there is an estimated lifetime of about 32 million $1 notes on each engraved plate.

Plate wear is first seen on Washington's right shoulder, and the assistant general manager for operations was quoted as saying that it was not uncommon for some wear to be shown on the dollar bill, progressively, before the die is taken out of service. A second press run handles the green reverse.

Loads on the press run include 20,000 sheets, valued at $640,000, before they enter the COPE separator produced by the Baumfolder Corporation of Sidney, Ohio. This separates the sheets from 32-unit large size to 16-unit sized.

These 16-unit sheets are then counted on an Uchida automatic counter into lots of 500 pieces (8,000 notes); defective sheets are replaced by star notes that are from the same district, also bearing the Fort Worth marker.

Packaging of the currency notes consists of 1,000 notes per unit, packed into a 4,000-note brick. In turn, these bricks are loaded, four per package, into a shrink-wrapped bundle of 16,000 notes weighing 40 pounds. From there, packages are removed to the vault, which was built into the interior of the facility and sized out at 19,000 square feet. Only the vault of the Federal Reserve in Baltimore is larger. Presently, the Fort Worth currency vault holds upwards of $140 million in $1 notes.

Once in the vault, the currency is transferred to the property of the Federal Reserve; the Fed makes an instant profit of more than $950 per 1,000 notes, though the issuance of each note has an effect on inflation, the money supply, and the economy.

In 1997, at a cost of 3.8 cents each, more than 9.6 billion notes worth approximately $142 billion were produced by the BEP for circulation in the Federal Reserve System. Presently it's about three times that sum. About five percent of this represents an increase in the money supply; the remaining 95 percent replaces unfit notes. At any one time, $200 million in notes may be in production.

Of total production, notes currently produced are the $1 (46 percent of production time), $2 (1 percent), $5 (9 percent), $10 (11 percent), $20 (19 percent), $50 (5 percent), and $100 (7 percent). The $100 bill is a significant foreign currency abroad, which is to say that about two-thirds of $100 bills circulate outside the United States.

The BEP's migration to offset printing production is intended, no doubt, to increase speed and efficiency in production; offset is a much easier reproductive medium than intaglio printing with its stylized and mechanistic method of production.

Under current law, the fiscal year 2000 appropriation provides, "None of the funds appropriated in this Act or otherwise available to the Department of the Treasury or the Bureau of Engraving and Printing may be used to redesign the $1 Federal Reserve note." Time will tell whether this series continues or draws to an end.

The World at Our Fingertips

Most of us use paper money for one thing and one thing only: purchasing power. It comes as a surprise to many, then, that there is a whole other world right at our fingertips: the world of *collecting* paper money as a pastime—a world of discovery and enjoyment, of art and education, of buying and selling, of color, and at times, even a world of profit. For the informed and experienced collector, sometimes substantial profit.

Paper currency today is used in every country of the world. But it wasn't always that way. In some places where coins do not exist for even the smallest transactions, foot-high bundles of paper have been seen passed from hand to hand.

Nor is paper currency something relatively new. While its modern variants date back only a few hundred years at most, we know that the first such money dates back to China in the ninth century A.D. Its issue and acceptability in China is perhaps based on unique circumstances. Where American paper money would later bear the phrase "to counterfeit is death," Chinese paper money of the ninth century circulated under different compulsion: use and accept it, or be put to death by order of the emperor himself. Versions of Chinese paper currency were used by the likes of Marco Polo following his journey along the Silk Road long before Europeans even had a concept of paper money, the Orient, or a new world in America. Since it is cheap to produce, easy to carry, and simple to identify, it is not hard to see why it's now the currency of choice for most governments.

The Bank of the United States

Among the notes of the period preceding the Civil War is the famous Bank of the United States $1,000 note. It is really just one of many broken bank notes, but because of its name, as a successor to the First Bank of the United States, its attractive design, and the fact that virtually every note one sees is a fake with the serial number "8894," it has become a popular conversation piece. Its story is a simple one. It is a replica made in the 1960s as a promotional piece. It is colored a beautifully aged yellow, is on crinkly-crisp parchment paper, and was made at least in the tens of thousands. Questions about its worth have been among the most commonly asked of dealers for more than 30 years. The answer has been and will always remain the same—nothing.

The U.S. Treasury Department's Web site picks up the story, and the history, in context. Currency notes from the Bank of the United States are something that the U.S. Treasury has seen many times. Their office receives many inquiries concerning the authenticity of these pieces. It is important to understand, first, that the Treasury Department did not issue notes intended for circulation as currency until 1862. This being the case, these notes are not obligations of the U.S. government.

A brief history of the Bank of the United States is in order. Research shows that the "first" Bank of the United States was founded in 1791 and existed until 1811; the "second" bank operated from 1816 to 1836. The U.S. government held 20 percent of the bank's stock, named five of the 25 trustees, and granted the charter to the bank.

In 1836, however, President Andrew Jackson vetoed a bill to renew the bank's charter, withdrew U.S. Treasury funds from the bank, and ceased all government involvement in the bank's operations. In 1837, the trustees of the bank secured a charter from the State of Pennsylvania, then paid the U.S. government for its outstanding interest and swapped old stock for new stock on a one-to-one share basis. The bank's name was changed to the Bank of the United States of Pennsylvania.

After 1837, the history of the bank was very rocky. On February 4, 1841, the bank closed its doors. This action left many creditors, including the London Merchant Bank, Baring Brothers, and the Rothschild family, with more than $25 million in claims, for which they were lucky to receive one-third value.

Returning to the present, because the Treasury did not issue the $1,000 Bank of the United States notes, they say that they have no way of verifying their authenticity or figuring out their value. The Treasury Department says, however, that it is likely, that bank notes with serial number 8894 are part of a series of antiqued reproductions issued in various denominations and forms for use in advertising campaigns by, notably, Cheerios breakfast cereal.

The notes this book is concerned about, from their first issue in 1861 until today, have always been worth something. In fact, the legal tender issues of the U.S. government are unique in the history of paper money in that they have never been demonetized. A three-cent note from 1862 may still be legally spent anywhere in America. Of course, since its collector's value is about a thousand times its face value, a reasonable person would not do that.

This illustrates some of the lure of collecting U.S. paper money. Add to that the notion that under close examination these notes are intricate works of art in miniature. Think of the histories told by their designs and of the tales they tell of their times. I am certain that this book will help you become more familiar with all of this, and it will help you discover the world of collecting paper money as a pastime.

How to Collect United States Paper Money

There is no single method for collecting paper money, but three rules stand out. First, collect what you can afford; second, buy in the best quality your budget allows; and, third, confine yourself at least initially to a limited area of specialization. While the first two of these should require no explanation, the third offers possibilities limited only by your own creativity. Here are some examples, which in many cases can be mixed and matched to meet your preferences:

- Type. By "type," in this case, we mean the design of the note. Most currency exists with a variety of different signatures of government officials. In a type collection you will try to find usually the nicest, but also the most common, representative for each design.

- Type of Issue. Today we are used to having only one form of U.S. currency, Federal Reserve Notes, in our wallets. As you turn through the pages to follow you will quickly see that for most of our history, this was far from the case. There were also, among others, Silver Certificates, Gold Certificates, Treasury Notes, and Legal Tender (United States) Notes. These existed in many types and many denominations. For more information on these, see the section on "Types of U.S. Currency."

  You can collect today's notes in any number of ways, including limiting yourself to star notes or to notes of only a particular Federal Reserve district.

- Seal. The green seals and serial numbers prevalent today were once in the minority. The full range of colors spans the spectrum—blue, red, yellow, gold, or brown. The seals themselves came in numerous shapes and sizes. A collection of these could be attractive and extensive. One famous wealthy collector used to enjoy displaying his collection of $500 notes, which he had arranged according to the shade of green displayed on the seal!

- Denomination. You can also collect all the note issues of a particular denomination— $2 notes, for instance. You can do this by design type, issue type, or signature combination.

- Signature. Many collectors enjoy pursuing and accumulating issues of a particular signature or signature combination.

- People. One popular collecting theme is that of particular portraits—presidents, statesmen, generals, real and allegorical women, and so on. Remember, more than the "Big Seven" (Washington, Jefferson, Lincoln, Hamilton, Jackson, Grant, and Franklin) have appeared on our nation's currency.

- Theme. Among the possibilities are Civil War generals, transportation, eagles and other animals, or vignettes highlighting scenes from American history.

- National Bank Notes. These are among the most fascinating of all, since each note bears the name of a distinct city, state, and bank. You can collect the notes of your hometown or of your ancestors, places where you have previously lived or where your family visited. Some states offer a realm of possibilities for accumulating a group of interesting city and bank names.

Use your imagination and devise your own plan. The "right" collection is the one that will bring you a lifetime of enjoyment pursuing it.

GRADING U.S. CURRENCY

Beauty, it has been said often enough, is in the eye of the beholder, a subjective decision based on individual biases and preferences. Assessing the grade, or state of preservation, of a note depends on a number of factors. In the end, grades, too, are subjective, even though they are based on certain standards (which will be explained shortly). Look at each note carefully. Check it for crispness, brightness, and depth of color. How well is it the printed area centered? Are there small folds or creases that may have been artificially suppressed? Does it look like any corners may have been repaired? Hold an older note up to the light and see if there are any pinholes.

Most notes are priced in conditions ranging from Very Good to Gem Uncirculated condition, based on these standards (from *Paper Money of the United States*, also by the authors):

Gem Uncirculated. A note that is flawless, with the same freshness, crispness, and bright color as when it was first printed. It must be perfectly centered, with full margins, and free of any marks, blemishes, or traces of handling.

Choice Uncirculated. An uncirculated note that is fresher and brighter than the norm for its particular issue. Almost as nice as Gem Uncirculated, but not quite there. Must be reasonably well centered.

Uncirculated. A note that shows no trace of circulation. It may not have perfect centering and may have one or more pinholes, counting-smudges, or other evidence of improper handling, but still retains its original crispness.

Sometimes large-size notes will be encountered that were obviously not circulated, but that have some pinholes. It was customary in the old days to spindle or pin new notes together, and that is why so many uncirculated notes may show these tiny holes. Such imperfections do not generally impair the choice appearance of a new note, and such notes are to be regarded as being in Uncirculated condition, although they generally command slightly lower prices than notes in perfect condition. (Note that some dealers and collectors prefer to substitute the term "new" for "Uncirculated" when describing paper money. The latter is more consistent with established numismatic standards and is generally recognized across various collecting subjects, and will be the term used herein.)

About Uncirculated. A bright, crisp note that appears new but upon close examination shows a trace of very light use, such as a corner fold or faint crease. About Uncirculated is a borderline condition, applied to a note that may not be quite Uncirculated, but yet is obviously better than an average Extremely Fine note. Such a note will command a price only slightly below that of a new note and is highly desirable.

Extremely Fine. A note that shows some faint evidence of circulation, although it will still be bright and will retain nearly full crispness. It may have two or three minor folds or creases but no tears or stains and no discolorations.

Very Fine. A note that has been in circulation, but not actively or for long. It still retains some crispness and is choice enough in its condition to be altogether desirable. It may show folds or creases, or some light smudges from the hands of a past generation. Sometimes Very Fine notes are the best available in certain rare issues, and they should accordingly be cherished just as much as uncirculated notes.

Fine. A note that shows evidence of much more circulation, has lost its crispness and very fine detail, and has creases that are more pronounced. The note still is not seriously soiled or stained.

Very Good. A note that has had considerable wear or circulation. It may be limp, soiled, or dark in appearance and may even have a small tear or two on an edge.

Good. A note that is badly worn, with margin or body tears, frayed margins, and missing corners.

Collectors will usually shun notes in less than Fine condition because they are often frightfully unappealing to the eye. Nonetheless, an exceptionally rare note has a ready market in even poor condition, because it may not otherwise exist, or (if it is in nicer condition) will have a price out of the reach of most collectors.

STORAGE AND CARE OF PAPER MONEY

Coin collectors who are used to a specific album already preprinted for a denomination and type will get to display a new creativity in coming up with a plan for housing a paper-money collection. There are no printed albums. Collectors today, however, are more fortunate than those of yesteryear, who would often use plain paper envelopes, scrapbooks, or makeshift albums. These provided neither security nor protection and were even harmful at times.

The most common way to store paper money today is in acetate sleeves. These offer a number of advantages. They allow both sides of the note to be seen. They are chemically inert and do not react with the paper. They are rigid enough to protect against the note's being bent or otherwise damaged, yet flexible enough to be practical. The individual sleeves may be stored in any order that pleases you and are small enough to fit conveniently into a safe-deposit box.

Another common method of storage is in loose-leaf-style vinyl pages configured for inclusion in a standard three-ring binder. However, if you choose this method it is important that your notes be placed in acetate sleeves first. The vinyl is not inert and under certain conditions can release an oil or a film that will damage anything it touches. The acetate sleeves prevent this.

TYPES OF U.S. CURRENCY

Since the federal government began printing paper money, it has produced many different kinds of currency notes. Collectors will appreciate how easily each one can be identified and evaluated with the assistance of this book. Legal Tender Notes, Demand Notes, Federal Reserve Notes, and others are all easily identified by their Friedberg numbers—a proprietary numbering system, devised by Robert Friedberg, that paper-money collectors use for easy identification of their notes.

The types of U.S. currency are listed below in the order of the first passage of the legislation authorizing them. The notes in this book are arranged by denomination in this order.

Interest Bearing Notes

Interest Bearing issues were authorized by Congress because of the financial emergencies caused by the Civil War, and are the rarest of all issues of American currency—not surprising, since they had to be turned in for the interest due on them to be collected. Nearly all were, and few are available for collectors.

The length of time for which interest on them was computed resulted in issues of 60-day, one-year, two-year, and three-year notes.

The 60-day notes were issued under the Act of March 2, 1861, and bore interest at six percent. Only proofs (no actual notes) are known of any of the three denominations: $50, $100, and $500.

The one-year notes bore interest at five percent for one year. They were issued under the Act of March 3, 1863, in seven denominations from $10 to $5,000.

The two-year notes bore interest at five percent for two years and were issued under the same act as the one-year notes, in denominations of $50, $100, $500, and $1,000.

There are three issues of three-year notes. All bore interest at 7.3 percent for a period of three years. The acts of Congress that authorized these issues are those of July 17, 1861; June 30, 1864; and March 3, 1865. They were issued in five denominations from $50 to $5,000, and the interest earned per day is stated on the notes.

An interesting feature of the Interest Bearing Notes is that they are the only issue of U.S. currency that originally had coupons attached to them. These had to be clipped and redeemed for payment at six months.

The Demand Notes of 1861

As a type, these are among the rarest off all currency issues and, in collectible condition, are out of the reach of most casual collectors. The term "greenback" owes its name to these notes, which are the first and earliest issue of U.S. currency as we have come to know it. They were issued in denominations of $5, $10, and $20, authorized by the congressional acts of July 17 and August 5, 1861. All are imprinted with the first date, "Act of July 17, 1861," as well as "Aug. 10th, 1861," probably the date of issue. Demand Notes are the only U.S. currency type to have neither the Treasury seal nor the actual names of the treasurer and the register of the Treasury. They also have the serial number printed just one time.

The first plates made for the various denominations had spaces for two signatures, and below these the words "Register of the Treasury" and "Treasurer of the United States" were engraved. Obviously, these high officials could not personally sign each note, so a clerical staff was employed to sign their names in their stead. The staff also wrote the words "For the" in addition to the own names. The impracticality of this was quickly noted and the printing plates were then changed to say "For the Register of the Treasury" and "For the Treasurer of the United States."

Legal Tender Notes (United States Notes)

There are five issues of large-size Legal Tender Notes.

First Issue. These notes are dated March 10, 1862, and were issued in all denominations from $5 to $1,000. There are two varieties in the wording on the reverse of these notes.

> *First Obligation.* Earlier issues read, "This note is a legal tender for all debts, public and private, except duties on imports and interest on the public debt, and is exchangeable for U.S. six per cent twenty year bonds, redeemable at the pleasure of the United States after five years."

> *Second Obligation.* Later issues bear this obligation, which reads, "This note is a legal tender for all debts, public and private, except duties on imports and interest on the public debt, and is receivable in payment of all loans made to the United States."

These notes are without the headings of either "Treasury Note" or "United States Note."

Second Issue. These are dated August 1, 1862. Only $1 and $2 notes were issued.

Third Issue. These are dated March 10, 1863. All denominations from $5 to $1,000 were released.

Fourth Issue. The largest and most extensive of the Legal Tender issues was printed under the Act of March 3, 1863. It included every possible denomination from $1 to $10,000 and comprised the 1869, 1874, 1878, 1880, 1907, 1917, and 1923 series.

The notes of 1869 are titled "Treasury Notes." Notes of this series are also known to collectors as "rainbow notes" because of the vivid, multicolored design on their face side. The issues from 1874 to 1923 are titled "United States notes." However, the obligation on all series is the same.

Fifth Issue. Only one note, the$10 series of 1901 (the Bison note), makes up this issue, which used as its authority the Legal Tender acts of 1862 and 1863.

Legal Tender Notes continued to be printed after the conversion to small-size currency in 1928 with $2, $50, and $100 denominations extending to the mid- to late 1960s. These are the "Red Seal" notes that prompt so many inquiries from novice collectors today.

National Bank Notes

Certainly the broadest, most diverse, and (many would argue) most interesting of all our money, National Bank Notes were issued from 1863 to 1929 by thousands of banks in every state and even in the territories. These notes had three distinct issuing authorizations, which are known as the First, Second, and Third Charter Periods. Although they look startlingly different from most other notes, they were fully legal tender and as completely negotiable as any other issue. The main design elements are the same for all banks. Variations occur only in the name of the bank, the charter number, the signatures, and the coat of arms of the state in which the bank was located.

These notes were created by the National Banking Act of 1863, followed by the Act of June 3, 1864. This allowed the government to give charters to banks that could then issue their own notes, in an amount up to 90 percent of the value of the U.S. government bonds the bank had on deposit with the Treasury as security. Each bank was given a unique charter number, which was printed on all notes issued after 1875. These charters were valid for 20 years from the time they were granted. After that time expired, the bank could renew the charter for another 20 years and keep issuing notes.

National Bank Notes are unusual in that the dates they were actually issued are not always consistent with the dates in office of those Treasury officials whose signatures appear on the notes. This is because, most likely to save time and money, the original printing plates were saved and used when needed at a later date. It was possible, then, for a note to be printed with the signatures of men long out of office, even after they had died.

Until July 1875, all National Bank Notes were printed in New York City by three private companies—the American, Continental, and National Bank Note companies—whose names appear on the notes. These did all the preparatory work, and, for a while, even used their own paper. The only task done in Washington was the overprinting of the seal and serial number. After March 1875, the special paper used for all other currency was designated for National Bank Notes as well. From then until the end of 1877, production was slowly transferred in stages until all printing of both face and back was being done at the Bureau of Engraving and Printing in Washington.

Another unique characteristic of National Bank Notes is that they have two different serial numbers. The first is the Treasury serial number; the other is the bank serial number. The former indicates the running total of such sheets (usually four notes per sheet) printed for all banks, while the latter represents the total number of sheets printed for the particular bank. After August 22, 1925, the Treasury serial number was discontinued, and instead there were two printings of the bank serial number.

National Bank Notes were usually printed in sheets of four notes, with the same serial numbers on each. The only difference besides the denomination was the addition of a "check" or "plate" letter, which indicated the note's original position on the sheet. It is normally a script capital letter from A to D, and appears twice on the face of each note. If all four notes on the sheet were of the same denomination, the letters appeared in order as A, B, C, D. If different denominations were printed on each sheet, the first note of each denomination began with the check letter A. When notes were printed in large quantities, they have check letters beyond D. In the most common printing configurations, three $1 notes were printed on a sheet with a $2 note; $5 notes were printed by themselves; $10 notes were by themselves or with a single $20 note (otherwise, $20 notes were by themselves on a sheet); $50 and $100 notes were either on a two-note sheet with one of each denomination, or on four-note sheet with one of the former and three of the latter. Other combinations, such as two-note or one-note sheets, exist, but they were not as popular with banks.

An oft-asked question is about the large capital letter (N, E, S, M, W, or P) seen on the face of some notes. From about 1902 to 1924, these letters were used to make the sorting of notes easier when they were being redeemed at the Treasury. They stand for an issuing bank's location in a region of the country, namely (in order) New England, the East, the South, the Midwest, the West, and the Pacific.

The Charter Periods of National Bank Notes

First Charter Period. Date span: February 25, 1863, to July 11, 1882. Issue Dates: 1863–1902. The notes of the First Charter Period are among the most beautiful currency ever issued, with the added bonus that each one is a lesson in American history. The faces contain one or two vignettes of either historical or allegorical themes. The backs, which are all black and green, depict famous scenes and are based on the murals that hang in the rotunda of the U.S. Capitol building.

The First Charter Period is the only one that contains the $1, $2, $500, and $1,000 denominations (the latter two exceedingly rare and, it is safe to say, impossible to obtain).

Two series of notes were issued under the First Charter Period: the "Original Series" and the Series of 1875. The notes of the Original Series were issued from 1863 to 1875 and did not bear the charter number of the bank, except in some rare instances. The Series of 1875 came into being after the Act of June 30, 1874, which mandated the charter number of the bank to be printed on all National Bank Notes.

The charter numbers were normally printed in red or blue (the latter being a bit scarcer), but a few banks issued $5 notes with the charter number printed in black and in script numerals rather than block numerals. These notes, called "Black Charters," are very rare.

Second Charter Period. Date span: July 12, 1882, to April 11, 1902. Issue dates: 1882–1922. The Second Charter Period was authorized by the Act of July 12, 1882, and notes issued under it are labeled "Series of 1882." The act came into existence because when a bank's initial charter expired, it needed to be renewed. It also allowed new banks to receive their first charter. There were three types of notes issues under the Second Charter Period:

Brown Backs. These very popular notes were first issued in 1882 by banks originally chartered in 1863 and re-chartered in 1882, and by new banks organized and chartered between July 12, 1882, and April 11, 1902. They were issued from 1882 to 1908. Stylistically, the faces of these notes resemble those of the First Charter Period; the backs are obviously brown, with the central design feature being each bank's charter number in a bluish-green hue.

Date Backs. These have a large "1882–1908" in the center panel on the green back. These are considered "emergency money," because, in order to increase the money in circulation, banks were allowed to deposit as collateral with the Treasury other types of securities besides government bonds. These were issued mostly from June 1908 to July 1916.

Value Backs. The rarest of all National Bank Notes and also an "emergency" issue. On these the denomination of the note is written out where the dates were on the preceding issue. These notes were released only from 1916 to 1922 and were issued only by those banks that had been issuing the type with "1882–1908" on back, and whose charters were still in force.

Third Charter Period. Date range: April 12, 1902, to April 11, 1922. Issue Dates: 1902–1929. Notes of the Third Charter Period, called the "Series of 1902," were issued under the Act of April 12, 1902. As were its predecessors, this act was required to renew expiring charters. This was the last charter period, since after 1922 Congress gave all National Banks permanent corporate status. There were three varieties issued:

Red seals. These were issued from 1902 to 1908, and were replaced after that by the Date Backs with blue seals for the same reason as for Date Backs under the Second Charter. These notes are the rarest of the Third Charter issues.

Blue seals with dates on back. The rationale for these is identical to that for the Date Backs of the Second Charter period but for banks which already were due for a third charter.

Blue seals without dates on back. These were issued from 1915 to 1929 and are the most frequently encountered of all National Bank Notes. They differ from the previous type by the absence of the dates "1902–1908" from the back. These notes were also the last issued before the conversion to small-size currency in 1929.

Gold Certificates

These are quite easily recognized since, instead of the usually common green reverse, all Gold Certificates are colored an intensely brilliant, golden shade of orange.

There were nine issues of Gold Certificates, but only four of these circulated. The others were primarily intended for use in bank transactions, and, with the exception of one extremely rare $20 note, all were high denominations.

The notes of the Series of 1882 were the first for regular circulation and include all denominations from $20 to $10,000.

The Series of 1905, 1906, and 1907 had only $10 and $20 issues, including what is now known as the "Technicolor Note" (Series of 1905) because of its vivid color with red seals and gold ink in the background. The most common Gold Certificates are the $50 note from the Series of 1913 and the notes of the Series of 1922, which had every denomination from $10 to $1,000.

For many years, from 1933 into the 1960s, the Treasury claimed that the Gold Certificates were illegal to own. The theory was that a series of executive orders from the Roosevelt administration made ownership of non-numismatic gold coins and all Gold Certificates illegal to own. The Treasury Department changed those regulations and their interpretation in 1964. The Treasury's Web site acknowledges some of this, presenting their own take on the matter.

Gold Certificates were withdrawn from circulation along with all gold coins and gold bullion as required by the Gold Reserve Act of 1934. Gold Certificates circulated until December 28, 1933. That is when the president ordered private owners of Gold Certificates to deliver their notes to the treasurer of the United States by midnight on January 17, 1934. It was then illegal to hold Gold Certificates. C. Douglas Dillon, the 57th secretary of the Treasury, removed the restrictions on the acquisition or holding of these notes on April 24, 1964.

Under 31 U.S.C. 5118(b) as amended, "The United States Government may not pay out any gold coin. A person lawfully holding United States coins and currency may present the coins for currency . . . for exchange (dollar for dollar) for other United States coins and currency (other than gold and silver coins) that" citizens may lawfully own. Although Gold Certificates are no longer produced and are not redeemable in gold, they still maintain their legal-tender status. You may redeem the notes you have through the Treasury Department or any financial institution. The redemption, however, will be at the face value on the note. These notes may, however, have a premium value to coin and currency collectors or dealers.

Compound Interest Treasury Notes

These were authorized by Congress in the acts of March 3, 1863, and June 30, 1864, and were issued strictly to raise money for the dual purposes of helping to finance the remaining years of the Civil War and trying to alleviate the terrible shortage of currency. Thus, these notes are really Legal Tender Notes (discussed previously), which paid interest at six percent after three years. Until redeemed, they could circulate at their face values, which were all denominations from $10 to $1,000. They were issued in denominations of $10, $20, $50, $100, $500, and $1,000, and were legal tender at their face value. The date of issue is printed in red on each note and the full interest would be paid only at the end of three years. An interesting feature of these notes is the gold overprint of the words "Compound Interest Treasury Note" and the denomination.

National Gold Bank Notes

The Act of July 12, 1870, authorized these notes as a response to the Gold Rush in California and the need of banks to efficiently manage the large number of transactions in gold that were occurring on a daily basis. What these notes did, in effect, was act as circulating currency that the bank named on the note would redeem in gold coin upon presentation.

Since these were essentially National Bank Notes, the faces are similar to those of the First Charter Period, except that the paper is tinted a golden hue. The backs all have a collage of contemporary American gold coins. Denominations issued range from $5 to $500.

All the banks were in California, with the exception of the Kidder National Gold Bank of Boston, from which no actual notes are known to exist. These notes circulated widely and are very seldom seen in better than Very Good condition.

Silver Certificates

Perhaps no other issue of American paper money has captured as much of the public's fascination and interest as have Silver Certificates. Their issues are numerous and could probably be considered the most widely collected of all our currency. All Silver Certificates issued were under the Acts of February 28, 1878, and August 4, 1886. Under these acts, there were five different issues, all of which were payable is silver dollars (much later amended to silver bullion), as follows:

First issue. The first issue, Series 1878 and 1880, had notes in denominations of $10 to $1,000. They are called "Certificates of Deposit" to indicate that the requisite silver dollars had been deposited by the government with the Treasury. These early issues do not have any green printing on their backs.

Second issue. The second issue of Silver Certificates, the Series of 1886, 1891, and 1908, had notes from $1 to $1,000.

Third issue. This issue was the famous "Educational Series" of 1896 and consisted only of $1, $2, and $5 notes. These are universally recognized as the most artistically enchanting U.S. paper money ever.

Fourth issue. The $1, $2, and $5 notes of the Series of 1899 composed the fourth issue.

Fifth issue. The fifth issue consisted only of the $1 and $5 notes of the Series of 1923.

Silver Certificates were issued as small- (current-) size notes from their inception in 1929 until they were discontinued.

On March 25, 1964, Secretary Dillon announced that Silver Certificates would no longer be redeemable in silver dollars. This decision was pursuant to the Act of June 4, 1963 (31 U.S.C. 405a-1). The act allowed the exchange of Silver Certificates for silver bullion until June 24, 1968, the deadline set by Congress. Since that date, there has been no obligation to issue silver in any form in exchange for these certificates.

Congress took this action because there were approximately 2.9 million silver dollars remaining in the Treasury Department's vaults. These coins had high numismatic values, and there was no way to make an equitable distribution of them among the many people holding Silver Certificates.

Silver Certificates are still legal tender and do still circulate at their face value. Depending upon the age and condition of the certificates, however, they may have a greater numismatic value to collectors and dealers.

Refunding Certificates

The Act of February 26, 1879, allowed the Treasury to issue these $10 Refunding Certificates. They bore interest at the rate of four percent a year with no time limit at the time of issue for the accrual of interest. This way, it was hoped, the public would hold on to them rather than turn them in. The goal was to popularize government securities with the general public, and it was felt that notes of this low denomination would do so.

In 1907, Congress stopped the interest as of July 1 of that year; by that time, the interest had more than doubled the value of the note.

There were two types issued; only one is considered collectible.

Treasury (Coin) Notes

The Legal Tender Act of July 14, 1890, authorized the secretary of the Treasury to issue these notes in payment for the Treasury Department's purchases of silver bullion. As with the Silver Certificates, discussed earlier, these notes were supported by precious metal and could be redeemed for coin, but it was up to the secretary of the Treasury whether the coin would be in gold or silver.

These notes were issued under the Series of 1890 and 1891 in denominations of $1, $2, $5, $10, $20, $50, $100, and $1,000.

Federal Reserve Bank Notes

With the creation of the Federal Reserve System by the Federal Reserve Act of December 23, 1913, two new types of currency, Federal Reserve Bank Notes and Federal Reserve Notes, were born. The Federal Reserve Bank Notes were also labeled "national currency" and were payable only at the named bank; the Federal Reserve Notes (green seals) are currency of the Federal Reserve System proper, not its individual banks.

There were two issues of Federal Reserve Bank Notes. The Series of 1915 consisted only of $5, $10, and $20 notes, which were issued only by the Federal Reserve Banks of Atlanta, Chicago, Kansas City, Dallas, and (for the $5 notes only) San Francisco.

The second issue, the Series of 1918, was authorized by the Act of April 23, 1918, and included all denominations from $1 to $50, although not every bank issued all of those denominations.

These notes gave birth to the letter and number designations for the 12 Federal Reserve Districts, which have remained unchanged to this day. They are:

1-A   Boston
2-B   New York
3-C   Philadelphia
4-D   Cleveland
5-E   Richmond
6-F   Atlanta
7-G   Chicago
8-H   St. Louis
9-I   Minneapolis
10-J   Kansas City
11-K   Dallas
12-L   San Francisco

Federal Reserve Notes

These were also issued under the Federal Reserve Act of December 23, 1913, and all denominations were issued from $5 to $10,000. The $5 to $100 notes are from the Series of 1914; all higher denominations are from the Series of 1918.

These notes were issued by the United States to all 12 Federal Reserve Banks and not by the banks themselves. They were then distributed to the member banks to be placed into circulation.

The reverses are similar to those of the Federal Reserve Bank Notes, except that the words "National Currency" and "Bank" have been removed.

Federal Reserve Notes continued with the changeover to the current small-size notes and are now the only form of U.S. currency in production. Today no denomination higher than $100 is printed.

SMALL-SIZE CURRENCY

By the 1920s, the Treasury Department was purchasing tons of the high-grade, specially prepared paper required to print currency. It was soon realized that millions of dollars could be saved if the notes were reduced in size. On July 10, 1929, the first of the current, reduced-size notes were placed in circulation. The types of notes issued were National Bank Notes (brown seals), Legal Tender Notes (red seals), Gold Certificates (gold seals), Silver Certificates (blue seals), Federal Reserve Bank Notes (brown seals), and Federal Reserve Notes (green seals).

Small-Size National Bank Notes

These were issued from July 1929 to May 1935, when the issue of National Bank Notes was halted by the Treasury recall of bonds used to secure them. The only denominations issued were $5, $10, $20, $50, and $100. There are two types for each denomination: Type One, issued from July 1929 to May 1933, has the charter number appearing two times in heavy black numerals on each note's face. The Type Two variety, issued from May 1933 to May 1935, has the charter number four times, with the additional two printed in brown ink next to the two printings of the serial number.

All are Series of 1929 with the signatures of Jones and Woods and a small brown seal. The notes also have two signatures from the issuing National Bank: those of its president and cashier.

Legal Tender Notes

The only ones issued were $1, $2, $5, and $100 notes. The $1 note was issued only in the Series of 1928 and the $100 note only in the Series of 1966, when it was printed to comply with the requirement in the Act of May 3, 1878, that the total value of United States notes outstanding be maintained at $346,681,016.

Although the $5 note was printed in the largest quantities, the $2 note is today the most commonly recognized note of these issues, perhaps because it has long been considered unlucky—or lucky, depending on who you ask.

Gold Certificates

The Great Depression ensured that this would not be a long-term issue. The Gold Reserve Act of 1933 ordered the surrender of all Gold Certificates, both large- and small-size. It was not until April 24, 1964, that the secretary of the Treasury removed all restrictions on the acquisition or holding of them, making it once again legal to collect them. Unlike their large-size counterparts, the reverses of small-size Gold Certificates are green.

Silver Certificates

The only denominations issued were $1, $5, and $10. This form of currency was abolished by the Act of June 4, 1963; and on June 24, 1968, the Treasury stopped redeeming Silver Certificates with silver bullion. Notes of the Series of 1935-A have a red "R" or "S" printed on them. These were used as control letters in a test printing of a different kind of paper. The motto "In God We Trust" appears on the reverse of $1 notes beginning with the Series of 1935-G. This series, however, appears with and without the motto.

Federal Reserve Bank Notes

All of these notes are Series of 1929 with signatures of Jones and Woods. The denominations issued were $5, $10, $20, $50, and $100. These have a larger brown seal than the one on National Bank Notes. The notes also have two signatures from the issuing Federal Reserve Bank: those of its governor and cashier deputy governor (New York), of its governor and assistant deputy governor (Chicago), or of its governor and controller (St. Louis).

Federal Reserve Notes

Federal Reserve Notes form the largest issues of our contemporary currency and are the only notes issued in today's currency system. All denominations from $1 to $10,000 have been issued, but the printing of $500 notes and above was discontinued in 1946. The wording on notes in the 1928 series says that they were "redeemable in gold." This was negated by the Gold Reserve Act of 1933 (see the earlier discussion under "Gold Certificates"), and the wording was suitably amended.

Notes Issued for Use During World War II

The shock and trauma of the Japanese attack on Pearl Harbor on December 7, 1941, inadvertently created one of the great paper-money-collecting curiosities of the 20th century: the famous brown seal notes with "HAWAII" overprint. These notes ($1 Silver Certificates and $5, $10, and $20 Federal Reserve Notes) were created because in early 1942 the danger of a Japanese invasion of the Hawaiian Islands was real. Had regular U.S. currency fallen into the invader's hands, the damage would have been incalculable. These notes, on the other hand, could have been immediately declared worthless, and for the only time since 1861, demonetized. From August 15, 1942, until October 21, 1944, no other currency could be used on the islands without special license.

Another three Silver Certificates were made in 1942 for use in the North African (and, later, Italian) invasions. These are distinguishable by a yellow seal and blue serial numbers.

Star Notes

If a note is found defective when inspected after printing, it is replaced with a "star" note—that is, a note with a star before or after the serial number. On Federal Reserve Notes, the star is placed after the serial number; on all other issues, before it. A star note is also used for the 100-millionth note in a series, since the numbering machines cannot print more than eight digits.

Star notes are indicated in the Small-Size Notes section by a (★) after the catalog number.

The use of the star on large-size notes for this purpose did not commence until 1910. Prior to that, the star was merely a part of the design, as on the Treasury Notes.

Fractional Currency

It may come as a shock to the layman that even today he can legally spend paper money with face values of 3 to 50 cents. Collectors know these items as "Fractional Currency," which (in five issues from 1862 to 1876) constituted an integral part of our currency system. As with our earliest large-size currency, these items owe their genesis to the economic turbulence created by the Civil War.

One of the side effects of the war was the hoarding of coins—not only gold and silver, but also copper. Banks and the Treasury both had suspended payments in metal, so those coins already in circulation became even more precious than their nominal value, and thus they disappeared. While those doing the hoarding were preserving their wealth, those trying to conduct business found it impossible. Merchants could not even give small change to their customers. Neither barter, locally issued scrip, nor tokens were of any long-term use. The encasing of postage stamps in a metal frame and mica face, pioneered by John Gault, remains interesting to this day, but it was of no practical effect.

On the recommendation of the U.S. Treasurer, Francis E. Spinner, Congress passed the Act of July 17, 1862, which gave postage monetary standing. The immediate effect was a disaster, as stamps were unsuitable for commerce. Next, the Treasury authorized an issue of 5¢, 10¢, 25¢, and 50¢ notes. These became known as Postage Currency, because they showed facsimiles of the contemporary 5¢ and 10¢ stamps. The four later issues were called Fractional Currency, and were authorized by another act of Congress (that of March 3, 1863). In general, all issues of Postage and Fractional Currency were receivable for all U.S. postage stamps.

In total, nearly $369 million in Fractional Currency was issued. Finally, Congress passed the acts of January 14, 1875, and April 17, 1876, authorizing the redemption of Fractional Currency in silver coins. It is estimated that not quite $2 million in all types of Fractional Currency is still outstanding.

First Issue. August 21, 1862, to May 27, 1863. These are the 5¢, 10¢, 25¢, and 50¢ "Postage Currency" notes mentioned above. Both sides were originally printed by the National Bank Note Company of New York. Later, to increase security, the government had the backs printed by the American Bank Note Company of New York, who added the "ABN" monogram to the lower right corner of the back. The notes exist with both perforated and straight edges.

Second Issue. October 10, 1863, to February 23, 1867. This issue consisted of 5¢, 10¢, 25¢, and 50¢ notes. The faces of all denominations have the bust of Washington in a bronze oval frame, but the backs each are in a different color.

Third Issue. December 5, 1864, to August 16, 1869. This issue consisted of the only 3¢ denomination and of 5¢, 10¢, 25¢, and 50¢ notes. Each has a different design.

Fourth Issue. July 14, 1869, to February 16, 1875. The notes of this issue consist of the 10¢, 15¢, 25¢, and 50¢ denominations, each of a different design. The Treasury seal appears for the first time on the Fractional Currency.

Fifteen-cent notes exist only as part of this issue. They are much scarcer than the other denominations.

Fifth Issue. February 26, 1874, to February 15, 1876. The notes of this issue consist only of 10¢, 25¢, and 50¢ denominations, each of a different design.

NOTES

1. *The Writings of Thomas Jefferson*, volume 10, pp. 64–65. Washington: The Thomas Jefferson Memorial Association, 1903.

2. The number preceding "U.S." is the volume of the *United States Reports* in which the case appears; the second number to the right of "U.S." is the page number that the case begins on.

COLLECTING $1 NOTES

Although the $1 denomination was not the first one made, it is by far the most plentiful. By virtue of its low face value and ready availability, it is the most collectible currency denomination. In fact, of all the notes printed today, from $1 to $100, $1 notes comprise about 45 percent of the total. Current Federal Reserve Notes, usually printed by all 12 Federal Reserve districts, are readily available as star notes (discussed later), and have constant changes in signature combinations as officeholders change. They are by far the easiest paper money to collect from circulation. In many ways, collecting them is analogous to the way beginning collectors started with Lincoln cents many years ago. Catch them early, though—the average life span of a $1 bill today is about 18 months!

Large-Size Notes

$1 Legal Tender Notes (United States Notes), Large-Size. Even though these were the first $1 notes issued, they did not make their appearance until the second issue of Legal Tender Notes, which consisted only of $1 and $2 denominations. Series of 1862 issues are recognizable by ornate patterns on the face: in the center, at the upper right, and most notably at the bottom right where the signatures are located (the "Patented April 23rd 1860" statement on the note refers to this design). Today these notes are encountered relatively frequently, with at least a few specimens seen at every auction. According to recent Track and Price™ data, more than 1,200 of these have been reported, with the first (F-16) being by far the most common.

The next major type, the Series of 1869 Legal Tender Note, is commonly called the "Rainbow Note." In fact, all denominations in the Series of 1869 owe this appellation to the colorful tint of their paper. The face of the $1 note features the familiar portrait of George Washington at the center, which of course remains on the $1 denomination today. More than 700 notes have been recorded, and they are available in all conditions, from Very Good up to Gem Uncirculated.

The basic Series of 1869 face design was used on all Legal Tender $1 notes from the Series of 1874 to 1917. There are five variations of the Treasury seal, multiple signature combinations, and serial numbers in either red or blue. The colorful tint of 1869 was taken off, and the back was changed. The large "X" upon which "United States of America" is engraved has resulted in this being called the "Sawhorse Reverse." Some earlier signature combinations are quite rare, but as a type, this note is fairly easy to acquire in any condition. There are more than 3,000 pieces reported of F-39 alone; the total population of the type approximately doubles that number.

The final large-size Legal Tender Note is that of the Series of 1923. This was the last issue before the changeover to small-size currency, and its design, for the most part, was retained by its more diminutive successor. Thousands of 1923 large-size notes have entered the marketplace; in low grade, it is one of the most affordable large-size notes.

$1 National Bank Notes, Original Series and Series of 1875, Large-Size. These were the only National Bank Notes issued for this denomination, and in popular nomenclature, they are referred to as "Aces." Extremely difficult to find in superior condition, they were printed on four-subject sheets, with the top three notes being of the $1 denomination and the final of the $2 denomination (F-387–F-393). These two issues are essentially the same type; the only difference is that, on the latter, the words "Series of 1875" are printed vertically in red on the left side of the note.

As with all National Bank Notes, these are primarily collected by location. More than a dozen states printed none of these notes; in at least a half-dozen other states, along with the Western territories, fewer than six banks are known to have issued them. The prices herein reflect the prices for specimens from common banks in larger states, such as New York, Ohio, or Massachusetts. As with all National Bank Notes, the rarity of a particular bank's note is as much a value factor as state of origin and grade.

$1 Silver Certificates, Large-Size. The first $1 Silver Certificate is known as the "Martha Washington Note." The wife of the nation's first president remains to this day the only non-allegorical female to be given a place on U.S. paper money. The face designs of the Series of 1886 and 1891 are similar, excepting variations in color (red or brown) and design of the Treasury seal. All nine notes in the two series are relatively common, with well over 100 notes recorded for each. The scarcest is F-220, but even this is available in the full range of conditions.

The most popular Silver Certificate—and perhaps the most popular single issue in the annals of U.S. currency—is the Series of 1896 Educational Note. Along with its $2 and $5 counterparts, it has long been recognized as the apex of artistic achievement in currency. The $1 note has a vignette, entitled "History Instructing Youth," in front of a panoramic view of Washington, D.C. To the right is a copy of the U.S. Constitution, and in wreaths around the border are the names of 23 great contributors to the American story: Longfellow, Sherman, Lincoln, Irving, Cooper, Fulton, Calhoun, Clay, Jackson, Adams, Jefferson, Washington, Franklin, Hamilton, Perry, Marshall, Webster, Morse, Hawthorne, Bancroft, Grant, Farragut, and Emerson. The reverse features portraits of George and Martha Washington also found on the faces of other notes. Values of these Educational Notes are strictly a function of popularity, not rarity; there are more than 2,200 known for F-224 alone, and close to 1,000 for F-225.

But the Series of 1896 bills, while beautiful, were problematic for banking and commerce; their intricate design, while beautiful, made them difficult to identify and more susceptible to counterfeiting. They were replaced by the Series of 1899 issues, popularly known today (for obvious reasons) as "Black Eagle" notes. Made in a dozen signature combinations, these were produced for three decades until being succeeded by the Series of 1923. Friedberg-229a is by far the rarest of the series, with a known population of just over 100. The others are relatively plentiful. With somewhere around 10,000 notes reported, the "Black Eagle" is a favorite in sales promotions.

The Series of 1923 Silver Certificate, featuring the bust of Washington, is the ancestor of our current $1 note. It was the last large-format Silver Certificate and remains available today in prodigious numbers. Only the final issue, F-239, with the signatures of Woods and Tate, has an element of scarcity to it, and that only in comparison to the other two.

$1 Treasury or Coin Notes, Large-Size. The reverse of the Treasury Notes (also called Coin Notes) of the Series of 1890 is among the most attractive examples of U.S. currency. The denomination—in this case, the word ONE—is placed in large letters against a background of lathework in shades of green. Regrettably for the art lover, the notes did not last long. Officials felt that the complicated nature of their design abetted counterfeiting rather than discouraged it, and decided a more effective deterrent would be a more open design with increased white space. This was instituted on the successor Series of 1891.

The portrait of an exquisitely bearded Edwin M. Stanton, secretary of war during the Civil War, is on the face of each of the two series. The Series of 1890 issues are much more valuable, with only one-third as many notes reported as for the Series of 1891.

$1 Federal Reserve Bank Notes, Large-Size. These Series of 1918 one-dollar notes are sometimes called "Green Eagles." Their distinguishing feature is the name of the issuing Federal Reserve Bank on the face with Washington's portrait in an oval at left. The back features an eagle clutching an American flag. They were produced in many different combinations (F-708 through F-746) and are notable because, in addition to the typical signatures of the treasurer and the register of the treasury, they bear two others: those of the governor and cashier of the issuing bank. All have the date of May 18, 1914, except those from San Francisco, which are dated May 20, 1914. They can be collected either by type, by bank, or by signature combinations. These notes exist in the thousands and more are being discovered almost daily.

Small-Size $1 Notes

$1 Legal Tender Notes, Small-Size. Sometimes called "1928 Red Seals," these are a single-issue type and were among the first small-size currency issued.. Recently they have become enormously popular, and their price has skyrocketed. A 1928 Red Seal, essentially, is a requisite item for anyone seeking to complete a type set of small-size currency.

$1 Silver Certificates, Small-Size. First issued in the Series of 1928, $1 Silver Certificates are distinguished by blue Treasury seals and arguably are the most recognized small-size currency collectibles. There are 22 different signature combinations, with the most elusive being those of Series 1928-C, D, and E. The latter, bearing the signatures of W.A. Julian and Henry Morgenthau Jr., is key to the series. Only Series of 1935 notes have the series designation printed twice on the face.

One-dollar Silver Certificates were produced for many years before being discontinued in 1963. However, they remained in circulation, and until June 1968, any bearer of a Silver Certificate was entitled to redeem it for face value in silver bullion. With the price of silver escalating, there was a mad rush by the public to redeem certificates for silver worth far more than the notes' face value. Dealers actually halted all other business to participate in this great "silver rush." In the end, untold millions of notes were redeemed at enormous profits for all involved, until June 25, 1968, after which the Treasury stopped redeeming the notes.

Among the more interesting issues of Silver Certificates are those for use in Hawaii and North Africa during World War II (F-2300 with brown Treasury seal and HAWAII overprinting, and F-2306 with a yellow seal, respectively). These have always been popular with collectors and a subject of intense curiosity when found by the general public. Other varieties of the Series of 1935-A include those with a bright red "R" or "S" printed on the face. This was a test of paper, with "R" signifying regular paper and "S" standing for special.

$1 Federal Reserve Notes, Small-Size. The era of today's small-size $1 Federal Reserve Notes with green seals began with the Series of 1963. With a few exceptions, every series was issued by all 12 Federal Reserve Banks. A frequent subject of conversation is the Series of 1963-B, with the signatures of Katherine Granahan and Joseph Barr. Their joint terms of office lasted only 28 days, leading to hoarding and speculation in the belief that these notes would be rare (they actually were made in large quantities and are still common today).

Starting with the completion of a second printing facility, a branch in Fort Worth, Texas (known as the Western (Facility), bills were produced there. See the text for a guide as to how to identify these issues.

On certain printings of the Series of 1988-A, 1993, and 1995 (F-1917, F-1920, F-1923), a test was done in which $1 notes were printed on a web-fed press that took paper from a large roll (rather than in individual sheets) and used a cylinder plate with 96 notes instead of the normal 32. This experiment lasted for eight years until it was ultimately declared a failure. See the listing for a guide to identification of these "web" notes; some from the first issue have become quite valuable.

On the pages that follow, an asterisk (*) after a number indicates a "star note"—that is, one printed to replace another made in error and then destroyed. These are always more valuable than the corresponding regular issue.

LARGE-SIZE $1 NOTES

Legal Tender Notes
Series of 1862

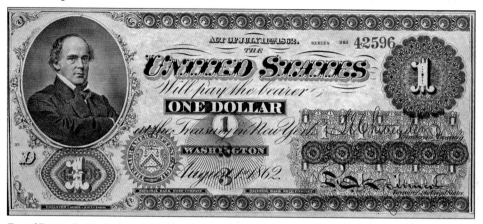

Face of F-16 to F-17b. Portrait of Treasury Secretary Salmon P. Chase. "National Bank Note Company" imprinted twice above lower border. Printed Treasury signatures of Chittenden and Spinner. "Patented April 23rd 1860" at lower left refers to the National Bank Note Co. patent for the security overprint.

Back of F-16 to F-17b.

No.		VG-8	F-12	VF-20	EF-40	Unc-63
Series of 1862, with signatures of Chittenden and Spinner and a small red seal						
F-16	National Bank Note Co. twice above lower border; left serial number over denomination	$200	$375	$650	$900	$2,250
F-16a	National Bank Note Co. twice above lower border, plus ABNCo monogram near center at right edge of face; left serial number over denomination	350	575	900	1,500	3,750
F-17	National Bank Note Co. and American Bank Note Co. above lower border; left serial number over Treasury seal	Rare	—	—	—	—
F-17a	ABNCo monogram near center at right edge of face; left serial number over denomination	210	400	700	1,000	2,350
F-17b	As above, but with ABNCo monogram added; left serial number over Treasury seal	Rare	12,000	—	—	—

Legal Tender Notes
Series of 1869

Face of F-18. Rainbow Note. Christopher Columbus making sight of land at left; portrait of Washington at center. Engraved by Albert Sealey from the painting by Gilbert Stuart.

Back of F-18, the only use of this design.

No.	Signatures		Seal	VG-8	F-12	VF-20	EF-40	Unc-63
F-18	Allison	Spinner	Large red	$300	$485	$800	$1,800	$3,400

Legal Tender Notes, *Series of 1874 to 1917*

Face of F-19 to F-39.

Back of F-19 to F-39.

No.	Series	Signatures		Seal	VG-8	F-12	VF-20	EF-40	Unc-63
F-19	1874	Allison	Spinner	Small red, rays	$140	$195	$325	$660	$1,500
F-20	1875	Allison	New	Small red, rays	125	175	275	500	1,100
F-21		Same but Series A			600	1,000	2,100	3,100	5,250
F-22		Same but Series B			1,000	1,550	2,500	3,500	7,500
F-23		Same but Series C			600	1,000	1,850	2,600	5,000
F-24		Same but Series D			600	1,000	2,850	4,250	11,000
F-25		Same but Series E			600	1,000	2,300	3,500	7,000
F-26	1875	Allison	Wyman	Small red, rays	135	180	250	450	1,035
F-27	1878	Allison	Gilfillan	Small red, rays	115	170	250	425	1,100
Large seal in place of floral ornament at right; red serial numbers									
F-28	1880	Scofield	Gilfillan	Large brown	125	175	275	435	1,000
F-29	1880	Bruce	Gilfillan	Large brown	125	175	275	435	1,000
F-30	1880	Bruce	Wyman	Large brown	125	175	275	400	950
As above, except serial numbers are blue									
F-31	1880	Rosecrans	Huston	Large red	300	525	875	1,500	3,300
F-32	1880	Rosecrans	Huston	Large brown	350	550	1,175	1,750	4,500
F-33	1880	Rosecrans	Nebeker	Large brown	375	600	1,200	1,750	4,500
Small seal is moved to left side of note; blue serial numbers									
F-34	1880	Rosecrans	Nebeker	Small red, scalloped	100	165	250	425	975
F-35	1880	Tillman	Morgan	Small red, scalloped	100	150	225	375	925
Serial numbers are red, no longer in ornamental frames									
F-36	1917	Teehee	Burke	Small red, scalloped	85	90	110	145	325
F-37	1917	Elliott	Burke	Small red, scalloped	85	90	110	145	325
F-37a	1917	Burke	Elliott (signatures reversed)		400	500	625	750	1,550
F-38	1917	Elliott	White	Small red, scalloped	85	90	115	150	325
F-39	1917	Speelman	White	Small red, scalloped	75	85	95	135	300

Legal Tender Notes
Series of 1923

Face of F-40. Portrait of Washington engraved by G.F.C. Smillie.

Back of F-40.

No.	Signatures		Seal	VG-8	F-12	VF-20	EF-40	Unc-63
F-40	Speelman	White	Small red, scalloped	$115	$150	$300	$390	$700

National Bank Notes
Original Series ("First Charter Period")

Face of F-380 to F-382. Red Treasury seal with rays. Printed by the American Bank Note Co. and National Bank Note Co., each firm doing one side. The imprint of the American Bank Note Co. is on the face of the note. The central vignette, "Concordia," by T.A. Liebler and Charles Burt, depicts two maidens before an altar, an allegorical representation of Union and Peace. Some notes of this type lack the charter number or have it printed only once. The bank officers signed in ink at the bottom.

Back of F-380 to F-382. At the left is the State Seal; at the center is "Landing of the Pilgrims," engraved by Charles Burt.

No.	Signatures		Seal	VG-8	F-12	VF-20	EF-40	Unc-63
F-380	Colby	Spinner	Red, rays	$550	$900	$1,175	$1,800	$3,700
F-381	Jeffries	Spinner	Red, rays	2,500	4,000	8,000	—	—
F-382	Allison	Spinner	Red, rays	550	900	1,200	1,800	3,700

Note: First Charter Period notes are the only National Bank Notes of the $1 denomination.

National Bank Notes
Series of 1875
("First Charter Period")

Face of F-383 to F-386. Printed at the Bureau of Engraving and Printing, this differs from the preceding in that the seal is scalloped and the words SERIES 1875 are added. The 672 represents the charter number.

Back of F-383 to F-386. Vignette "Landing of the Pilgrims" by Charles Burt.

No.	Signatures		Seal	VG-8	F-12	VF-20	EF-40	Unc-63
F-383	Allison	New	Red, scalloped	$550	$875	$1,175	$1,750	$3,500
F-384	Allison	Wyman	Red, scalloped	550	900	1,200	1,800	3,600
F-385	Allison	Gilfillan	Red, scalloped	550	900	1,225	1,850	3,700
F-386	Scofield	Gilfillan	Red, scalloped	575	950	1,350	1,950	4,000

Note: First Charter Period notes are the only National Bank Notes of the $1 denomination.

Silver Certificates
Series of 1886

Face of F-215 to F-221. "Martha Washington Note." The portrait was engraved by Charles Burt. There are four variations on the seal.

Back of F-215 to F-221.

No.	Signatures		Seal	VG-8	F-12	VF-20	EF-40	Unc-63
F-215	Rosecrans	Jordan	Small red, plain	$215	$335	$475	$675	$1,600
F-216	Rosecrans	Hyatt	Small red, plain	280	400	550	800	1,800
F-217	Rosecrans	Hyatt	Large red	225	350	485	685	1,650
F-218	Rosecrans	Huston	Large red	225	350	525	775	1,750
F-219	Rosecrans	Huston	Large brown	225	350	550	850	1,900
F-220	Rosecrans	Nebeker	Large brown	225	350	550	800	1,850
F-221	Rosecrans	Nebeker	Small red, scalloped	225	350	575	875	1,950

Silver Certificates
Series of 1891

Face of F-222 and F-223.

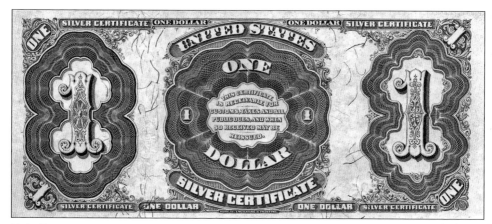

Back of F-222 and F-223.

No.	Signatures		Seal	VG-8	F-12	VF-20	EF-40	Unc-63
F-222	Rosecrans	Nebeker	Small red, scalloped	$250	$350	$500	$625	$1,275
F-223	Tillman	Morgan	Small red, scalloped	205	325	425	575	1,200

Silver Certificates
Series of 1896

Face of F-224 and F-225, the famous "Educational Note" with "History Instructing Youth." Washington, DC, is in the distance. Perhaps the most popular large-size note.

Back of F-224 and F-225, with portraits of Martha and George Washington.

No.	Signatures		Seal	VG-8	F-12	VF-20	EF-40	Unc-63
F-224	Tillman	Morgan	Small red, rays	$210	$325	$485	$900	$1,750
F-225	Bruce	Roberts	Small red, rays	225	350	485	900	1,750

Silver Certificates
Series of 1899

Face of F-226 to F-236, the popular "Black Eagle Note," with the vignette officially known as "Eagle of the Capitol." Small portraits of Lincoln and Grant are below. These were issued over a long period of years in over a dozen different varieties. The series date appears above, below, or to the right of the seal.

Back of F-226 to F-236.

No.	Signatures		Seal	VG-8	F-12	VF-20	EF-40	Unc-63
F-226	Lyons	Roberts	Blue; date above serial no.	$115	$140	$170	$230	$675
F-226a	Lyons	Roberts	Blue; date below serial no.	100	130	150	210	500
F-227	Lyons	Treat	Blue; date below serial no.	110	135	155	225	575
F-228	Vernon	Treat	Blue; date below serial no.	110	130	145	215	525
F-229	Vernon	McClung	Blue; date below serial no.	110	130	145	215	525
F-229a	Vernon	McClung	Blue; date to right of seal	875	1,750	2,850	3,900	7,900
F-230	Napier	McClung	Blue; date to right of seal	95	125	140	200	500
F-231	Napier	Thompson	Blue; date to right of seal	300	475	625	1,000	2,500
F-232	Parker	Burke	Blue; date to right of seal	85	115	135	200	485
F-233	Teehee	Burke	Blue; date to right of seal	85	110	130	195	475
F-234	Elliott	Burke	Blue; date to right of seal	85	115	135	200	485
F-235	Elliott	White	Blue; date to right of seal	85	110	130	195	475
F-236	Speelman	White	Blue; date to right of seal	85	110	130	195	475

Silver Certificates
Series of 1923

Face of F-237 to F-239, one of three different signature combinations within this type.

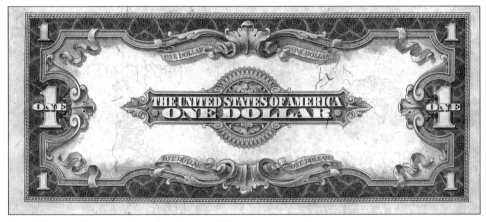

Back of F-237 to F-239, similar to the other notes of this type.

No.	Signatures		Seal	VG-8	F-12	VF-20	EF-40	Unc-63
F-237	Speelman	White	Blue	$21	$30	$45	$55	$110
F-238	Woods	White	Blue	23	35	50	60	125
F-239	Woods	Tate	Blue	120	180	300	425	950

Treasury or Coin Notes
Series of 1890

Face of F-347 to F-349. Bust of Edwin M. Stanton, Secretary of War during the Civil War. The star at the serial number is an ornament.

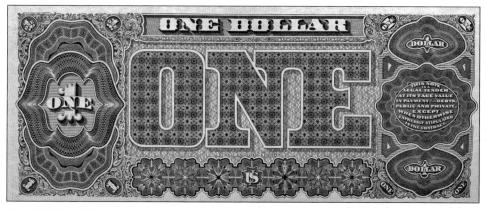

Back of F-347 to F-349, with ornate detailed features.

No.	Signatures		Seal	VG-8	F-12	VF-20	EF-40	Unc-63
F-347	Rosecrans	Huston	Large brown	$240	$475	$925	$1,950	$3,900
F-348	Rosecrans	Nebeker	Large brown	300	625	1,500	3,500	6,200
F-349	Rosecrans	Nebeker	Small red	250	475	925	1,950	3,600

Treasury or Coin Notes
Series of 1891

Face of F-350 to F-352. Same design as the preceding.

Back of F-350 to F-352. With "open," non-ornate design. On new security paper with two vertical columns of distributed fibers.

No.	Signatures		Seal	VG-8	F-12	VF-20	EF-40	Unc-63
F-350	Rosecrans	Nebeker	Small red	$175	$215	$400	$575	$1,125
F-351	Tillman	Morgan	Small red	160	250	350	525	1,025
F-352	Bruce	Roberts	Small red	175	215	400	575	1,125

Federal Reserve Bank Notes
Series of 1918

Face of F-708 to F-746. The letter B (New York district) appears in the corners and as a prefix to the serial numbers.

Back of F-708 to F-746, sometimes called the "Green Eagle Note."

No.	Issuing Bank	Treasury Signatures		Bank Signatures		VG-8	F-12	VF-20	EF-40	Unc-63
F-708	Boston	Teehee	Burke	Bullen	Morss	$90	$115	$150	$190	$425
F-709	Boston	Teehee	Burke	Willett	Morss	120	165	220	300	600
F-710	Boston	Elliott	Burke	Willett	Morss	75	85	125	190	400
F-711	New York	Teehee	Burke	Sailer	Strong	80	90	140	185	425
F-712	New York	Teehee	Burke	Hendricks	Strong	75	85	125	180	375
F-713	New York	Elliott	Burke	Hendricks	Strong	75	85	125	180	375
F-714	Philadelphia	Teehee	Burke	Hardt	Passmore	80	95	130	190	450
F-715	Philadelphia	Teehee	Burke	Dyer	Passmore	75	90	130	185	425
F-716	Philadelphia	Elliott	Burke	Dyer	Passmore	90	130	160	205	500
F-717	Philadelphia	Elliott	Burke	Dyer	Norris	75	90	130	185	425
F-718	Cleveland	Teehee	Burke	Baxter	Fancher	75	90	125	185	425
F-719	Cleveland	Teehee	Burke	Davis	Fancher	90	120	140	200	465
F-720	Cleveland	Elliott	Burke	Davis	Fancher	75	90	125	185	425
F-721	Richmond	Teehee	Burke	Keesee	Seay	85	110	140	200	450
F-722	Richmond	Elliott	Burke	Keesee	Seay	120	145	185	250	525
F-723	Atlanta	Teehee	Burke	Pike	McCord	90	120	170	250	525
F-724	Atlanta	Teehee	Burke	Bell	McCord	120	185	285	500	1,600
F-725	Atlanta	Teehee	Burke	Bell	Wellborn	110	165	210	275	600
F-726	Atlanta	Elliott	Burke	Bell	Wellborn	80	90	125	220	470
F-727	Chicago	Teehee	Burke	McCloud	McDougal	80	90	125	185	400
F-728	Chicago	Teehee	Burke	Cramer	McDougal	90	110	140	190	460
F-729	Chicago	Elliott	Burke	Cramer	McDougal	80	90	125	185	400

Chart continued on next page.

No.	Issuing Bank	Treasury Signatures		Bank Signatures		VG-8	F-12	VF-20	EF-40	Unc-63
F-730	St. Louis	Teehee	Burke	Attebery	Wells	$90	$130	$150	$210	$440
F-731	St. Louis	Teehee	Burke	Attebery	Biggs	110	160	250	375	950
F-732	St. Louis	Elliott	Burke	Attebery	Biggs	110	160	250	375	950
F-733	St. Louis	Elliott	Burke	White	Biggs	90	130	150	210	440
F-734	Minneapolis	Teehee	Burke	Cook	Wold	95	125	160	250	500
F-735	Minneapolis	Teehee	Burke	Cook	Young	150	230	550	875	1,950
F-736	Minneapolis	Elliott	Burke	Cook	Young	100	130	185	275	800
F-737	Kansas City	Teehee	Burke	Anderson	Miller	90	120	150	185	400
F-738	Kansas City	Elliott	Burke	Anderson	Miller	90	120	150	185	400
F-739	Kansas City	Elliott	Burke	Helm	Miller	90	120	150	185	400
F-740	Dallas	Teehee	Burke	Talley	Van Zandt	95	135	165	225	550
F-741	Dallas	Elliott	Burke	Talley	Van Zandt	120	250	400	625	3,800
F-742	Dallas	Elliott	Burke	Lawder	Van Zandt	100	145	180	250	700
F-743	San Francisco	Teehee	Burke	Clerk	Lynch	85	110	145	200	500
F-744	San Francisco	Teehee	Burke	Clerk	Calkins	100	140	180	325	800
F-745	San Francisco	Elliott	Burke	Clerk	Calkins	110	150	200	375	1,200
F-746	San Francisco	Elliott	Burke	Ambrose	Calkins	90	120	155	235	650

SMALL-SIZE $1 NOTES

Legal Tender Notes
Series of 1928,
Red Seal

Face of F-1500. Portrait of Washington.

Back of F-1500.

No.	Signatures	Quantity Printed	VF-20	Unc-63	No.	Signatures	Quantity Printed	VF-20	Unc-63
F-1500	Woods Woodin	1,872,012	$180	$425	F-1500★	Woods Woodin	8,000	$5,750	$25,000

Silver Certificates
Series of 1928 to 1928-E, Blue Seal

Face of F-1600 to F-1605.

Back of F-1600 to F-1605.

No.	Series	Signatures		Qty Printed	VF-20	Unc-63	No.	Series	Signatures		Qty Printed	VF-20	Unc-63
F-1600	1928	Tate	Mellon	638,296,908	$32	$85	F-1603	1928-C	Woods	Woodin	5,364,348	$225	$675
F-1600★	1928	Tate	Mellon		90	475	F-1603★	1928-C	Woods	Woodin		6,750	Rare
F-1601	1928-A	Woods	Mellon	2,267,809,500	32	70	F-1604	1928-D	Julian	Woodin	14,451,372	100	400
F-1601★	1928-A	Woods	Mellon		175	750	F-1604★	1928-D	Julian	Woodin		6,500	20,000
F-1602	1928-B	Woods	Mills	674,597,808	32	80	F-1605	1928-E	Julian	Morgenthau	3,519,324	600	2,000
F-1602★	1928-B	Woods	Mills		160	950	F-1605★	1928-E	Julian	Morgenthau		11,000	Rare

Silver Certificates
Series of 1934, Blue Seal

Face of F-1606.

Back of F-1606.

No.	Signatures		Quantity Printed	VF-20	Unc-63	No.	Signatures		Quantity Printed	VF-20	Unc-63
F-1606	Julian	Morgenthau	682,176,000	$35	$105	F-1606★	Julian	Morgenthau	7,680,000	$95	$750

Silver Certificates
Series of 1935 to 1935-G, Blue Seal, No Motto

Face of F-1607 to F-1610. Only Series 1935 has "Series 1935" twice on the face; others have the series designation only once.

Back of F-1607 to F-1610.

No.	Series	Signatures		Quantity Printed	VF-20	Unc-63
F-1607	1935	Julian	Morgenthau	1,681,552,000	$7.50	$30
F-1607★	1935	Julian	Morgenthau		75.00	650
F-1608	1935-A	Julian	Morgenthau	6,111,832,000	3.50	20
F-1608★	1935-A	Julian	Morgenthau		22.00	150
Red "R" surcharge						
F-1609	1935-A	Julian	Morgenthau	1,184,000	150.00	425
F-1609★	1935-A	Julian	Morgenthau	12,000	1,500.00	6,000
Red "S" surcharge						
F-1610	1935-A	Julian	Morgenthau	1,184,000	125.00	425
F-1610★	1935-A	Julian	Morgenthau	12,000	2,500.00	5,500

Silver Certificates
Series of 1935-A, Brown Seal, Hawaii

Face of F-2300 with HAWAII overprinted at the left and right ends and with Treasury seal and serial numbers in brown.

Back of F-2300 with large HAWAII overprint.

No.	Series	Quantity Printed	VF-20	Unc-63	No.	Series	Quantity Printed	VF-20	Unc-63
F-2300	1935-A	35,052,000	$50	$195	F-2300★	1935-A	204,000	$350	$2,500

Silver Certificates
Series of 1935-A, Yellow Seal for North Africa

Face of F-2306 with Treasury seal printed in yellow, to signify its use in the European and North African theaters of war.

Back of F-2306. The back design is the same type used on F-1607 to F-1616.

No.	Series	Quantity Printed	VF-20	Unc-63	No.	Series	Quantity Printed	VF-20	Unc-63
F-2306	1935-A	26,916,000	$60	$195	F-2306★	1935-A	144,000	$400	$3,000

Silver Certificates
Series of 1935 to 1935-G (continued from F-1610)

Detail of the top border "Wide" style (F-1613W).   *Detail of the top border "Narrow" style (F-1613N).*

No.	Series	Signatures		Quantity Printed	VF-20	Unc-63
F-1611	1935-B	Julian	Vinson	806,612,000	$3.50	$20.00
F-1611★	1935-B	Julian	Vinson		40.00	200.00
F-1612	1935-C	Julian	Snyder	3,088,108,000	3.00	20.00
F-1612★	1935-C	Julian	Snyder		20.00	60.00
F-1613W	1935-D	Clark	Snyder	4,656,968,000	3.00	15.00
F-1613W★	1935-D	Clark	Snyder		10.00	80.00
F-1613N	1935-D	Clark	Snyder		4.00	25.00
F-1613N★	1935-D	Clark	Snyder		12.50	75.00
F-1614	1935-E	Priest	Humphrey	5,134,056,000	3.00	10.00
F-1614★	1935-E	Priest	Humphrey		7.00	22.50
F-1615	1935-F	Priest	Anderson	1,173,360,000	3.00	10.00
F-1615★	1935-F	Priest	Anderson	53,200,000	7.00	20.00
No motto						
F-1616	1935-G	Smith	Dillon	194,600,000	3.50	10.00
F-1616★	1935-G	Smith	Dillon	8,640,000	12.50	60.00

Note: The Series 1935-D notes were produced with backs of two different heights, the Wide as used on earlier notes, and the Narrow type, 1/16 inch shorter than the Wide.

Silver Certificates
Series of 1935-G to 1957-B,
Blue Seal, With Motto

Face of F-1617 to F-1621.
Same as the preceding.

Back of F-1617 to F-1621
with IN GOD WE TRUST.

No.	Series	Signatures		Quantity Printed	VF-20	Unc-63
No motto						
F-1617	1935-G	Smith	Dillon	31,320,000	$4	$40
F-1617★	1935-G	Smith	Dillon	1,080,000	40	150
Motto						
F-1618	1935-H	Granahan	Dillon	30,520,000	3	15
F-1618★	1935-H	Granahan	Dillon	1,436,000	5	50
F-1619	1957	Priest	Anderson	2,609,600,000	3	13
F-1619★	1957	Priest	Anderson	307,640,000	4	25
F-1620	1957-A	Smith	Dillon	1,594,080,000	3	13
F-1620★	1957-A	Smith	Dillon	94,720,000	6	18
F-1621	1957-B	Granahan	Dillon	718,400,000	3	12
F-1621★	1957-B	Granahan	Dillon	49,280,000	4	15

Federal Reserve Notes
Series of 1963 to 1963-B,
Green Seal

Face of F-1900 to date. Beginning
with the Series of 1969, a modified
Treasury seal was used.

Back of F-1900 to date.

Series of 1963—Signatures of Granahan and Dillon

No.	Issuing Bank	Quantity Printed	VF-20	Unc-63	No.	Issuing Bank	Quantity Printed	VF-20	Unc-63
F-1900A	Boston	87,680,000		$6	F-1900G	Chicago	279,360,000		$6
F-1900A★	Boston	6,400,000	$4	9	F-1900G★	Chicago	19,840,000	$4	9
F-1900B	New York	219,200,000		6	F-1900H	St. Louis	99,840,000		6
F-1900B★	New York	15,360,000	4	9	F-1900H★	St. Louis	9,600,000	4	10
F-1900C	Philadelphia	123,680,000		6	F-1900I	Minneapolis	44,800,000		6
F-1900C★	Philadelphia	10,880,000	4	9	F-1900I★	Minneapolis	5,120,000	4	13
F-1900D	Cleveland	108,320,000		6	F-1900J	Kansas City	88,960,000		6
F-1900D★	Cleveland	8,320,000	4	9	F-1900J★	Kansas City	8,960,000	4	10
F-1900E	Richmond	159,520,000		6	F-1900K	Dallas	85,760,000		6
F-1900E★	Richmond	12,160,000	4	9	F-1900K★	Dallas	8,960,000	4	9
F-1900F	Atlanta	221,120,000		6	F-1900L	San Francisco	199,999,999		6
F-1900F★	Atlanta	19,200,000	4	9	F-1900L★	San Francisco	14,720,000	9	32

Series of 1963-A—Signatures of Granahan and Fowler

No.	Issuing Bank	Quantity Printed	VF-20	Unc-63	No.	Issuing Bank	Quantity Printed	VF-20	Unc-63
F-1901A	Boston	319,840,000		$5	F-1901G	Chicago	784,480,000		$5
F-1901A★	Boston	19,840,000	$4	10	F-1901G★	Chicago	52,640,000	$4	10
F-1901B	New York	657,600,000		5	F-1901H	St. Louis	264,000,000		5
F-1901B★	New York	47,680,000	4	10	F-1901H★	St. Louis	17,920,000	4	10
F-1901C	Philadelphia	375,520,000		5	F-1901I	Minneapolis	112,160,000		5
F-1901C★	Philadelphia	26,240,000	4	10	F-1901I★	Minneapolis	7,040,000	4	12
F-1901D	Cleveland	337,120,000		5	F-1901J	Kansas City	219,200,000		5
F-1901D★	Cleveland	21,120,000	4	10	F-1901J★	Kansas City	14,720,000	4	10
F-1901E	Richmond	532,000,000		5	F-1901K	Dallas	288,960,000		5
F-1901E★	Richmond	41,600,000	4	10	F-1901K★	Dallas	19,184,000	4	10
F-1901F	Atlanta	636,480,000		5	F-1901L	San Francisco	576,800,000		5
F-1901F★	Atlanta	40,960,000	4	10	F-1901L★	San Francisco	43,040,000	4	10

Series of 1963-B—Signatures of Granahan and Barr

No.	Issuing Bank	Quantity Printed	VF-20	Unc-63	No.	Issuing Bank	Quantity Printed	VF-20	Unc-63
F-1902B	New York	123,040,000	$2	$7.00	F-1902G★	Chicago	2,400,000	$3	$17.50
F-1902B★	New York	3,680,000	3	17.50	F-1902J	Kansas City	44,800,000	2	7.00
F-1902E	Richmond	93,600,000	2	7.00	F-1902L	San Francisco	106,400,000	2	7.00
F-1902E★	Richmond	3,200,000	3	17.50	F-1902L★	San Francisco	3,040,000	3	17.50
F-1902G	Chicago	91,040,000	2	7.00					

Federal Reserve Notes
Series of 1969 to Date, Green Seal

Series of 1969 (with new Treasury seal)—Signatures of Elston and Kennedy

No.	Issuing Bank	Quantity Printed	VF-20	Unc-63	No.	Issuing Bank	Quantity Printed	VF-20	Unc-63
F-1903A	Boston	99,200,000		$6	F-1903G	Chicago	359,520,000		$6
F-1903A★	Boston	5,120,000	$3	9	F-1903G★	Chicago	12,160,000	$3	9
F-1903B	New York	269,120,000		6	F-1903H	St. Louis	74,880,000		6
F-1903B★	New York	14,080,000	3	9	F-1903H★	St. Louis	3,840,000	3	9
F-1903C	Philadelphia	68,480,000		6	F-1903I	Minneapolis	48,000,000		6
F-1903C★	Philadelphia	3,776,000	3	9	F-1903I★	Minneapolis	1,920,000	6	18
F-1903D	Cleveland	120,480,000		6	F-1903J	Kansas City	95,360,000		6
F-1903D★	Cleveland	5,760,000	3	9	F-1903J★	Kansas City	5,760,000	3	9
F-1903E	Richmond	250,560,000		6	F-1903K	Dallas	113,440,000		6
F-1903E★	Richmond	10,880,000	3	9	F-1903K★	Dallas	5,120,000	3	9
F-1903F	Atlanta	185,120,000		6	F-1903L	San Francisco	226,240,000		6
F-1903F★	Atlanta	7,680,000	3	9	F-1903L★	San Francisco	9,600,000	3	9

Series of 1969-A—Signatures of Kabis and Kennedy

No.	Issuing Bank	Quantity Printed	VF-20	Unc-63	No.	Issuing Bank	Quantity Printed	VF-20	Unc-63
F-1904A	Boston	40,480,000		$5.00	F-1904G	Chicago	75,680,000		$5.00
F-1904A★	Boston	1,120,000	$3	7.50	F-1904G★	Chicago	4,480,000	$3	7.50
F-1904B	New York	122,400,000		5.00	F-1904H	St. Louis	41,420,000		5.00
F-1904B★	New York	6,240,000	3	7.50	F-1904H★	St. Louis	1,280,000	3	9.00
F-1904C	Philadelphia	44,960,000		5.00	F-1904I	Minneapolis	21,760,000		5.00
F-1904C★	Philadelphia	1,760,000	3	7.50	F-1904I★	Minneapolis	640,000	7	25.00
F-1904D	Cleveland	30,080,000		5.00	F-1904J	Kansas City	40,480,000		5.00
F-1904D★	Cleveland	1,280,000	3	7.50	F-1904J★	Kansas City	1,120,000	5	12.00
F-1904E	Richmond	66,080,000		5.00	F-1904K	Dallas	27,520,000		5.00
F-1904E★	Richmond	3,200,000	3	7.50	F-1904L	San Francisco	51,840,000		5.00
F-1904F	Atlanta	70,560,000		5.00	F-1904L★	San Francisco	3,840,000	3	7.50
F-1904F★	Atlanta	2,400,000	3	7.50					

Series of 1969-B—Signatures of Kabis and Connally

No.	Issuing Bank	Quantity Printed	VF-20	Unc-63	No.	Issuing Bank	Quantity Printed	VF-20	Unc-63
F-1905A	Boston	94,720,000		$5	F-1905G	Chicago	204,480,000		$5
F-1905A★	Boston	1,920,000	$3	9	F-1905G★	Chicago	4,480,000	$3	9
F-1905B	New York	329,440,000		5	F-1905H	St. Louis	59,520,000		5
F-1905B★	New York	7,040,000	3	9	F-1905H★	St. Louis	1,920,000	3	9
F-1905C	Philadelphia	133,280,000		5	F-1905I	Minneapolis	33,920,000		5
F-1905C★	Philadelphia	3,200,000	3	9	F-1905I★	Minneapolis	640,000	7	25
F-1905D	Cleveland	91,520,000		5	F-1905J	Kansas City	67,200,000		5
F-1905D★	Cleveland	4,480,000	3	9	F-1905J★	Kansas City	2,560,000	3	9
F-1905E	Richmond	180,000,000		5	F-1905K	Dallas	116,640,000		5
F-1905E★	Richmond	3,840,000	3	9	F-1905K★	Dallas	5,120,000	3	9
F-1905F	Atlanta	200,000,000		5	F-1905L	San Francisco	208,960,000		5
F-1905F★	Atlanta	3,840,000	3	9	F-1905L★	San Francisco	5,760,000	3	9

Series of 1969-C—Signatures of Banuelos and Connally

No.	Issuing Bank	Quantity Printed	VF-20	Unc-63	No.	Issuing Bank	Quantity Printed	VF-20	Unc-63
F-1906B	New York	49,920,000		$6	F-1906H★	St. Louis	640,000	$5	$25
F-1906D	Cleveland	15,520,000		6	F-1906I	Minneapolis	25,600,000		6
F-1906D★	Cleveland	480,000	$12	25	F-1906I★	Minneapolis	640,000	5	30
F-1906E	Richmond	61,600,000		6	F-1906J	Kansas City	38,560,000		6
F-1906E★	Richmond	480,000	5	35	F-1906J★	Kansas City	1,120,000	5	25
F-1906F	Atlanta	60,960,000		6	F-1906K	Dallas	29,440,000		6
F-1906F★	Atlanta	3,680,000	5	25	F-1906K★	Dallas	640,000	12	35
F-1906G	Chicago	137,120,000		6	F-1906L	San Francisco	101,280,000		6
F-1906G★	Chicago	1,748,000	5	25	F-1906L★	San Francisco	2,400,000	50	180
F-1906H	St. Louis	23,680,000		6					

Series of 1969-D—Signatures of Banuelos and Shultz

No.	Issuing Bank	Quantity Printed	VF-20	Unc-63	No.	Issuing Bank	Quantity Printed	VF-20	Unc-63
F-1907A	Boston	187,040,000		$6.50	F-1907G	Chicago	378,080,000		$6.50
F-1907A★	Boston	1,120,000	$3	14.00	F-1907G★	Chicago	5,270,000	$3	10.00
F-1907B	New York	468,480,000		6.50	F-1907H	St. Louis	168,480,000		6.50
F-1907B★	New York	4,480,000	3	10.00	F-1907H★	St. Louis	1,760,000	3	12.00
F-1907C	Philadelphia	218,560,000		6.50	F-1907I	Minneapolis	83,200,000		6.50
F-1907C★	Philadelphia	4,320,000	3	10.00	F-1907J	Kansas City	185,760,000		6.50
F-1907D	Cleveland	161,440,000		6.50	F-1907J★	Kansas City	3,040,000	3	10.00
F-1907D★	Cleveland	2,400,000	3	10.00	F-1907K	Dallas	158,240,000		6.50
F-1907E	Richmond	374,240,000		6.50	F-1907K★	Dallas	6,240,000	3	10.00
F-1907E★	Richmond	8,480,000	3	10.00	F-1907L	San Francisco	400,640,000		6.50
F-1907F	Atlanta	377,440,000		6.50	F-1907L★	San Francisco	6,400,000	3	10.00
F-1907F★	Atlanta	5,280,000	3	10.00					

Series of 1974—Signatures of Neff and Simon

No.	Issuing Bank	Quantity Printed	VF-20	Unc-63	No.	Issuing Bank	Quantity Printed	VF-20	Unc-63
F-1908A	Boston	269,760,000		$5	F-1908G	Chicago	473,600,000		$5
F-1908A★	Boston	2,400,000	$3	9	F-1908G★	Chicago	4,992,000	$3.00	9
F-1908B	New York	740,320,000		5	F-1908H	St. Louis	291,520,000		5
F-1908B★	New York	8,800,000	3	9	F-1908H★	St. Louis	2,880,000	3.00	12
F-1908C	Philadelphia	308,800,000		5	F-1908I	Minneapolis	144,160,000		5
F-1908C★	Philadelphia	1,600,000	3	20	F-1908I★	Minneapolis	480,000	17.50	35
F-1908D	Cleveland	240,960,000		5	F-1908J	Kansas City	223,520,000		5
F-1908D★	Cleveland	960,000	13	25	F-1908J★	Kansas City	2,144,000	3.00	10
F-1908E	Richmond	644,000,000		5	F-1908K	Dallas	330,560,000		5
F-1908E★	Richmond	4,960,000	3	9	F-1908K★	Dallas	1,216,000	3.00	10
F-1908F	Atlanta	599,680,000		5	F-1908L	San Francisco	736,960,000		5
F-1908F★	Atlanta	5,632,000	3	9	F-1908L★	San Francisco	3,520,000	3.00	9

Series of 1977—Signatures of Morton and Blumenthal

No.	Issuing Bank	Quantity Printed	VF-20	Unc-63	No.	Issuing Bank	Quantity Printed	VF-20	Unc-63
F-1909A	Boston	188,160,000		$5	F-1909G	Chicago	615,680,000		$5
F-1909A★	Boston	3,072,000	$8	20	F-1909G★	Chicago	9,472,000	$3	8
F-1909B	New York	635,520,000		5	F-1909H	St. Louis	199,680,000		5
F-1909B★	New York	10,112,000	3	8	F-1909H★	St. Louis	2,048,000	3	8
F-1909C	Philadelphia	216,960,000		5	F-1909I	Minneapolis	115,200,000		5
F-1909C★	Philadelphia	4,480,000	3	8	F-1909I★	Minneapolis	2,944,000	3	8
F-1909D	Cleveland	213,120,000		5	F-1909J	Kansas City	223,360,000		5
F-1909D★	Cleveland	3,328,000	3	8	F-1909J★	Kansas City	3,840,000	3	8
F-1909E	Richmond	418,560,000		5	F-1909K	Dallas	289,280,000		5
F-1909E★	Richmond	6,400,000	3	8	F-1909K★	Dallas	4,608,000	3	8
F-1909F	Atlanta	565,120,000		5	F-1909L	San Francisco	516,480,000		5
F-1909F★	Atlanta	8,960,000	3	8	F-1909L★	San Francisco	8,320,000	3	8

Series of 1977-A—Signatures of Morton and Miller

No.	Issuing Bank	Quantity Printed	VF-20	Unc-63	No.	Issuing Bank	Quantity Printed	VF-20	Unc-63
F-1910A	Boston	204,800,000		$5	F-1910G	Chicago	250,680,000		$5
F-1910A★	Boston	2,432,000	$3.50	25	F-1910G★	Chicago	2,560,000	$3.50	8
F-1910B	New York	592,000,000		5	F-1910H	St. Louis	103,680,000		5
F-1910B★	New York	9,472,000	3.50	8	F-1910H★	St. Louis	1,664,000	3.50	8
F-1910C	Philadelphia	196,480,000		5	F-1910I	Minneapolis	38,400,000		5
F-1910C★	Philadelphia	2,688,000	3.50	8	F-1910I★	Minneapolis	384,000	3.50	8
F-1910D	Cleveland	174,720,000		5	F-1910J	Kansas City	266,880,000		5
F-1910D★	Cleveland	2,560,000	3.50	8	F-1910J★	Kansas City	4,864,000	3.50	8
F-1910E	Richmond	377,600,000		5	F-1910K	Dallas	313,600,000		5
F-1910E★	Richmond	6,400,000	3.50	8	F-1910K★	Dallas	6,016,000	3.50	8
F-1910F	Atlanta	396,160,000		5	F-1910L	San Francisco	432,280,000		5
F-1910F★	Atlanta	5,376,000	3.50	8	F-1910L★	San Francisco	5,888,000	3.50	8

Series of 1981—Signatures of Buchanan and Regan

No.	Issuing Bank	Quantity Printed	VF-20	Unc-63	No.	Issuing Bank	Quantity Printed	VF-20	Unc-63
F-1911A	Boston	308,480,000		$5	F-1911G	Chicago	629,760,000		$5
F-1911A★	Boston	3,200,000	$5.00	12	F-1911G★	Chicago	5,184,000	$5.00	16
F-1911B	New York	963,840,000		5	F-1911H	St. Louis	163,840,000		5
F-1911B★	New York	11,776,000	5.00	12	F-1911H★	St. Louis	1,056,000	7.50	12
F-1911C	Philadelphia	359,680,000		5	F-1911I	Minneapolis	105,600,000		5
F-1911C★	Philadelphia	1,536,000	5.00	140	F-1911I★	Minneapolis	1,152,000	7.50	12
F-1911D	Cleveland	295,680,000		5	F-1911J	Kansas City	302,080,000		5
F-1911D★	Cleveland	1,792,000	7.50	12	F-1911J★	Kansas City	3,216,000	5.00	12
F-1911E	Richmond	603,520,000		5	F-1911K	Dallas	385,920,000		5
F-1911E★	Richmond	3,840,000	5.00	16	F-1911K★	Dallas	1,920,000	5.00	16
F-1911F	Atlanta	741,760,000		5	F-1911L	San Francisco	677,760,000		5
F-1911F★	Atlanta	3,200,000	5.00	16	F-1911L★	San Francisco	4,992,000	5.00	12

Series of 1981-A—Signatures of Ortega and Regan

No.	Issuing Bank	Quantity Printed	VF-20	Unc-63	No.	Issuing Bank	Quantity Printed	VF-20	Unc-63
F-1912A	Boston	204,800,000		$5.00	F-1912G★	Chicago	3,200,000	$5	$17.50
F-1912B	New York	537,600,000		5.00	F-1912H	St. Louis	182,400,000		5.00
F-1912B★	New York	9,216,000	$5	17.50	F-1912I	Minneapolis	122,400,000		5.00
F-1912C	Philadelphia	99,200,000		5.00	F-1912J	Kansas City	176,000,000		5.00
F-1912D	Cleveland	188,800,000		5.00	F-1912K	Dallas	188,800,000		5.00
F-1912E	Richmond	441,600,000		5.00	F-1912K★	Dallas	3,200,000	225	1,150.00
F-1912E★	Richmond	6,400,000	5	17.50	F-1912L	San Francisco	659,600,000		5.00
F-1912F	Atlanta	483,200,000		5.00	F-1912L★	San Francisco	3,200,000	5	17.50
F-1912G	Chicago	482,000,000		5.00					

Series of 1985—Signatures of Ortega and Baker

No.	Issuing Bank	Quantity Printed	VF-20	Unc-63	No.	Issuing Bank	Quantity Printed	VF-20	Unc-63
F-1913A	Boston	553,600,000		$5.00	F-1913H	St. Louis	400,000,000		$5.00
F-1913B	New York	1,795,200,000		5.00	F-1913H★	St. Louis	640,000	$375	1,150.00
F-1913C	Philadelphia	422,400,000		5.00	F-1913I	Minneapolis	246,400,000		5.00
F-1913D	Cleveland	636,800,000		5.00	F-1913I★	Minneapolis	3,200,000	6	13.50
F-1913E	Richmond	1,190,400,000		5.00	F-1913J	Kansas City	390,400,000		5.00
F-1913E★	Richmond	6,400,000	$6	13.50	F-1913K	Dallas	697,600,000		5.00
F-1913F	Atlanta	1,414,400,000		5.00	F-1913K★	Dallas	3,200,000	5	12.00
F-1913G	Chicago	1,190,400,000		5.00	F-1913L	San Francisco	1,881,600,000		5.00
F-1913G★	Chicago	5,120,000	5	12.00	F-1913L★	San Francisco	9,600,000	5	12.00

Series of 1988—Signatures of Ortega and Brady

No.	Issuing Bank	Quantity Printed	VF-20	Unc-63	No.	Issuing Bank	Quantity Printed	VF-20	Unc-63
F-1914A	Boston	214,400,000		$8	F-1914G	Chicago	416,400,000		$8
F-1914A★	Boston	3,200,000		20	F-1914H	St. Louis	396,800,000		8
F-1914B	New York	921,600,000		8	F-1914I	Minneapolis	246,400,000		8
F-1914B★	New York	2,560,000		18	F-1914J	Kansas City	390,400,000		8
F-1914C	Philadelphia	96,000,000		8	F-1914J★	Kansas City	3,200,000		18
F-1914D	Cleveland	195,200,000		8	F-1914K	Dallas	80,000,000		8
F-1914E	Richmond	728,800,000		8	F-1914K★	Dallas	1,248,000		30
F-1914E★	Richmond	2,688,000		18	F-1914L	San Francisco	585,600,000		8
F-1914F	Atlanta	390,400,000		8	F-1914L★	San Francisco	3,200,000		18
F-1914F★	Atlanta	3,840,000	$325	1,325					

Series of 1988-A—Signatures of Villalpando and Brady
Printed in Washington, DC, on sheet-fed presses

No.	Issuing Bank	Quantity Printed	VF-20	Unc-63	No.	Issuing Bank	Quantity Printed	VF-20	Unc-63
F-1915A	Boston	582,400,000		$5	F-1915G	Chicago	1,728,000,000		$5
F-1915B	New York	2,161,344,000		5	F-1915G★	Chicago	19,200,000	$6	15
F-1915B★	New York	12,800,000	$3	9	F-1915H	St. Louis	410,400,000		5
F-1915C	Philadelphia	472,320,000		5	F-1915H★	St. Louis	3,200,000	7	20
F-1915D	Cleveland	454,400,000		5	F-1915I	Minneapolis	76,800,000		5
F-1915D★	Cleveland	6,400,000	3	9	F-1915I★	Minneapolis	5,760,000	6	15
F-1915E	Richmond	1,593,600,000		5	F-1915J	Kansas City	96,000,000		5
F-1915E★	Richmond	10,880,000	3	9	F-1915K	Dallas	211,200,000		5
F-1915F	Atlanta	1,747,200,000		5	F-1915L	San Francisco	280,600,000		5
F-1915F★	Atlanta	12,800,000	3	9					

Series of 1988-A—Signatures of Villalpando and Brady
Printed at the Western Facility (Fort Worth, Texas)

Face of F-1916 and later notes printed at the Western Facility in Fort Worth, Texas. These may be identified by a small "FW" on the right of the face, adjacent on the left to the plate letter and number. Back (not shown) features minor changes including new location of back plate number in the field to the lower right of the motto (on earlier issues the number was at the inside border below the lower right corner of the E in ONE).

No.	Issuing Bank	Quantity Printed	VF-20	Unc-63	No.	Issuing Bank	Quantity Printed	VF-20	Unc-63
F-1916F	Atlanta	533,000,000		$5	F-1916J	Kansas City	300,800,000		$5
F-1916G	Chicago	748,800,000		5	F-1916K	Dallas	761,000,000		5
F-1916G★	Chicago	6,400,000	$3	10	F-1916K★	Dallas	3,200,000	$3	10
F-1916H	St. Louis	326,400,000		5	F-1916L	San Francisco	2,009,600,000		5
F-1916I	Minneapolis	844,800,000		5	F-1916L★	San Francisco	19,200,000	3	10
F-1916I★	Minneapolis	7,680,000	7	15					

Series of 1988-A—Signatures of Villalpando and Brady
Printed in Washington, DC, on web-fed presses

Back of F-1917 and later web-fed issues. Notes printed by this method may
be identified by the absence of the check letter-number on the face (not shown)
and the placement of a check number only (no letter) on the back, to the right
of "In God We Trust."

No.	Issuing Bank	Quantity Printed	VF-20	Unc-63	No.	Issuing Bank	Quantity Printed	VF-20	Unc-63
F-1917A	Boston	64,000,000				Block FM		$45	$110
	Blocks AE, AF, AG		$15	$35		Block FN		350	800
F-1917B	New York	1,920,000				Block FU		65	125
	Block BL		300	1,200		Block FV		15	35
F-1917C	Philadelphia	12,800,000			F-1917F★	Atlanta	640,000	500	1,150
	Block CA		15	35	F-1917G	Chicago	19,200,000		
F-1917E	Richmond	38,400,000				Block GP		50	150
	Blocks EI, EK		15	35		Block GQ		75	175
F-1917F	Atlanta	89,600,000							
	Block FL		90	180					

Series of 1993—Signatures of Withrow and Bentsen
Printed in Washington, DC, on sheet-fed presses

No.	Issuing Bank	Quantity Printed	VF-20	Unc-63	No.	Issuing Bank	Quantity Printed	VF-20	Unc-63
F-1918A	Boston	140,800,000		$4.50	F-1918E	Richmond	524,800,000		$4.50
F-1918B	New York	716,800,000		4.50	F-1918F	Atlanta	787,200,000		4.50
F-1918B★	New York	2,240,000	$4	9.00	F-1918F★	Atlanta	16,000,000	$4	9.00
F-1918C	Philadelphia	70,400,000		4.50	F-1918G	Chicago	96,000,000		4.50
F-1918C★	Philadelphia	640,000	40	175.00	F-1918H	St. Louis	76,800,000		4.50
F-1918D	Cleveland	108,800,000		4.50	F-1918L	San Francisco	128,000,000		4.50

Series of 1993—Signatures of Withrow and Bentsen
Printed at the Western Facility (Fort Worth, Texas)

No.	Issuing Bank	Quantity Printed	VF-20	Unc-63	No.	Issuing Bank	Quantity Printed	VF-20	Unc-63
F-1919G	Chicago	646,400,000		$4.50	F-1919K	Dallas	620,800,000		$4.50
F-1919G★	Chicago	8,960,000	$3	9.00	F-1919K★	Dallas	19,200,000	$3	9.00
F-1919H	St. Louis	121,600,000		4.50	F-1919L	San Francisco	1,171,200,000		4.50
F-1919I	Minneapolis	25,600,000	20	150.00					

Series of 1993—Signatures of Withrow and Bentsen
Printed in Washington, DC, on web-fed presses

No.	Issuing Bank	Quantity Printed	VF-20	Unc-63	No.	Issuing Bank	Quantity Printed	VF-20	Unc-63
F-1920B	New York	12,800,000			F-1920C	Philadelphia	12,800,000		
	Block BH		$8	$20		Block CA		$8	$20

Series of 1995—Signatures of Withrow and Rubin
Printed in Washington, DC, on sheet-fed presses

No.	Issuing Bank	Quantity Printed	Unc-63	No.	Issuing Bank	Quantity Printed	Unc-63
F-1921A	Boston	1,134,745,600	$3.50	F-1921E★	Richmond	7,040,000	$6.50
F-1921A★	Boston	12,160,000	6.50	F-1921F	Atlanta	1,279,360,000	3.50
F-1921B	New York	2,062,080,000	3.50	F-1921F★	Atlanta	19,840,000	6.50
F-1921B★	New York	9,600,000	6.50	F-1921G	Chicago	38,400,000	3.50
F-1921C	Philadelphia	428,800,000	3.50	F-1921H	St. Louis	76,800,000	3.50
F-1921C★	Philadelphia	9,600,000	6.50	F-1921I	Minneapolis	160,000	30.00
F-1921D	Cleveland	1,452,800,000	3.50	F-1921J	Kansas City	83,200,000	3.50
F-1921D★	Cleveland	7,040,000	6.50	F-1921L	San Francisco	44,800,000	3.50
F-1921E	Richmond	1,831,400,000	3.50	F-1921L★	San Francisco		6.50

Series of 1995—Signatures of Withrow and Rubin
Printed at the Western Facility (Fort Worth, Texas)

No.	Issuing Bank	Quantity Printed	VF-20	Unc-63	No.	Issuing Bank	Quantity Printed	VF-20	Unc-63
F-1922C	Philadelphia	76,800,000		$3.50	F-1922I	Minneapolis	1,310,720,000		$3.50
F-1922C★	Philadelphia	3,200,000		6.00	F-1922I★	Minneapolis	14,080,000		6.00
F-1922D	Cleveland	134,400,000		3.50	F-1922J	Kansas City	262,400,000		3.50
F-1922F	Atlanta	452,480,000		3.50	F-1922J★	Kansas City	6,400,000		6.00
F-1922F★	Atlanta	3,584,000		6.00	F-1922K	Dallas	1,273,600,000		3.50
F-1922G	Chicago	1,459,200,000		3.50	F-1922K★	Dallas	1,440,000	$8	25.00
F-1922G★	Chicago	10,240,000		6.00	F-1922L	San Francisco	2,252,800,000		3.50
F-1922H	St. Louis	921,600,000		3.50	F-1922L★	San Francisco	6,400,000		6.00

Series of 1995—Signatures of Withrow and Rubin
Printed in Washington, DC, on web-fed presses

No.	Issuing Bank	Quantity Printed	VF-20	Unc-63	No.	Issuing Bank	Quantity Printed	VF-20	Unc-63
F-1923A	Boston	18,560,000			F-1923D	Cleveland	6,400,000		
	Blocks AC, AD		$10	$30		Block DC		$7	$23
F-1923B	New York	12,800,000			F-1923F	Atlanta	12,800,000		
	Block BH		8	20		Block FD		7	20

Series of 1999—Signatures of Withrow and Summers
Printed in Washington, DC

No.	Issuing Bank	Quantity Printed	VF-20	Unc-63	No.	Issuing Bank	Quantity Printed	VF-20	Unc-63
F-1924A	Boston	556,800,000		$3	F-1924D	Cleveland	268,800,000		$3
F-1924A★	Boston	3,840,000		7	F-1924D★	Cleveland	640,000	$10	45
F-1924B	New York	1,497,600,000		3	F-1924E	Richmond	748,800,000		3
F-1924B★	New York	9,600,000		7	F-1924E★	Richmond	7,040,000		7
F-1924C	Philadelphia	1,062,400,000		3	F-1924F	Atlanta	780,800,000		3
F-1924C★	Philadelphia	13,760,000		7					

Series of 1999—Signatures of Withrow and Summers
Printed at the Western Facility (Fort Worth, Texas)

No.	Issuing Bank	Quantity Printed	VF-20	Unc-63	No.	Issuing Bank	Quantity Printed	VF-20	Unc-63
F-1925F	Atlanta	1,062,400,000		$3	F-1925I	Minneapolis	12,800,000		$3
F-1925F★	Atlanta	640,000	$13	60	F-1925J	Kansas City	339,200,000		3
F-1925G	Chicago	864,400,000		3	F-1925K	Dallas	934,400,000		3
F-1925H	St. Louis	89,600,000		3	F-1925L	San Francisco	1,920,000,000		3
F-1925H★	St. Louis	7,040,000		6	F-1925L★	San Francisco	19,840,000		6

Series of 2001—Signatures of Marin and O'Neill
Printed in Washington, DC

No.	Issuing Bank	Quantity Printed	VF-20	Unc-63	No.	Issuing Bank	Quantity Printed	VF-20	Unc-63
F-1926A	Boston	448,000,000		$3	F-1926F	Atlanta	499,200,000		$3
F-1926A★	Boston	3,520,000		6	F-1926F★	Atlanta	3,520,000		6
F-1926B	New York	678,400,000		3	F-1926H	St. Louis	147,200,000		3
F-1926C	Philadelphia	550,400,000		3	F-1926H★	St. Louis	640,000	$20	70
F-1926C★	Philadelphia	6,400,000		6	F-1926I	Minneapolis	6,400,000		10
F-1926D	Cleveland	307,200,000		3	F-1926J	Kansas City	19,200,000		3
F-1926E	Richmond	70,400,000		3					

Series of 2001—Signatures of Marin and O'Neill
Printed at the Western Facility (Fort Worth, Texas)

No.	Issuing Bank	Quantity Printed	Unc-63	No.	Issuing Bank	Quantity Printed	Unc-63
F-1927F	Atlanta	384,000,000	$3	F-1927J	Kansas City	160,000,000	$3
F-1927F★	Atlanta	3,840,000	6	F-1927K	Dallas	300,800,000	3
F-1927G	Chicago	358,400,000	3	F-1927K★	Dallas	3,200,000	9
F-1927G★	Chicago	4,480,000	6	F-1927L	San Francisco	1,152,000,000	3
F-1927H	St. Louis	128,000,000	3	F-1927L★	San Francisco	3,200,000	4
F-1927I	Minneapolis	57,600,000	4				

Series of 2003—Signatures of Marin and Snow
Printed in Washington, DC

No.	Issuing Bank	Quantity Printed	Unc-63	No.	Issuing Bank	Quantity Printed	Unc-63
F-1928A	Boston	384,000,000	$3	F-1928D*	Cleveland	320,000	$65
F-1928A*	Boston	3,200,000	5	F-1928E	Richmond	953,600,000	3
F-1928B	New York	610,600,000	3	F-1928E*	Richmond	6,880,000	10
F-1928B*	New York	5,760,000	5	F-1928F	Atlanta	153,600,000	3
F-1928C	Philadelphia	460,800,000	3	F-1928F*	Atlanta	320,000	7
F-1928D	Cleveland	326,400,000	3				

Series of 2003—Signatures of Marin and Snow
Printed at the Western Facility (Fort Worth, Texas)

No.	Issuing Bank	Quantity Printed	Unc-63	No.	Issuing Bank	Quantity Printed	Unc-63
F-1929F	Atlanta	140,800,000	$3	F-1929J	Kansas City	179,200,000	$3
F-1929F*	Atlanta	3,200,000	6	F-1929K	Dallas	704,000,000	3
F-1929G	Chicago	742,400,000	3	F-1929K*	Dallas	3,200,000	6
F-1929G*	Chicago	10,240,000	6	F-1929L	San Francisco	1,267,200,000	3
F-1929H	St. Louis	268,800,000	3	F-1929L*	San Francisco	3,200,000	6
F-1929I	Minneapolis	147,200,000	3				

Series of 2003-A—Signatures of Cabral and Snow
Printed in Washington, DC

No.	Issuing Bank	Unc-63	No.	Issuing Bank	Unc-63
F-1930A	Boston	$3	F-1930E	Richmond	$3
F-1930B	New York	3	F-1930E*	Richmond	6
F-1930B*	New York	6	F-1930F	Atlanta	3
F-1930C	Philadelphia	3	F-1930F*	Atlanta	6
F-1930D	Cleveland	3			

Series of 2003-A—Signatures of Cabral and Snow
Printed at the Western Facility (Fort Worth, Texas)

No.	Issuing Bank	Unc-63	No.	Issuing Bank	Unc-63
F-1931F	Atlanta	$3	F-1931J*	Kansas City	$6
F-1931G	Chicago	3	F-1931K	Dallas	3
F-1931H	St. Louis	3	F-1931K*	Dallas	6
F-1931I	Minneapolis	3	F-1931L	San Francisco	3
F-1931J	Kansas City	3			

Series of 2006—Signatures of Cabral and Paulson
Printed in Washington, DC

No.	Issuing Bank	Unc-63	No.	Issuing Bank	Unc-63
F-1932A	Boston	Current	F-1932D	Cleveland	Current
F-1932B	New York	Current	F-1932E	Richmond	Current
F-1932B*	New York	Current	F-1932F	Atlanta	Current
F-1932C	Philadelphia	Current	F-1932F*	Atlanta	Current

Series of 2006—Signatures of Cabral and Paulson
Printed at the Western Facility (Fort Worth, Texas)

No.	Issuing Bank	Unc-63	No.	Issuing Bank	Unc-63
F-1933B	New York	Current	F-1933G*	Chicago	Current
F-1933C	Philadelphia	Current	F-1933H	St. Louis	Current
F-1933D	Cleveland	Current	F-1933I	Minneapolis	Current
F-1933D*	Cleveland	Current	F-1933J	Kansas City	Current
F-1933E	Richmond	Current	F-1933K	Dallas	Current
F-1933F	Atlanta	Current	F-1933L	San Francisco	Current
F-1933F*	Atlanta	Current	F-1933L*	San Francisco	Current
F-1933G	Chicago	Current			

JEFFERSON.

COLLECTING $2 NOTES

Should the field of American currency ever need a candidate, deserving or not, for the role of "evil stepmother"—unwanted, unrespected, yet always there—it need look no further than the $2 bill. They have been a part of the paper currency system since the second issue of Legal Tender Notes (Series of 1862) but, particularly in recent times, seem to be more the subject of uninformed hoarding than widespread use. This applies both to the current $2 Federal Reserve Notes and their immediate predecessors, the Red Seal Legal Tender issues (Series 1928–1963), which were the currency of choice only at race-track betting windows.

Large-Size Notes

$2 Legal Tender Notes (United States Notes), Large-Size. The first $2 bills were issued concurrently with the $1 Legal Tender Notes of the Series of 1862 and are similar in style. This first type consists of just two notes, F-41 and F-41a. Though the first is four times as common (more than 500 notes have been recorded), both notes can be found in a range of conditions.

Thomas Jefferson made his first of many appearances on the $2 bill in the Series of 1869 (F-42), the Rainbow Note for this denomination. Just as prominent in the design as the third president is a view of the U.S. Capitol, whose exterior was completed only a few years earlier in 1863. The present population of this note is less than 500. The Series of 1874–1917 notes maintain the same face design as in 1869, but without the added color and with variations in the seal and color of the serial numbers. The back is more ornate than before and has the denomination repeated seven times. A quick glance at this note shows why it is referred to as the "Bracelet Reverse." The four Series of 1917 issues are quite common, with hundreds known of F-57 through F-59 and thousands of F-60. The earlier issues are much scarcer, with fewer than 200 known for any one number and only dozens for some.

$2 National Bank Notes, Original Series and Series of 1875, Large-Size. Known by everyone as the "Lazy Deuce" by virtue of the horizontal "2" occupying a third of the face, this is one of the most famous issues of American currency. At the left of the "2" is a female representation of "Stars and Stripes," and the back vignette is of Sir Walter Raleigh showing corn and tobacco to the English. These were normally printed on the same sheets as the $1 First Charter Period notes, but as the bottom note on a sheet of four. As with all National Bank Notes of the First Charter Period, the Original Series and Series of 1875 are essentially the same type. Since these were printed on the same sheets as the $1 notes, the issuing banks are similar. Population differences are a function not of how many were issued but of how many were preserved over the years; notes in top conditions are very difficult to find and, when encountered, command substantial premiums.

$2 Silver Certificates, Large-Size. Silver Certificates show the greatest diversity in design of all $2 notes. The first was the Series of 1886, featuring Civil War general and 1880 Democratic presidential candidate Winfield Scott Hancock. There were five issues, the most common of which is F-242, with nearly 400 specimens recorded.

The Series of 1891 features the portrait of William Windom—congressman, senator, two-time Treasury secretary, and great-grandfather of the actor of the same name. This popular type note is not very common—fewer than 600 specimens are known of both types, but a significant percentage of these are in the higher grades.

Next was the $2 issue in the Educational Series, Series of 1896. This note features an allegorical presentation of "Science Presenting Steam and Electricity to Commerce and Manufacture." On the back are two prominent inventors: Robert Fulton and Samuel F.B. Morse. Just as with the $1 Educational Note, its price is more a reflection of demand than true rarity. There have been more than 600 recordings of each of the two types, yet these are priced higher than the Windoms.

The final large-size $2 Silver Certificate is the Series of 1899, with George Washington making one of his rare appearances on a denomination other than $1. These were issued in 10 signature combinations, all relatively common.

$2 Treasury or Coin Notes, Large-Size. Similar to other Series of 1890 notes, the back is completely filled with ornate engraving and the denomination written out in large letters. The total cited population of the three notes (F-353 to F-355) is listed as less than 300, but up to a quarter of each issue is recorded as better than Extremely Fine.

The Series of 1891 is more readily available, but with a much more mundane design. The faces of the Series of 1890 and 1891 notes are the same excepting minor variations; all have a full facing bust of General James Birdseye McPherson, the highest ranking Union officer killed in the Civil War.

$2 Federal Reserve Bank Notes, Large-Size. These are by far the most popular of all Federal Reserve Bank Notes owing to the presence of a World War I–era battleship on the reverse. The face design is consistent with other denominations, featuring a standard left-side currency portrait of Thomas Jefferson. They were issued by all 12 Federal Reserve districts, and although there are a few "better" signature combinations, there are no outstanding rarities among the 34 different types. Some specimens (such as F-769 through F-770) may be extremely difficult to locate in uncirculated condition.

Small-Size $2 Notes

$2 Legal Tender Notes, Small-Size. From the introduction of small currency in 1929 until 1976, the only bills of the $2 denomination were these "Red Seals." They were produced steadily but never in gargantuan amounts through the Series of 1963-A, delivered to the Treasury in July 1965. In addition to having a relatively small number printed, these notes also were extensively hoarded, and one of the more common inquiries dealers receive today concerns the value of these "strange-looking" $2 bills. Every note has a corresponding star (replacement) note, which may be valued in multiples of the regular issue. There are small variations in the legal obligation printed on the notes.

$2 Federal Reserve Notes, Small-Size. After the last printing of $2 Red Seals in 1965, the note was considered extinct. Then, in December 1975, the Bureau of Engraving and Printing began production of Federal Reserve Notes of this denomination. The issues of the Series of 1976 were essentially commemorative banknotes celebrating the bicentennial of American independence. With a back-side design featuring John Trumbull's painting of Thomas Jefferson presenting the Declaration of Independence to John Hancock, they became popular keepsakes and were offered in any number of enterprising formats: with stamps as first-day covers, with coins as bicentennial sets, with commemorative medals, etc. There were more than 575 million notes printed in total for all 12 Federal Reserve districts, along with more than 15 million star notes. The lowest amounts were for the Minneapolis and Kansas City districts.

These were followed by three other issues: The Series of 1995, 2003, and 2003A. With the exception of notes for Atlanta in the Series of 1995 and Minneapolis in that of 2003, these issues were not meant to circulate but intended for sale to collectors. By the end of 2006, more than 230 million of the Series of 2003A had been printed, an indication perhaps of yet another effort to put this denomination into more common usage.

LARGE-SIZE $2 NOTES

Legal Tender Notes
Series of 1862

Face of F-41 and F-41a. Portrait of Alexander Hamilton, first secretary of the Treasury.

Face of F-41 and F-41a.

No.		VG-8	F-12	VF-20	EF-40	Unc-63
Series of 1862, with signatures of Chittenden and Spinner and a small red seal						
F-41	National Bank Note Company vertically at left	$385	$650	$1,250	$2,400	$4,200
F-41a	American Bank Note Company vertically at left	435	775	1,475	2,700	4,600

Legal Tender Notes
Series of 1869

Face of F-42, the Rainbow Note. Bust of Thomas Jefferson, view of the U.S. Capitol.

Back of F-42.

No.	Signatures		Seal	VG-8	F-12	VF-20	EF-40	Unc-63
F-42	Allison	Spinner	Large red	$475	$750	$1,150	$2,450	$4,750

Legal Tender Notes
Series of 1874 to 1917

Face of F-43 to F-60.

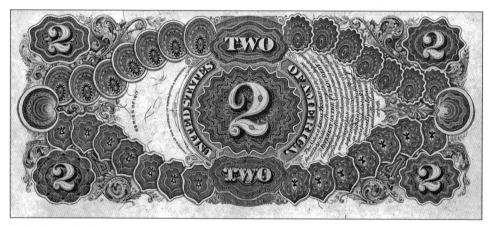

Back of F-43 to F-60.

No.	Series	Signatures		Seal	VG-8	F-12	VF-20	EF-40	Unc-63
Red floral ornament around "Washington, DC" at right; seal at left									
F-43	1874	Allison	Spinner	Small red with rays	$200	$390	$700	$1,375	$1,950
F-44	1875	Allison	New	Small red with rays	250	450	650	950	2,050
F-45				Same but Series A	750	1,300	1,750	3,250	9,250
F-46				Same but Series B	400	750	1,250	1,850	3,900
F-47	1875	Allison	Wyman	Small red with rays	220	425	675	1,100	1,800
F-48	1878	Allison	Gilfillan	Small red with rays	185	380	625	825	1,750
F-49	1878	Scofield	Gilfillan	Small red with rays	2,900	7,500	11,500	20,000	
Large seal replaces floral ornament at right; red serial numbers									
F-50	1880	Scofield	Gilfillan	Large brown	135	205	300	485	1,300
F-51	1880	Bruce	Gilfillan	Large brown	135	195	280	450	1,150
F-52	1880	Bruce	Wyman	Large brown	135	190	280	450	1,150
Same, except serial numbers are blue									
F-53	1880	Rosecrans	Huston	Large red	800	1,200	1,875	4,750	11,000
F-54	1880	Rosecrans	Huston	Large brown	1,750	3,250	9,500	17,500	35,000
F-55	1880	Rosecrans	Nebeker	Small red, scalloped	170	220	350	425	1,150
F-56	1880	Tillman	Morgan	Small red, scalloped	160	210	330	400	1,035
Same, except serial numbers are red									
F-57	1917	Teehee	Burke	Small red, scalloped	75	110	135	200	425
F-58	1917	Elliott	Burke	Small red, scalloped	75	110	135	200	425
F-59	1917	Elliott	White	Small red, scalloped	75	110	135	200	425
F-60	1917	Speelman	White	Small red, scalloped	75	100	120	180	350

National Bank Notes
Original Series
("First Charter Period")

Face of F-387 to F-389, the "Lazy Deuce." "Stars and Stripes" vignette at the left.

Back of F-387 to F-389. The vignette at the center shows Sir Walter Raleigh, having returned to England, displaying corn and tobacco.

No.	Signatures		Seal	VG-8	F-12	VF-20	EF-40	Unc-63
F-387	Colby	Spinner	Red with rays	$2,500	$3,150	$4,900	$6,500	$11,500
F-388	Jeffries	Spinner	Red with rays			Very rare		
F-389	Allison	Spinner	Red with rays	3,300	3,950	5,400	7,000	14,500

National Bank Notes
Series of 1875
("First Charter Period")

Face of F-390 to F-393, with SERIES 1875 vertical overprint left of center. The charter number of this bank is 524. This is the general type of F-390 to 393. The back is the same as that on the Original Series.

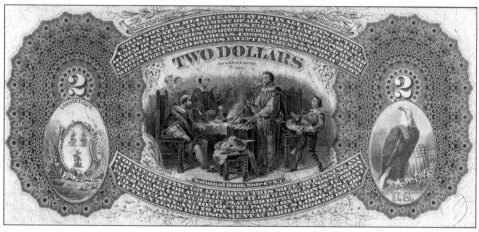

Back of F-390 to F-393.

No.	Signatures		Seal	VG-8	F-12	VF-20	EF-40	Unc-63
F-390	Allison	New	Red, scalloped	$3,150	$3,750	$4,900	$6,400	$11,500
F-391	Allison	Wyman	Red, scalloped	3,150	3,750	4,900	6,400	11,500
F-392	Allison	Gilfillan	Red, scalloped	3,150	3,750	4,900	6,400	11,500
F-393	Scofield	Gilfillan	Red, scalloped	3,150	3,750	4,900	6,400	11,500

Silver Certificates
Series of 1886

Face of F-240 to F-244. Bust of General Winfield Scott Hancock.

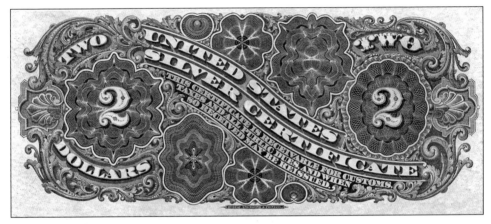

Back of F-240 to F-244.

No.	Signatures		Seal	VG-8	F-12	VF-20	EF-40	Unc-63
F-240	Rosecrans	Jordan	Small red	$335	$625	$875	$1,700	$3,350
F-241	Rosecrans	Hyatt	Small red	400	675	875	1,850	3,750
F-242	Rosecrans	Hyatt	Large red	300	575	875	1,500	2,550
F-243	Rosecrans	Huston	Large red	335	625	875	1,850	3,400
F-244	Rosecrans	Huston	Large brown	335	625	875	1,800	3,450

Silver Certificates
Series of 1891

Face of F-245 and F-246. Bust of William Windom, who served two terms as secretary of the Treasury (1881–1884 and 1889–1891).

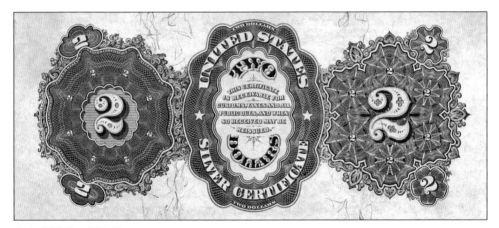

Back of F-245 and F-246.

No.	Signatures		Seal	VG-8	F-12	VF-20	EF-40	Unc-63
F-245	Rosecrans	Nebeker	Small red	$300	$550	$825	$1,900	$3,950
F-246	Tillman	Morgan	Small red	300	525	825	1,750	3,750

Silver Certificates
Series of 1896

Face of F-247 and F-248, the $2 note in the "Educational" series. Vignette "Science Presenting Steam and Electricity to Industry and Commerce." The engraving is the work of Charles Schlecht and G.F.C. Smillie. The Treasury Department felt that such a complicated motif aided counterfeiters, because the designs would not be scrutinized carefully. Bankers complained that the design was so elaborate that the denomination could not be instantly identified, making such bills difficult to count quickly.

Back of F-247 and F-248, showing inventor Robert Fulton and artist and inventor Samuel F.B. Morse. Engraved by Thomas F. Morris.

No.	Signatures		Seal	VG-8	F-12	VF-20	EF-40	Unc-63
F-247	Tillman	Morgan	Small red	$525	$875	$1,350	$2,750	$6,000
F-248	Bruce	Roberts	Small red	525	875	1,350	2,750	6,000

Silver Certificates
Series of 1899

Face of F-249 to F-258. Gilbert Stuart's portrait of Washington is flanked by figures representing Agriculture and Mechanics.

Back of F-249 to F-258.

No.	Signatures		Seal	VG-8	F-12	VF-20	EF-40	Unc-63
F-249	Lyons	Roberts	Blue	$185	$250	$325	$610	$1,450
F-250	Lyons	Treat	Blue	185	250	400	635	1,500
F-251	Vernon	Treat	Blue	185	250	325	610	1,450
F-252	Vernon	McClung	Blue	185	250	360	635	1,500
F-253	Napier	McClung	Blue	185	230	315	610	1,400
F-254	Napier	Thompson	Blue	375	575	900	1,250	3,400
F-255	Parker	Burke	Blue	185	225	315	575	1,300
F-256	Teehee	Burke	Blue	180	220	305	550	1,175
F-257	Elliott	Burke	Blue	200	250	375	650	1,500
F-258	Speelman	White	Blue	170	215	300	525	1,150

Treasury or Coin Notes
Series of 1890

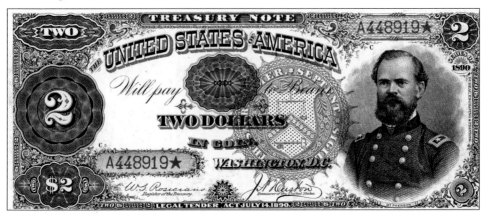

Face of F-353 to F-355. Portrait of Civil War general James McPherson.

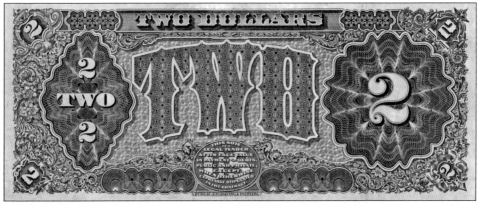

Ornate back of F-353 to F-355.

No.	Signatures		Seal	VG-8	F-12	VF-20	EF-40	Unc-63
F-353	Rosecrans	Huston	Large brown	$400	$950	$1,800	$4,000	$10,000
F-354	Rosecrans	Nebeker	Large brown	675	1,200	3,000	9,500	35,000
F-355	Rosecrans	Nebeker	Small red	400	950	2,100	4,350	10,000

Treasury or Coin Notes
Series of 1891

Face of F-356 to F-358.

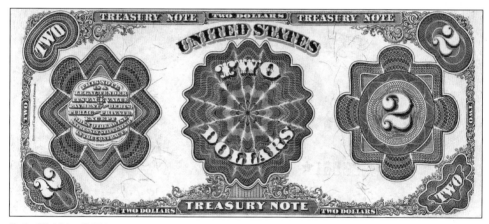

Back of F-356 to F-358.

No.	Signatures		Seal	VG-8	F-12	VF-20	EF-40	Unc-63
F-356	Rosecrans	Nebeker	Small red	$300	$525	$1,050	$1,500	$2,950
F-357	Tillman	Morgan	Small red	300	475	950	1,450	2,650
F-358	Bruce	Roberts	Small red	300	525	1,050	1,500	2,950

Federal Reserve Bank Notes
Series of 1918

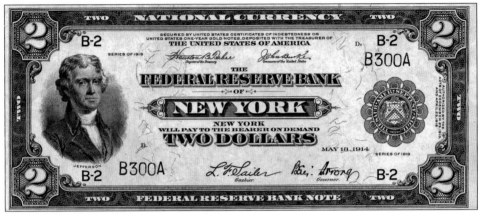

Face of F-747 to F-780. Portrait of Thomas Jefferson.

Back of F-747 to F-780. The famous "Battleship Note."

No.	Issuing Bank	Series	Treasury Signatures		Bank Signatures		VG-8	F-12	VF-20	EF-40	Unc-63
F-747	Boston	1918	Teehee	Burke	Bullen	Morss	$300	$430	$600	$950	$2,200
F-748	Boston	1918	Teehee	Burke	Willett	Morss	315	450	625	1,000	2,800
F-749	Boston	1918	Elliott	Burke	Willett	Morss	300	450	575	975	2,200
F-750	New York	1918	Teehee	Burke	Sailer	Strong	315	450	625	1,000	2,500
F-751	New York	1918	Teehee	Burke	Hendricks	Strong	315	450	625	1,000	2,500
F-752	New York	1918	Elliott	Burke	Hendricks	Strong	300	430	600	975	2,050
F-753	Philadelphia	1918	Teehee	Burke	Hardt	Passmore	315	450	600	975	2,050
F-754	Philadelphia	1918	Teehee	Burke	Dyer	Passmore	315	450	600	975	2,050
F-755	Philadelphia	1918	Elliott	Burke	Dyer	Passmore	500	900	1,800	2,950	14,500
F-756	Philadelphia	1918	Elliott	Burke	Dyer	Norris	315	450	600	975	2,050
F-757	Cleveland	1918	Teehee	Burke	Baxter	Fancher	315	450	600	975	2,050
F-758	Cleveland	1918	Teehee	Burke	Davis	Fancher	450	675	975	1,450	4,300
F-759	Cleveland	1918	Elliott	Burke	Davis	Fancher	325	475	625	1,050	2,000
F-760	Richmond	1918	Teehee	Burke	Keesee	Seay	400	550	725	1,350	3,400
F-761	Richmond	1918	Elliott	Burke	Keesee	Seay	350	500	650	1,175	3,200
F-762	Atlanta	1918	Teehee	Burke	Pike	McCord	350	500	650	1,175	3,000
F-763	Atlanta	1918	Teehee	Burke	Bell	McCord	800	1,450	2,250	4,500	
F-764	Atlanta	1918	Elliott	Burke	Bell	Wellborn	500	900	1,500	4,500	
F-765	Chicago	1918	Teehee	Burke	McCloud	McDougal	315	475	625	975	2,150
F-766	Chicago	1918	Teehee	Burke	Cramer	McDougal	335	525	650	1,175	3,400
F-767	Chicago	1918	Elliott	Burke	Cramer	McDougal	315	475	625	975	2,150
F-768	St. Louis	1918	Teehee	Burke	Attebery	Wells	400	675	925	1,450	3,900

No.	Issuing Bank	Series	Treasury Signatures		Bank Signatures		VG-8	F-12	VF-20	EF-40	Unc-63
F-769	St. Louis	1918	Teehee	Burke	Attebery	Biggs	$475	$975	$1,500	$2,750	
F-770	St. Louis	1918	Elliott	Burke	Attebery	Biggs	425	800	1,500	2,750	
F-771	St. Louis	1918	Elliott	Burke	White	Biggs	400	725	1,300	1,800	$4,100
F-772	Minneapolis	1918	Teehee	Burke	Cook	Wold	400	650	800	1,025	2,750
F-773	Minneapolis	1918	Elliott	Burke	Cook	Young	400	625	775	1,025	3,750
F-774	Kansas City	1918	Teehee	Burke	Anderson	Miller	375	525	725	1,000	2,700
F-775	Kansas City	1918	Elliott	Burke	Helm	Miller	400	625	900	1,600	3,250
F-776	Dallas	1918	Teehee	Burke	Talley	Van Zandt	425	625	875	1,200	3,250
F-777	Dallas	1918	Elliott	Burke	Talley	Van Zandt	525	700	975	1,300	3,900
F-778	San Francisco	1918	Teehee	Burke	Clerk	Lynch	375	550	700	1,400	5,000
F-779	San Francisco	1918	Elliott	Burke	Clerk	Calkins	450	700	1,000	1,650	5,000
F-780	San Francisco	1918	Elliott	Burke	Ambrose	Calkins	415	625	925	1,650	3,250

SMALL-SIZE $2 NOTES

Legal Tender Notes, *Series of 1928 to 1928-G, Red Seal*

Face of F-1501 to F-1508.

Back of F-1501 to F-1508.

No.	Series	Signatures		Qty Printed	VF-20	Unc-63	No.	Series	Signatures		Qty Printed	VF-20	Unc-63
F-1501	1928	Tate	Mellon	55,889,424	$13	$125	F-1505	1928-D	Julian	Morgenthau	146,381,364	$15.00	$80
F-1501★	1928	Tate	Mellon		265	1,000	F-1505★	1928-D	Julian	Morgenthau		100.00	400
F-1502	1928-A	Woods	Mellon	46,859,136	65	325	F-1506	1928-E	Julian	Vinson	5,261,016	15.00	125
F-1502★	1928-A	Woods	Mellon		1,750	8,000	F-1506★	1928-E	Julian	Vinson		2,750.00	12,000
F-1503	1928-B	Woods	Mills	9,001,632	150	850	F-1507	1928-F	Julian	Snyder	43,349,292	12.50	65
F-1503★	1928-B	Woods	Mills		20,000	Very rare	F-1507★	1928-F	Julian	Snyder		100.00	750
F-1504	1928-C	Julian	Morgenthau	86,584,008	25	100	F-1508	1928-G	Clark	Snyder	52,208,000	12.50	65
F-1504★	1928-C	Julian	Morgenthau		525	1,750	F-1508★	1928-G	Clark	Snyder		65.00	500

Legal Tender Notes, *Series of 1953 to 1953-C, Red Seal*

Face of F-1509 to F-1512.

Entry continued on next page.

Back of F-1509 to F-1512.

No.	Series	Signatures		Qty Printed	VF-20	Unc-63	No.	Series	Signatures		Qty Printed	VF-20	Unc-63
F-1509	1953	Priest	Humphrey	45,360,000	$9	$30	F-1511	1953-B	Smith	Dillon	10,800,000	$9	$20
F-1509★	1953	Priest	Humphrey	2,160,000	15	75	F-1511★	1953-B	Smith	Dillon	720,000	20	75
F-1510	1953-A	Priest	Anderson	18,000,000	9	20	F-1512	1953-C	Granahan	Dillon	5,760,000	9	20
F-1510★	1953-A	Priest	Anderson	720,000	17	60	F-1512★	1953-C	Granahan	Dillon	360,000	15	80

Legal Tender Notes
Series of 1963 and 1963-A, Red Seal, Motto Added

Face of F-1513 and F-1514.

Back of F-1513 and F-1514, with IN GOD WE TRUST above Monticello.

No.	Series	Signatures		Qty Printed	VF-20	Unc-63	No.	Series	Signatures		Qty Printed	VF-20	Unc-63
F-1513	1963	Granahan	Dillon	15,360,000	$9	$15	F-1514	1963-A	Granahan	Fowler	3,200,000	$9	$20
F-1513★	1963	Granahan	Dillon	640,000	12	40	F-1514★	1963-A	Granahan	Fowler	640,000	12	80

Federal Reserve Notes, *Series of 1976 to 2003-A, Green Seal*

Face of F-1935 to F-1938.

Back of F-1935 to F-1938.

Series of 1976—Signatures of Neff and Simon

No.	Issuing Bank	Quantity Printed	F-12	Unc-63	No.	Issuing Bank	Quantity Printed	F-12	Unc-63
F-1935A	Boston	29,440,000		$9	F-1935G	Chicago	84,480,000		$9.00
F-1935A★	Boston	1,280,000	$8	20	F-1935G★	Chicago	1,280,000	$20	60.00
F-1935B	New York	67,200,000		9	F-1935H	St. Louis	39,040,000		10.00
F-1935B★	New York	2,560,000	8	20	F-1935H★	St. Louis	1,280,000	8	25.00
F-1935C	Philadelphia	33,280,000		9	F-1935I	Minneapolis	23,680,000		18.00
F-1935C★	Philadelphia	1,280,000	8	20	F-1935I★	Minneapolis	640,000	80	250.00
F-1935D	Cleveland	31,360,000		9	F-1935J	Kansas City	24,960,000		22.00
F-1935D★	Cleveland	1,280,000	10	25	F-1935J★	Kansas City	640,000	70	200.00
F-1935E	Richmond	56,960,000		9	F-1935K	Dallas	41,600,000		12.50
F-1935E★	Richmond	640,000	10	75	F-1935K★	Dallas	1,280,000	8	20.00
F-1935F	Atlanta	60,800,000		9	F-1935L	San Francisco	82,560,000		9.00
F-1935F★	Atlanta	1,280,000	8	20	F-1935L★	San Francisco	1,920,000	10	30.00

Series of 1995—Signatures of Withrow and Rubin

No.	Issuing Bank	Quantity Printed	Unc-63	No.	Issuing Bank	Quantity Printed	Unc-63
F-1936A★	Boston	9,999	$75	F-1936G★	Chicago	9,999	$65
F-1936B★	New York	9,999	60	F-1936H★	St. Louis	9,999	60
F-1936C★	Philadelphia	9,999	60	F-1936I★	Minneapolis	9,999	70
F-1936D★	Cleveland	9,999	60	F-1936J★	Kansas City	9,999	65
F-1936E★	Richmond	9,999	60	F-1936K★	Dallas	9,999	65
F-1936F	Atlanta	153,600,000	9	F-1936L★	San Francisco	9,999	60
F-1936F★	Atlanta	1,216,000	17				

Series of 2003—Signatures of Marin and Snow

Printed at the Western Facility (Fort Worth, Texas)

No.	Issuing Bank	Quantity Printed	Unc-63	No.	Issuing Bank	Quantity Printed	Unc-63
F-1937A★	Boston	16,000	$40	F-1937H★	St. Louis	16,000	$40
F-1937B★	New York	16,000	40	F-1937I	Minneapolis	121,600,000	5
F-1937C★	Philadelphia	16,000	40	F-1937I★	Minneapolis	3,840,000	28
F-1937D★	Cleveland	16,000	40	F-1937J★	Kansas City	16,000	40
F-1937E★	Richmond	16,000	40	F-1937K★	Dallas	16,000	40
F-1937F★	Atlanta	16,000	40	F-1937L★	San Francisco	16,000	40
F-1937G★	Chicago	16,000	40				

Note: Notes not listed (B, F, G, and K without stars) were only made for sale to collectors by the Bureau of Engraving and Printing and not released to circulation.

Series of 2003-A—Signatures of Cabral and Snow

Printed at the Western Facility (Fort Worth, Texas)

No.	Issuing Bank	Unc-63	No.	Issuing Bank	Unc-63
F-1938A	Boston	Current	F-1938G	Chicago	Current
F-1938B	New York	Current	F-1938H	St. Louis	Current
F-1938C	Philadelphia	Current	F-1938I	Minneapolis	Current
F-1938D	Cleveland	Current	F-1938J	Kansas City	Current
F-1938E	Richmond	Current	F-1938K	Dallas	Current
F-1938F	Atlanta	Current	F-1938L	San Francisco	Current
F-1983F★	Atlanta	Current			

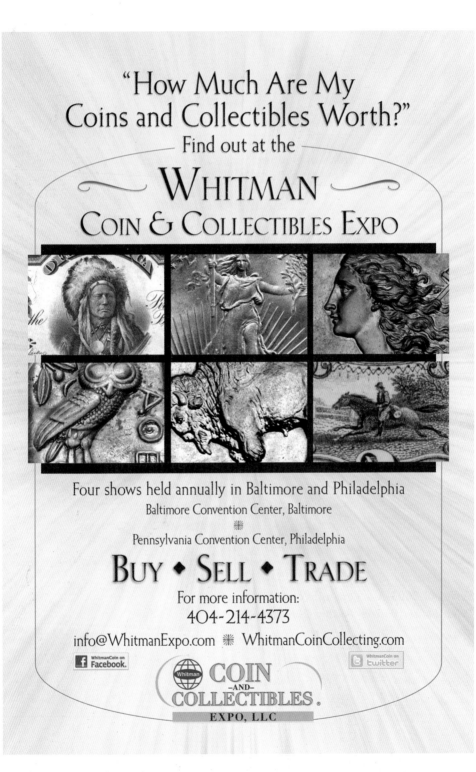

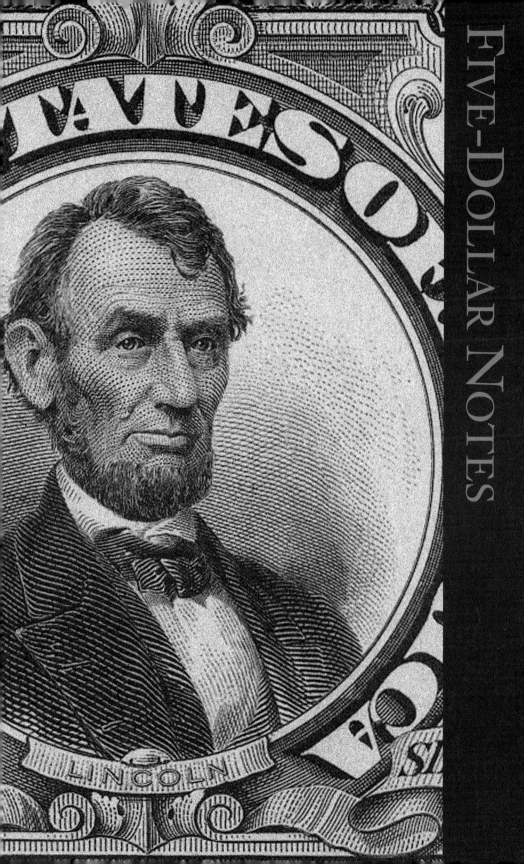

COLLECTING $5 NOTES

A collector wishing to combine the prospects of wide availability and affordable prices in U.S. paper money should look no further than the $5 denomination. Although, as we shall see later, there is a wider variety of $10 notes, so many of these are beyond the reach of normal collectors that they should be considered non-collectible for all save the wealthiest of specialists. Some of the most famous notes in U.S. history are described in this section, including the final issue of the Educational Series, the Indian Chief, the Porthole, the Woodchopper, and the only reasonably collectible National Gold Bank Note of California.

Large-Size Notes

$5 Demand Notes of 1861, Large-Size. These are the first denomination in the first issue of U.S. currency and are the notes that gave rise to the term "greenback," an American colloquialism we still use a century-and-a-half later. The notes were authorized by the Act of July 17, 1861, then privately printed by the American Bank Note Company. The front of the bill features the Capitol building's statue of Freedom and a small bust of Alexander Hamilton. The notes were intended to be hand-signed by the treasurer and register, a prospect that soon proved unworkable, leading clerks to sign for them (with "for the" dutifully written in, as well). These notes are very rare today; the only ones remotely collectible are of the type payable at New York (F-1a), of which nine specimens are known. The versions with "for the" engraved are more available, but of the several hundred in existence, few are above Very Fine condition.

$5 Legal Tender Notes (United States Notes), Large-Size. There are only three types of $5 Legal Tender Notes. The first, from the Series of 1862–1863, is very similar to the Demand Note, except for the change in obligation and the addition of the Treasury seal and engraved signatures. The backs of these notes bear what are known today as either the "First Obligation" or the "Second Obligation" (please see the introduction for more information). Despite the fact that these are among the first collectible notes, they are surprisingly plentiful, even in uncirculated condition. In fact, there are close to 600 examples known of F-61a alone, and of those, more than 300 are uncirculated, many with low serial numbers.

The "Woodchopper Note," featuring a pioneer family and their faithful dog in the center, is an American classic. It exists both as a "Rainbow Note" in the Series of 1869, for which there are more than 500 specimens recorded, and also in the Series of 1875, 1878, 1880, and 1907, which differ primarily in the placement and color of the seal and serial numbers. This is a case where wide availability has ensured popularity. There are a few scarcer signature varieties, but overall the population is more than 5,000 notes, half of them F-91.

$5 National Bank Notes, Large-Size. Five-dollar notes are the lowest National Bank Note denomination made available in the full range of types. For most issues of National Bank Notes, the lowest denomination produced is the most commonly available. However, the $5 notes of the First Charter Period (Original Series and Series of 1875) are more plentiful than either the $1 or $2 note, if for no other reason than they were printed four to a sheet and thus in greater quantities.

The $5 is the lowest denomination in the Second Charter Period, Series of 1882, and it is the only such denomination that has a face design different from its corresponding denomination in the First Charter Period. Artistically, the portrait of the recently assassinated President James A. Garfield makes this, hands-down, the least appealing note in the series.

It was, however, a precursor of things to come. There were three different backs on the Second Charter notes, as with the other issues in the series. The most interesting and appealing of these is what is known today as the "Brown Back," so called because its central design consists of the issuing bank's charter number set in blue against a brown background. See the introduction for a more detailed explanation of the three issues.

The Third Charter Period, Series of 1902, was the final large-size National Bank Note series and boasts three varieties of notes, as well. Most appealing to many is the first type, known as "Red Seals." They exist in just three signature combinations, as opposed to eight readily available ones for the second issue (known as "Date Backs") or the 15 varieties possible for the third, "Plain Back" type. Both of the latter have blue seals and serial numbers instead of red.

Valuation for all the above notes reflects that for the most common banks in the most populous states; notes issued by rare banks, states, or territories, particularly in the West, are considerably more expensive.

$5 National Gold Bank Notes, Large-Size. In the aftermath of the California Gold Rush, these rare notes were printed in four series (1870, 1872, 1873, and 1874) for California gold banks. Very few notes have survived, and the only remotely collectible one is F-1136 from the First National Gold Bank of San Francisco. It is extraordinarily difficult to locate one in a condition better than Very Good, which reflects the high degree of use they saw in commerce. They are similar in style to the National Bank Notes of the First Charter period. Most were printed on a yellow- or gold-tinted paper. They were redeemable by the issuing bank in gold coin, a fact illustrated on the back center panel of all Gold Bank Notes with a large montage of U.S. gold coins of the period days.

$5 Silver Certificates, Large-Size. This Silver Certificate issue has an established following among collectors. As a class, five of the six types have no equal in collecting popularity; in fact, they have served as an introduction to American paper money for countless collectors. They commence with the famous "Silver Dollar Back" notes of the Series of 1886, named for the arrangement of five Morgan Dollars on the back. Four of the coins display the reverse (Philadelphia Mint), while the center, fifth coin shows an obverse dated 1886, the same year as the note series. The note's features the portrait of Ulysses S. Grant. Friedberg-261 and F-263 are the most prevalent issues, with the latter frequently offered in uncirculated quality.

The same face design was continued in the Series of 1891 with a considerably more mundane back. It was issued with only two signature combinations and, despite lower overall availability, valuations normally do not approach those of the Series of 1886.

The Series of 1896 Silver Certificate is the final note in the "Educational Series." (Designs exist for a $10 note but none were issued.) This one depicts, in front of the Capitol building, an allegorical group representing "Electricity as the Dominant Force in the World." The back has portraits of Grant and Philip Sheridan, both Civil War generals. Of the three signature combinations, F-268 is by far the most common, with more than 600 reported, but there are several hundred of each of the other two, as well. They are available across the range of conditions, most commonly in Very Fine or below.

Another long-time favorite is the Series of 1899, with the portrait of Oncpapa Sioux Chief Ta-to-ka-in-yan-ka, more commonly known as "Running Antelope." Recent research has discovered that the headdress is of the Pawnee rather than the Sioux style, likely the result of artistic license taken by the engraver. These notes were produced with 11 signature combinations over a period spanning three decades. More than 3,500 notes have been recorded on the market. Excepting star notes, the only rare one is F-276, with the signatures of Napier and Thompson.

The final design is known as the "Porthole Note" because of the appearance of Lincoln's bust on the face in a perfectly round frame resembling a ship's window. This is a one-note type that soon was superseded by the first issues of small-size notes. There are close to a thousand recorded, with more than a quarter of them uncirculated.

$5 Treasury or Coin Notes, Large-Size. The Series of 1890 and 1891 Treasury Notes, or Coin Notes, follow the standard pattern for the category. The faces all show General George H. Thomas, a Virginian who nonetheless served with distinction as a Union general during the Civil War. He is best remembered today as the "Rock of Chickamauga," an appellation he earned by his epic leadership at the 1863 battle straddling the Tennessee-Georgia border. Friedberg-360, bearing the signatures of Rosecrans and Nebeker with a large brown seal, is rare (only 13 known, and just one uncirculated). There are hundreds known of each of the other two. The back of Series of 1891 has the same plain style as its contemporaries and is easy to find in the full range of grades.

$5 Federal Reserve Notes, Large-Size. The listing of Federal Reserve Notes, Series of 1914, is extensive and confusing. There are two varieties: Red Seal and Blue Seal. While the Red Seals all have the Burke-McAdoo signature combination, the Blue Seals have four different ones. To complicate things further, each Red Seal was produced for every Federal Reserve district with two styles of placement of the district letters and numbers. The Blue Seals don't get simpler; they get harder. Many types have up to three variations in the placement of district identifiers and seals. Those desiring more information may find it in the text, but most of these notes are collected by type and sometimes by bank and/or signature. Until recently, these were not widely collected; they were so common and uninteresting that many went unreported to the census takers. Only in the past few years have computerized, data-mining techniques made it possible to accumulate information on the number of notes extant. Some which at one time were thought scarce have been found to be quite common. Exercise caution with all but those notes creditably proven to be rare.

$5 Federal Reserve Bank Notes, Large-Size. Federal Reserve Bank Notes, Series of 1915 or 1918, have the Federal Reserve Bank's name at center with Lincoln's bust to the left. The back features two historical vignettes: Columbus in sight of land, and the landing of the Pilgrims. These were issued for 11 districts (Richmond excepted) and are quite common. Star notes, however, are exceedingly rare.

Small-Size $5 Notes

The design of the small-size $5 with Abraham Lincoln on the face and the Lincoln Memorial on the back was nearly constant until the security changes made in the Series of 1999. The only differences were in the color of the seal.

$5 Legal Tender Notes, Small-Size. These issues closely mirror those of the $2 Legal Tender Note except that none was made for the Series of 1928-G and 1963-A. With the notable exception of Series 1928-D, more $5 notes were printed than $2. The 1928 (1928–1928-E) issues are quite collectible and, in top condition, are becoming elusive. All $5 star notes are now valued in excess of $100 in top condition, with earlier star notes often fetching prices in the thousands of dollars. Regrettably, for those who find normal Legal Tender Notes hidden in their night tables in used condition, they are not worth much more than a small premium above their face value.

$5 National Bank Notes, Small-Size. This is the lowest-denominated small-size National Bank Note. The Type 1 variety (1929–1933) is considered more common than Type 2 (1933–1935); the two are easily differentiated, with the latter bearing the bank charter number in black and brown in different locations. These $5 bills are widely collected today, usually by geographical location. Except for issues by rare banks and states, such as Alaska, Hawaii, Arizona, Idaho, Nevada, and Wyoming, they are common. They should not be confused with the similar-looking Federal Reserve Bank Notes, which see.

$5 Silver Certificates, Small-Size. These are a relatively uninteresting issue, but nonetheless one that offers easy collectibility. They were only issued in two types, Series of 1934–1934-D and 1953–1953B, and even star notes are reasonably affordable. More than 90 million 1953-C notes were made but never released to circulation. Small-size $5 Silver Certificates also were issued (F-2307 with yellow Treasury seal) for use in North Africa during World War II.

$5 Federal Reserve Bank Notes, Small-Size. Federal Reserve Bank Notes of the Series of 1929, brown seal, are collectible from 11 of the 12 Federal Reserve districts. Regular issues and star notes were printed for every district except Richmond. No star notes from the San Francisco district have been reported as yet and should be considered extremely rare. The regular issue from San Francisco, with a printing of only 360,000 notes, is one of the keys to the entire Federal Reserve Bank Note series.

$5 Federal Reserve Notes, Small-Size. These commence with the Series of 1928 and continue through that of 1999 with little noticeable change. Not all districts issued notes for each series, and some—particularly 1928-C (F-1953-F) and 1928-D (F-1954-F)—are rare and difficult to obtain.

With the exception of the $1 Emergency Note for Hawaii, which was a Silver Certificate, the other Hawaii issues were Federal Reserve Notes with the same brown seals and other markings. The $5 Hawaii notes were part of the Series of 1934 (F-2301) and 1934-A (F-2302); they are about twice as valuable as the $1 notes. The corresponding star notes are valued in the thousands of dollars, even in lower grades.

The Western Facility in Fort Worth, Texas, began printing $5 notes in 1991 with the Series of 1988-A. Starting with the Series of 1999, anticounterfeiting efforts led to a modification of the face and back designs, as seen in the text. A newer version, with the addition of more security features (including light purple in the center of the bill blending into gray at the edges, and small, yellow "05"s printed in the field on both sides) went into circulation on March 13, 2008.

LARGE-SIZE $5 NOTES
Demand Notes of 1861

Face of F-1 to F-5a, payable at New York, with "for the" added in ink. The statue Freedom from the top of the Capitol building in Washington, DC, at left. At right is a portrait of Alexander Hamilton from a painting by Archibald Robertson.

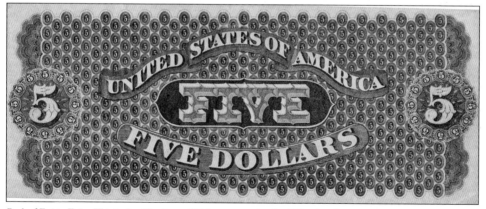

Back of F-1 to F-5a. This is the oldest issue of U.S. currency that is still legal tender.

No.	Payable at		VG-8	F-12	VF-20	EF-40	Unc-63
F-1	New York		$1,500	$3,000	$4,750	—	—
F-1a	New York; "For the" handwritten	Rare above F-12	12,000	22,500	—	—	—
F-2	Philadelphia		1,750	3,250	5,750		
F-2a	Philadelphia; "For the" handwritten	None issued	—	—			
F-3	Boston		1,900	3,300	6,000	—	—
F-3a	Boston; "For the" handwritten	Unique	—	—	—	—	
F-4	Cincinnati	5 known	11,000	—	—	—	
F-4a	Cincinnati; "For the" handwritten	Unknown	—	—	—	—	
F-5	St. Louis	9 known	7,500	20,000	—	—	
F-5a	St. Louis; "For the" handwritten	Unique	—	—	—	—	

Legal Tender Notes
Series of 1862

Face of F-61 to F-62. The vignettes are similar to those used on the $5 Demand Notes of 1861.

Back of F-61 with "First Obligation" on the reverse.

No.	Act	Signatures		Seal	VG-8	F-12	VF-20	EF-40	Unc-63
First Obligation on back, American Bank Note Co. on upper border									
F-61	1862	Chittenden	Spinner	Small red	$2,500	$5,000	$11,500	—	—
F-61a	1862	Chittenden	Spinner	Small red, "Series" on face	350	550	725	$1,050	$2,250
Second Obligation on back									
F-62	1862	Chittenden	Spinner	Small red	375	585	800	1,150	2,800

Legal Tender Notes
Series of 1863

Face of F-63 to F-63b.

Back of F-62 to F-63b with "Second Obligation" on the reverse.

No.	Act	Signatures		Seal	VG-8	F-12	VF-20	EF-40	Unc-63
Second Obligation on back, American Bank Note Co. and National Bank Note Co. on lower border									
F-63	1863	Chittenden	Spinner	Small red	$375	$550	$725	$1,100	$2,750
Second Obligation on back, American Bank Note Co. twice on lower border									
F-63a	1863	Chittenden	Spinner	Small red, one serial no.	375	550	725	1,100	2,300
F-63b	1863	Chittenden	Spinner	Small red, two serial nos.	375	550	725	1,100	2,300

Legal Tender Notes
Series of 1869

Face of F-64, the famous "Rainbow Note." Vignettes of Andrew Jackson and a "Pioneer Family." Also called the "Wood-chopper Note." The star at the serial number is decorative.

Back of F-64.

No.	Signatures			Seal	VG-8	F-12	VF-20	EF-40	Unc-63
F-64	Allison	Spinner	"Rainbow" Note	Large red	$265	$475	$1,050	$1,575	$2,850

Legal Tender Notes
Series of 1875 to 1907

Face of F-65 to F-92.

Back of F-65 to F-92.

No.	Series	Signatures		Seal	VG-8	F-12	VF-20	EF-40	Unc-63
Large red floral ornament around "Washington, D.C." at right; seal at left									
F-65	1875	Allison	New	Small red, rays	$175	$285	$500	$750	$1,500
F-66		As above but Series A			500	800	1,100	3,000	17,500
F-67		As above but Series B			140	200	350	600	1,500
F-68	1875	Allison	Wyman	Small red, rays	130	190	325	525	1,250
F-69	1878	Allison	Gilfillan	Small red, rays	140	240	425	675	1,375
Large seal replaces floral ornament; red serial numbers									
F-70	1880	Scofield	Gilfillan	Large brown	450	750	1,050	2,200	4,500
F-71	1880	Bruce	Gilfillan	Large brown	200	300	415	625	1,175
F-72	1880	Bruce	Wyman	Large brown	200	330	415	625	1,250
Same as above, blue serial numbers									
F-73	1880	Bruce	Wyman	Large red, plain	145	275	420	625	1,050
F-74	1880	Rosecrans	Jordan	Large red, plain	165	325	435	750	1,275
F-75	1880	Rosecrans	Hyatt	Large red, plain	450	700	1,000	3,500	35,000
F-76	1880	Rosecrans	Huston	Large red, spike	230	500	750	1,450	6,000
F-77	1880	Rosecrans	Huston	Large brown	240	525	775	1,500	15,000
F-78	1880	Rosecrans	Nebeker	Large brown	275	650	1,250	2,000	6,750
F-79	1880	Rosecrans	Nebeker	Small red, scalloped	140	170	225	375	675
F-80	1880	Tillman	Morgan	Small red, scalloped	140	170	225	400	700
F-81	1880	Bruce	Roberts	Small red, scalloped	170	200	300	525	800
F-82	1880	Lyons	Roberts	Small red, scalloped	175	220	340	575	1,300

Chart continued on next page.

No.	Series	Signatures		Seal	VG-8	F-12	VF-20	EF-40	Unc-63
Red "V" and "Dollars" added to left of design; red serial numbers									
F-83	1907	Vernon	Treat	Small red, scalloped	$135	$210	$280	$440	$775
F-84	1907	Vernon	McClung	Small red, scalloped	135	210	280	440	775
F-85	1907	Napier	McClung	Small red, scalloped	135	200	260	425	725
F-86	1907	Napier	Thompson	Small red, scalloped	175	300	600	950	1,800
F-87	1907	Parker	Burke	Small red, scalloped	125	185	240	385	625
F-88	1907	Teehee	Burke	Small red, scalloped	125	185	235	350	575
F-89	1907	Elliott	Burke	Small red, scalloped	125	185	240	400	700
F-90	1907	Elliott	White	Small red, scalloped	140	215	300	450	750
F-91	1907	Speelman	White	Small red, scalloped	100	140	200	340	535
F-92	1907	Woods	White	Small red, scalloped	140	215	300	450	750

National Bank Notes
Original Series
("First Charter Period")

Face of F-394 to F-399. At left is "Columbus Sighting Land"; at right, "America Presented to the Old World."

Back of F-394 to F-399. At center is "The Landing of Columbus."

No.	Signatures		Seal		VG-8	F-12	VF-20	EF-40	Unc-63
F-394	Chittenden	Spinner	Red, rays		$1,150	$1,400	$1,750	$2,400	$4,600
F-397	Colby	Spinner	Red, rays		1,150	1,400	1,750	2,400	4,600
F-398	Jeffries	Spinner	Red, rays	11 known	5,000	7,500	8,500	10,000	—
F-399	Allison	Spinner	Red, rays		1,225	1,450	1,850	2,700	5,250

National Bank Notes
Series of 1875
("First Charter Period")

Face of F-401 to F-408b. Charter numbers are usually red, but may sometimes be in black ink.

Back of F-401 to F-408b.

The small Bureau, Engraving & Printing seal is found on Series 1875 notes, indicating that they were printed in Washington, DC.

No.	Signatures		Seal		VG-8	F-12	VF-20	EF-40	Unc-63
F-401	Allison	New	Red, scalloped		$1,175	$1,400	$1,650	$2,300	$4,500
F-402	Allison	Wyman	Red, scalloped		1,250	1,500	1,850	2,900	5,250
F-403	Allison	Gilfillan	Red, scalloped		1,250	1,550	1,950	3,100	5,600
F-404	Scofield	Gilfillan	Red, scalloped		1,200	1,425	1,725	2,350	4,600
F-405	Bruce	Gilfillan	Red, scalloped		1,200	1,425	1,750	2,400	4,600
F-406	Bruce	Wyman	Red, scalloped	4 known	—	—	—	—	—
F-406a	Bruce	Jordan	Red, scalloped	4 known	—	—	—	—	—
F-407	Rosecrans	Huston	Red, scalloped		1,400	1,700	2,400	3,400	—
F-408	Rosecrans	Jordan	Red, scalloped	6 known	—	—	—	—	—
F-408a	Rosecrans	Nebeker	Red, scalloped	Unique	—	—	—	—	—
F-408b	Tillman	Morgan	Red, scalloped	2 known	—	—	—	—	—

National Bank Notes
Series of 1882 Brown Back
("Second Charter Period")

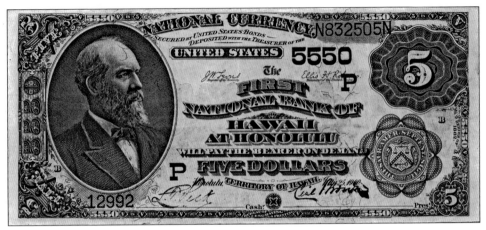

Face of F-466 to F-478. Portrait of President James A. Garfield. The bank names vary widely in style.

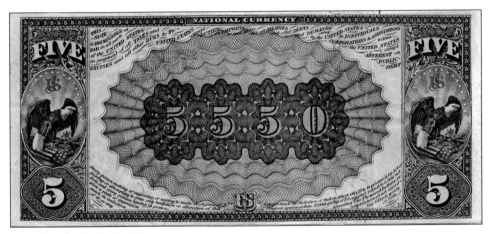

Back of F-466 to F-478. Bank charter number at center.

No.	Signatures			VG-8	F-12	VF-20	EF-40	Unc-63
F-466	Bruce	Gilfillan		$400	$525	$700	$975	$1,850
F-467	Bruce	Wyman		390	500	675	925	1,750
F-468	Bruce	Jordan		425	575	725	1,050	2,150
F-469	Rosecrans	Jordan		400	525	700	975	1,850
F-470	Rosecrans	Hyatt		425	575	725	1,050	2,150
F-471	Rosecrans	Huston		400	525	700	975	1,850
F-472	Rosecrans	Nebeker		400	525	700	975	1,850
F-473	Rosecrans	Morgan		550	800	1,150	2,350	3,900
F-474	Tillman	Morgan		400	525	700	975	1,850
F-475	Tillman	Roberts		425	600	750	1,150	2,300
F-476	Bruce	Roberts		450	650	800	1,275	2,600
F-477	Lyons	Roberts		450	650	800	1,275	2,600
F-477a	Lyons	Treat	Unknown	—	—	—	—	—
F-478	Vernon	Treat	7 known	—	—	—	—	—

National Bank Notes
Series of 1882 Date Back
("Second Charter Period")

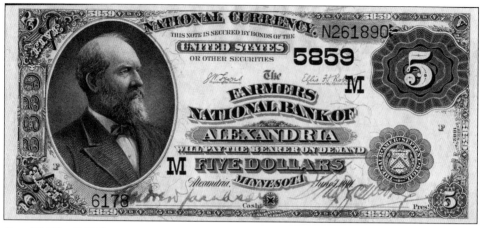

Face of F-532 to F-538b.

Back of F-532 to F-538b.

No.	Signatures			VG-8	F-12	VF-20	EF-40	Unc-63
F-532	Rosecrans	Huston		$425	$525	$675	$1,150	$2,300
F-533	Rosecrans	Nebeker		415	515	600	900	2,100
F-533a	Rosecrans	Morgan	3 known	—	—	—	—	—
F-534	Tillman	Morgan		415	515	600	900	2,050
F-535	Tillman	Roberts		450	600	750	1,000	—
F-536	Bruce	Roberts		450	600	700	1,350	2,750
F-537	Lyons	Roberts		400	500	585	850	1,900
F-538	Vernon	Treat		450	600	850	1,100	—
F-538a	Vernon	McClung	Unknown	—	—	—	—	—
F-538b	Napier	McClung	7 known	1,100	2,200	2,750	3,500	—

National Bank Notes
Series of 1882 Value Back
("Second Charter Period")

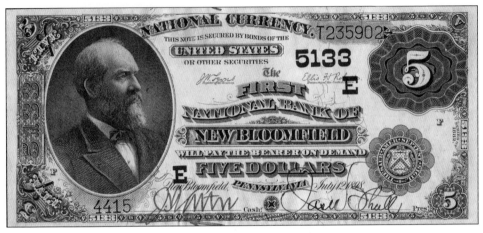

Face of F-573 to F-575b.

Back of F-573 to F-575b.

No.	Signatures			VG-8	F-12	VF-20	EF-40	Unc-63
F-573	Tillman	Morgan		$650	$850	$1,300	—	—
F-573a	Tillman	Roberts	6 known	800	1,000	1,400	$2,200	—
F-574	Lyons	Roberts	8 known	500	640	800	1,175	$2,450
F-574a	Bruce	Roberts	Unknown	—	—	—	—	—
F-574b	Lyons	Treat		—	—	—	—	—
F-575	Vernon	Treat		650	850	1,300	—	—
F-575a	Napier	McClung	11 known	675	875	1,350	—	—
F-575b	Teehee	Burke	6 known	—	—	—	—	—

Note: These notes were issued from 1916 to 1922 in sheets of 5-5-5-5.

National Bank Notes
Series of 1902 Red Seal
("Third Charter Period")

Face of F-587 to F-589. Portrait of President Benjamin Harrison.

Back of F-587 to F-589.

No.	Signatures		VG-8	F-12	VF-20	EF-40	Unc-63
F-587	Lyons	Roberts	$450	$550	$725	$925	$2,100
F-588	Lyons	Treat	575	675	800	1,100	2,500
F-589	Vernon	Treat	625	725	875	1,250	2,750

National Bank Notes
Series of 1902 Blue Seal, Date Back
("Third Charter Period")

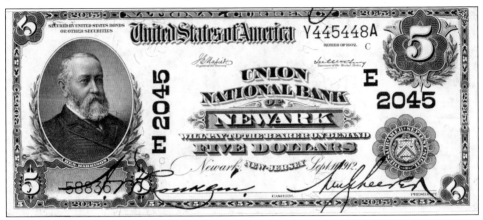

Face of F-590 to F-597a.

Back of F-590 to F-597a.

No.	Signatures			VG-8	F-12	VF-20	EF-40	Unc-63
F-590	Lyons	Roberts		$120	$140	$215	$330	$650
F-591	Lyons	Treat		125	150	225	350	700
F-592	Vernon	Treat		120	140	215	330	675
F-593	Vernon	McClung		120	140	215	330	675
F-594	Napier	McClung		125	150	225	350	700
F-595	Napier	Thompson		160	215	285	430	825
F-596	Napier	Burke		150	200	275	400	775
F-597	Parker	Burke		140	170	250	385	750
F-597a	Teehee	Burke	Unique	—	—	—	—	—

National Bank Notes
Series of 1902 Blue Seal, Plain Back ("Third Charter Period")

Face of F-598 to F-612.

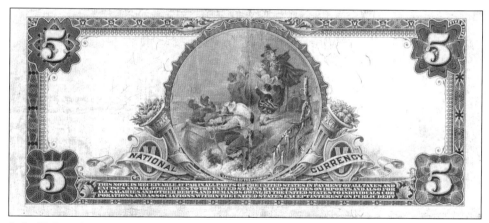

Back of F-598 to F-612.

No.	Signatures		VG-8	F-12	VF-20	EF-40	Unc-63
F-598	Lyons	Roberts	$100	$120	$150	$285	$550
F-599	Lyons	Treat	100	120	150	285	600
F-600	Vernon	Treat	100	120	150	285	550
F-601	Vernon	McClung	100	120	150	285	575
F-602	Napier	McClung	100	120	150	285	600
F-603	Napier	Thompson	125	150	190	375	725
F-604	Napier	Burke	110	130	170	330	650
F-605	Parker	Burke	100	120	160	320	650
F-606	Teehee	Burke	100	120	150	285	550
F-607	Elliott	Burke	100	120	150	285	575
F-608	Elliott	White	100	120	150	285	600
F-609	Speelman	White	100	120	150	285	575
F-610	Woods	White	115	135	175	350	675
F-611	Woods	Tate	115	135	175	350	675
F-612	Jones	Woods	375	500	675	1,250	2,750

National Gold Bank Notes

Face of F-1136 to F-1141. This is the same design as used on Original Series $5 notes F-394 to F-399. Printed on paper tinted to impart a "golden" appearance.

Back of F-1136 to F-1141. An assortment of contemporary gold coins.

No.	Date	Name of Bank	City		Fair	VG-8	F-12	VF-20	EF-40
F-1136	1870	First National Gold Bank	San Francisco		$1,150	$2,600	$5,900	$12,500	$25,000
F-1137	1872	National Gold Bank and Trust Company	San Francisco	Rare above F-12	1,600	4,000	10,500	—	—
F-1138	1872	National Gold Bank of D.O. Mills and Co.	Sacramento	Rare above F-12	1,800	4,500	12,500	—	—
F-1139	1873	First National Gold Bank	Santa Barbara	Rare above VG-8	2,750	8,250	—	—	—
F-1140	1873	First National Gold Bank	Stockton	Rare above VG-8	2,750	8,250	15,000	—	—
F-1141	1874	Farmer's National Gold Bank	San Jose		1,600	4,000	10,000	25,000	—

Silver Certificates
Series of 1886

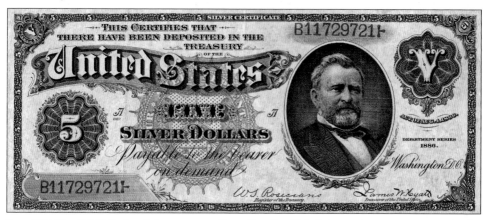

Face of F-259 to F-265. Seals and placements vary. Bust of President U.S. Grant.

Back of F-259 to F-265, the "Silver Dollar Note." The center coin shows the date of the series, 1886.

No.	Signatures		Seal	VG-8	F-12	VF-20	EF-40	Unc-63
F-259	Rosecrans	Jordan	Small red, plain	$900	$1,650	$3,500	$6,500	$10,000
F-260	Rosecrans	Hyatt	Small red, plain	850	1,350	2,600	6,000	10,000
F-261	Rosecrans	Hyatt	Large red	800	1,300	2,400	5,400	10,000
F-262	Rosecrans	Huston	Large red	975	1,450	3,000	6,200	11,000
F-263	Rosecrans	Huston	Large brown	800	1,300	2,400	5,400	10,000
F-264	Rosecrans	Nebeker	Large brown	1,000	1,500	3,200	7,000	10,000
F-265	Rosecrans	Nebeker	Small red, scalloped	1,250	2,000	4,000	8,750	21,000

Silver Certificates
Series of 1891

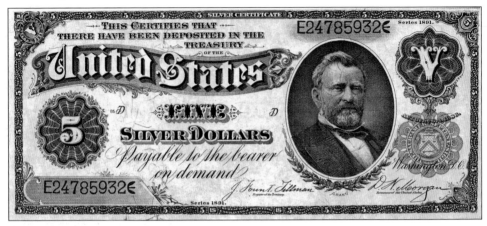

Face of F-266 and F-267. Bust of President U.S. Grant.

Back of F-266 and F-267.

No.	Signatures		Seal	VG-8	F-12	VF-20	EF-40	Unc-63
F-266	Rosecrans	Nebeker	Small red, scalloped	$400	$775	$1,050	$2,300	$4,250
F-267	Tillman	Morgan	Small red	400	650	900	1,800	3,850

Silver Certificates
Series of 1896

Face of F-268 to F-270. The third and final note in the "Educational Series," with "Electricity Presenting Light to the World."

Back of F-268 to F-270. Busts of President U.S. Grant and General Philip Sheridan.

No.	Signatures		Seal	VG-8	F-12	VF-20	EF-40	Unc-63
F-268	Tillman	Morgan	Small red	$725	$1,175	$2,300	$4,800	$9,600
F-269	Bruce	Roberts	Small red	800	1,300	2,300	4,950	10,000
F-270	Lyons	Roberts	Small red	925	1,500	2,750	6,000	12,500

Silver Certificates
Series of 1899

Face of F-271 to F-281. "Indian Chief Note" featuring the chief colloquially known as "Running Antelope."

Back of F-271 to F-281.

No.	Signatures		Seal	VG-8	F-12	VF-20	EF-40	Unc-63
F-271	Lyons	Roberts	Blue	$450	$550	$675	$1,300	$2,650
F-272	Lyons	Treat	Blue	485	625	800	1,500	3,450
F-273	Vernon	Treat	Blue	475	600	750	1,450	3,100
F-274	Vernon	McClung	Blue	485	625	800	1,500	3,450
F-275	Napier	McClung	Blue	460	575	700	1,325	2,900
F-276	Napier	Thompson	Blue	575	835	1,400	2,750	6,000
F-277	Parker	Burke	Blue	460	575	700	1,325	2,900
F-278	Teehee	Burke	Blue	460	575	700	1,325	2,900
F-279	Elliott	Burke	Blue	460	600	725	1,400	2,950
F-280	Elliott	White	Blue	430	550	650	1,265	2,550
F-281	Speelman	White	Blue	430	550	650	1,250	2,500

Silver Certificates
Series of 1923

Face of F-282, the "Porthole Note." Portrait of President Abraham Lincoln.

Back of F-282. The Great Seal of the United States.

No.	Signatures		Seal	VG-8	F-12	VF-20	EF-40	Unc-63
F-282	Speelman	White	Blue	$600	$725	$1,150	$2,100	$4,050

Treasury or Coin Notes
Series of 1890

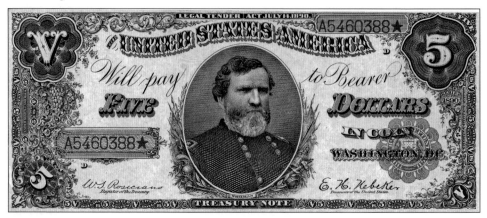

Face of F-359 to F-361. Bust of Civil War General George H. Thomas.

Back of F-359 to F-361.

No.	Signatures		Seal	VG-8	F-12	VF-20	EF-40	Unc-63
F-359	Rosecrans	Huston	Large brown	$400	$700	$1,500	$2,400	$8,500
F-360	Rosecrans	Nebeker	Large brown	2,200	5,000	10,000	50,000	Rare
F-361	Rosecrans	Nebeker	Small red	375	600	1,300	2,100	7,500

Treasury or Coin Notes
Series of 1891

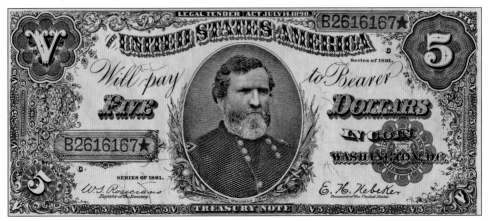

Face of F-362 to F-365.

Back of F-362 to F-365.

No.	Signatures		Seal	VG-8	F-12	VF-20	EF-40	Unc-63
F-362	Rosecrans	Nebeker	Small red	$325	$500	$800	$1,175	$2,600
F-363	Tillman	Morgan	Small red	325	485	775	1,150	2,550
F-364	Bruce	Roberts	Small red	325	500	800	1,175	2,600
F-365	Lyons	Roberts	Small red	450	750	1,500	3,000	15,000

Federal Reserve Notes, *Series of 1914, Red Seal*

Suffix Letters on Types F-832A to F-891C

Red Seals—"*A*" *suffix:* Large district letter and numeral at top right and bottom left. Small letter at top left and bottom right. *B suffix:* As above, but with small district letter and numeral added above letter at top left. Red Seals are scarcer than Blue Seals.

Blue Seals—"*A*" *suffix:* Large district letter and numeral at top left and bottom right. *B suffix:* Large letter and numeral at top right with small district letters and numerals in the other three corners. *C suffix:* Again, a large pair of letters and numerals, but positioned both vertically, more toward the center of the note and closer to the outside edge. Also, the seals to the sides of the portrait are closer to the note's center than on the Blue Seal notes with A suffix.

Face of F-832A to F-843B.

Back of F-832A to F-843B.

No.	Issuing Bank	VG-8	F-12	VF-20	EF-40	Unc-63
Signatures of Burke and McAdoo						
F-832A	Boston	$225	$425	$700	$800	—
F-832B	Boston	190	325	525	800	$2,700
F-833A	New York	200	375	575	800	2,000
F-833B	New York	175	225	375	800	1,650
F-834A	Philadelphia	225	400	575	800	3,650
F-834B	Philadelphia	190	250	375	875	3,300
F-835A	Cleveland	275	475	700	800	3,750
F-835B	Cleveland	190	350	475	975	2,700
F-836A	Richmond	350	550	825	1,350	4,000
F-836B	Richmond	275	475	700	1,150	3,750
F-837A	Atlanta	225	425	700	800	3,400
F-837B	Atlanta	190	350	525	800	2,700
F-838A	Chicago	200	385	600	800	2,350
F-838B	Chicago	190	325	500	800	1,900
F-839A	St. Louis	225	425	700	800	3,000
F-839B	St. Louis	200	375	550	800	2,700
F-840A	Minneapolis	250	450	650	800	3,400
F-840B	Minneapolis	200	375	575	800	3,100
F-841A	Kansas City	275	450	650	800	5,400
F-841B	Kansas City	350	575	850	1,150	—
F-842A	Dallas	800	1,350	2,200	3,750	—
F-842B	Dallas	350	575	1,100	2,400	9,000
F-843A	San Francisco	750	1,200	2,100	4,250	—
F-843B	San Francisco	225	425	650	800	5,000

Federal Reserve Notes
Series of 1914, Blue Seal

Face of F-844 to F-891C. Back is the same as the preceding.

No.	Issuing Bank	Signatures		VG-8	F-12	VF-20	EF-40	Unc-63
F-844	Boston	Burke	McAdoo	$60	$75	$105	$160	$375
F-845	Boston	Burke	Glass	75	95	125	300	650
F-846	Boston	Burke	Houston	55	65	75	115	250
F-847A	Boston	White	Mellon	55	65	75	115	250
F-847B	Boston	White	Mellon	80	100	125	190	450
F-848	New York	Burke	McAdoo	55	65	75	125	375
F-849	New York	Burke	Glass	70	95	120	160	425
F-850	New York	Burke	Houston	55	65	75	125	300
F-851A	New York	White	Mellon	55	65	75	115	250
F-851B	New York	White	Mellon	60	75	100	145	400
F-851C	New York	White	Mellon	55	65	75	115	300
F-852	Philadelphia	Burke	McAdoo	65	75	105	190	450
F-853	Philadelphia	Burke	Glass	75	95	120	160	400
F-854	Philadelphia	Burke	Houston	60	70	85	150	375
F-855A	Philadelphia	White	Mellon	55	65	75	115	250
F-855B	Philadelphia	White	Mellon	75	85	110	150	450
F-855C	Philadelphia	White	Mellon	55	65	75	115	250
F-856	Cleveland	Burke	McAdoo	65	75	115	190	450
F-857	Cleveland	Burke	Glass	75	105	185	245	700
F-858	Cleveland	Burke	Houston	60	70	85	125	350
F-859A	Cleveland	White	Mellon	55	65	75	115	250
F-859B	Cleveland	White	Mellon	65	75	90	160	375
F-859C	Cleveland	White	Mellon	60	70	80	125	290
F-860	Richmond	Burke	McAdoo	65	85	110	170	450
F-861	Richmond	Burke	Glass	85	100	180	350	1,250
F-862	Richmond	Burke	Houston	60	70	85	160	425
F-863A	Richmond	White	Mellon	55	65	75	125	350
F-863B	Richmond	White	Mellon	300	800	1,750	3,000	—
F-864	Atlanta	Burke	McAdoo	65	75	105	160	475
F-865	Atlanta	Burke	Glass	100	150	225	300	750
F-866	Atlanta	Burke	Houston	65	80	110	165	400
F-867A	Atlanta	White	Mellon	55	65	75	135	375
F-867B	Atlanta	White	Mellon	475	600	800	1,400	—
F-868	Chicago	Burke	McAdoo	65	75	90	125	350
F-869	Chicago	Burke	Glass	70	80	100	145	400
F-870	Chicago	Burke	Houston	60	70	80	125	325
F-871A	Chicago	White	Mellon	55	65	75	115	290
F-871B	Chicago	White	Mellon	60	70	80	125	325
F-871C	Chicago	White	Mellon	70	80	90	150	375
F-872	St. Louis	Burke	McAdoo	70	80	105	140	375
F-873	St. Louis	Burke	Glass	80	110	185	250	600
F-874	St. Louis	Burke	Houston	70	80	105	140	375
F-875A	St. Louis	White	Mellon	70	80	100	135	350
F-875B	St. Louis	White	Mellon	75	85	110	160	425

Chart continued on next page.

No.	Issuing Bank	Signatures		VG-8	F-12	VF-20	EF-40	Unc-63
F-876	Minneapolis	Burke	McAdoo	$75	$90	$110	$160	$450
F-877	Minneapolis	Burke	Glass	90	115	145	250	700
F-878	Minneapolis	Burke	Houston	75	90	120	170	575
F-879A	Minneapolis	White	Mellon	60	80	115	160	425
F-880	Kansas City	Burke	McAdoo	70	85	110	170	450
F-881	Kansas City	Burke	Glass	85	105	130	200	750
F-882	Kansas City	Burke	Houston	65	80	100	150	375
F-883A	Kansas City	White	Mellon	65	80	100	140	350
F-883B	Kansas City	White	Mellon	100	180	325	500	—
F-884	Dallas	Burke	McAdoo	90	150	275	400	1,200
F-885	Dallas	Burke	Glass	190	350	550	1,400	—
F-886	Dallas	Burke	Houston	80	105	150	225	750
F-887A	Dallas	White	Mellon	60	80	105	165	400
F-887B	Dallas	White	Mellon	90	115	175	300	750
F-888	San Francisco	Burke	McAdoo	70	85	110	200	—
F-889	San Francisco	Burke	Glass	150	210	400	900	—
F-890	San Francisco	Burke	Houston	70	85	110	150	400
F-891A	San Francisco	White	Mellon	60	70	90	135	350
F-891B	San Francisco	White	Mellon	70	85	115	150	400
F-891C	San Francisco	White	Mellon	130	200	400	875	2,300

Federal Reserve Bank Notes
Series of 1918

Face of F-781 to F-809a. Bust of Abraham Lincoln.

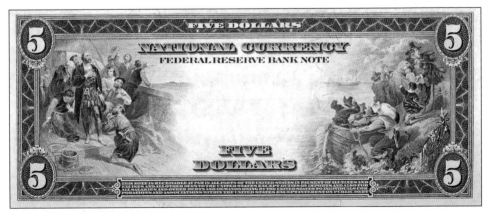

Back of F-781 to F-809a. "Columbus in Sight of Land" at left, "Landing of the Pilgrims" at right.

No.	Issuing Bank	Treasury Signatures		Bank Signatures		VG-8	F-12	VF-20	EF-40	Unc-63
F-781	Boston	Teehee	Burke	Bullen	Morss	$250	$400	$800	$1,800	$3,500
F-782	New York	Teehee	Burke	Hendricks	Strong	150	250	425	675	1,100
F-783	Philadelphia	Teehee	Burke	Hardt	Passmore	150	325	475	700	1,100
F-784	Philadelphia	Teehee	Burke	Dyer	Passmore	175	350	550	1,000	2,250
F-785	Cleveland	Teehee	Burke	Baxter	Fancher	150	235	350	475	1,100
F-786	Cleveland	Teehee	Burke	Davis	Fancher	275	450	675	1,000	2,000
F-787	Cleveland	Elliott	Burke	Davis	Fancher	150	300	475	750	1,100
F-788	Atlanta	Teehee	Burke	Bell	Wellborn	250	400	1,100	2,500	—
F-789	Atlanta	Teehee	Burke	Pike	McCord	150	325	475	675	—
F-790	Atlanta	Teehee	Burke	Pike	McCord	150	325	475	675	1,100
F-791	Atlanta	Teehee	Burke	Bell	Wellborn	250	400	1,100	2,500	4,500
F-792	Atlanta	Elliott	Burke	Bell	Wellborn	385	600	1,250	2,750	4,500
F-793	Chicago	Teehee	Burke	McLallen	McDougal	225	375	575	925	1,850
F-794	Chicago	Teehee	Burke	McCloud	McDougal	150	275	375	600	1,300
F-795	Chicago	Teehee	Burke	Cramer	McDougal	575	1,250	2,750	5,000	—
F-796	St. Louis	Teehee	Burke	Attebery	Wells	165	300	400	650	1,100
F-797	St. Louis	Teehee	Burke	Attebery	Biggs	200	375	550	800	1,750
F-798	St. Louis	Elliott	Burke	White	Biggs	300	475	675	925	1,750
F-799	Minneapolis	Teehee	Burke	Cook	Wold	250	325	575	1,000	1,750
F-800	Kansas City	Teehee	Burke	Anderson	Miller	250	325	525	775	1,100
F-801	Kansas City	Teehee	Burke	Cross	Miller	450	900	1,700	3,000	—
F-802	Kansas City	Teehee	Burke	Helm	Miller	575	1,250	2,000	3,000	5,000
F-803	Kansas City	Teehee	Burke	Anderson	Miller	200	325	550	775	1,100
F-804	Kansas City	Elliott	Burke	Helm	Miller	200	300	500	750	1,100
F-805	Dallas	Teehee	Burke	Hoopes	Van Zandt	325	575	950	1,400	3,000
F-806	Dallas	Teehee	Burke	Talley	Van Zandt	550	1,100	2,600	6,500	—
F-807	Dallas	Teehee	Burke	Talley	Van Zandt	350	600	950	1,400	4,250
With date May 20, 1914										
F-808	San Francisco	Teehee	Burke	Clerk	Lynch	250	500	800	1,200	2,600
F-809	San Francisco	Teehee	Burke	Clerk	Lynch	525	800	1,350	2,750	5,000
With date May 18, 1914										
F-809a	San Francisco	Teehee	Burke	Clerk	Lynch	500	750	1,250	2,500	5,500

Note: The Richmond Bank did not issue notes.

SMALL-SIZE $5 NOTES

Legal Tender Notes
Series of 1928 to 1928-F, Red Seal at Left

Face of F-1525 to F-1531.

Back of F-1525 to F-1535.

See next page for chart.

No.	Series	Signatures		Quantity Printed	VF-20	Unc-63
F-1525	1928	Woods	Mellon	267,209,616	$24	$100
F-1525★	1928	Woods	Mellon		400	2,000
F-1526	1928-A	Woods	Mills	58,194,600	30	175
F-1526★	1928-A	Woods	Mills		550	7,000
F-1527	1928-B	Julian	Morgenthau	147,827,340	20	80
F-1527★	1928-B	Julian	Morgenthau		225	900
F-1528	1928-C	Julian	Morgenthau	214,735,765	20	80
F-1528★	1928-C	Julian	Morgenthau		120	775
F-1529	1928-D	Julian	Vinson	9,297,120	55	300
F-1529★	1928-D	Julian	Vinson		1,350	5,750
F-1530	1928-E	Julian	Snyder	109,952,760	20	75
F-1530★	1928-E	Julian	Snyder		130	900
F-1531	1928-F	Clark	Snyder	104,194,704	18	60
F-1531★	1928-F	Clark	Snyder		80	575

Legal Tender Notes
Series of 1953 to 1953-C,
Red Seal at Right

Face of F-1532 to F-1535, the type of Series 1953 to 1963 with red Treasury seal at right. Back type of all $5 notes, all series through the 1950s.

No.	Series	Signatures		Quantity Printed	VF-20	Unc-63
F-1532	1953	Priest	Humphrey	120,880,000	$12	$50
F-1532★	1953	Priest	Humphrey	5,760,000	50	300
F-1533	1953-A	Priest	Anderson	90,280,000	12	50
F-1533★	1953-A	Priest	Anderson	5,400,000	40	175
F-1534	1953-B	Smith	Dillon	44,640,000	12	35
F-1534★	1953-B	Smith	Dillon	2,160,000	45	175
F-1535	1953-C	Granahan	Dillon	8,640,000	15	40
F-1535★	1953-C	Granahan	Dillon	320,000	65	175

Legal Tender Notes
Series of 1963,
Red Seal at Right, Motto Added

Face of F-1536, type as preceding.

Back of F-1536 with IN GOD WE TRUST above Lincoln Memorial.

No.	Signatures		Quantity Printed	VF-20	Unc-63
F-1536	Granahan	Dillon	63,360,000	$12	$25
F-1536★	Granahan	Dillon	3,840,000	20	75

National Bank Notes
Series of 1929, Type 1

Face of F-1800-1. Bank charter number in black at left and right borders. Back type is the same as on all other $5 notes, through the 1950s.

No.		VF-20	Unc-60
F-1800-1	Issued from 1929 to 1935 in sheets of 6 notes	$75	$225

National Bank Notes
Series of 1929, Type 2

Face of F-1800-2. Bank charter number now also in brown at lower left and upper right of portrait. Back type is the same as on all other $5 notes, through the 1950s.

No.		VF-20	Unc-60
F-1800-2	Issued from 1929 to 1935 in sheets of 6 notes	$75	$225

Silver Certificates
Series of 1934 to 1934-D,
Blue Seal

Face of F-1650 to F-1654. Back type is the same as on all other $5 notes, through the 1950s.

No.	Series	Signatures		Quantity Printed	VF-20	Unc-63
F-1650	1934	Julian	Morgenthau	393,088,368	$15	$40
F-1650★	1934	Julian	Morgenthau		70	450
F-1651	1934-A	Julian	Morgenthau	656,265,948	12	25
F-1651★	1934-A	Julian	Morgenthau		45	300
F-1652	1934-B	Julian	Vinson	59,128,500	12	50
F-1652★	1934-B	Julian	Vinson		100	900
F-1653	1934-C	Julian	Snyder	403,146,148	12	30
F-1653★	1934-C	Julian	Snyder		55	200
F-1654	1934-D	Clark	Snyder	486,146,148	12	50
F-1654★	1934-D	Clark	Snyder		45	275

Silver Certificates
Series of 1934-A,
Yellow Seal for North Africa

Face of F-2307 with yellow Treasury seal. These were produced for distribution during World War II, around the Mediterranean Sea and North Africa. Back type is the same as on all other $5 notes, through the 1950s.

No.	Series	Quantity Printed	VF-20	Unc-63	No.	Series	Quantity Printed	VF-20	Unc-63
F-2307	1934-A	16,710,000	$75	$300	F-2307★	1934-A		$375	$3,000

Silver Certificates
Series of 1953 to 1953-C,
Blue Seal

Face of F-1655 to F-1658. Back type is the same as on all other $5 notes, through the 1950s.

No.	Series	Signatures		Quantity Printed	VF-20	Unc-63
F-1655	1953	Priest	Humphrey	339,600,000	$12	$33
F-1655★	1953	Priest	Humphrey	15,120,000	20	110
F-1656	1953-A	Priest	Anderson	232,400,000	12	30
F-1656★	1953-A	Priest	Anderson	12,960,000	25	70
F-1657	1953-B	Smith	Dillon	73,000,000†	12	30
F-1657★	1953-B	Smith	Dillon	3,240,000	2,000	15,000
F-1658	1953-C	Granahan	Dillon	Not released	—	—

†Only 14,196,000 notes were released.

Federal Reserve Bank Notes
Series of 1929,
Brown Seal

Face of F-1850, similar to others in this series. Incomplete sheets intended for National Bank Notes were overprinted to provide paper money to satisfy possible demand for paper money after the Bank Holiday of March 1933. Back type is the same as on all other $5 notes, through the 1950s.

No.	Issuing Bank	Quantity Printed	VF-20	Unc-63	No.	Issuing Bank	Quantity Printed	VF-20	Unc-63
F-1850A	Boston	3,180,000	$45	$150	F-1850H	St. Louis	276,000	$650	$5,750
F-1850B	New York	2,100,000	45	150	F-1850I	Minneapolis	684,000	150	750
F-1850C	Philadelphia	3,096,000	45	175	F-1850J	Kansas City	2,460,000	55	200
F-1850D	Cleveland	4,236,000	45	175	F-1850K	Dallas	996,000	45	200
F-1850F	Atlanta	1,884,000	45	200	F-1850L	San Francisco	360,000	2,900	11,250
F-1850G	Chicago	5,988,000	40	150	F-1850★	Most common districts		525	3,250

Federal Reserve Notes
Series of 1928 and 1928-A, Green Seal

Face of F-1950 to F-1951. The face printing notes that the bill is payable "in gold or lawful money," a provision since rescinded. Bank location at left represented by the district number.

Series of 1928—Signatures of Tate and Mellon

No.	Issuing Bank	Quantity Printed	VF-20	Unc-63	No.	Issuing Bank	Quantity Printed	VF-20	Unc-63
F-1950A	Boston	8,025,300	$75	$450	F-1950G	Chicago	12,320,052	$35	$235
F-1950A★	Boston		325	1,500	F-1950G★	Chicago		200	1,200
F-1950B	New York	14,701,884	35	275	F-1950H	St. Louis	4,675,200	165	1,200
F-1950B★	New York		375	1,975	F-1950H★	St. Louis		700	3,100
F-1950C	Philadelphia	11,819,712	50	400	F-1950I	Minneapolis	4,284,300	160	1,250
F-1950C★	Philadelphia		250	1,500	F-1950I★	Minneapolis		900	4,500
F-1950D	Cleveland	9,049,500	55	450	F-1950J	Kansas City	4,480,800	60	450
F-1950D★	Cleveland		350	1,800	F-1950J★	Kansas City		425	2,200
F-1950E	Richmond	6,027,600	35	275	F-1950K	Dallas	8,137,824	40	225
F-1950E★	Richmond		675	3,750	F-1950K★	Dallas		400	2,200
F-1950F	Atlanta	10,964,400	45	360	F-1950L	San Francisco	9,792,000	35	300
F-1950F★	Atlanta		350	2,750	F-1950L★	San Francisco		750	3,000

Series of 1928-A—Signatures of Woods and Mellon

No.	Issuing Bank	Quantity Printed	VF-20	Unc-63	No.	Issuing Bank	Quantity Printed	VF-20	Unc-63
F-1951A	Boston	9,404,352	$45	$300	F-1951F★	Atlanta		$550	$2,250
F-1951A★	Boston		900	2,000	F-1951G	Chicago	37,882,176	35	175
F-1951B	New York	42,878,196	40	200	F-1951G★	Chicago		325	1,625
F-1951B★	New York		600	1,450	F-1951H	St. Louis	2,731,824	50	250
F-1951C	Philadelphia	10,806,012	40	200	F-1951H★	St. Louis		625	2,500
F-1951C★	Philadelphia		750	2,125	F-1951I	Minneapolis	652,800	400	2,000
F-1951D	Cleveland	6,822,000	40	200	F-1951J	Kansas City	3,572,400	60	450
F-1951D★	Cleveland		450	2,125	F-1951K	Dallas	2,564,400	425	3,500
F-1951E	Richmond	2,409,900	50	225	F-1951K★	Dallas		1,700	4,200
F-1951E★	Richmond		400	2,400	F-1951L	San Francisco	6,565,500	55	350
F-1951F	Atlanta	3,537,600	150	1,550	F-1951L★	San Francisco		300	2,250

Federal Reserve Notes
Series of 1928-B to 1928-D, Green Seal

Face of F-1952 to F-1954, similar in style to the preceding, but now with the location at left represented by the district letter. The face printing notes that the bill is payable "in gold or lawful money." This style was continued through Series 1928-D.

Series of 1928-B—Signatures of Woods and Mellon

No.	Issuing Bank	Quantity Printed	VF-20	Unc-63	No.	Issuing Bank	Quantity Printed	VF-20	Unc-63
F-1952A	Boston	28,430,724	$25	$70	F-1952C	Philadelphia	25,698,396	$20	$65
F-1952A★	Boston		400	1,600	F-1952C★	Philadelphia		200	775
F-1952B	New York	51,157,536	25	85	F-1952D	Cleveland	24,874,272	20	65
F-1952B★	New York		275	1,250	F-1952D★	Cleveland		400	1,250

No.	Issuing Bank	Quantity Printed	VF-20	Unc-63	No.	Issuing Bank	Quantity Printed	VF-20	Unc-63
F-1952E	Richmond	15,151,932	$25	$95	F-1952I	Minneapolis	6,954,060	$45	$160
F-1952E★	Richmond		400	1,500	F-1952I★	Minneapolis		500	1,250
F-1952F	Atlanta	13,386,420	25	100	F-1952J	Kansas City	10,677,636	35	130
F-1952F★	Atlanta		275	900	F-1952J★	Kansas City		400	1,250
F-1952G	Chicago	17,157,036	25	100	F-1952K	Dallas	4,334,400	25	110
F-1952G★	Chicago		400	1,500	F-1952K★	Dallas		400	1,500
F-1952H	St. Louis	20,251,716	20	65	F-1952L	San Francisco	28,840,000	30	120
F-1952H★	St. Louis		290	1,250	F-1952L★	San Francisco		400	1,500

Series of 1928-C—Signatures of Woods and Mills

No.	Issuing Bank	Quantity Printed		VF-20	Unc-63
F-1953D	Cleveland	3,293,640	Unknown	—	—
F-1953F	Atlanta	2,056,200		$1,100	$4,500
F-1953L	San Francisco	266,304	Unknown	—	—

Series of 1928-D—Signatures of Woods and Woodin

No.	Issuing Bank	Quantity Printed	VF-20	Unc-63
F-1954F	Atlanta	1,281,600	$2,200	$7,500

Federal Reserve Notes
Series of 1934 to 1934-D, Green Seal

Face of F-1955 to F-1960.
The mention of gold removed.

Series of 1934—Signatures of Julian and Morgenthau

No.	Issuing Bank	Quantity Printed	VF-20	Unc-63	No.	Issuing Bank	Quantity Printed	VF-20	Unc-63
Notes with a vivid, light green seal					Notes with a darker and duller blue-green seal				
F-1955A	Boston	30,510,036	$15	$80	F-1956A	Boston		$20.00	$60
F-1955A★	Boston		125	850	F-1956A★	Boston		75.00	350
F-1955B	New York	47,888,760	15	80	F-1956B	New York		17.50	55
F-1955B★	New York		125	850	F-1956B★	New York		75.00	350
F-1955C	Philadelphia	47,327,760	15	80	F-1956C	Philadelphia		17.50	55
F-1955C★	Philadelphia		125	850	F-1956C★	Philadelphia		75.00	350
F-1955D	Cleveland	62,273,508	15	80	F-1956D	Cleveland		15.00	50
F-1955D★	Cleveland		175	1,000	F-1956D★	Cleveland		75.00	350
F-1955E	Richmond	62,128,452	15	80	F-1956E	Richmond		15.00	50
F-1955E★	Richmond		175	1,000	F-1956E★	Richmond		75.00	350
F-1955F	Atlanta	50,548,608	15	80	F-1956F	Atlanta		17.50	55
F-1955F★	Atlanta		200	1,000	F-1956F★	Atlanta		125.00	400
F-1955G	Chicago	31,299,156	15	80	F-1956G	Chicago		17.50	60
F-1955G★	Chicago		125	750	F-1956G★	Chicago		75.00	350
F-1955H	St. Louis	48,737,280	15	80	F-1956H	St. Louis		15.00	50
F-1955H★	St. Louis		125	850	F-1956H★	St. Louis		75.00	350
F-1955I	Minneapolis	16,795,392	30	100	F-1956I	Minneapolis		25.00	75
F-1955I★	Minneapolis		200	1,000	F-1956I★	Minneapolis		225.00	900
F-1955J	Kansas City	31,854,432	15	80	F-1956J	Kansas City		20.00	60
F-1955J★	Kansas City		175	1,000	F-1956J★	Kansas City		125.00	400
F-1955K	Dallas	33,332,208	15	80	F-1956K	Dallas		25.00	65
F-1955K★	Dallas		200	1,000	F-1956K★	Dallas		125.00	450
F-1955L	San Francisco	39,324,168	15	80	F-1956L	San Francisco		17.50	60
F-1955L★	San Francisco		125	1,000	F-1956L★	San Francisco		125.00	400

Note: The quantity printed is the combined total for both light- and dark-seal notes.

Federal Reserve Notes
Series of 1934 and 1934-A, Brown Seal, Hawaii

Face of F-2301 to F-2302 with HAWAII overprinted at the left and right ends and with Treasury seal and serial numbers in brown.

Back of F-2301 to F-2302 with large HAWAII overprint.

No.	Series	Quantity Printed	VF-20	Unc-63	No.	Series	Quantity Printed	VF-20	Unc-63
F-2301	1934	9,416,000	$125	$750	F-2302	1934-A	Incl. in F-2301	$100	$650
F-2301★	1934		3,175	10,000	F-2302★	1934-A		7,500	Rare

Federal Reserve Notes
(continued from F-1956L★)

Series of 1934-A—Signatures of Julian and Morgenthau

No.	Issuing Bank	Quantity Printed	VF-20	Unc-63	No.	Issuing Bank	Quantity Printed	VF-20	Unc-63
F-1957A	Boston	23,231,568	$12.50	$25	F-1957E★	Richmond		$90.00	$400
F-1957A★	Boston		45.00	275	F-1957F	Atlanta	22,811,916	30.00	150
F-1957B	New York	143,199,336	12.50	30	F-1957F★	Atlanta		90.00	450
F-1957B★	New York		45.00	275	F-1957G	Chicago	88,376,376	12.50	30
F-1957C	Philadelphia	30,691,632	12.50	30	F-1957G★	Chicago		45.00	275
F-1957C★	Philadelphia		50.00	300	F-1957H	St. Louis	7,843,452	30.00	85
F-1957D	Cleveland	1,610,676	15.00	35	F-1957H★	St. Louis		90.00	300
F-1957D★	Cleveland		90.00	425	F-1957L	San Francisco	72,118,452	15.00	40
F-1957E	Richmond	6,555,168	15.00	35	F-1957L★	San Francisco		90.00	275

Series of 1934-B—Signatures of Julian and Vinson

No.	Issuing Bank	Quantity Printed	VF-20	Unc-63	No.	Issuing Bank	Quantity Printed	VF-20	Unc-63
F-1958A	Boston	3,457,800	$20	$90	F-1958F★	Atlanta		$200	$950
F-1958A★	Boston		125	800	F-1958G	Chicago	9,070,932	20	100
F-1958B	New York	14,099,580	15	75	F-1958G★	Chicago		110	675
F-1958B★	New York		110	625	F-1958H	St. Louis	4,307,712	20	100
F-1958C	Philadelphia	8,306,820	15	80	F-1958H★	St. Louis		125	675
F-1958C★	Philadelphia		150	700	F-1958I	Minneapolis	2,482,500	30	150
F-1958D	Cleveland	11,348,184	15	80	F-1958I★	Minneapolis		125	800
F-1958D★	Cleveland		110	800	F-1958J	Kansas City	73,800	1,200	2,750
F-1958E	Richmond	5,902,848	25	110	F-1958J★	Kansas City		Rare	—
F-1958E★	Richmond		110	950	F-1958L	San Francisco	9,910,296	15	90
F-1958F	Atlanta	4,314,048	25	110	F-1958L★	San Francisco		350	1,600

Series of 1934-C—Signatures of Julian and Snyder

No.	Issuing Bank	Quantity Printed	VF-20	Unc-63	No.	Issuing Bank	Quantity Printed	VF-20	Unc-63
F-1959A	Boston	14,463,600	$20	$50	F-1959G	Chicago	60,598,812	$15	$45
F-1959A★	Boston		90	600	F-1959G★	Chicago		90	500
F-1959B	New York	74,383,248	15	45	F-1959H	St. Louis	20,393,340	25	60
F-1959B★	New York		90	500	F-1959H★	St. Louis		90	600
F-1959C	Philadelphia	22,879,212	15	45	F-1959I	Minneapolis	5,089,200	30	125
F-1959C★	Philadelphia		110	600	F-1959I★	Minneapolis		125	800
F-1959D	Cleveland	19,898,256	15	45	F-1959J	Kansas City	8,313,504	25	60
F-1959D★	Cleveland		80	450	F-1959J★	Kansas City		150	600
F-1959E	Richmond	23,800,524	15	45	F-1959K	Dallas	5,107,800	30	65
F-1959E★	Richmond		110	550	F-1959K★	Dallas		175	800
F-1959F	Atlanta	23,572,968	15	45	F-1959L	San Francisco	9,451,944	25	60
F-1959F★	Atlanta		110	675	F-1959L★	San Francisco		110	600

Series of 1934-D—Signatures of Clark and Snyder

No.	Issuing Bank	Quantity Printed	VF-20	Unc-63	No.	Issuing Bank	Quantity Printed	VF-20	Unc-63
F-1960A	Boston	12,660,552	$20	$60	F-1960G	Chicago	36,601,680	$15	$65
F-1960A★	Boston		100	700	F-1960G★	Chicago		80	500
F-1960B	New York	50,976,576	15	50	F-1960H	St. Louis	8,093,412	25	65
F-1960B★	New York		80	550	F-1960H★	St. Louis		125	650
F-1960C	Philadelphia	12,106,740	15	50	F-1960I	Minneapolis	3,594,900	50	425
F-1960C★	Philadelphia		80	625	F-1960I★	Minneapolis		400	1,550
F-1960D	Cleveland	8,969,052	15	60	F-1960J	Kansas City	6,538,740	25	80
F-1960D★	Cleveland		125	1,100	F-1960J★	Kansas City		125	750
F-1960E	Richmond	13,333,032	25	65	F-1960K	Dallas	4,139,016	25	135
F-1960E★	Richmond		125	1,250	F-1960K★	Dallas		150	775
F-1960F	Atlanta	9,599,352	200	1,200	F-1960L	San Francisco	11,704,200	20	70
F-1960F★	Atlanta		400	3,100	F-1960L★	San Francisco		125	775

Federal Reserve Notes
Series of 1950 to 1950-E,
Green Seal

Face of F-1961 to F-1985. The seal was modified starting with F-1969.

Series of 1950—Signatures of Clark and Snyder

No.	Issuing Bank	Quantity Printed	VF-20	Unc-63	No.	Issuing Bank	Quantity Printed	VF-20	Unc-63
F-1961A	Boston	30,672,000	$15.00	$60	F-1961G	Chicago	85,104,000	$15.00	$60
F-1961A★	Boston	408,000	45.00	325	F-1961G★	Chicago	1,176,000	45.00	300
F-1961B	New York	106,768,000	12.50	50	F-1961H	St. Louis	36,864,000	12.50	55
F-1961B★	New York	1,464,000	40.00	275	F-1961H★	St. Louis	552,000	45.00	325
F-1961C	Philadelphia	44,784,000	12.50	50	F-1961I	Minneapolis	11,796,000	12.50	70
F-1961C★	Philadelphia	600,000	45.00	325	F-1961I★	Minneapolis	144,000	125.00	625
F-1961D	Cleveland	54,000,000	12.50	55	F-1961J	Kansas City	25,428,000	12.50	60
F-1961D★	Cleveland	744,000	45.00	325	F-1961J★	Kansas City	360,000	45.00	475
F-1961E	Richmond	47,088,000	12.50	50	F-1961K	Dallas	22,848,000	12.50	65
F-1961E★	Richmond	684,000	60.00	425	F-1961K★	Dallas	372,000	80.00	525
F-1961F	Atlanta	52,416,000	12.50	55	F-1961L	San Francisco	55,008,000	12.50	60
F-1961F★	Atlanta	696,000	45.00	325	F-1961L★	San Francisco	744,000	60.00	325

Series of 1950-A—Signatures of Priest and Humphrey

No.	Issuing Bank	Quantity Printed	VF-20	Unc-63	No.	Issuing Bank	Quantity Printed	VF-20	Unc-63
F-1962A	Boston	53,568,000	$10.00	$25	F-1962G	Chicago	129,296,000	$10.00	$25
F-1962A★	Boston	2,808,000	20.00	75	F-1962G★	Chicago	6,264,000	15.00	65
F-1962B	New York	186,472,000	10.00	25	F-1962H	St. Louis	54,936,000	10.00	25
F-1962B★	New York	9,216,000	17.50	60	F-1962H★	St. Louis	3,384,000	35.00	115
F-1962C	Philadelphia	69,616,000	10.00	25	F-1962I	Minneapolis	11,232,000	15.00	35
F-1962C★	Philadelphia	4,320,000	20.00	75	F-1962I★	Minneapolis	864,000	55.00	325
F-1962D	Cleveland	45,360,000	10.00	25	F-1962J	Kansas City	29,952,000	12.50	30
F-1962D★	Cleveland	2,376,000	20.00	75	F-1962J★	Kansas City	1,088,000	30.00	90
F-1962E	Richmond	76,672,000	10.00	25	F-1962K	Dallas	24,984,000	15.00	35
F-1962E★	Richmond	5,400,000	35.00	115	F-1962K★	Dallas	1,368,000	35.00	125
F-1962F	Atlanta	86,464,000	10.00	25	F-1962L	San Francisco	90,712,000	10.00	25
F-1962F★	Atlanta	5,040,000	20.00	75	F-1962L★	San Francisco	744,000	20.00	75

Series of 1950-B—Signatures of Priest and Anderson

No.	Issuing Bank	Quantity Printed	VF-20	Unc-63	No.	Issuing Bank	Quantity Printed	VF-20	Unc-63
F-1963A	Boston	30,880,000	$8	$25	F-1963G	Chicago	104,320,000	$8.00	$25
F-1963A★	Boston	2,520,000	15	65	F-1963G★	Chicago	6,120,000	15.00	65
F-1963B	New York	85,960,000	8	25	F-1963H	St. Louis	25,840,000	8.00	25
F-1963B★	New York	4,680,060	15	55	F-1963H★	St. Louis	1,440,000	20.00	75
F-1963C	Philadelphia	43,560,000	8	25	F-1963I	Minneapolis	20,880,000	12.50	40
F-1963C★	Philadelphia	2,880,000	15	65	F-1963I★	Minneapolis	792,000	45.00	125
F-1963D	Cleveland	38,800,000	8	25	F-1963J	Kansas City	32,400,000	8.00	25
F-1963D★	Cleveland	2,880,000	15	65	F-1963J★	Kansas City	2,520,000	20.00	75
F-1963E	Richmond	52,920,000	8	25	F-1963K	Dallas	52,120,000	10.00	25
F-1963E★	Richmond	2,080,000	25	90	F-1963K★	Dallas	3,240,000	20.00	75
F-1963F	Atlanta	80,560,000	8	25	F-1963L	San Francisco	56,080,000	8.00	25
F-1963F★	Atlanta	3,960,000	20	80	F-1963L★	San Francisco	3,600,000	20.00	75

Series of 1950-C—Signatures of Smith and Dillon

No.	Issuing Bank	Quantity Printed	VF-20	Unc-63	No.	Issuing Bank	Quantity Printed	VF-20	Unc-63
F-1964A	Boston	20,880,000	$8	$20	F-1964G	Chicago	56,880,000	$8	$20
F-1964A★	Boston	720,000	40	165	F-1964G★	Chicago	3,240,000	20	75
F-1964B	New York	47,440,000	8	20	F-1964H	St. Louis	22,680,000	10	25
F-1964B★	New York	2,880,000	15	60	F-1964H★	St. Louis	720,000	35	120
F-1964C	Philadelphia	29,520,000	8	20	F-1964I	Minneapolis	12,960,000	20	40
F-1964C★	Philadelphia	1,800,000	20	75	F-1964I★	Minneapolis	720,000	45	165
F-1964D	Cleveland	33,840,000	8	20	F-1964J	Kansas City	24,760,000	8	20
F-1964D★	Cleveland	1,800,000	25	80	F-1964J★	Kansas City	1,800,000	25	80
F-1964E	Richmond	33,480,000	8	20	F-1964K	Dallas	3,960,000	20	75
F-1964E★	Richmond	2,160,000	25	80	F-1964K★	Dallas	360,000	45	160
F-1964F	Atlanta	54,360,000	8	20	F-1964L	San Francisco	25,920,000	8	20
F-1964F★	Atlanta	3,240,000	20	75	F-1964L★	San Francisco	1,440,000	35	125

Series of 1950-D—Signatures of Granahan and Dillon

No.	Issuing Bank	Quantity Printed	VF-20	Unc-63	No.	Issuing Bank	Quantity Printed	VF-20	Unc-63
F-1965A	Boston	25,200,000	$8	$20	F-1965G	Chicago	67,240,000	$8	$20
F-1965A★	Boston	1,080,000	25	110	F-1965G★	Chicago	3,600,000	15	55
F-1965B	New York	102,160,000	8	20	F-1965H	St. Louis	20,160,000	8	20
F-1965B★	New York	5,040,000	15	55	F-1965H★	St. Louis	720,000	30	90
F-1965C	Philadelphia	21,520,000	8	20	F-1965I	Minneapolis	7,920,000	10	30
F-1965C★	Philadelphia	1,080,000	20	65	F-1965I★	Minneapolis	360,000	40	180
F-1965D	Cleveland	23,400,000	8	20	F-1965J	Kansas City	11,160,000	8	20
F-1965D★	Cleveland	1,080,000	20	80	F-1965J★	Kansas City	720,000	30	90
F-1965E	Richmond	42,960,000	8	20	F-1965K	Dallas	7,200,000	10	25
F-1965E★	Richmond	1,080,000	25	110	F-1965K★	Dallas	360,000	35	135
F-1965F	Atlanta	35,200,000	8	25	F-1965L	San Francisco	53,280,000	8	20
F-1965F★	Atlanta	1,800,000	20	90	F-1965L★	San Francisco	3,600,000	20	80

Series of 1950-E—Signatures of Granahan and Fowler

No.	Issuing Bank	Quantity Printed	VF-20	Unc-63	No.	Issuing Bank	Quantity Printed	VF-20	Unc-63
F-1966B	New York	82,000,000	$10	$35	F-1966G★	Chicago	1,080,000	$45.00	$240
F-1966B★	New York	6,678,000	20	80	F-1966L	San Francisco	24,400,000	12.50	50
F-1966G	Chicago	14,760,000	15	70	F-1966L★	San Francisco	1,800,000	45.00	175

Federal Reserve Notes
Series of 1963 to 1963-A,
Green Seal, Motto Added

Back with IN GOD WE TRUST added. Back type of F-1967 to F-1985.

Series of 1963—Signatures of Granahan and Dillon

No.	Issuing Bank	Quantity Printed	VF-20	Unc-63	No.	Issuing Bank	Quantity Printed	VF-20	Unc-63
F-1967A	Boston	4,480,000	$7	$30	F-1967G	Chicago	22,400,000	$7.00	$20
F-1967A★	Boston	640,000	25	115	F-1967G★	Chicago	3,200,000	12.50	55
F-1967B	New York	12,160,000	7	25	F-1967H	St. Louis	14,080,000	7.00	25
F-1967B★	New York	1,280,000	20	75	F-1967H★	St. Louis	1,920,000	15.00	55
F-1967C	Philadelphia	8,320,000	7	25	F-1967J	Kansas City	1,920,000	7.00	25
F-1967C★	Philadelphia	1,920,000	15	65	F-1967J★	Kansas City	640,000	25.00	85
F-1967D	Cleveland	10,240,000	7	25	F-1967K	Dallas	5,760,000	7.00	25
F-1967D★	Cleveland	1,920,000	15	65	F-1967K★	Dallas	1,920,000	20.00	80
F-1967F	Atlanta	17,920,000	7	25	F-1967L	San Francisco	18,560,000	7.00	25
F-1967F★	Atlanta	2,560,000	15	65	F-1967L★	San Francisco	1,920,000	15.00	60

Series of 1963-A—Signatures of Granahan and Fowler

No.	Issuing Bank	Quantity Printed	VF-20	Unc-63	No.	Issuing Bank	Quantity Printed	VF-20	Unc-63
F-1968A	Boston	77,440,000	$6.00	$25	F-1968G	Chicago	213,440,000	$7.00	$25
F-1968A★	Boston	5,760,000	12.00	45	F-1968G★	Chicago	16,640,000	10.00	30
F-1968B	New York	98,080,000	6.00	20	F-1968H	St. Louis	56,960,000	7.00	25
F-1968B★	New York	7,680,000	10.00	35	F-1968H★	St. Louis	5,120,000	12.50	45
F-1968C	Philadelphia	106,400,000	6.00	20	F-1968I	Minneapolis	32,640,000	10.00	35
F-1968C★	Philadelphia	10,240,000	10.00	35	F-1968I★	Minneapolis	3,200,000	20.00	70
F-1968D	Cleveland	83,840,000	6.00	20	F-1968J	Kansas City	55,040,000	7.00	30
F-1968D★	Cleveland	7,040,000	9.00	30	F-1968J★	Kansas City	5,760,000	12.50	45
F-1968E	Richmond	118,560,000	6.00	20	F-1968K	Dallas	64,000,000	7.00	25
F-1968E★	Richmond	10,880,000	10.00	35	F-1968K★	Dallas	3,840,000	15.00	50
F-1968F	Atlanta	117,920,000	7.00	25	F-1968L	San Francisco	128,900,000	7.00	25
F-1968F★	Atlanta	9,600,000	12.50	45	F-1968L★	San Francisco	12,153,000	12.50	45

Federal Reserve Notes
Series of 1969 to 1995,
Green Seal

Series of 1969 (with new Treasury seal)—Signatures of Elston and Kennedy

No.	Issuing Bank	Quantity Printed	VF-20	Unc-63	No.	Issuing Bank	Quantity Printed	VF-20	Unc-63
F-1969A	Boston	51,200,000	$6	$20.00	F-1969G	Chicago	125,600,000	$6	$17.50
F-1969A★	Boston	1,920,000	9	50.00	F-1969G★	Chicago	5,120,000	10	32.50
F-1969B	New York	198,560,000	6	17.50	F-1969H	St. Louis	27,520,000	6	20.00
F-1969B★	New York	8,960,000	9	32.50	F-1969H★	St. Louis	1,280,000	10	50.00
F-1969C	Philadelphia	69,120,000	6	17.50	F-1969I	Minneapolis	16,640,000	6	22.50
F-1969C★	Philadelphia	2,560,000	9	32.50	F-1969I★	Minneapolis	640,000	15	70.00
F-1969D	Cleveland	56,320,000	6	17.50	F-1969J	Kansas City	48,640,000	6	17.50
F-1969D★	Cleveland	2,560,000	10	32.50	F-1969J★	Kansas City	3,192,000	10	32.50
F-1969E	Richmond	84,480,000	6	17.50	F-1969K	Dallas	39,680,000	6	17.50
F-1969E★	Richmond	3,200,000	10	32.50	F-1969K★	Dallas	1,920,000	10	40.00
F-1969F	Atlanta	84,480,000	6	17.50	F-1969L	San Francisco	103,840,000	6	17.50
F-1969F★	Atlanta	3,840,000	10	32.50	F-1969L★	San Francisco	4,480,000	10	35.00

Series of 1969-A—Signatures of Kabis and Connally

No.	Issuing Bank	Quantity Printed	VF-20	Unc-63	No.	Issuing Bank	Quantity Printed	VF-20	Unc-63
F-1970A	Boston	23,040,000	$8.00	$22.50	F-1970G	Chicago	60,800,000	$8.00	$22.50
F-1970A★	Boston	1,280,000	12.50	55.00	F-1970G★	Chicago	1,920,000	12.50	45.00
F-1970B	New York	62,240,000	8.00	22.50	F-1970H	St. Louis	15,360,000	8.00	22.50
F-1970B★	New York	1,760,000	12.50	45.00	F-1970H★	St. Louis	640,000	15.00	60.00
F-1970C	Philadelphia	41,160,000	8.00	22.50	F-1970I	Minneapolis	8,960,000	8.00	35.00
F-1970C★	Philadelphia	1,920,000	12.50	45.00	F-1970I★	Minneapolis	640,000	20.00	80.00
F-1970D	Cleveland	21,120,000	8.00	22.50	F-1970J	Kansas City	17,920,000	8.00	22.50
F-1970D★	Cleveland	640,000	15.00	65.00	F-1970J★	Kansas City	640,000	15.00	70.00
F-1970E	Richmond	37,920,000	8.00	22.50	F-1970K	Dallas	21,120,000	8.00	22.50
F-1970E★	Richmond	1,120,000	12.50	60.00	F-1970K★	Dallas	640,000	17.50	70.00
F-1970F	Atlanta	25,120,000	8.00	22.50	F-1970L	San Francisco	44,800,000	8.00	22.50
F-1970F★	Atlanta	480,000	17.50	90.00	F-1970L★	San Francisco	1,920,000	15.00	50.00

Series of 1969-B—Signatures of Banuelos and Connally

No.	Issuing Bank	Quantity Printed	VF-20	Unc-63	No.	Issuing Bank	Quantity Printed	VF-20	Unc-63
F-1971A	Boston	5,760,000	$17.50	$100	F-1971G	Chicago	27,040,000	$15.00	$80
F-1971B	New York	34,560,000	15.00	65	F-1971G★	Chicago	480,000	40.00	200
F-1971B★	New York	634,000	30.00	200	F-1971H	St. Louis	5,120,000	17.50	90
F-1971C	Philadelphia	5,120,000	15.00	100	F-1971I	Minneapolis	8,320,000	17.50	90
F-1971D	Cleveland	12,160,000	15.00	80	F-1971J	Kansas City	8,320,000	17.50	90
F-1971E	Richmond	15,360,000	15.00	80	F-1971J★	Kansas City	640,000	50.00	200
F-1971E★	Richmond	640,000	30.00	175	F-1971K	Dallas	12,160,000	15.00	75
F-1971F	Atlanta	18,560,000	15.00	80	F-1971L	San Francisco	23,160,000	15.00	75
F-1971F★	Atlanta	640,000	40.00	200	F-1971L★	San Francisco	640,000	30.00	200

Series of 1969-C—Signatures of Banuelos and Shultz

No.	Issuing Bank	Quantity Printed	VF-20	Unc-63	No.	Issuing Bank	Quantity Printed	VF-20	Unc-63
F-1972A	Boston	50,720,000	$7.00	$20	F-1972F★	Atlanta	3,200,000	$10.00	$45
F-1972A★	Boston	1,920,000	12.50	60	F-1972G	Chicago	54,400,000	7.00	20
F-1972B	New York	120,000,000	7.00	20	F-1972H	St. Louis	37,760,000	7.00	20
F-1972B★	New York	2,400,000	10.00	45	F-1972H★	St. Louis	1,280,000	12.50	55
F-1972C	Philadelphia	53,760,000	7.00	20	F-1972I	Minneapolis	14,080,000	10.00	45
F-1972C★	Philadelphia	1,280,000	10.00	50	F-1972J	Kansas City	41,120,000	7.00	20
F-1972D	Cleveland	43,680,000	7.00	20	F-1972J★	Kansas City	1,920,000	12.50	55
F-1972D★	Cleveland	1,120,000	12.50	65	F-1972K	Dallas	41,120,000	7.00	20
F-1972E	Richmond	73,760,000	7.00	20	F-1972K★	Dallas	1,920,000	12.50	65
F-1972E★	Richmond	640,000	12.50	60	F-1972L	San Francisco	80,800,000	7.00	20
F-1972F	Atlanta	81,440,000	7.00	20	F-1972L★	San Francisco	3,680,000	10.00	55

Series of 1974—Signatures of Neff and Simon

No.	Issuing Bank	Quantity Printed	VF-20	Unc-63	No.	Issuing Bank	Quantity Printed	VF-20	Unc-63
F-1973A	Boston	58,240,000	$7.00	$12.50	F-1973G	Chicago	95,520,000	$7.00	$12.50
F-1973A★	Boston	1,408,000	12.50	50.00	F-1973G★	Chicago	1,760,000	10.00	35.00
F-1973B	New York	153,120,000	7.00	12.50	F-1973H	St. Louis	64,800,000	7.00	12.50
F-1973B★	New York	2,656,000	10.00	35.00	F-1973H★	St. Louis	1,760,000	20.00	65.00
F-1973C	Philadelphia	53,920,000	7.00	12.50	F-1973I	Minneapolis	41,600,000	7.00	12.50
F-1973C★	Philadelphia	3,040,000	10.00	35.00	F-1973I★	Minneapolis	2,560,000	12.50	35.00
F-1973D	Cleveland	78,080,000	7.00	12.50	F-1973J	Kansas City	42,240,000	7.00	12.50
F-1973D★	Cleveland	1,920,000	10.00	40.00	F-1973J★	Kansas City	2,176,000	10.00	35.00
F-1973E	Richmond	135,200,000	7.00	12.50	F-1973K	Dallas	57,600,000	7.00	12.50
F-1973E★	Richmond	1,760,000	10.00	40.00	F-1973K★	Dallas	1,408,000	12.50	45.00
F-1973F	Atlanta	127,520,000	7.00	12.50	F-1973L	San Francisco	139,680,000	7.00	12.50
F-1973F★	Atlanta	3,040,000	10.00	40.00	F-1973L★	San Francisco	5,088,000	10.00	40.00

Series of 1977—Signatures of Morton and Blumenthal

No.	Issuing Bank	Quantity Printed	VF-20	Unc-63	No.	Issuing Bank	Quantity Printed	VF-20	Unc-63
F-1974A	Boston	60,800,000	$7.00	$12.50	F-1974G	Chicago	177,920,000	$7.00	$12.50
F-1974A★	Boston	1,664,000	35.00	100.00	F-1974G★	Chicago	2,816,000	10.00	40.00
F-1974B	New York	183,040,000	7.00	12.50	F-1974H	St. Louis	46,080,000	7.00	12.50
F-1974B★	New York	3,072,000	10.00	35.00	F-1974H★	St. Louis	128,000	55.00	150.00
F-1974C	Philadelphia	78,720,000	7.00	12.50	F-1974I	Minneapolis	21,760,000	7.00	15.00
F-1974C★	Philadelphia	1,280,000	12.50	50.00	F-1974J	Kansas City	78,080,000	7.00	12.50
F-1974D	Cleveland	72,960,000	7.00	12.50	F-1974J★	Kansas City	1,408,000	12.50	50.00
F-1974D★	Cleveland	1,152,000	12.50	55.00	F-1974K	Dallas	60,800,000	7.00	12.50
F-1974E	Richmond	110,720,000	7.00	15.00	F-1974K★	Dallas	2,408,000	20.00	55.00
F-1974E★	Richmond	2,816,000	12.50	45.00	F-1974L	San Francisco	135,040,000	7.00	12.50
F-1974F	Atlanta	127,360,000	7.00	12.50	F-1974L★	San Francisco	2,432,000	12.50	50.00
F-1974F★	Atlanta	1,920,000	12.50	50.00					

Series of 1977-A—Signatures of Morton and Miller

No.	Issuing Bank	Quantity Printed	VF-20	Unc-63	No.	Issuing Bank	Quantity Printed	VF-20	Unc-63
F-1975A	Boston	48,000,000	$6	$15	F-1975G	Chicago	80,640,000	$6	$15
F-1975A★	Boston	512,000	20	65	F-1975G★	Chicago	1,408,000	15	45
F-1975B	New York	113,920,000	6	15	F-1975H	St. Louis	42,240,000	6	15
F-1975B★	New York	2,304,000	15	45	F-1975H★	St. Louis	640,000	20	60
F-1975C	Philadelphia	55,680,000	6	15	F-1975I	Minneapolis	10,240,000	6	15
F-1975C★	Philadelphia	640,000	15	45	F-1975I★	Minneapolis	256,000	30	75
F-1975D	Cleveland	58,880,000	6	15	F-1975J	Kansas City	52,480,000	6	15
F-1975D★	Cleveland	1,280,000	15	50	F-1975J★	Kansas City	1,024,000	20	55
F-1975E	Richmond	77,440,000	6	15	F-1975K	Dallas	76,160,000	6	15
F-1975E★	Richmond	768,000	35	90	F-1975K★	Dallas	1,408,000	20	50
F-1975F	Atlanta	76,160,000	6	15	F-1975L	San Francisco	106,880,000	6	15
F-1975F★	Atlanta	1,152,000	15	50	F-1975L★	San Francisco	1,152,000	20	55

Series of 1981—Signatures of Buchanan and Regan

No.	Issuing Bank	Quantity Printed	VF-20	Unc-63	No.	Issuing Bank	Quantity Printed	VF-20	Unc-63
F-1976A	Boston	109,000,000	$10.00	$25	F-1976G	Chicago	241,280,000	$10.00	$25
F-1976B	New York	250,880,000	10.00	25	F-1976G★	Chicago	768,000	20.00	65
F-1976B★	New York	4,464,000	20.00	70	F-1976H	St. Louis	199,680,000	10.00	25
F-1976C	Philadelphia	112,640,000	10.00	25	F-1976H★	St. Louis	628,000	30.00	95
F-1976C★	Philadelphia	640,000	25.00	95	F-1976I	Minneapolis	109,440,000	10.00	25
F-1976D	Cleveland	122,240,000	10.00	25	F-1976I★	Minneapolis	640,000	45.00	125
F-1976D★	Cleveland	1,268,000	25.00	95	F-1976J	Kansas City	125,440,000	10.00	25
F-1976E	Richmond	234,880,000	10.00	25	F-1976J★	Kansas City	960,000	30.00	95
F-1976E★	Richmond	640,000	20.00	70	F-1976K	Dallas	138,240,000	10.00	25
F-1976F	Atlanta	234,880,000	10.00	25	F-1976K★	Dallas	640,000	22.50	95
F-1976F★	Atlanta	1,644,000	22.50	90	F-1976L	San Francisco	263,680,000	10.00	25

Series of 1981-A—Signatures of Ortega and Regan

No.	Issuing Bank	Quantity Printed	VF-20	Unc-63	No.	Issuing Bank	Quantity Printed	VF-20	Unc-63
F-1977A	Boston	192,000,000	$15	$40	F-1977G	Chicago	345,600,000	$15	$35
F-1977B	New York	448,000,000	15	35	F-1977H	St. Louis	128,000,000	15	40
F-1977B★	New York	3,200,000	40	165	F-1977I	Minneapolis	73,800,000	15	40
F-1977C	Philadelphia	169,600,000	15	35	F-1977J	Kansas City	134,400,000	25	70
F-1977D	Cleveland	214,400,000	15	35	F-1977K	Dallas	176,000,000	20	50
F-1977E	Richmond	332,800,000	15	35	F-1977L	San Francisco	438,400,000	20	50
F-1977F	Atlanta	352,000,000	15	35	F-1977L★	San Francisco	3,200,000	40	165

Series of 1985—Signatures of Ortega and Baker

No.	Issuing Bank	Quantity Printed	VF-20	Unc-63	No.	Issuing Bank	Quantity Printed	VF-20	Unc-63
F-1978A	Boston	192,000,000	$7.50	$17.50	F-1978G	Chicago	348,000,000	$7.50	$17.50
F-1978B	New York	451,200,000	7.50	17.50	F-1978G★	Chicago	6,400,000	20.00	70.00
F-1978B★	New York	3,200,000	30.00	90.00	F-1978H	St. Louis	128,000,000	7.50	17.50
F-1978C	Philadelphia	170,400,000	7.50	17.00	F-1978I	Minneapolis	173,600,000	7.50	17.50
F-1978C★	Philadelphia	6,400,000	20.00	70.00	F-1978J	Kansas City	135,200,000	7.50	17.50
F-1978D	Cleveland	216,000,000	7.50	17.50	F-1978K	Dallas	176,800,000	7.50	17.50
F-1978E	Richmond	335,200,000	7.50	17.50	F-1978K★	Dallas	3,200,000	20.00	70.00
F-1978E★	Richmond	3,200,000	25.00	85.00	F-1978L	San Francisco	460,800,000	7.50	17.50
F-1978F	Atlanta	354,400,000	7.50	17.50	F-1978L★	San Francisco	3,200,000	25.00	80.00
F-1978F★	Atlanta	6,400,000	20.00	70.00					

Series of 1988—Signatures of Ortega and Brady

No.	Issuing Bank	Quantity Printed	VF-20	Unc-63	No.	Issuing Bank	Quantity Printed	VF-20	Unc-63
F-1979A	Boston	86,400,000	$7.50	$17.50	F-1979F★	Atlanta	6,400,000	$20.00	$60.00
F-1979A★	Boston	768,000	35.00	100.00	F-1979G	Chicago	134,400,000	7.50	17.50
F-1979B	New York	185,600,000	7.50	17.50	F-1979H	St. Louis	51,200,000	7.50	17.50
F-1979B★	New York	3,200,000	20.00	60.00	F-1979I	Minneapolis	9,600,000	15.00	40.00
F-1979C	Philadelphia	54,400,000	7.50	17.50	F-1979J	Kansas City	44,800,000	7.50	17.50
F-1979D	Cleveland	111,200,000	7.50	17.50	F-1979K	Dallas	54,500,000	7.50	17.50
F-1979E	Richmond	131,200,000	7.50	17.50	F-1979L	San Francisco	70,400,000	7.50	17.50
F-1979F	Atlanta	137,200,000	7.50	17.50					

Series of 1988-A—Signatures of Villalpando and Brady
Printed in Washington, DC

No.	Issuing Bank	Quantity Printed	VF-20	Unc-63	No.	Issuing Bank	Quantity Printed	VF-20	Unc-63
F-1980A	Boston	140,800,000	$7.50	$17.50	F-1980F★	Atlanta	2,640,000	$15.00	$45.00
F-1980A★	Boston	3,200,000	15.00	55.00	F-1980G	Chicago	633,600,000	7.50	17.50
F-1980B	New York	640,000,000	7.50	17.50	F-1980H	St. Louis	185,600,000	7.50	17.50
F-1980B★	New York	4,608,000	12.50	40.00	F-1980H★	St. Louis	1,280,000	15.00	55.00
F-1980C	Philadelphia	70,400,000	7.50	17.50	F-1980I	Minneapolis	73,600,000	7.50	17.50
F-1980D	Cleveland	166,000,000	7.50	17.50	F-1980I★	Minneapolis	3,200,000	20.00	75.00
F-1980D★	Cleveland	4,864,000	12.50	40.00	F-1980J	Kansas City	115,200,000	7.50	17.50
F-1980E	Richmond	486,400,000	7.50	17.50	F-1980K	Dallas	128,000,000	7.50	17.50
F-1980E★	Richmond	3,020,000	12.50	40.00	F-1980L	San Francisco	492,800,000	7.50	17.50
F-1980F	Atlanta	192,000,000	7.50	17.50					

Series of 1988-A—Signatures of Villalpando and Brady
Printed at the Western Facility (Fort Worth, Texas)

No.	Issuing Bank	Quantity Printed	VF-20	Unc-63	No.	Issuing Bank	Quantity Printed	VF-20	Unc-63
F-1981C	Philadelphia	25,600,000	$6	$15	F-1981J	Kansas City	25,600,000	$6	$15
F-1981F	Atlanta	282,400,000	6	15	F-1981K	Dallas	44,800,000	6	15
F-1981F★	Atlanta	640,000	15	40	F-1981L	San Francisco	179,200,000	6	15
F-1981G	Chicago	76,800,000	6	15	F-1981L★	San Francisco	3,200,000	15	40
F-1981G★	Chicago	1,280,000	15	40					

Note: The notes that are printed in Fort Worth may be identified by a small FW on the right front side next to the plate check letter-number. See illustration under "One-Dollar Notes."

Series of 1993—Signatures of Withrow and Bentsen
Printed in Washington, DC

No.	Issuing Bank	Quantity Printed	VF-20	Unc-63	No.	Issuing Bank	Quantity Printed	VF-20	Unc-63
F-1982A	Boston	38,400,000	$6	$15	F-1982E	Richmond	76,800,000	$6	$15
F-1982B	New York	102,400,000	6	15	F-1982E★	Richmond	1,920,000	15	35
F-1982B★	New York	2,816,000	15	35	F-1982F	Atlanta	70,400,000	6	15
F-1982C	Philadelphia	38,400,000	6	15					

Series of 1993—Signatures of Withrow and Bentsen
Printed at the Western Facility (Fort Worth, Texas)

No.	Issuing Bank	Quantity Printed	VF-20	Unc-63	No.	Issuing Bank	Quantity Printed	VF-20	Unc-63
F-1983G	Chicago	64,000,000	$6	$15	F-1983J	Kansas City	32,000,000	$6.00	$15
F-1983G★	Chicago	1,280,000	15	40	F-1983K	Dallas	57,600,000	6.00	15
F-1983H	St. Louis	64,000,000	6	15	F-1983L	San Francisco	185,600,000	6.00	15
F-1983H★	St. Louis	2,560,000	15	40	F-1983L★	San Francisco	2,560,000	12.50	35
F-1983I	Minneapolis	6,400,000	75	250					

Series of 1995—Signatures of Withrow and Rubin
Printed in Washington, DC

No.	Issuing Bank	Quantity Printed	VF-20	Unc-63	No.	Issuing Bank	Quantity Printed	VF-20	Unc-63
F-1984A	Boston	160,000,000	$6	$15	F-1984C	Philadelphia	128,000,000	$6	$15
F-1984A★	Boston	640,000	25	115	F-1984D	Cleveland	89,600,000	6	15
F-1984B	New York	390,040,444	6	15	F-1984E	Richmond	300,800,000	6	10
F-1984B★	New York	3,840,000	10	35	F-1984F	Atlanta	179,200,000	6	10

Series of 1995—Signatures of Withrow and Rubin
Printed at the Western Facility (Fort Worth, Texas)

No.	Issuing Bank	Quantity Printed	VF-20	Unc-63	No.	Issuing Bank	Quantity Printed	VF-20	Unc-63
F-1985A	Boston	57,600,000	$6.00	$13	F-1985G	Chicago	524,800,000	$6	$13
F-1985B	New York	76,800,000	6.00	13	F-1985G★	Chicago	9,600,000	15	35
F-1985C	Philadelphia	38,000,000	6.00	13	F-1985H	St. Louis	204,800,000	6	13
F-1985D	Cleveland	64,000,000	6.00	13	F-1985I	Minneapolis	64,000,000	6	18
F-1985D★	Cleveland	3,200,000	12.50	35	F-1985J	Kansas City	160,000,000	6	13
F-1985E	Richmond	108,000,000	6.00	13	F-1985K	Dallas	204,800,000	6	13
F-1985F	Atlanta	448,000,000	6.00	13	F-1985L	San Francisco	706,800,000	6	13
F-1985F★	Atlanta	70,400,000	15.00	40					

Federal Reserve Notes
Series of 1999 to 2006,
Green Seal, Security Features

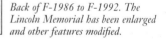

Face of F-1986 to F-1992, the type used from Series 1999 to 2006. Lincoln's portrait is modified as are other aspects, and security features have been added.

Back of F-1986 to F-1992. The Lincoln Memorial has been enlarged and other features modified.

Series of 1999—Signatures of Withrow and Summers
Printed in Washington, DC

No.	Issuing Bank	Quantity Printed	Unc-63	No.	Issuing Bank	Quantity Printed	Unc-63
F-1986A	Boston	19,200,000	$12.50	F-1986D	Cleveland	25,600,000	$12.50
F-1986B	New York	76,800,000	12.50	F-1986E	Richmond	96,000,000	12.50
F-1986B★	New York	35,200	25.00	F-1986E★	Richmond	739,200	30.00
F-1986C	Philadelphia	57,600,000	12.50				

Series of 1999—Signatures of Withrow and Summers
Printed at the Western Facility (Fort Worth, Texas)

No.	Issuing Bank	Quantity Printed	Unc-63	No.	Issuing Bank	Quantity Printed	Unc-63
F-1987A	Boston	70,400,000	$12.50	F-1987G	Chicago	140,800,000	$12.50
F-1987A★	Boston	3,200,000	25.00	F-1987G★	Chicago	3,200,000	25.00
F-1987B	New York	256,000,000	12.50	F-1987H	St. Louis	44,800,000	12.50
F-1987B★	New York	3,840,000	25.00	F-1987I	Minneapolis	12,800,000	17.50
F-1987C	Philadelphia	89,600,000	12.50	F-1987J	Kansas City	32,000,000	12.50
F-1987D	Cleveland	12,800,000	12.50	F-1987J★	Kansas City	3,200,000	25.00
F-1987E	Richmond	185,600,000	12.50	F-1987K	Dallas	121,600,000	12.50
F-1987E★	Richmond	3,200,000	25.00	F-1987K★	Dallas	3,200,000	25.00
F-1987F	Atlanta	211,200,000	12.50	F-1987L	San Francisco	243,200,000	12.50
F-1987F★	Atlanta	10,915,200	25.00				

Series of 2001—Signatures of Marin and O'Neill
All printed at the Western Facility (Fort Worth, Texas)

No.	Issuing Bank	Quantity Printed	Unc-63	No.	Issuing Bank	Quantity Printed	Unc-63
F-1988A	Boston	128,000,000	$15.00	F-1988H	St. Louis	102,400,000	$15.00
F-1988B	New York	121,600,000	15.00	F-1988I	Minneapolis	32,000,000	17.50
F-1988C	Philadelphia	64,000,000	15.00	F-1988J	Kansas City	76,800,000	15.00
F-1988D	Cleveland	83,200,000	15.00	F-1988K	Dallas	211,200,000	15.00
F-1988E	Richmond	51,200,000	17.50	F-1988K★	Dallas	3,200,000	35.00
F-1988F	Atlanta	224,000,000	15.00	F-1988L	San Francisco	281,600,000	15.00
F-1988G	Chicago	185,600,000	15.00	F-1988L★	San Francisco	5,120,000	35.00

Series of 2003—Signatures of Marin and Snow
Printed in Washington, DC

No.	Issuing Bank	Quantity Printed	Unc-63	No.	Issuing Bank	Quantity Printed	Unc-63
F-1989A	Boston	32,000,000	$15	F-1989F	Atlanta	89,600,000	$15
F-1989C	Philadelphia	32,000,000	15	F-1989G	Chicago	32,000,000	15
F-1989D	Cleveland	32,000,000	15	F-1989G★	Chicago	1,600,000	60

Series of 2003—Signatures of Marin and Snow
Printed at the Western Facility (Fort Worth, Texas)

No.	Issuing Bank	Quantity Printed	Unc-63	No.	Issuing Bank	Quantity Printed	Unc-63
F-1990A	Boston	25,600,000	$15	F-1990G	Chicago	89,600,000	$15
F-1990B	New York	147,200,000	15	F-1990H	St. Louis	51,200,000	15
F-1990C	Philadelphia	38,400,000	15	F-1990I	Minneapolis	32,000,000	20
F-1990C★	Philadelphia		40	F-1990J	Kansas City	51,200,000	15
F-1990D	Cleveland	32,000,000	15	F-1990K	Dallas	96,000,000	15
F-1990E	Richmond	108,800,000	15	F-1990L	San Francisco	300,800,000	15
F-1990F	Atlanta	96,000,000	15	F-1990L★	San Francisco	3,200,000	40

Series of 2003-A—Signatures of Cabral and Snow
Printed at the Western Facility (Fort Worth, Texas)

No.	Issuing Bank	Unc-63	No.	Issuing Bank	Unc-63
F-1991A	Boston	$15	F-1991G	Chicago	$15
F-1991B	New York	15	F-1991G★	Chicago	25
F-1991B★	New York	25	F-1991H	St. Louis	15
F-1991C	Philadelphia	15	F-1991I	Minneapolis	15
F-1991D	Cleveland	15	F-1991J	Kansas City	15
F-1991E	Richmond	15	F-1991K	Dallas	15
F-1991F	Atlanta	15	F-1991L	San Francisco	15
F-1991F★	Atlanta	25	F-1991L★	San Francisco	25

Series of 2006—Signatures of Cabral and Paulson
Printed at the Western Facility (Fort Worth, Texas)

No.	Issuing Bank	Unc-63	No.	Issuing Bank	Unc-63
F-1992F	Atlanta	Current	F-1992I	Minneapolis	Current
F-1992G	Chicago	Current			

Federal Reserve Notes
Series of 2006 to Date, Green Seal, Additional Features

Face of F-1993 to date. Similar to the preceding, but with color and other security features added, including tiny yellow "05" numbers at left.

Back of F-1993 to date. Similar to the preceding, but with color and other security features added, including tiny yellow "05" numbers at right.

Series of 2006 (color added)—Signatures of Cabral and Paulson
Printed at the Western Facility (Fort Worth, Texas)

No.	Issuing Bank	Unc-63	No.	Issuing Bank	Unc-63
F-1993A	Boston	Current	F-1993G	Chicago	Current
F-1993A★	Boston	Current	F-1993G★	Chicago	Current
F-1993B★	New York	Current	F-1993H	St. Louis	Current
F-1993C	Philadelphia	Current	F-1993I	Minneapolis	Current
F-1993D	Cleveland	Current	F-1993J	Kansas City	Current
F-1993E	Richmond	Current	F-1993K	Dallas	Current
F-1993F	Atlanta	Current	F-1993L	San Francisco	Current
F-1993F★	Atlanta	Current	F-1993L★	San Francisco	Current

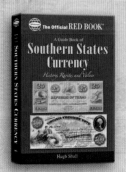
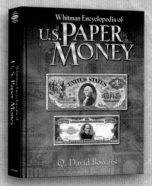
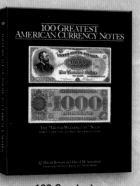

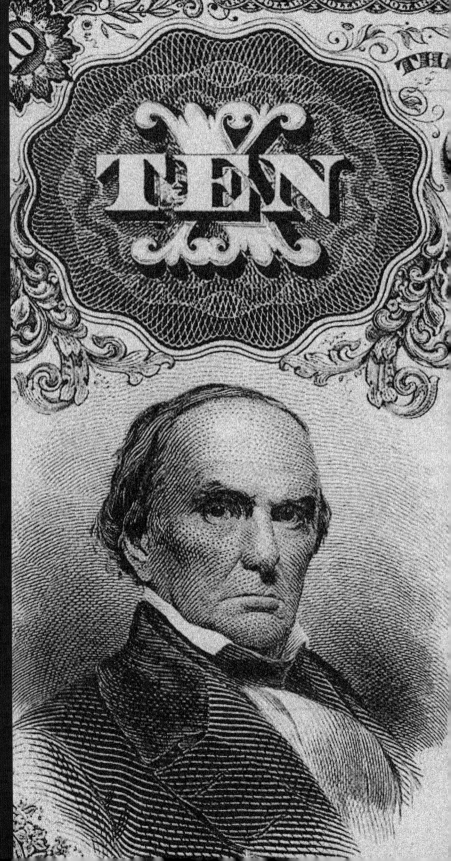

COLLECTING $10 NOTES

If you are looking to form a collection of United States paper money that includes a sample of every type of issue—from the horse blanket Demand Notes of 1861 up to the current-size Federal Reserve Notes—your only choice is to collect $10 bills. No other denomination has an example of every type of currency issued in the century-and-a-half since our present currency system was established.

Large-Size Notes

$10 Demand Notes of 1861, Large-Size. These were part of the first issues of "greenback" notes, used during the financial upheaval created by the Civil War. The three denominations were not legal tender at issue and were only declared so later. They were redeemable in coin "on demand," hence the name. See the $5 denomination chapter for an explanation of notes with "for the" handwritten on their face; there are 10 of these notes known in total, and in high grades they are virtually unknown. None has yet been reported in uncirculated condition. There have been a few recorded in Extremely Fine or About Uncirculated, but the vast majority of the 100-plus notes in our database are in Fine condition or lower.

$10 Interest-Bearing Notes, Large-Size. Interest-Bearing Notes are probably the single rarest class of American paper currency. The $10 Interest-Bearing Notes were produced under the Act of March 3, 1863, and earned interest, payable to the bearer upon presentation, at a rate of 5% only for a fixed period of one year. This was the lowest denomination issued in this category. As rare as these $10 notes are, they have to be considered the most common of any Interest-Bearing Notes in any denomination. They were only two issues, F-196 and F-196a, with the first being three times as scarce. There are only two notes known to be in better than Extremely Fine condition and two-thirds are Very Fine or less. These were held more by institutions than individuals and were quickly redeemed once interest earning ceased.

$10 Compound Interest Treasury Notes, Large-Size. The $10 denomination is also the lowest-valued note in this category. It is commonly stated that these notes, issued under the acts of March 3, 1863, and June 20, 1864, were intended to raise money to fight the Civil War. They were an important tool in alleviating a scarcity of money caused by the near-bankruptcy of the U.S. Treasury. While these notes circulated, they also drew interest payable to the bearer as stated on their back. An interesting feature (unique to these notes and some Fractional Currency issues) is the way "Compound Interest Treasury Note" and the numerical face value were printed on the face. A bronze powder was applied via a convoluted process in which a rubber plate was used to "print" a type of sizing compound on the note, upon which, while still wet, the powder was sprinkled. All three types are rare. The most available is F-190b, of which almost 100 notes are known to exist.

$10 Legal Tender Notes (United States Notes), Large-Size. The faces of the Series of 1862 and 1863 $10 Legal Tender Notes are virtually identical to that of the Demand Note. While not cheap, they are a collectible issue, thanks in particular to F-93 and F-95b. Various printing company imprints exist, and the notes' backs bear either the First or Second Obligation.

Even a trivia addict would be stumped were she posed the question, "What do you get when you cross a jackass with a rainbow?" The answer, of course, is a Series of 1869 Legal Tender Note. Even with a stern portrait of the legendary secretary of state, senator, orator, and fictional devil-fighter Daniel Webster at lower left, and an attractive vignette of Pocahontas Presented at Court at right, the small eagle at bottom center is what causes all the fuss. If you turn the note upside down, it looks like a donkey from the neck up, hence the nickname "Jackass Note." This same eagle was used on Fractional Currency shields of the late 1860s. With their attractive blue-green hue, large red seal, and topicality, these notes are perfectly suited to form the centerpiece of a new collection—and, luckily, more than a third of the notes reported are uncirculated.

Although the faces of the Series of 1875, 1878, and 1880 are also "Jackass Notes," these are nowhere near as colorful as the Series of 1869 since they were printed on standard banknote paper. There are two rarities in the 17 signature combinations run on these notes: Only 13 specimens are extant of F-97, and only two of F-109, one of which sold in 2006 for $184,000 in Very Fine to Extremely Fine condition.

The Series of 1901 "Bison Note" is another classic, avidly sought for its imagery as a piece of Americana. The horned, ready-to-charge bison, posed standing on the Great Plains at the note's center, is flanked by portraits of William Clark and Meriwether Lewis, the two explorers Jefferson sent on the famous 1804 expedition through terra incognita to the Pacific coast. Also called the "Buffalo Bill," the note is said to have been designed to stimulate interest in the Lewis and Clark Centennial Exposition of 1905, held in Portland, Oregon. In recent years, a certain Montana ranch owner (and well-known sports and cable television entrepreneur) tried to no avail to persuade the government to reissue this design. His reasoning was that a $10 bill featuring his favorite animal, the American bison, would be so actively collected and hoarded that there would be a considerable reduction in the national debt.

Prices for these notes in the choicest condition have recently approached stratospheric levels, with superb specimens of some signature combinations going for well into five figures. They are easily available in all grades, however, to any collector who wants one.

The Series of 1923 Legal Tender Notes, with Andrew Jackson on the face, are a one-Friedberg-number type. The presentation of the "10"s on the back has given rise to the moniker "Poker Chip Note." There are several hundred specimens in the population surveys, about a third of them uncirculated.

$10 National Bank Notes, Large-Size. The notes of the "First Charter Period" have lightning as a theme, with Benjamin Franklin flying a kite into stormy skies at left and Liberty grasping hold of a lightning bolt at right. The vignette in the back panel shows DeSoto Discovering the Mississippi. Many of these issues are rare. Only two notes are known from just one bank in Reno, Nevada, making this one of the rarest of all National Bank Notes.

The remaining National Bank Notes are unremarkable compared to other denominations, with the exception of different designs and portraits on the face of each denomination. The Series of 1882 Second Charter Period notes continue the electrical motif on their face, but their value is not much different from the corresponding $5 issues.

The Series of 1902 Third Charter Period issues are also widely available and, once again, at a cost not far from that of the $5s. True rarity is found only by bank and state or territory. Only one bank, the First National Bank of Puerto Rico at San Juan, issued notes. There are 12 known Red Seals from this bank, one with a unique Date Back that, when last sold in 2002, brought $74,750 in only Very Good condition.

These were issued as four-subject sheets ($10-$10-$10-$20 and, rarely, $10-$10-$10-$10). If a letter "D" is found on the face of the note, it would be of the latter.

$10 National Gold Bank Notes, Large-Size. Eleven California gold banks issued National Gold Bank Notes in the $10 denomination, as opposed to just six for the $5. Nonetheless they are both scarcer and more expensive, even in the lowest of conditions, since nearly all were redeemed. Designs are consistent with others in the series.

$10 Silver Certificates, Large-Size. Starting with the $10 Silver Certificates, we enter a more rarified air of collectibility. There are only two basic designs, each divided into two subtypes by their backs. The first is the Series of 1878 and 1880, featuring the signers of the Declaration of Independence and "Financier of the Revolution" Robert Morris on the face, and the word SILVER in large block letters on the back. These are printed in black on the back rather than the customary green. Please see the charts herein for a description of the differences in signatures, counter-signatures, obligations, and embellishments. None of the Series of 1878 is within the price range of an average collector.

Friedberg-287 through F-290 are the issues usually offered for sale, and of these F-289 (more than 150 pieces known) is the most common, but not enough to result in a substantial price difference since these notes are usually collected by type.

The Series of 1886 Silver Certificates are known as "Tombstone Notes" because of the style of the frame used to surround the portrait of Grover Cleveland's first vice president, Thomas A. Hendricks, who died in office in late 1885. He is the only vice president who did not also serve as president whose portrait is on U.S. paper money. This is the only commonly collected large-size

Silver Certificate, and can usually be found, albeit less frequently in higher grades. The total known census is a little more than 400 pieces.

$10 Refunding Certificates, Large-Size. Refunding Certificates exist only as part of the $10 denomination, and there were only two issues. Just two specimens are known of F-213 (one of which sold for more than $425,000 in 2005) and about 150 of F-214. Upon issue, these drew interest at 4 percent, which continued to accrue until July 1, 1907.

$10 Treasury or Coin Notes, Large-Size. Both the Series of 1890 and 1891 are virtually identical to the $5 Treasury Notes but with the portrait of a different Union general, Philip H. Sheridan (George H. Thomas is on the $5). Sheridan is best known for his scorched-earth battle policy that ravaged Virginia's Shenandoah Valley in 1864, and also for his role in the final defeat of the Confederacy at Appomattox. Overall, F-366–F-368 are a bit more expensive than F-369–F-371, even though the amount known of each is similar.

$10 Federal Reserve Notes, Large-Size. See the discussion under $5 notes for an explanation of the various types and subtypes. Any Red Seal variety is considerably scarcer than all but the rarest Blue Seals. Star replacement notes exist for nearly all of the Blue Seal issues, but are very difficult to find, with only one or two known for some issues.

$10 Federal Reserve Bank Notes, Large-Size. Federal Reserve Bank Notes of 1915 and 1918 follow the pattern of their $5 counterparts and of Federal Reserve Notes. There are only five notes known of F-817a from the Kansas City district. These were not issued by the Boston, Philadelphia, Cleveland, Richmond, Minneapolis, or San Francisco banks.

$10 Gold Certificates, Large-Size. Ten-dollar Gold Certificates were only made for the Series of 1907 and 1922 with the same design: a bust of Michael Hillegas, a merchant and sugar refiner whose success (together with his financial gifts and loans to the Army) qualified him to become the first treasurer of the United States in 1775. The notes exist with nine signature combinations and, as a type, are quite common except in uncirculated, the scarcity of which is gaining recognition in the market. There are more than 2,700 pieces recorded of F-1173, making this an easy mark for the type collector.

Small-Size $10 Notes

All small-size $10 notes have Alexander Hamilton on the face and the Treasury Building on the back. They were printed without serious modification for more than 70 years until the security enhancements (the Bureau of Engraving and Printing's term) of the Series of 1999 Federal Reserve Notes.

$10 National Bank Notes, Small-Size. See the section on the $5 denomination. These are primarily collected by state and bank. Again, do not confuse these with the Federal Reserve Bank Notes discussed below.

$10 Silver Certificates, Small-Size. Here are found two of the great small-size note rarities: the regular issue and star note of the Series of 1933. The star note is unique. Treasury records indicate that only 216,000 were printed and not widely released. These were issued after the gold recall of March 1933 and intended to help put silver into the market to replace the recalled gold. Later series were those of 1934–1934-D and 1953–1953-B. There are changes in the redemption and certification language after 1933, allowing redemption in silver bullion as well as silver dollars. Silver Certificates of the series of 1934 and 1934-A also exist with a yellow seal; these were made for use during World War II in North Africa. The 1934 issue (F-2308) is rare, and the star of this note (F-2308*) is unique.

$10 Gold Certificates, Small-Size. These were made in the Series of 1928 and 1928-A. The latter were never released as they were produced at nearly the same time as the gold recall. Examples of the Series of 1928 are fairly common.

$10 Federal Reserve Bank Notes, Small-Size. These brown-seal notes of the Series of 1929 were printed for all 12 Federal Reserve districts as both regular issues and star replacement notes. The Dallas district's (504,000 regular and 12,000 stars) are the scarcest. The star note from the Boston district (F-1860-A*) is also rare.

$10 Federal Reserve Notes, Small-Size. Small-size $10 Federal Reserve Notes have for the most part been issued by all 12 districts since their inception, though none were made for the Series of 1988. The Series of 1928-C (F-2003) was only printed for New York, Cleveland, Richmond, and Chicago, and are the key issues for the series. The 1950-E notes were produced for just three districts: New York, Chicago, and San Francisco. These, too, command a higher premium than normal. The HAWAII emergency notes, with overprints and brown seals, are from the Series of 1934-A.

Starting with the Series of 1999, security considerations led to design modifications, as with the other higher denomination notes. This process was expanded in the Series of 2004-A with the addition of background colors of orange, yellow, and red; small, yellow "10"s on front and back; an updated Hamilton portrait with no frame; watermarked paper; and other devices.

LARGE-SIZE $10 NOTES

Demand Notes of 1861

Face of F-6 to F-10a. Portrait of Abraham Lincoln at left, eagle and shield at top center, and an allegory of Art at right.

Back of F-6 to F-10a.

No.	Payable at		VG-8	F-12	VF-20
F-6	New York		$3,250	$6,000	$12,500
F-6a	New York; "For the" handwritten	5 known	—	—	—
F-7	Philadelphia		3,250	6,000	12,500
F-7a	Philadelphia; "For the" handwritten	3 known	—	—	—
F-8	Boston		3,250	6,000	12,500
F-8a	Boston; "For the" handwritten	2 known	—	—	—
F-9	Cincinnati		5 known	—	—
F-9a	Cincinnati; "For the" handwritten	Unique	—	—	—
F-10	St. Louis	4 known	—	—	—
F-10a	St. Louis; "For the" handwritten	Unknown	—	—	—

Interest-Bearing Notes of 1863

Face of F-196 and F-196a, with American Bank Note Company imprint. Portrait of Secretary of the Treasury Salmon P. Chase at left, "Eagle of the Capitol" at center, and allegory of Peace at right.

Back of F-196 and F-196a.

No.	Printed by		VG-8	F-12	VF-20
F-196	American Bank Note Co.	9 known	—	—	—
F-196a	Treasury Department	About 25 known	$2,000	$5,000	$12,500

Compound Interest Treasury Notes of 1863 and 1864

Face of F-190 to F-190b.

Back of F-190 to F-190b.

No.	Act	Overprint Date	Signatures		VG-8	F-12	VF-20	EF-40
F-190	1863	June 10, 1864	Chittenden	Spinner	$2,350	$4,600	$11,500	—
F-190a	1864	July 15, 1864	Chittenden	Spinner	2,100	4,900	12,500	—
F-190b	1864	Aug.15–Dec. 15, 1864	Colby	Spinner	1,900	3,950	7,000	$11,000

Legal Tender Notes
Series of 1862,
First Obligation

Face of F-93 to F-93b. Portrait of President Lincoln at left, an eagle and shield at center, and "Art" at right, similar to those on contemporary Demand Notes.

Back of F-93 to F-93b.

Detail of small starburst at the center of the bottom border.

No.	Printing Order	Signatures		Seal		VG-8	F-12	VF-20	EF-40	Unc-63
Treasury seal centered near right border; starburst at center of bottom border; face plate nos. 7–26										
F-93	Last printed	Chittenden	Spinner	Small red		$800	$1,100	$1,650	$2,700	$6,750
Treasury seal at upper right corner; no starburst										
F-93a	First printed	Chittenden	Spinner	Small red	About 5 known					
Treasury seal centered near right border; no starburst										
F-93b	Second printed	Chittenden	Spinner	Small red		2,500	4,000	6,000	8,000	

Legal Tender Notes
Series of 1862 and 1863, Second Obligation

Face of F-94 to F-95b.

Back of F-94 to F-95b with "Second Obligation."

No.	Act	Signatures		Seal	VG-8	F-12	VF-20	EF-40	Unc-63
F-94	1862	Chittenden	Spinner	Small red	$950	$1,450	$2,050	$3,200	$9,500
National Bank Note Co. on lower border									
F-95	1863	Chittenden	Spinner	Small red	950	1,450	2,050	3,300	9,500
American Bank Note Co. on lower border									
F-95a	1863	Chittenden	Spinner	Small red, one serial no.	975	1,500	2,150	3,300	9,500
F-95b	1863	Chittenden	Spinner	Small red, two serial nos.	750	1,150	1,650	2,650	6,000

Legal Tender Notes
Series of 1869

Face of F-96, the "Rainbow Note." Vignettes of Daniel Webster and Indian princess Pocahontas being presented to Europeans. At the lower center is an eagle, which if viewed upside down resembles a jackass. This note, as well as those of the next type, are also called "Jackass Notes."

Back of F-96.

The eagle on the Series of 1869 Note when viewed upside down. This eagle appeared on certain later notes and on Fractional Currency Shields.

No.	Act	Signatures		Seal		VG-8	F-12	VF-20	EF-40	Unc-63
F-96	1869	Allison	Spinner	Large red	"Rainbow" Note	$415	$775	$1,150	$1,700	$5,400

Legal Tender Notes
Series of 1875 to 1880

Face of F-97 to F-113. There are multiple signature and seal varieties. Vignettes as preceding, but without green overprint.

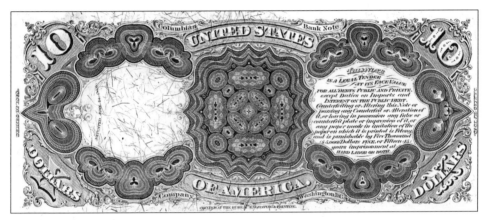

Back of F-97 to F-113.

No.	Series	Signatures		Seal		VG-8	F-12	VF-20	EF-40	Unc-63
Red TEN in red ornamental design at right center; seal at left										
F-97	1875	Allison	New	Small red, rays		$4,250	$7,250	$14,000	$26,000	—
F-98	1875	Same as above, but Series A				700	1,300	2,200	2,850	$7,900
F-99	1878	Allison	Gilfillan	Small red, rays		450	750	1,050	1,500	4,500
Large seal replaces TEN; red serial numbers										
F-100	1880	Scofield	Gilfillan	Large brown		310	525	775	1,000	2,200
F-101	1880	Bruce	Gilfillan	Large brown		310	525	825	1,200	2,200
F-102	1880	Bruce	Wyman	Large brown		310	525	825	1,200	2,200
Same, but with blue serial numbers										
F-103	1880	Bruce	Wyman	Large red, plain		300	500	750	1,050	2,200
F-104	1880	Rosecrans	Jordan	Large red, plain		375	650	850	1,375	3,000
F-105	1880	Rosecrans	Hyatt	Large red, plain		400	675	850	1,400	2,200
F-106	1880	Rosecrans	Hyatt	Large red, spike		300	475	750	1,075	2,200
F-107	1880	Rosecrans	Huston	Large red, spike		300	475	750	1,075	2,200
F-108	1880	Rosecrans	Huston	Large brown		300	475	750	1,075	2,200
F-109	1880	Rosecrans	Nebeker	Large brown	2 known	—	—	—	—	—
F-110	1880	Rosecrans	Nebeker	Small red, scalloped		265	435	685	1,025	2,050
F-111	1880	Tillman	Morgan	Small red, scalloped		265	435	685	1,025	1,950
F-112	1880	Bruce	Roberts	Small red, scalloped		400	575	900	1,500	5,750
F-113	1880	Lyons	Roberts	Small red, scalloped		265	435	685	1,025	1,900

Legal Tender Notes
Series of 1901

Face of F-114 to F-122, the "Bison Note." The bison at center is flanked by portraits of explorers Meriwether Lewis and William Clark.

Back of F-114 to F-122. Standing figure of Columbia.

No.	Signatures		Seal	VG-8	F-12	VF-20	EF-40	Unc-63
F-114	Lyons	Roberts	Small red, scalloped	$525	$680	$1,050	$2,000	$4,900
F-115	Lyons	Treat	Small red, scalloped	525	690	1,100	2,200	5,200
F-116	Vernon	Treat	Small red, scalloped	525	690	1,100	2,200	5,200
F-117	Vernon	McClung	Small red, scalloped	575	750	1,275	2,450	7,250
F-118	Napier	McClung	Small red, scalloped	525	690	1,100	2,200	5,200
F-119	Parker	Burke	Small red, scalloped	525	680	1,050	2,100	5,050
F-120	Teehee	Burke	Small red, scalloped	515	625	1,000	2,000	4,900
F-121	Elliott	White	Small red, scalloped	500	600	1,000	1,950	4,800
F-122	Speelman	White	Small red, scalloped	500	600	1,000	1,900	4,800

Legal Tender Notes
Series of 1923

Face of F-123. Bust of Andrew Jackson.

Back of F-123. Also called the "Poker Chip Note," because of the appearance of the denomination at left and right.

No.	Signatures		Seal	VG-8	F-12	VF-20	EF-40	Unc-63
F-123	Speelman	White	Small red, scalloped	$650	$1,300	$3,100	$4,700	$8,500

National Bank Notes
Original Series
("First Charter Period")

Face of F-409 to F-414. At left is "Franklin and Electricity." At right is "America Seizing the Lightning," with the goddess riding on the back of an eagle.

Back of F-409 to F-414. Vignette "De Soto Discovering the Mississippi."

No.	Signatures		Seal		VG-8	F-12	VF-20	EF-40	Unc-63
F-409	Chittenden	Spinner	Red, rays		$1,425	$1,900	$2,250	$2,750	$5,500
F-412	Colby	Spinner	Red, rays		1,425	1,900	2,250	2,750	5,500
F-413	Jeffries	Spinner	Red, rays	Unique	—	—	—	—	—
F-414	Allison	Spinner	Red, rays		1,550	2,000	2,400	3,200	7,500

National Bank Notes
Series of 1875
("First Charter Period")

Face of F-416 to F-423a. Same as the preceding, but with SERIES 1875 overprinted in red vertically to left of center and with three-line Bureau of Engraving and Printing imprint vertically at border at upper left.

Back of F-416 to F-423a. Same as the preceding.

No.	Signatures		Seal		VG-8	F-12	VF-20	EF-40	Unc-63
F-416	Allison	New	Red, scalloped		$1,375	$1,750	$2,300	$2,750	$5,500
F-417	Allison	Wyman	Red, scalloped		1,400	1,800	2,400	2,850	5,500
F-418	Allison	Gilfillan	Red, scalloped		1,400	1,850	2,450	2,900	5,500
F-419	Scofield	Gilfillan	Red, scalloped		1,375	1,700	2,200	2,750	5,500
F-420	Bruce	Gilfillan	Red, scalloped		1,375	1,700	2,200	2,750	5,500
F-421	Bruce	Wyman	Red, scalloped		1,950	2,500	3,500	5,250	
F-422	Rosecrans	Huston	Red, scalloped		1,750	2,150	2,600	3,250	5,500
F-423	Rosecrans	Nebeker	Red, scalloped		1,900	2,400	3,250	4,750	
F-423a	Tillman	Morgan	Red, scalloped	Unique	—	—	—	—	—

National Bank Notes
Series of 1882 Brown Back
("Second Charter Period")

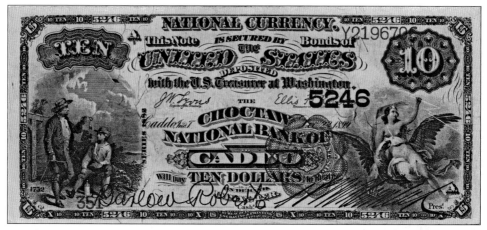

Face of F-479 to F-492. Same design as that created for the First Charter Period notes.

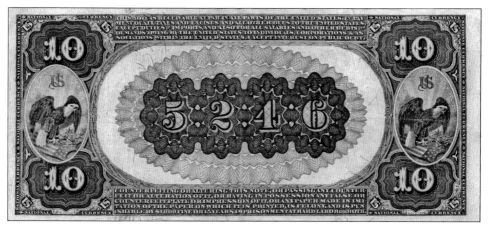

Back of F-479 to F-492. At center is the charter number of the issuing bank.

No.	Signatures		VG-8	F-12	VF-20	EF-40	Unc-63
F-479	Bruce	Gilfillan	$500	$675	$900	$1,250	$2,750
F-480	Bruce	Wyman	500	675	900	1,250	2,200
F-481	Bruce	Jordan	500	675	925	1,275	2,750
F-482	Rosecrans	Jordan	500	675	925	1,250	2,750
F-483	Rosecrans	Hyatt	500	675	925	1,250	2,750
F-484	Rosecrans	Huston	500	675	925	1,250	2,500
F-485	Rosecrans	Nebeker	500	675	925	1,250	2,500
F-486	Rosecrans	Morgan	1,250	1,900	2,750	3,500	—
F-487	Tillman	Morgan	500	675	925	1,250	2,500
F-488	Tillman	Roberts	500	725	1,000	1,350	3,000
F-489	Bruce	Roberts	500	725	1,000	1,350	3,000
F-490	Lyons	Roberts	500	675	900	1,200	2,500
F-491	Lyons	Treat	975	1,350	2,750	—	—
F-492	Vernon	Treat	950	1,300	2,000	2,900	—

National Bank Notes
Series of 1882 Date Back
("Second Charter Period")

Face of F-539 to F-548a. Same as the preceding.

Back of F-539 to F-548a. At left is portrait of Secretary of the Treasury William P. Fessenden. At right, a mechanic is shown.

No.	Signatures			VG-8	F-12	VF-20	EF-40	Unc-63
F-539	Rosecrans	Huston		$600	$775	$850	$1,300	$2,800
F-540	Rosecrans	Nebeker		575	750	850	1,150	2,600
F-541	Rosecrans	Morgan	Extremely rare (2 known)					
F-542	Tillman	Morgan		575	750	850	1,150	2,600
F-543	Tillman	Roberts		625	800	900	1,350	—
F-544	Bruce	Roberts		650	825	950	1,450	—
F-545	Lyons	Roberts		550	675	800	1,050	2,500
F-546	Vernon	Treat		600	775	900	1,400	—
F-547	Vernon	McClung	Extremely rare (2 known)					
F-548	Napier	McClung		—	—	—		
F-548a	Napier	McClung	Unique					

National Bank Notes
Series of 1882 Value Back
("Second Charter Period")

Face of F-576 to F-579b. Same as the preceding, with a blue Treasury seal.

Back of F-576 to F-579b.

No.	Signatures			VG-8	F-12	VF-20	EF-40	Unc-63
F-576	Tillman	Morgan		$1,000	$1,350	$2,000	$3,000	$5,000
F-576a	Tillman	Roberts		1,200	1,750	2,500	3,000	5,000
F-576b	Bruce	Roberts		1,200	1,750	2,500	3,000	5,000
F-577	Lyons	Roberts		675	825	1,000	1,300	2,650
F-577a	Lyons	Treat	Unknown	—	—	—	—	—
F-578	Vernon	Treat		750	950	1,175	1,850	—
F-579	Napier	McClung		750	950	1,175	1,850	3,000
F-579a	Parker	Burke	Unknown	—	—	—	—	—
F-579b	Teehee	Burke		875	1,125	1,500	—	—

National Bank Notes
Series of 1902 Red Seal
("Third Charter Period")

Face of F-613 to F-615. At left is the recently assassinated President William McKinley.

Back of F-613 to F-615. A standing figure dividing two oceans.

No.	Signatures		VG-8	F-12	VF-20	EF-40	Unc-63
F-613	Lyons	Roberts	$625	$725	$900	$1,350	$2,600
F-614	Lyons	Treat	650	725	1,000	1,400	3,250
F-615	Vernon	Treat	650	750	1,000	1,400	3,250

National Bank Notes
Series of 1902 Blue Seal, Date Back
("Third Charter Period")

Face of F-616 to F-623a.

Back of F-616 to F-623a.

No.	Signatures		VG-8	F-12	VF-20	EF-40	Unc-63
F-616	Lyons	Roberts	$150	$175	$250	$350	$575
F-617	Lyons	Treat	150	175	250	350	575
F-618	Vernon	Treat	150	175	250	350	575
F-619	Vernon	McClung	150	175	250	350	575
F-620	Napier	McClung	150	175	250	350	575
F-621	Napier	Thompson	225	280	350	375	1,450
F-622	Napier	Burke	170	200	275	400	700
F-623	Parker	Burke	160	185	260	400	625
F-623a	Teehee	Burke	215	275	360	500	1,500

National Bank Notes
Series of 1902 Blue Seal, Plain Back
("Third Charter Period")

Face of F-624 to F-638.

Back of F-624 to F-638.

No.	Signatures		VG-8	F-12	VF-20	EF-40	Unc-63
F-624	Lyons	Roberts	$110	$135	$170	$315	$550
F-625	Lyons	Treat	110	140	175	325	575
F-626	Vernon	Treat	110	140	175	325	575
F-627	Vernon	McClung	110	140	175	325	575
F-628	Napier	McClung	110	140	175	325	575
F-629	Napier	Thompson	250	300	370	500	1,150
F-630	Napier	Burke	175	250	315	425	950
F-631	Parker	Burke	110	140	175	325	575
F-632	Teehee	Burke	110	140	175	325	575
F-633	Elliott	Burke	110	140	175	325	575
F-634	Elliott	White	110	140	175	325	575
F-635	Speelman	White	110	140	175	325	575
F-636	Woods	White	140	165	250	400	950
F-637	Woods	Tate	140	165	250	400	950
F-638	Jones	Woods	575	650	750	1,050	—

National Gold Bank Notes

Face of F-1142 to F-1151a. Same basic design as the National Bank Notes of the First Charter Period.

Back of F-1142 to F-1151a. An assortment of contemporary gold coins.

No.	Date	Name of Bank	City	G-4	VG-8	F-12	VF-20
F-1142	1870	First National Gold Bank	San Francisco	$2,750	$4,250	$8,000	$40,000
F-1143	1872	National Gold Bank and Trust Company	San Francisco	3,500	6,000	20,000	—
F-1144	1872	National Gold Bank of D.O. Mills and Co.	Sacramento	3,500	6,000	12,000	Rare
F-1145	1873	First National Gold Bank	Santa Barbara	10,000	22,500	50,000	—
F-1146	1873	First National Gold Bank	Stockton	3,500	7,500	15,000	—
F-1147	1875	First National Gold Bank	Stockton	3,500	7,500	20,000	—
F-1148	1874	Farmer's National Gold Bank	San Jose	3,500	7,500	27,500	—
F-1149	1874	First National Gold Bank	Petaluma	7,000	16,000	30,000	80,000
F-1150	1875	First National Gold Bank	Petaluma	7,000	19,500	38,500	—
F-1151	1875	First National Gold Bank	Oakland	7,000	16,000	30,000	—
F-1151a	1875	Union National Gold Bank	Oakland	50,000	—	—	—

Silver Certificates
Series of 1878 and 1880,
With Countersignatures

Face of F-283 to F-286a. Portrait of Robert Morris, secretary of finance from 1781 to 1784. Standard Treasury Department signatures are above each other at the right. Left of center is space for a countersignature to be added in ink by another official.

Back of F-283 to F-286a.

No.	Series	Countersignature	Payable At	Deposited With		VG-8	F-12	VF-20
Large red seal								
F-283	1878	W.G. White	New York	Asst. Treasurer of the U.S.	*2005 Heritage Auction, sold for $253,000*			Unique
F-284	1878	J.C. Hopper	New York	Asst. Treasurer of the U.S.				4 known
F-284a	1878	T. Hillhouse	New York	Asst. Treasurer of the U.S.	Handwritten signature			Unknown
F-284b	1878	T. Hillhouse	New York	Asst. Treasurer of the U.S.	Engraved signature			2 known
F-284c	1878	R.M. Anthony	San Francisco	Asst. Treasurer of the U.S.	Handwritten signature			Unknown
F-285	1878	A.U. Wyman	Washington, D.C.	Treasurer of the U.S.	Engraved signature			2 known
F-285a	1878	A.U. Wyman	Washington, D.C.	Treasurer of the U.S.	Infrequently traded			8 known
Large brown seal at top; large "X" below								
F-286	1880	T. Hillhouse	New York	Asst. Treasurer of the U.S.		$5,500	$9,500	$17,000
F-286a	1880	A.U. Wyman	Washington, D.C.	Treasurer of the U.S.				Unknown

Note: All these notes are countersigned; all have the signatures of Scofield and Gilfillan and a large red seal; and all are without the legend "Series of 1878." All have engraved countersignatures except for the notes F-284a, F-284c, and F-285, which are hand-signed.

Silver Certificates
Series of 1880,
No Countersignatures

Face of F-287 to F-290. No countersignature.

Back of F-287 to F-290.

No.	Signatures		Seal	VG-8	F-12	VF-20	EF-40	Unc-63
Large brown seal at top; large "X" below								
F-287	Scofield	Gilfillan	Large brown	$1,600	$2,300	$3,850	$6,500	$17,500
F-288	Bruce	Gilfillan	Large brown	1,550	2,250	3,750	6,500	15,500
F-289	Bruce	Wyman	Large brown	1,500	2,200	3,500	5,750	13,000
Similar to above, but with seal in center and no large "X"								
F-290	Bruce	Wyman	Large red	1,500	2,500	3,500	15,000	125,000

Silver Certificates
Series of 1886

Face of F-291 to F-297. "The Tombstone Note." Portrait of the recently deceased (1885) vice president under Grover Cleveland, Thomas A. Hendricks.

Back of F-291 to F-297.

No.	Signatures		Seal	VG-8	F-12	VF-20	EF-40	Unc-63
F-291	Rosecrans	Jordan	Small red, plain	$700	$1,350	$2,750	$4,750	$17,500
F-292	Rosecrans	Hyatt	Small red, plain	600	1,100	2,450	4,750	13,000
F-293	Rosecrans	Hyatt	Large red	575	975	2,150	4,400	11,000
F-294	Rosecrans	Huston	Large red	600	1,100	2,450	4,750	13,000
F-295	Rosecrans	Huston	Large brown	600	1,100	2,450	4,750	15,000
F-296	Rosecrans	Nebeker	Large brown	600	1,100	2,450	4,750	13,000
F-297	Rosecrans	Nebeker	Small red, scalloped	700	1,350	2,750	4,750	15,000

Silver Certificates
Series of 1891 and 1908

Face of F-298 to F-304. Same as the preceding.

Back of F-298 to F-304.

No.	Series	Signatures		Seal	VG-8	F-12	VF-20	EF-40	Unc-63
F-298	1891	Rosecrans	Nebeker	Small red	$300	$650	$1,200	$1,900	$4,600
F-299	1891	Tillman	Morgan	Small red	275	500	1,000	1,700	3,800
F-300	1891	Bruce	Roberts	Small red	285	600	1,100	1,750	4,300
F-301	1891	Lyons	Roberts	Small red	285	600	1,100	1,750	4,300
With large blue "X" at left center of face									
F-302	1908	Vernon	Treat	Blue	350	575	975	1,550	3,250
F-303	1908	Vernon	McClung	Blue	350	575	975	1,550	3,250
F-304	1908	Parker	Burke	Blue	325	550	925	1,500	3,100

Refunding Certificates
Series of 1879

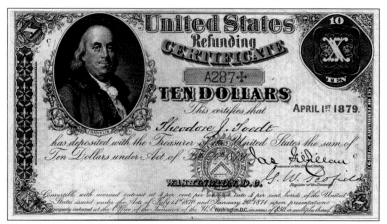

Face of F-213. Portrait of Benjamin Franklin. This note has a bearer's name inked on the face. Only two examples are known, one of which is held by the Treasury Department.

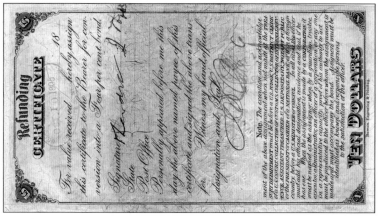

Back of F-213.

No.		
F-213	Payable to order	Extremely rare

Refunding Certificates
Series of 1879, Modified Back

Face of F-214. Similar to the preceding.

Back of F-214.

No.		VG-8	F-12	VF-20	EF-40	Unc-63
F-214	Payable to bearer	$1,350	$1,850	$3,400	$4,900	$9,500

Treasury or Coin Notes
Series of 1890

Face of F-366 to F-368. Bust of General Philip D. Sheridan. The star at the serial number is decorative.

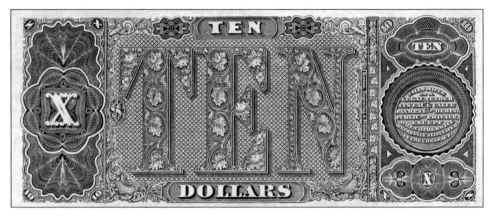

Back of F-366 to F-368.

No.	Signatures		Seal	VG-8	F-12	VF-20	EF-40	Unc-63
F-366	Rosecrans	Huston	Large brown	$800	$1,150	$1,675	$3,300	$6,500
F-367	Rosecrans	Nebeker	Large brown	975	1,375	2,050	3,900	9,500
F-368	Rosecrans	Nebeker	Small red	800	1,150	1,675	3,300	6,500

Treasury or Coin Notes
Series of 1891

Face of F-369 to F-371.

Back of F-369 to F-371.

No.	Signatures		Seal	VG-8	F-12	VF-20	EF-40	Unc-63
F-369	Rosecrans	Nebeker	Small red	$450	$850	$1,200	$1,750	$3,750
F-370	Tillman	Morgan	Small red	500	850	1,200	1,750	3,750
F-371	Bruce	Roberts	Small red	450	850	1,200	1,750	4,000

Gold Certificates
Series of 1907 and 1922

Face of F-1167 to F-1173a. Bust of Michael Hillegas, treasurer of the United States from 1775 to 1789.

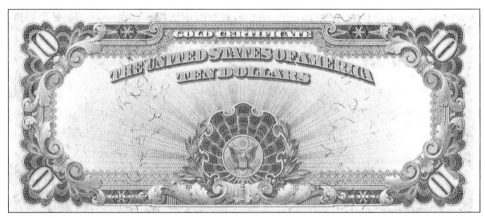

Back of F-1167 to F-1173a.

No.	Series	Signatures		Seal	VG-8	F-12	VF-20	EF-40	Unc-63
F-1167	1907	Vernon	Treat	Gold	$155	$185	$275	$625	$1,850
F-1168	1907	Vernon	McClung	Gold	155	235	310	690	1,850
F-1169	1907	Napier	McClung	Gold Act of 1882	155	185	275	625	1,800
F-1169a	1907	Napier	McClung	Gold Act of 1907	155	185	275	625	1,900
F-1170	1907	Napier	Thompson	Gold Act of 1882	275	400	575	1,500	3,000
F-1170a	1907	Napier	Thompson	Gold Act of 1907	200	275	475	1,350	4,500
F-1171	1907	Parker	Burke	Gold	145	170	235	575	1,750
F-1172	1907	Teehee	Burke	Gold	145	170	235	575	1,725
F-1173	1922	Speelman	White	Gold	100	150	200	435	1,150
F-1173a	1922	Speelman	White	Gold, small serial numbers	125	175	250	525	1,750

Federal Reserve Notes
Series of 1914, Red Seal

Friedberg Suffix Letters on Types F-892A to F-951C

Red Seals—*"A" suffix:* Large district letter and numeral at top right and bottom left. Small letter at top left and bottom right. *B suffix:* As above, but with small district letter and numeral added above letter at top left. As a class Red Seals are scarcer than Blue Seals.

Blue Seals—*"A" suffix:* Large district letter and numeral at top left and bottom right. *B suffix:* Large letter and numeral at top right with small district letters and numerals in the other three corners. *C suffix:* Again, a large pair of letters and numerals, but positioned both vertically, more toward the center of the note and closer to the outside edge. Also, the seals to the sides of the portrait are closer to the note's center than on the Blue Seal notes with A suffix.

Face of F-892A to F-903B.

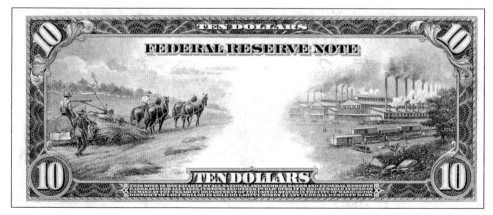

Back of F-892A to F-903B. Representations of agriculture at left and commerce at right.

No.	Issuing Bank	VG-8	F-12	VF-20	EF-40	Unc-63
F-892A	Boston	$275	$550	$700	$1,100	—
F-892B	Boston	700	1,000	2,000	—	—
F-893A	New York	250	475	750	1,375	$2,950
F-893B	New York	200	325	600	1,100	2,750
F-894A	Philadelphia	300	400	700	1,200	4,500
F-894B	Philadelphia	225	350	625	1,125	3,200

Chart continued on next page.

No.	Issuing Bank	VG-8	F-12	VF-20	EF-40	Unc-63
F-895A	Cleveland	$425	$900	$1,800	$2,450	$7,500
F-895B	Cleveland	235	375	675	1,250	—
F-896A	Richmond	425	825	—	—	—
F-896B	Richmond	450	850	2,250	4,750	—
F-897A	Atlanta	375	575	1,050	2,000	6,000
F-897B	Atlanta	650	1,250	1,900	4,000	7,500
F-898A	Chicago	250	425	675	1,125	2,850
F-898B	Chicago	250	425	675	1,125	2,850
F-899A	St. Louis	250	450	700	1,150	2,850
F-899B	St. Louis	275	500	900	2,000	4,500
F-900A	Minneapolis	250	450	700	1,150	2,850
F-900B	Minneapolis	385	725	1,250	—	—
F-901A	Kansas City	275	500	775	1,400	—
F-901B	Kansas City	325	575	975	1,900	—
F-902A	Dallas	325	525	1,350	3,000	—
F-902B	Dallas	500	1,000	2,300	4,900	—
F-903A	San Francisco	350	525	1,350	2,500	—
F-903B	San Francisco	350	550	1,350	2,500	—

Federal Reserve Notes
Series of 1914, Blue Seal

Face of F-904 to F-951C.

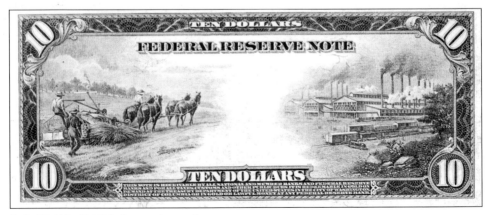

Back of F-904 to F-951C. Same as the preceding.

No.	Issuing Bank	Signatures		VG-8	F-12	VF-20	EF-40	Unc-63
F-904	Boston	Burke	McAdoo	$65	$75	$100	$140	$325
F-905	Boston	Burke	Glass	70	85	110	185	400
F-906	Boston	Burke	Houston	65	75	100	140	325
F-907A	Boston	White	Mellon	65	75	100	140	325
F-907B	Boston	White	Mellon	70	90	110	175	350
F-908	New York	Burke	McAdoo	65	75	100	140	325
F-909	New York	Burke	Glass	70	80	110	165	400
F-910	New York	Burke	Houston	65	75	95	130	325
F-911A	New York	White	Mellon	60	70	90	125	300
F-911B	New York	White	Mellon	70	85	110	150	350
F-911C	New York	White	Mellon	65	70	95	130	325
F-912	Philadelphia	Burke	McAdoo	65	75	100	135	325
F-913	Philadelphia	Burke	Glass	75	90	115	155	625
F-914	Philadelphia	Burke	Houston	65	75	110	165	675
F-915A	Philadelphia	White	Mellon	65	75	100	155	325
F-915C	Philadelphia	White	Mellon	70	85	105	160	350
F-916	Cleveland	Burke	McAdoo	70	90	110	155	400
F-917	Cleveland	Burke	Glass	70	85	110	155	500
F-918	Cleveland	Burke	Houston	65	75	100	145	350
F-919A	Cleveland	White	Mellon	65	75	100	145	325
F-919B	Cleveland	White	Mellon	70	85	110	165	650
F-919C	Cleveland	White	Mellon	70	85	110	165	650
F-920	Richmond	Burke	McAdoo	70	85	110	175	1,000
F-921	Richmond	Burke	Glass	80	100	175	325	1,250
F-922	Richmond	Burke	Houston	70	85	110	160	500
F-923	Richmond	White	Mellon	65	75	100	145	325
F-924	Atlanta	Burke	McAdoo	75	90	125	170	600
F-925	Atlanta	Burke	Glass	80	125	200	375	750
F-926	Atlanta	Burke	Houston	70	90	110	165	350
F-927A	Atlanta	White	Mellon	65	75	100	140	400
F-927B	Atlanta	White	Mellon	75	100	125	200	—
F-928	Chicago	Burke	McAdoo	65	75	100	140	325
F-929	Chicago	Burke	Glass	65	75	105	160	450
F-930	Chicago	Burke	Houston	65	75	100	140	325
F-931A	Chicago	White	Mellon	65	75	100	140	325
F-931B	Chicago	White	Mellon	70	90	110	165	365
F-931C	Chicago	White	Mellon	70	85	115	175	450
F-932	St. Louis	Burke	McAdoo	75	90	120	190	—
F-933	St. Louis	Burke	Glass	70	85	110	165	450
F-934	St. Louis	Burke	Houston	65	75	100	140	325
F-935	St. Louis	White	Mellon	70	85	110	165	450
F-936	Minneapolis	Burke	McAdoo	70	85	115	175	450
F-937	Minneapolis	Burke	Glass	80	90	140	210	750
F-938	Minneapolis	Burke	Houston	85	105	150	—	—
F-939	Minneapolis	White	Mellon	65	75	100	140	325
F-940	Kansas City	Burke	McAdoo	65	75	100	140	325
F-941	Kansas City	Burke	Glass	130	240	420	580	1,200
F-942	Kansas City	Burke	Houston	65	75	100	140	325
F-943A	Kansas City	White	Mellon	65	75	100	140	325
F-944	Dallas	Burke	McAdoo	65	70	105	150	350
F-945	Dallas	Burke	Glass	525	850	1,300	3,500	—
F-946	Dallas	Burke	Houston	80	95	150	235	—
F-947	Dallas	White	Mellon	75	90	145	230	525
F-948	San Francisco	Burke	McAdoo	110	180	325	675	—
F-949	San Francisco	Burke	Glass	110	180	325	675	—
F-950	San Francisco	Burke	Houston	90	110	165	250	—
F-951A	San Francisco	White	Mellon	65	75	100	140	350
F-951B	San Francisco	White	Mellon	90	125	175	260	—
F-951C	San Francisco	White	Mellon	75	115	145	200	—

Federal Reserve Bank Notes
Series of 1915 and 1918

Face of F-810 to F-821. Portrait of Andrew Jackson at left.

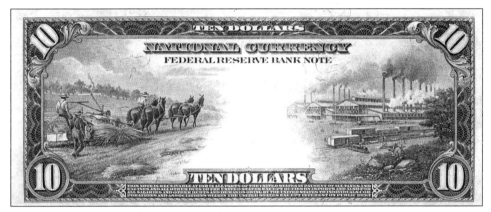

Back of F-810 to F-821.

No.	Issuing Bank	Series	Treasury Signatures		Bank Signatures		VG-8	F-12	VF-20	EF-40	Unc-63
F-810	New York	1918	Teehee	Burke	Hendricks	Strong	$1,250	$1,900	$2,250	$3,950	$8,500
F-811	Atlanta	1915	Teehee	Burke	Bell	Wellborn	2,250	5,000	12,000	22,500	—
F-812	Atlanta	1918	Elliott	Burke	Bell	Wellborn	1,400	1,850	2,250	3,950	8,500
F-813	Chicago	1915	Teehee	Burke	McLallen	McDougal	1,300	1,600	2,250	3,950	8,500
F-814	Chicago	1918	Teehee	Burke	McCloud	McDougal	1,400	1,700	2,250	3,950	8,500
F-815	St. Louis	1918	Teehee	Burke	Attebery	Wells	1,500	1,750	2,250	3,950	—
F-816	Kansas City	1915	Teehee	Burke	Anderson	Miller	1,400	1,750	2,250	3,950	—
F-817	Kansas City	1915	Teehee	Burke	Cross	Miller	1,400	1,750	2,250	3,950	6,500
Bank signatures plate engraved											
F-817a	Kansas City	1915	Teehee	Burke	Cross	Miller	—	—	—	—	—
Bank signatures hand stamped in red with Cross as "acting" secretary											
F-818	Kansas City	1915	Teehee	Burke	Helm	Miller	4,000	8,750	15,000	—	—
F-819	Dallas	1915	Teehee	Burke	Hoopes	Van Zandt	1,400	2,000	2,500	4,000	8,500
F-820	Dallas	1915	Teehee	Burke	Gilbert	Van Zandt	4,500	8,500	—	—	—
F-821	Dallas	1915	Teehee	Burke	Talley	Van Zandt	2,750	4,750	9,500	15,000	—

SMALL-SIZE $10 NOTES
National Bank Notes
Series of 1929, Type 1

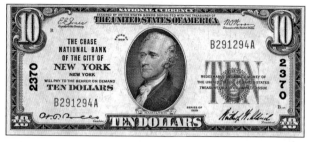

Face of F-1801-1. Bank charter number in black at left and right borders.

Back of F-1801-1. The Treasury Department. Back type of all small-size $10 series through the 1950s.

No.		VF-20	EF-40	Unc-63
F-1801-1		$75	$100	$175

National Bank Notes
Series of 1929, Type 2

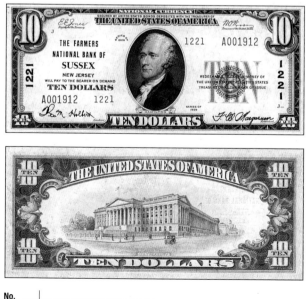

Face of F-1801-2. As preceding, but with brown bank and charter number added to lower left and upper right of portrait.

Back of F-1801-2.

No.		VF-20	EF-40	Unc-63
F-1801-2		$75	$100	$200

Silver Certificates
Series of 1933, Blue Seal

Face of F-1700 to F-1700a.

Back of F-1700 to F-1700a.

No.	Series	Signatures		Quantity Printed	VF-20	Unc-63
F-1700	1933	Julian	Woodin	216,000	$4,750	$12,500
F-1700★	1933	Julian	Woodin			Unique
F-1700a	1933-A	Julian	Morgenthau	336,000	Not released	

Silver Certificates
Series of 1934 to 1934-D,
Blue Seal

Face of F-1701 to F-1705.

Back of F-1701 to F-1705.

No.	Series	Signatures		Quantity Printed	VF-20	Unc-63
F-1701	1934	Julian	Morgenthau	88,692,864	$40	$125
F-1701★	1934	Julian	Morgenthau		180	1,375

Silver Certificates
Series of 1934 and 1934-A, Yellow Seal for North Africa

Face of F-2308 to F-2309, with yellow Treasury seal. These notes were produced for distribution during World War II in and around the Mediterranean Sea and North Africa.

Back of F-2308 to F-2309.

No.	Series	Quantity Printed	VF-20	Unc-63
F-2308	1934		$3,150	$15,000
F-2308★	1934			Unique
F-2309	1934-A	21,860,000	70	265
F-2309★	1934-A		300	1,350

Silver Certificates
Series of 1934 to 1934-D, Blue Seal (continued from F-1701)

No.	Series	Signatures		Quantity Printed	VF-20	Unc-63
F-1702	1934-A	Julian	Morgenthau	42,346,428	$45	$150
F-1702★	1934-A	Julian	Morgenthau		225	900
F-1703	1934-B	Julian	Vinson	337,740	225	900
F-1703★	1934-B	Julian	Vinson		2,750	Rare
F-1704	1934-C	Julian	Snyder	20,032,632	40	120
F-1704★	1934-C	Julian	Snyder		100	450
F-1705	1934-D	Clark	Snyder	11,801,112	45	225
F-1705★	1934-D	Clark	Snyder		325	2,250

Silver Certificates
Series of 1953 to 1953-B, Blue Seal

Face of F-1706 to F-1708.

Back of F-1706 to F-1708.

No.	Series	Signatures		Quantity Printed	VF-20	Unc-63
F-1706	1953	Priest	Humphrey	10,440,000	$55	$165
F-1706★	1953	Priest	Humphrey	576,000	100	600
F-1707	1953-A	Priest	Anderson	1,080,000	55	275
F-1707★	1953-A	Priest	Anderson	144,000	150	900
F-1708	1953-B	Smith	Dillon	720,000	55	200

Gold Certificates
Series of 1928 and 1928-A, Gold Seal

Face of F-2400 to F-2401.

Back of F-2400 to F-2401.

No.	Series	Signatures		Quantity Printed	VG-8	F-12	VF-20	EF-40	Unc-63
F-2400	1928	Wood	Mellon	130,812,000	$70	$100	$150	$250	$675
F-2400★	1928	Woods	Mellon		175	325	575	1,000	3,375
F-2401	1928-A	Woods	Mellon	2,544,000			Not issued		

Federal Reserve Bank Notes
Series of 1929, Brown Seal

Face of F-1860. The plates are the same as for National Bank Notes (F-1800-1). Back type is the same as on all small-size $10 series through the 1950s.

No.	Issuing Bank	Quantity Printed	VF-20	Unc-63	No.	Issuing Bank	Quantity Printed	VF-20	Unc-63
F-1860A	Boston	1,680,000	$50	$175	F-1860H	St. Louis	1,584,000	$45	$175
F-1860B	New York	5,556,000	45	175	F-1860I	Minneapolis	58,000	65	350
F-1860C	Philadelphia	1,416,000	45	175	F-1860J	Kansas City	1,284,000	45	200
F-1860D	Cleveland	2,412,000	45	175	F-1860K	Dallas	504,000	500	1,000
F-1860E	Richmond	1,356,000	65	200	F-1860L	San Francisco	1,080,000	65	1,500
F-1860F	Atlanta	1,056,000	45	200	F-1860★	Most common districts		400	2,450
F-1860G	Chicago	3,156,000	45	175					

Federal Reserve Notes
Series of 1928 and 1928-A, Green Seal

Face of F-2000 to F-2001. Type of Series of 1928 and 1928-A. The face printing notes that the bill is payable (since rescinded) "in gold or lawful money."

Back of F-2000 to F-2001.

See next page for chart.

Series of 1928—Signatures of Tate and Mellon

No.	Issuing Bank	Quantity Printed	VF-20	Unc-63	No.	Issuing Bank	Quantity Printed	VF-20	Unc-63
F-2000A	Boston	9,804,552	$60	$400	F-2000G	Chicago	8,130,000	$40	$375
F-2000A★	Boston		750	2,525	F-2000G★	Chicago		400	1,400
F-2000B	New York	11,295,796	75	875	F-2000H	St. Louis	4,124,100	40	265
F-2000B★	New York		300	2,500	F-2000H★	St. Louis		250	1,250
F-2000C	Philadelphia	8,114,412	40	250	F-2000I	Minneapolis	3,874,440	70	500
F-2000C★	Philadelphia		350	1,200	F-2000I★	Minneapolis		550	2,200
F-2000D	Cleveland	75,708,120	30	350	F-2000J	Kansas City	3,620,400	40	300
F-2000D★	Cleveland		350	1,250	F-2000J★	Kansas City		325	1,600
F-2000E	Richmond	4,534,800	50	475	F-2000K	Dallas	4,855,500	60	600
F-2000E★	Richmond		750	3,250	F-2000K★	Dallas		1,500	6,000
F-2000F	Atlanta	6,807,720	40	300	F-2000L	San Francisco	7,086,900	45	375
F-2000F★	Atlanta		450	6,500	F-2000L★	San Francisco		1,250	3,750

Series of 1928-A—Signatures of Woods and Mellon

No.	Issuing Bank	Quantity Printed	VF-20	Unc-63	No.	Issuing Bank	Quantity Printed	VF-20	Unc-63
F-2001A	Boston	2,893,440	$55	$450	F-2001F★	Atlanta		$2,100	$6,000
F-2001A★	Boston		800	9,000	F-2001G	Chicago	8,715,000	50	350
F-2001B	New York	18,631,056	50	275	F-2001G★	Chicago		425	2,000
F-2001B★	New York		325	1,400	F-2001H	St. Louis	531,600	70	350
F-2001C	Philadelphia	2,710,680	55	450	F-2001H★	St. Louis		375	1,000
F-2001C★	Philadelphia		1,500	6,000	F-2001I	Minneapolis	102,600	675	6,000
F-2001D	Cleveland	5,610,000	50	275	F-2001J	Kansas City	410,400	300	2,950
F-2001D★	Cleveland		450	1,800	F-2001K	Dallas	961,800	350	2,250
F-2001E	Richmond	552,300	100	800	F-2001L	San Francisco	2,547,900	90	650
F-2001E★	Richmond		400	2,000	F-2001L★	San Francisco		350	1,500
F-2001F	Atlanta	3,033,480	60	500					

Federal Reserve Notes
Series of 1928-B and 1928-C, Green Seal

Face of F-2002 to F-2003, similar to the preceding but with the bank represented by the district letter. The face printing notes that the bill is payable (since rescinded) "in gold or lawful money." Type of Series of 1928-B and 1928-C.

Back of F-2002 to F-2003.

Series of 1928-B—Signatures of Woods and Mellon

No.	Issuing Bank	Quantity Printed	VF-20	Unc-63	No.	Issuing Bank	Quantity Printed	VF-20	Unc-63
F-2002A	Boston	33,218,088	$20	$75	F-2002E	Richmond	12,714,504	$25	$100
F-2002A★	Boston		185	950	F-2002E★	Richmond		175	600
F-2002B	New York	44,808,308	20	75	F-2002F	Atlanta	5,246,700	25	100
F-2002B★	New York		125	600	F-2002F★	Atlanta		225	1,250
F-2002C	Philadelphia	22,689,216	20	75	F-2002G	Chicago	38,035,000	20	75
F-2002C★	Philadelphia		125	600	F-2002G★	Chicago		95	425
F-2002D	Cleveland	17,418,024	20	75	F-2002H	St. Louis	10,814,664	20	100
F-2002D★	Cleveland		175	900	F-2002H★	St. Louis		200	1,300

No.	Issuing Bank	Quantity Printed	VF-20	Unc-63	No.	Issuing Bank	Quantity Printed	VF-20	Unc-63
F-2002I	Minneapolis	5,294,460	$25	$125	F-2002K	Dallas	3,396,096	$65	$300
F-2002I★	Minneapolis		150	800	F-2002L	San Francisco	22,695,300	25	125
F-2002J	Kansas City	7,748,040	20	75	F-2002L★	San Francisco		350	1,200
F-2002J★	Kansas City		325	1,500					

Series of 1928-C—Signatures of Woods and Mills

No.	Issuing Bank	Quantity Printed	VF-20	Unc-63	No.	Issuing Bank	Quantity Printed	VF-20	Unc-63
F-2003B	New York	2,902,678	$90	$550	F-2003E	Richmond	304,800	$3,650	—
F-2003D	Cleveland	4,230,428	525	3,150	F-2003F	Atlanta	688,380	Unknown	
F-2003D★	Cleveland		15,000	50,000	F-2003G	Chicago	2,423,400	70	$475

Federal Reserve Notes
Series of 1934 to 1934-D, Green Seal

Face of F-2004 to F-2009. The mention of gold no longer appears.

Back of F-2004 to F-2009.

Series of 1934—Signatures of Julian and Morgenthau

No.	Issuing Bank	Quantity Printed	VF-20	Unc-63	No.	Issuing Bank	Quantity Printed	VF-20	Unc-63
Notes with a vivid, light green seal					**Notes with a darker and duller blue-green seal**				
F-2004A	Boston	46,276,152	$20	$80	F-2005A	Boston		$15	$65
F-2004A★	Boston		75	700	F-2005A★	Boston		80	400
F-2004B	New York	117,298,008	20	75	F-2005B	New York		15	75
F-2004B★	New York		90	475	F-2005B★	New York		50	250
F-2004C	Philadelphia	34,770,768	20	85	F-2005C	Philadelphia		15	65
F-2004C★	Philadelphia		90	700	F-2005C★	Philadelphia		75	400
F-2004D	Cleveland	28,764,108	20	90	F-2005D	Cleveland		15	75
F-2004D★	Cleveland		90	800	F-2005D★	Cleveland		80	500
F-2004E	Richmond	16,437,252	20	110	F-2005E	Richmond		15	90
F-2004E★	Richmond		300	1,600	F-2005E★	Richmond		65	700
F-2004F	Atlanta	20,656,872	25	125	F-2005F	Atlanta		15	80
F-2004F★	Atlanta		175	1,000	F-2005F★	Atlanta		65	700
F-2004G	Chicago	69,962,064	20	75	F-2005G	Chicago		15	65
F-2004G★	Chicago		85	450	F-2005G★	Chicago		65	350
F-2004H	St. Louis	22,593,204	20	100	F-2005H	St. Louis		20	80
F-2004H★	St. Louis		100	750	F-2005H★	St. Louis		65	400
F-2004I	Minneapolis	16,840,980	25	150	F-2005I	Minneapolis		20	100
F-2004I★	Minneapolis		275	1,250	F-2005I★	Minneapolis		125	550
F-2004J	Kansas City	22,627,824	20	100	F-2005J	Kansas City		15	80
F-2004J★	Kansas City		100	900	F-2005J★	Kansas City		65	400
F-2004K	Dallas	21,403,488	25	250	F-2005K	Dallas		20	100
F-2004K★	Dallas		300	2,000	F-2005K★	Dallas		75	500
F-2004L	San Francisco	37,402,308	20	100	F-2005L	San Francisco		15	75
F-2004L★	San Francisco		180	1,400	F-2005L★	San Francisco		65	500

Series of 1934-A—Signatures of Julian and Morgenthau

No.	Issuing Bank	Quantity Printed	VF-20	Unc-63	No.	Issuing Bank	Quantity Printed	VF-20	Unc-63
F-2006A	Boston	104,540,088	$12	$40	F-2006G	Chicago	177,285,960	$12	$35
F-2006A★	Boston		40	250	F-2006G★	Chicago		40	200
F-2006B	New York	281,940,996	12	40	F-2006H	St. Louis	50,694,312	12	40
F-2006B★	New York		55	300	F-2006H★	St. Louis		45	250
F-2006C	Philadelphia	95,338,032	12	40	F-2006I	Minneapolis	16,340,016	15	50
F-2006C★	Philadelphia		35	250	F-2006I★	Minneapolis		70	350
F-2006D	Cleveland	93,332,004	12	40	F-2006J	Kansas City	31,069,978	12	45
F-2006D★	Cleveland		35	250	F-2006J★	Kansas City		40	250
F-2006E	Richmond	101,037,912	12	40	F-2006K	Dallas	28,263,156	14	55
F-2006E★	Richmond		40	225	F-2006K★	Dallas		75	400
F-2006F	Atlanta	85,478,160	12	40	F-2006L	San Francisco	125,537,592	12	50
F-2006F★	Atlanta		40	350	F-2006L★	San Francisco		50	275

Federal Reserve Notes
Series 1934 and 1934-A, Brown Seal, Hawaii

Face of F-2303 with HAWAII overprinted at the left and right ends and with Treasury seal and serial numbers in brown.

Back of F-2303 with large HAWAII overprint.

No.	Series	Quantity Printed	VF-20	Unc-63	No.	Series	Quantity Printed	VF-20	Unc-63
F-2303	1934-A	10,424,000	$130	$900	F-2303★	1934-A		$1,600	$11,000

Federal Reserve Notes
Series of 1934 to 1934-D, Green Seal (continued from F-2006)

Series of 1934-B—Signatures of Julian and Vinson

No.	Issuing Bank	Quantity Printed	EF-40	Unc-63	No.	Issuing Bank	Quantity Printed	EF-40	Unc-63
F-2007A	Boston	3,999,600	$40	$125	F-2007E	Richmond	4,018,272	$30	$135
F-2007A★	Boston		175	600	F-2007E★	Richmond		225	1,000
F-2007B	New York	34,815,948	25	65	F-2007F	Atlanta	6,746,076	25	85
F-2007B★	New York		150	400	F-2007F★	Atlanta		300	1,000
F-2007C	Philadelphia	10,339,020	25	80	F-2007G	Chicago	18,130,836	25	60
F-2007C★	Philadelphia		150	750	F-2007G★	Chicago		100	400
F-2007D	Cleveland	1,394,700	30	135	F-2007H	St. Louis	6,849,348	40	90
F-2007D★	Cleveland		350	1,200	F-2007H★	St. Louis		175	750

No.	Issuing Bank	Quantity Printed	EF-40	Unc-63	No.	Issuing Bank	Quantity Printed	EF-40	Unc-63
F-2007I	Minneapolis	2,254,800	$50	$145	F-2007K	Dallas	3,085,200	$50	$145
F-2007I★	Minneapolis		350	1,400	F-2007K★	Dallas		250	1,400
F-2007J	Kansas City	3,835,764	35	90	F-2007L	San Francisco	9,076,800	35	85
F-2007J★	Kansas City		200	800	F-2007L★	San Francisco		150	600

Series of 1934-C—Signatures of Julian and Snyder

No.	Issuing Bank	Quantity Printed	EF-40	Unc-63	No.	Issuing Bank	Quantity Printed	EF-40	Unc-63
F-2008A	Boston	42,431,404	$25	$65	F-2008G	Chicago	105,875,412	$20	$40
F-2008A★	Boston		100	365	F-2008G★	Chicago		75	300
F-2008B	New York	115,675,644	20	40	F-2008H	St. Louis	36,541,404	20	55
F-2008B★	New York		100	335	F-2008H★	St. Louis		100	380
F-2008C	Philadelphia	46,874,760	20	40	F-2008I	Minneapolis	11,944,848	20	80
F-2008C★	Philadelphia		100	330	F-2008I★	Minneapolis		300	950
F-2008D	Cleveland	332,400	20	45	F-2008J	Kansas City	20,874,072	20	55
F-2008D★	Cleveland		125	360	F-2008J★	Kansas City		100	365
F-2008E	Richmond	37,422,600	20	50	F-2008K	Dallas	25,642,620	20	55
F-2008E★	Richmond		100	450	F-2008K★	Dallas		150	365
F-2008F	Atlanta	44,838,264	20	55	F-2008L	San Francisco	49,164,480	20	40
F-2008F★	Atlanta		100	500	F-2008L★	San Francisco		100	410

Series of 1934-D—Signatures of Clark and Snyder

No.	Issuing Bank	Quantity Printed	EF-40	Unc-63	No.	Issuing Bank	Quantity Printed	EF-40	Unc-63
F-2009A	Boston	19,917,900	$20	$60	F-2009G	Chicago	55,943,844	$15	$55
F-2009A★	Boston		175	650	F-2009G★	Chicago		110	550
F-2009B	New York	64,067,904	20	60	F-2009H	St. Louis	15,828,048	20	75
F-2009B★	New York		110	450	F-2009H★	St. Louis		125	650
F-2009C	Philadelphia	18,432,000	20	60	F-2009I	Minneapolis	5,237,220	30	100
F-2009C★	Philadelphia		110	450	F-2009I★	Minneapolis		200	850
F-2009D	Cleveland	20,291,316	20	60	F-2009J	Kansas City	7,992,000	25	80
F-2009D★	Cleveland		110	600	F-2009J★	Kansas City		150	750
F-2009E	Richmond	18,090,312	20	60	F-2009K	Dallas	7,178,196	25	80
F-2009E★	Richmond		650	1,100	F-2009K★	Dallas		110	900
F-2009F	Atlanta	17,064,816	20	60	F-2009L	San Francisco	23,956,584	20	70
F-2009F★	Atlanta		175	850	F-2009L★	San Francisco		300	875

Federal Reserve Notes
Series of 1950 to 1950-E,
Green Seal

Face of F-2010 to F-2013.

Back of F-2010 to F-2013.

See next page for chart.

Series of 1950—Signatures of Clark and Snyder

No.	Issuing Bank	Quantity Printed	EF-40	Unc-63	No.	Issuing Bank	Quantity Printed	EF-40	Unc-63
F-2010A	Boston	70,992,000	$18	$65	F-2010G	Chicago	161,056,000	$18	$60
F-2010A★	Boston	1,008,000	100	525	F-2010G★	Chicago	2,088,000	75	350
F-2010B	New York	218,576,000	18	60	F-2010H	St. Louis	47,808,000	18	65
F-2010B★	New York	2,586,000	100	400	F-2010H★	St. Louis	648,000	125	525
F-2010C	Philadelphia	76,320,000	18	65	F-2010I	Minneapolis	18,864,000	20	85
F-2010C★	Philadelphia	1,008,000	150	525	F-2010I★	Minneapolis	552,000	225	950
F-2010D	Cleveland	76,032,000	18	65	F-2010J	Kansas City	36,332,000	18	60
F-2010D★	Cleveland	1,008,000	150	525	F-2010J★	Kansas City	456,000	150	600
F-2010E	Richmond	61,776,000	18	60	F-2010K	Dallas	33,264,000	18	65
F-2010E★	Richmond	876,000	150	525	F-2010K★	Dallas	480,000	150	600
F-2010F	Atlanta	63,792,000	18	65	F-2010L	San Francisco	76,896,000	18	60
F-2010F★	Atlanta	864,000	150	525	F-2010L★	San Francisco	1,152,000	125	525

Series of 1950-A—Signatures of Priest and Humphrey

No.	Issuing Bank	Quantity Printed	EF-40	Unc-63	No.	Issuing Bank	Quantity Printed	EF-40	Unc-63
F-2011A	Boston	104,248,000	$20	$75	F-2011G	Chicago	235,064,000	$20	$70
F-2011A★	Boston	5,112,000	80	200	F-2011G★	Chicago	11,160,000	80	200
F-2011B	New York	356,664,000	20	70	F-2011H	St. Louis	46,512,000	25	100
F-2011B★	New York	16,992,000	75	180	F-2011H★	St. Louis	2,880,000	80	200
F-2011C	Philadelphia	71,920,000	20	75	F-2011I	Minneapolis	8,136,000	20	75
F-2011C★	Philadelphia	3,672,000	75	250	F-2011I★	Minneapolis	432,000	100	315
F-2011D	Cleveland	75,088,000	20	70	F-2011J	Kansas City	25,488,000	20	70
F-2011D★	Cleveland	3,672,000	75	250	F-2011J★	Kansas City	2,304,000	80	300
F-2011E	Richmond	82,144,000	20	75	F-2011K	Dallas	21,816,000	20	80
F-2011E★	Richmond	4,392,000	80	275	F-2011K★	Dallas	1,584,000	90	315
F-2011F	Atlanta	73,288,000	20	65	F-2011L	San Francisco	101,584,000	20	70
F-2011F★	Atlanta	3,816,000	80	200	F-2011L★	San Francisco	6,408,000	80	200

Series of 1950-B—Signatures of Priest and Anderson

No.	Issuing Bank	Quantity Printed	EF-40	Unc-63	No.	Issuing Bank	Quantity Printed	EF-40	Unc-63
F-2012A	Boston	49,240,000	$15	$40.00	F-2012G	Chicago	165,080,000	$15	$32.50
F-2012A★	Boston	2,880,000	65	150.00	F-2012G★	Chicago	6,480,000	65	150.00
F-2012B	New York	170,840,000	15	32.50	F-2012H	St. Louis	33,040,000	15	35.00
F-2012B★	New York	8,280,000	55	150.00	F-2012H★	St. Louis	1,800,000	65	185.00
F-2012C	Philadelphia	66,880,000	15	32.50	F-2012I	Minneapolis	13,320,000	20	47.50
F-2012C★	Philadelphia	3,240,000	65	145.00	F-2012I★	Minneapolis	720,000	95	350.00
F-2012D	Cleveland	55,360,000	15	35.00	F-2012J	Kansas City	33,480,000	15	50.00
F-2012D★	Cleveland	2,880,000	65	150.00	F-2012J★	Kansas City	2,520,000	80	150.00
F-2012E	Richmond	51,120,000	15	35.00	F-2012K	Dallas	26,280,000	15	45.00
F-2012E★	Richmond	2,880,000	80	160.00	F-2012K★	Dallas	1,440,000	65	300.00
F-2012F	Atlanta	66,520,000	15	35.00	F-2012L	San Francisco	55,000,000	15	40.00
F-2012F★	Atlanta	2,880,000	55	200.00	F-2012L★	San Francisco	2,880,000	65	140.00

Series of 1950-C—Signatures of Smith and Dillon

No.	Issuing Bank	Quantity Printed	EF-40	Unc-63	No.	Issuing Bank	Quantity Printed	EF-40	Unc-63
F-2013A	Boston	51,120,000	$15	$40	F-2013G	Chicago	69,400,000	$15	$35
F-2013A★	Boston	2,160,000	100	300	F-2013G★	Chicago	3,600,000	70	175
F-2013B	New York	126,520,000	15	35	F-2013H	St. Louis	23,040,000	15	55
F-2013B★	New York	6,840,000	90	275	F-2013H★	St. Louis	1,080,000	75	250
F-2013C	Philadelphia	25,200,000	15	40	F-2013I	Minneapolis	9,000,000	20	85
F-2013C★	Philadelphia	720,000	75	300	F-2013I★	Minneapolis	720,000	115	325
F-2013D	Cleveland	33,120,000	15	40	F-2013J	Kansas City	23,320,000	15	70
F-2013D★	Cleveland	1,800,000	125	275	F-2013J★	Kansas City	800,000	90	250
F-2013E	Richmond	45,640,000	15	40	F-2013K	Dallas	17,640,000	15	65
F-2013E★	Richmond	1,800,000	140	350	F-2013K★	Dallas	720,000	100	250
F-2013F	Atlanta	38,880,000	15	40	F-2013L	San Francisco	35,640,000	15	65
F-2013F★	Atlanta	2,880,000	125	375	F-2013L★	San Francisco	1,800,000	90	250

Face of F-2014 to F-2015.
Type of Series of 1950 to
1963-A. The wording above
the seal is slightly different.

Back of F-2014 to F-2015, the back type of all small-size $10 series through the 1950s

Series of 1950-D—Signatures of Granahan and Dillon

No.	Issuing Bank	Quantity Printed	EF-40	Unc-63	No.	Issuing Bank	Quantity Printed	EF-40	Unc-63
F-2014A	Boston	38,800,000	$15	$50	F-2014F★	Atlanta	1,440,000	$70	$200
F-2014A★	Boston	1,800,000	80	200	F-2014G	Chicago	115,480,000	15	40
F-2014B	New York	150,320,000	15	40	F-2014G★	Chicago	5,040,000	50	150
F-2014B★	New York	6,840,000	50	150	F-2014H	St. Louis	10,440,000	15	50
F-2014C	Philadelphia	19,080,000	15	50	F-2014H★	St. Louis	720,000	60	200
F-2014C★	Philadelphia	1,080,000	60	200	F-2014J	Kansas City	15,480,000	15	50
F-2014D	Cleveland	24,120,000	15	50	F-2014J★	Kansas City	1,080,000	60	200
F-2014D★	Cleveland	360,000	60	200	F-2014K	Dallas	18,280,000	15	50
F-2014E	Richmond	33,840,000	15	50	F-2014K★	Dallas	800,000	75	250
F-2014E★	Richmond	720,000	70	225	F-2014L	San Francisco	62,560,000	15	50
F-2014F	Atlanta	36,000,000	15	50	F-2014L★	San Francisco	3,600,000	60	200

Series of 1950-E—Signatures of Granahan and Fowler

No.	Issuing Bank	Quantity Printed	EF-40	Unc-63	No.	Issuing Bank	Quantity Printed	EF-40	Unc-63
F-2015B	New York	12,600,000	$45	$100	F-2015G★	Chicago	4,320,000	$150	$300
F-2015B★	New York	2,621,000	150	275	F-2015L	San Francisco	17,280,000	50	120
F-2015G	Chicago	65,080,000	45	100	F-2015L★	San Francisco	720,000	175	375

Federal Reserve Notes
Series of 1963 and 1963-A, Green Seal

Face of F-2016 to F-2032. Same as the preceding. The seal was modified starting with F-2018.

Back of F-2016 to F-2032. The motto "In God We Trust" is added above the Treasury Department.

See next page for chart.

Series of 1963 (IN GOD WE TRUST added)—Signatures of Granahan and Dillon

No.	Issuing Bank	Quantity Printed	EF-40	Unc-63	No.	Issuing Bank	Quantity Printed	EF-40	Unc-63
F-2016A	Boston	5,760,000	$15	$60	F-2016F★	Atlanta	1,280,000	$50	$120
F-2016A★	Boston	640,000	50	125	F-2016G	Chicago	35,200,000	15	45
F-2016B	New York	24,960,000	15	50	F-2016G★	Chicago	2,560,000	40	110
F-2016B★	New York	1,920,000	45	100	F-2016H	St. Louis	13,440,000	15	75
F-2016C	Philadelphia	6,400,000	15	60	F-2016H★	St. Louis	1,280,000	40	100
F-2016C★	Philadelphia	1,280,000	45	100	F-2016J	Kansas City	3,840,000	15	75
F-2016D	Cleveland	7,040,000	15	60	F-2016J★	Kansas City	640,000	50	150
F-2016D★	Cleveland	640,000	45	100	F-2016K	Dallas	5,120,000	15	75
F-2016E	Richmond	4,480,000	15	60	F-2016K★	Dallas	640,000	50	150
F-2016E★	Richmond	640,000	50	125	F-2016L	San Francisco	14,080,000	15	60
F-2016F	Atlanta	10,880,000	15	60	F-2016L★	San Francisco	1,280,000	50	125

Series of 1963-A—Signatures of Granahan and Fowler

No.	Issuing Bank	Quantity Printed	EF-40	Unc-63	No.	Issuing Bank	Quantity Printed	EF-40	Unc-63
F-2017A	Boston	131,360,000	$15	$40	F-2017G	Chicago	195,520,000	$15	$35
F-2017A★	Boston	6,400,000	25	80	F-2017G★	Chicago	9,600,000	20	75
F-2017B	New York	199,360,000	15	35	F-2017H	St. Louis	43,520,000	15	40
F-2017B★	New York	9,600,000	20	75	F-2017H★	St. Louis	1,920,000	30	85
F-2017C	Philadelphia	100,000,000	15	40	F-2017I	Minneapolis	16,640,000	18	50
F-2017C★	Philadelphia	4,480,000	20	80	F-2017I★	Minneapolis	640,000	30	95
F-2017D	Cleveland	72,960,000	15	40	F-2017J	Kansas City	31,360,000	15	40
F-2017D★	Cleveland	3,840,000	20	80	F-2017J★	Kansas City	1,920,000	30	85
F-2017E	Richmond	114,720,000	15	40	F-2017K	Dallas	51,200,000	15	40
F-2017E★	Richmond	5,120,000	20	80	F-2017K★	Dallas	1,920,000	30	85
F-2017F	Atlanta	80,000,000	15	40	F-2017L	San Francisco	87,200,000	15	40
F-2017F★	Atlanta	3,840,000	20	85	F-2017L★	San Francisco	5,120,000	20	80

Federal Reserve Notes
Series of 1969 to 1995,
Green Seal

Series of 1969 (with new Treasury seal)—Signatures of Elston and Kennedy

No.	Issuing Bank	Quantity Printed	EF-40	Unc-63	No.	Issuing Bank	Quantity Printed	EF-40	Unc-63
F-2018A	Boston	71,880,000	$15	$35	F-2018G	Chicago	142,240,000	$15	$35
F-2018A★	Boston	2,560,000	30	70	F-2018G★	Chicago	6,400,000	30	70
F-2018B	New York	247,360,000	15	35	F-2018H	St. Louis	22,400,000	15	35
F-2018B★	New York	10,240,000	30	70	F-2018H★	St. Louis	640,000	75	200
F-2018C	Philadelphia	56,960,000	15	35	F-2018I	Minneapolis	12,800,000	15	35
F-2018C★	Philadelphia	2,560,000	30	70	F-2018I★	Minneapolis	1,280,000	40	80
F-2018D	Cleveland	57,600,000	15	35	F-2018J	Kansas City	31,360,000	15	35
F-2018D★	Cleveland	2,560,000	30	70	F-2018J★	Kansas City	1,280,000	30	70
F-2018E	Richmond	56,960,000	15	35	F-2018K	Dallas	30,080,000	15	35
F-2018E★	Richmond	2,560,000	30	70	F-2018K★	Dallas	1,280,000	30	70
F-2018F	Atlanta	53,760,000	15	35	F-2018L	San Francisco	56,320,000	15	35
F-2018F★	Atlanta	2,560,000	30	70	F-2018L★	San Francisco	3,185,000	30	70

Series of 1969-A—Signatures of Kabis and Connally

No.	Issuing Bank	Quantity Printed	EF-40	Unc-63	No.	Issuing Bank	Quantity Printed	EF-40	Unc-63
F-2019A	Boston	41,120,000	$15	$35	F-2019F★	Atlanta	640,000	$30	$100
F-2019A★	Boston	1,920,000	20	65	F-2019G	Chicago	80,160,000	15	35
F-2019B	New York	111,840,000	15	35	F-2019G★	Chicago	3,560,000	25	65
F-2019B★	New York	3,840,000	20	65	F-2019H	St. Louis	15,360,000	15	35
F-2019C	Philadelphia	24,320,000	15	35	F-2019H★	St. Louis	640,000	25	75
F-2019C★	Philadelphia	1,920,000	20	65	F-2019I	Minneapolis	8,320,000	15	50
F-2019D	Cleveland	23,680,000	15	35	F-2019J	Kansas City	10,880,000	15	35
F-2019D★	Cleveland	1,276,000	20	65	F-2019K	Dallas	20,480,000	15	35
F-2019E	Richmond	25,600,000	15	35	F-2019K★	Dallas	640,000	25	70
F-2019E★	Richmond	640,000	30	100	F-2019L	San Francisco	23,840,000	15	35
F-2019F	Atlanta	13,440,000	15	35	F-2019L★	San Francisco	640,000	20	70

Series of 1969-B—Signatures of Banuelos and Connally

No.	Issuing Bank	Quantity Printed	EF-40	Unc-63	No.	Issuing Bank	Quantity Printed	EF-40	Unc-63
F-2020A	Boston	16,640,000	$60	$180	F-2020G*	Chicago	1,268,000	$80	$250
F-2020B	New York	60,320,000	60	125	F-2020H	St. Louis	8,960,000	60	125
F-2020B*	New York	1,920,000	75	175	F-2020H*	St. Louis	1,280,000	100	300
F-2020C	Philadelphia	16,000,000	60	125	F-2020I	Minneapolis	3,200,000	80	200
F-2020D	Cleveland	12,800,000	60	125	F-2020J	Kansas City	5,120,000	60	150
F-2020E	Richmond	12,160,000	60	125	F-2020J*	Kansas City	640,000	125	350
F-2020E*	Richmond	640,000	125	400	F-2020K	Dallas	5,760,000	70	140
F-2020F	Atlanta	13,440,000	60	125	F-2020L	San Francisco	23,840,000	60	125
F-2020F*	Atlanta	640,000	125	250	F-2020L*	San Francisco	640,000	125	350
F-2020G	Chicago	32,640,000	60	125					

Series of 1969-C—Signatures of Banuelos and Shultz

No.	Issuing Bank	Quantity Printed	EF-40	Unc-63	No.	Issuing Bank	Quantity Printed	EF-40	Unc-63
F-2021A	Boston	44,800,000	$15	$40	F-2021G	Chicago	55,200,000	$12	$35
F-2021A*	Boston	640,000	45	125	F-2021G*	Chicago	880,000	35	110
F-2021B	New York	203,200,000	12	35	F-2021H	St. Louis	29,800,000	15	40
F-2021B*	New York	7,040,000	25	70	F-2021H*	St. Louis	1,280,000	40	100
F-2021C	Philadelphia	69,920,000	15	45	F-2021I	Minneapolis	11,520,000	15	45
F-2021C*	Philadelphia	1,280,000	30	80	F-2021I*	Minneapolis	640,000	55	120
F-2021D	Cleveland	46,880,000	15	40	F-2021J	Kansas City	23,040,000	15	40
F-2021D*	Cleveland	2,400,000	30	75	F-2021J*	Kansas City	640,000	30	70
F-2021E	Richmond	45,600,000	15	40	F-2021K	Dallas	24,960,000	15	40
F-2021E*	Richmond	1,120,000	35	110	F-2021K*	Dallas	640,000	30	70
F-2021F	Atlanta	46,240,000	15	40	F-2021L	San Francisco	56,960,000	15	35
F-2021F*	Atlanta	1,920,000	30	80	F-2021L*	San Francisco	640,000	30	65

Series of 1974—Signatures of Neff and Simon

No.	Issuing Bank	Quantity Printed	EF-40	Unc-63	No.	Issuing Bank	Quantity Printed	EF-40	Unc-63
F-2022A	Boston	104,480,000	$15	$35	F-2022G	Chicago	104,320,000	$12	$30
F-2022A*	Boston	2,560,000	30	65	F-2022G*	Chicago	4,480,000	20	60
F-2022B	New York	239,040,000	12	30	F-2022H	St. Louis	46,240,000	15	35
F-2022B*	New York	4,460,000	20	65	F-2022H*	St. Louis	1,280,000	20	75
F-2022C	Philadelphia	69,280,000	15	35	F-2022I	Minneapolis	27,520,000	15	35
F-2022C*	Philadelphia	2,560,000	20	65	F-2022I*	Minneapolis	2,560,000	40	125
F-2022D	Cleveland	82,080,000	15	35	F-2022J	Kansas City	24,320,000	15	35
F-2022D*	Cleveland	1,920,000	20	65	F-2022J*	Kansas City	640,000	20	65
F-2022E	Richmond	105,760,000	15	35	F-2022K	Dallas	39,840,000	15	35
F-2022E*	Richmond	1,920,000	20	65	F-2022K*	Dallas	1,920,000	20	65
F-2022F	Atlanta	75,520,000	15	35	F-2022L	San Francisco	1,920,000	15	35
F-2022F*	Atlanta	3,200,000	20	65	F-2022L*	San Francisco	1,760,000	20	65

Series of 1977—Signatures of Morton and Blumenthal

No.	Issuing Bank	Quantity Printed	EF-40	Unc-63	No.	Issuing Bank	Quantity Printed	EF-40	Unc-63
F-2023A	Boston	96,640,000	$15	$40	F-2023G	Chicago	174,720,000	$15	$35
F-2023A*	Boston	2,688,000	30	100	F-2023G*	Chicago	3,968,000	30	80
F-2023B	New York	277,120,000	15	40	F-2023H	St. Louis	46,720,000	15	35
F-2023B*	New York	7,168,000	25	70	F-2023H*	St. Louis	896,000	30	85
F-2023C	Philadelphia	83,200,000	15	35	F-2023I	Minneapolis	10,240,000	20	50
F-2023C*	Philadelphia	896,000	30	80	F-2023I*	Minneapolis	256,000	45	150
F-2023D	Cleveland	83,200,000	15	35	F-2023J	Kansas City	50,560,000	15	35
F-2023D*	Cleveland	768,000	25	75	F-2023J*	Kansas City	896,000	35	85
F-2023E	Richmond	71,040,000	15	35	F-2023K	Dallas	53,760,000	15	40
F-2023E*	Richmond	1,920,000	25	80	F-2023K*	Dallas	640,000	35	100
F-2023F	Atlanta	88,960,000	15	35	F-2023L	San Francisco	73,600,000	15	35
F-2023F*	Atlanta	1,536,000	30	80	F-2023L*	San Francisco	1,792,000	30	80

Series of 1977-A—Signatures of Morton and Miller

No.	Issuing Bank	Quantity Printed	EF-40	Unc-63	No.	Issuing Bank	Quantity Printed	EF-40	Unc-63
F-2024A	Boston	83,840,000	$15.00	$40	F-2024G	Chicago	108,160,000	$12.50	$35
F-2024A*	Boston	1,664,000	40.00	95	F-2024G*	Chicago	3,200,000	15.00	50
F-2024B	New York	259,280,000	12.50	35	F-2024H	St. Louis	27,520,000	12.50	35
F-2024B*	New York	5,248,000	20.00	55	F-2024H*	St. Louis	640,000	30.00	90
F-2024C	Philadelphia	96,000,000	12.50	35	F-2024I	Minneapolis	7,680,000	12.50	50
F-2024C*	Philadelphia	2,048,000	20.00	65	F-2024I*	Minneapolis	128,000	50.00	150
F-2024D	Cleveland	44,800,000	12.50	35	F-2024J	Kansas City	40,320,000	15.00	45
F-2024D*	Cleveland	2,048,000	20.00	65	F-2024J*	Kansas City	2,136,000	30.00	100
F-2024E	Richmond	104,320,000	12.50	35	F-2024K	Dallas	60,160,000	12.50	35
F-2024E*	Richmond	3,072,000	25.00	90	F-2024K*	Dallas	4,224,000	20.00	55
F-2024F	Atlanta	33,920,000	12.50	35	F-2024L	San Francisco	59,520,000	12.50	35
F-2024F*	Atlanta	640,000	40.00	135	F-2024L*	San Francisco	2,048,000	20.00	60

Series of 1981—Signatures of Buchanan and Regan

No.	Issuing Bank	Quantity Printed	EF-40	Unc-63	No.	Issuing Bank	Quantity Printed	EF-40	Unc-63
F-2025A	Boston	172,160,000	$15	$40	F-2025F★	Atlanta	1,908,000	$30	$100
F-2025A★	Boston	1,280,000	25	90	F-2025G	Chicago	254,080,000	15	40
F-2025B	New York	434,560,000	15	40	F-2025G★	Chicago	1,280,000	30	100
F-2025B★	New York	1,920,000	35	125	F-2025H	St. Louis	55,280,000	20	55
F-2025C	Philadelphia	131,840,000	15	40	F-2025I	Minneapolis	23,680,000	20	60
F-2025C★	Philadelphia	632,000	35	125	F-2025I★	Minneapolis	256,000	50	150
F-2025D	Cleveland	122,240,000	15	45	F-2025J	Kansas City	53,120,000	20	40
F-2025D★	Cleveland	1,268,000	25	115	F-2025K	Dallas	50,560,000	20	45
F-2025E	Richmond	131,840,000	15	40	F-2025L	San Francisco	144,000,000	15	40
F-2025E★	Richmond	2,576,000	25	90	F-2025L★	San Francisco	1,280,000	25	90
F-2025F	Atlanta	131,840,000	15	40					

Series of 1981-A—Signatures of Ortega and Regan

No.	Issuing Bank	Quantity Printed	EF-40	Unc-63	No.	Issuing Bank	Quantity Printed	EF-40	Unc-63
F-2026A	Boston	112,000,000	$15	$40	F-2026F★	Atlanta	4,736,000	$35	$100
F-2026B	New York	259,000,000	15	30	F-2026G	Chicago	183,600,000	15	40
F-2026B★	New York	3,200,000	35	100	F-2026H	St. Louis	25,600,000	15	40
F-2026C	Philadelphia	48,000,000	15	40	F-2026I	Minneapolis	19,200,000	15	40
F-2026D	Cleveland	80,000,000	15	40	F-2026J	Kansas City	48,000,000	15	40
F-2026E	Richmond	92,800,000	15	40	F-2026K	Dallas	48,000,000	15	40
F-2026E★	Richmond	3,200,000	30	90	F-2026L	San Francisco	115,200,000	15	40
F-2026F	Atlanta	83,200,000	15	40					

Series of 1985—Signatures of Ortega and Baker

No.	Issuing Bank	Quantity Printed	EF-40	Unc-63	No.	Issuing Bank	Quantity Printed	EF-40	Unc-63
F-2027A	Boston	380,800,000	$20	$35	F-2027G	Chicago	358,400,000	$20	$30
F-2027A★	Boston	7,296,000	30	70	F-2027H	St. Louis	131,200,000	20	35
F-2027B	New York	1,027,200,000	20	30	F-2027H★	St. Louis	3,200,000	30	75
F-2027B★	New York	3,200,000	25	60	F-2027I	Minneapolis	64,000,000	20	35
F-2027C	Philadelphia	163,200,000	20	35	F-2027J	Kansas City	86,400,000	20	35
F-2027D	Cleveland	304,000,000	20	35	F-2027K	Dallas	115,200,000	20	35
F-2027D★	Cleveland	3,200,000	35	100	F-2027K★	Dallas	3,136,000	35	90
F-2027E	Richmond	211,200,000	20	35	F-2027L	San Francisco	300,800,000	20	30
F-2027F	Atlanta	297,600,000	20	35	F-2027L★	San Francisco	3,200,000	35	90
F-2027F★	Atlanta	3,200,000	45	135					

Series of 1988-A—Signatures of Villalpando and Brady

No.	Issuing Bank	Quantity Printed	EF-40	Unc-63	No.	Issuing Bank	Quantity Printed	EF-40	Unc-63
F-2028A	Boston	198,400,000	$20	$35	F-2028F	Atlanta	236,800,000	$20	$35
F-2028A★	Boston	6,400,000	35	95	F-2028G	Chicago	236,800,000	20	35
F-2028B	New York	339,200,000	20	35	F-2028H	St. Louis	70,400,000	20	35
F-2028B★	New York	3,200,000	35	95	F-2028I	Minneapolis	19,200,000	20	35
F-2028C	Philadelphia	57,600,000	20	35	F-2028J	Kansas City	51,200,000	20	35
F-2028D	Cleveland	128,000,000	20	35	F-2028K	Dallas	115,200,000	20	40
F-2028D★	Cleveland	3,200,000	35	95	F-2028L	San Francisco	217,600,000	20	35
F-2028E	Richmond	105,600,000	20	35	F-2028L★	San Francisco	3,200,000	35	95

Series of 1990—Signatures of Villalpando and Brady

Printed in Washington, DC

Security thread and micro-size printing introduced

No.	Issuing Bank	Quantity Printed	EF-40	Unc-63	No.	Issuing Bank	Quantity Printed	EF-40	Unc-63
F-2029A	Boston	128,000,000	$12.50	$20	F-2029G	Chicago	307,200,000	$12.50	$20
F-2029B	New York	742,400,000	12.50	20	F-2029G★	Chicago	2,560,000	20.00	50
F-2029B★	New York	16,874,000	20.00	50	F-2029H	St. Louis	70,400,000	12.50	20
F-2029C	Philadelphia	19,200,000	12.50	20	F-2029H★	St. Louis	1,920,000	20.00	50
F-2029C★	Philadelphia	2,560,000	20.00	50	F-2029I	Minneapolis	12,800,000	12.50	20
F-2029D	Cleveland	89,600,000	12.50	20	F-2029J	Kansas City	70,400,000	12.50	20
F-2029E	Richmond	105,600,000	12.50	20	F-2029K	Dallas	57,600,000	12.50	20
F-2029F	Atlanta	160,000,000	12.50	20	F-2029L	San Francisco	83,200,000	12.50	20

Series of 1993—Signatures of Withrow and Bentsen
Printed in Washington, DC

No.	Issuing Bank	Quantity Printed	EF-40	Unc-63	No.	Issuing Bank	Quantity Printed	EF-40	Unc-63
F-2030A	Boston	147,200,000	$12.50	$20	F-2030F	Atlanta	121,600,000	$12.50	$20
F-2030B	New York	480,000,000	12.50	20	F-2030G	Chicago	128,000,000	12.50	20
F-2030B★	New York	5,120,000	20.00	50	F-2030G★	Chicago	2,176,000	20.00	50
F-2030C	Philadelphia	83,200,000	12.50	20	F-2030H	St. Louis	89,600,000	12.50	20
F-2030C★	Philadelphia	1,920,000	20.00	50	F-2030J	Kansas City	19,200,000	12.50	20
F-2030D	Cleveland	115,200,000	12.50	20	F-2030L	San Francisco	192,000,000	12.50	20

Series of 1995—Signatures of Withrow and Rubin
Printed in Washington, DC

No.	Issuing Bank	Quantity Printed	EF-40	Unc-63	No.	Issuing Bank	Quantity Printed	EF-40	Unc-63
F-2031A	Boston	192,000,000	$12.50	$25	F-2031E	Richmond	153,600,000	$12.50	$25
F-2031B	New York	358,400,000	12.50	25	F-2031E★	Richmond	1,280,000	25.00	55
F-2031C	Philadelphia	57,600,000	12.50	25	F-2031F	Atlanta	70,400,000	12.50	25
F-2031D	Cleveland	108,000,000	12.50	25	F-2031F★	Atlanta	640,000	50.00	100

Series of 1995—Signatures of Withrow and Rubin
Printed at the Western Facility (Fort Worth, Texas)

No.	Issuing Bank	Quantity Printed	EF-40	Unc-63	No.	Issuing Bank	Quantity Printed	EF-40	Unc-63
F-2032B	New York	76,800,000	$12.50	$25	F-2032G★	Chicago	3,200,000	$15.00	$35
F-2032C	Philadelphia	89,600,000	12.50	25	F-2032H	St. Louis	153,600,000	12.50	25
F-2032D	Cleveland	70,400,000	12.50	25	F-2032H★	St. Louis	6,400,000	15.00	40
F-2032D★	Cleveland	1,920,000	20.00	50	F-2032I	Minneapolis	70,400,000	15.00	35
F-2032E	Richmond	134,400,000	12.50	25	F-2032J	Kansas City	147,200,000	12.50	25
F-2032E★	Richmond	1,280,000	20.00	50	F-2032K	Dallas	166,400,000	12.50	25
F-2032F	Atlanta	377,600,000	12.50	25	F-2032L	San Francisco	275,200,000	12.50	25
F-2032F★	Atlanta	320,000	35.00	110	F-2032L★	San Francisco	3,200,000	15.00	50
F-2032G	Chicago	448,000,000	12.50	25					

Federal Reserve Notes
Series of 1999 to 2003, Green Seal, Security Features

Face of F-2033 to F-2038. Hamilton's portrait is modified as are other aspects, and security features have been added.

Back of F-2033 to F-2038. The Treasury Department has been enlarged and certain other features modified.

See next page for chart.

Series of 1999—Signatures of Withrow and Summers
Printed in Washington, DC

No.	Issuing Bank	Quantity Printed	Unc-63	No.	Issuing Bank	Quantity Printed	Unc-63
F-2033A	Boston	83,200,000	$20	F-2033E★	Richmond	675,200	$85
F-2033A★	Boston	3,200,000	35	F-2033F	Atlanta	96,000,000	20
F-2033B	New York	300,800,000	20	F-2033G	Chicago	83,200,000	20
F-2033B★	New York	3,200,000	35	F-2033H	St. Louis	38,400,000	20
F-2033C	Philadelphia	64,000,000	20	F-2033I	Minneapolis	6,400,000	65
F-2033C★	Philadelphia	3,520,000	35	F-2033J	Kansas City	12,800,000	20
F-2033D	Cleveland	51,520,000	20	F-2033K	Dallas	44,800,000	20
F-2033D★	Cleveland	2,240,000	45	F-2033L	San Francisco	32,000,000	20
F-2033E	Richmond	112,800,000	20				

Series of 1999—Signatures of Withrow and Summers
Printed at the Western Facility (Fort Worth, Texas)

No.	Issuing Bank	Quantity Printed	Unc-63	No.	Issuing Bank	Quantity Printed	Unc-63
F-2034A★	Boston	3,200,000	$40	F-2034J	Kansas City	51,200,000	$25
F-2034B★	New York	3,200,000	40	F-2034K	Dallas	128,000,000	20
F-2034F	Atlanta	83,200,000	20	F-2034K★	Dallas	12,800,000	30
F-2034F★	Atlanta	7,715,200	30	F-2034L	San Francisco	76,800,000	20
F-2034G	Chicago	44,800,000	20				

Series of 2001—Signatures of Marin and O'Neill
Printed in Washington, DC

No.	Issuing Bank	Quantity Printed	Unc-63	No.	Issuing Bank	Quantity Printed	Unc-63
F-2035A	Boston	19,200,000	$20	F-2035E	Richmond	117,760,000	$20
F-2035B	New York	121,600,000	20	F-2035F	Atlanta	38,400,000	20
F-2035B★	New York	320,000	110	F-2035G	Chicago	51,200,000	20
F-2035C	Philadelphia	108,800,000	20	F-2035G★	Chicago	640,000	70
F-2035D	Cleveland	57,600,000	20	F-2035H	St. Louis	12,800,000	25
F-2035D★	Cleveland	1,280,000	40	F-2035I	Minneapolis	6,400,000	30

Series of 2001—Signatures of Marin and O'Neill
Printed at the Western Facility (Fort Worth, Texas)

No.	Issuing Bank	Quantity Printed	Unc-63	No.	Issuing Bank	Quantity Printed	Unc-63
F-2036A	Boston	147,200,000	$20	F-2036H	St. Louis	64,000,000	$20
F-2036B	New York	121,600,000	20	F-2036I	Minneapolis	32,000,000	25
F-2036C	Philadelphia	32,000,000	20	F-2036K	Dallas	38,400,000	25
F-2036E	Richmond	44,800,000	20	F-2036K★	Dallas	3,200,000	40
F-2036F	Atlanta	76,800,000	20	F-2036L	San Francisco	44,800,000	20
F-2036G	Chicago	640,000	90	F-2036L★	San Francisco	3,200,000	40

Series of 2003—Signatures of Marin and Snow
Printed in Washington, DC

No.	Issuing Bank	Quantity Printed	Unc-63	No.	Issuing Bank	Quantity Printed	Unc-63
F-2037A	Boston	32,000,000	$20	F-2037H	St. Louis	38,400,000	$20
F-2037A★	Boston	416,000	65	F-2037H★	St. Louis	768,000	50
F-2037B	New York	57,600,000	20	F-2037I	Minneapolis	6,400,000	35
F-2037C	Philadelphia	32,000,000	20	F-2037J	Kansas City	51,200,000	20
F-2037D	Cleveland	38,400,000	20	F-2037J★	Kansas City	2,920,000	40
F-2037D★	Cleveland	1,280,000	40	F-2037K	Dallas	76,800,000	20
F-2037E	Richmond	38,400,000	20	F-2037K★	Dallas	320,000	65
F-2037F	Atlanta	57,600,000	20	F-2037L	San Francisco	108,800,000	20
F-2037G	Chicago	140,800,000	20				

Series of 2003—Signatures of Marin and Snow
Printed at the Western Facility (Fort Worth, Texas)

No.	Issuing Bank	Quantity Printed	Unc-63	No.	Issuing Bank	Quantity Printed	Unc-63
F-2038A	Boston	32,000,000	$20	F-2038E	Richmond	44,800,000	$20
F-2038B	New York	89,600,000	20	F-2038F	Atlanta	38,400,000	20
F-2038C	Philadelphia	44,800,000	20	F-2038G	Chicago	6,400,000	20
F-2038D	Cleveland	32,000,000	20	F-2038I	Minneapolis	6,400,000	40

Federal Reserve Notes
Series of 2004-A to Date,
Green Seal, Additional Features

Face of F-2039 to date. Similar to the preceding, but with color and other security features added and with an additional seal to the lower right of the portrait.

Back of F-2039 to date. Similar to the preceding, but with tiny yellow "10" numbers and other security features added.

Series of 2004-A (color added)—Signatures of Cabral and Snow
Printed at the Western Facility (Fort Worth, Texas)

No.	Issuing Bank	Unc-63	No.	Issuing Bank	Unc-63
F-2039A	Boston	$20	F-2039F★	Atlanta	$110
F-2039A★	Boston	50	F-2039G	Chicago	20
F-2039B	New York	20	F-2039G★	Chicago	85
F-2039B★	New York	85	F-2039H	St. Louis	20
F-2039C	Philadelphia	20	F-2039I	Minneapolis	25
F-2039D	Cleveland	20	F-2039J	Kansas City	20
F-2039E	Richmond	20	F-2039L★	San Francisco	100
F-2039F	Atlanta	20			

Series of 2006—Signatures of Cabral and Paulson
Printed at the Western Facility (Fort Worth, Texas)

No.	Issuing Bank	Unc-63	No.	Issuing Bank	Unc-63
F-2040A	Boston	Current	F-2040G	Chicago	Current
F-2040B	New York	Current	F-2040G★	Chicago	Current
F-2040C	Philadelphia	Current	F-2040H	St. Louis	Current
F-2040C★	Philadelphia	Current	F-2040I	Minneapolis	Current
F-2040D	Cleveland	Current	F-2040J	Kansas City	Current
F-2040E	Richmond	Current	F-2040K	Dallas	Current
F-2040F	Atlanta	Current	F-2040L	San Francisco	Current

226★

20

COLLECTING $20 NOTES

The $20 denomination is one which demands seriousness and resources should it be the focus of a collection. The number of types, both large size and small size, are broadly represented but are not as widely pursued as similar notes in lower denominations. Some $20 issues, such as large size Silver Certificates and Treasury Notes, become prohibitively expensive in the highest states of preservation. The high face value becomes a factor when collecting small size issues.

Large-Size Notes

$20 Interest-Bearing Notes, Large-Size. There is only one note in this category, a One Year Note authorized under the Act of March 3, 1863. There are two varieties, the first (F-197) printed under contract with "ABN Co. and NBN Co." on the face—one of which sold for more than $32,000 in 2007—and the second (F-197a) printed at the Treasury in Washington. Today, there are only nine known of the first and 25 of the second.

$20 Demand Notes of 1861, Large-Size. This is the third-highest denominated, and most valuable, of the Demand Notes. The issue was similar to the $10. The only specimen known with "For the" handwritten is from the bank in New York and last sold in 1999 for more than $40,000. Of the 20 others now known, eight are payable at New York and seven at Philadelphia.

$20 Legal Tender Notes (United States Notes), Large-Size. Starting with this denomination, the issues are more limited than for the lower ones. The $20 Legal Tender Series of 1862 and 1863 continue the pattern of using the same face design as the Demand Notes of 1861 (essentially incorporating their design). There are seven varieties based on design factors, printers, and the form of the obligation. These are mainly collected by type, with the more common numbers (especially F-124 and F-126b) appearing with relative frequency. It is interesting, and fortuitous for those with the budget, that more than a third of the F-126b pieces known are in uncirculated condition.

The Series of 1869, 1875, 1878, and 1880 $20 Legal Tender Notes all have a right-facing portrait of Alexander Hamilton at left, and a standing figure of Liberty holding a sword and shield at right. The 1869 issue is another example of the colorful "Rainbow Note" and one of the more common of the 21 notes of this type of face. The rarest known today, with about a dozen extant, is F-130, bearing the signatures of Scofield and Gilfillan and a large brown seal. Later-printed issues are not hard to find, even in the best states of preservation.

$20 National Bank Notes, Large-Size. The First and Second Charter Period notes of this issue assume a more patriotic aura than their $10 counterparts, with two depictions—of the Battle of Lexington and of Columbia leading a procession of citizens—flanking the bank information in the center of the face. The back of the First Charters shows a part of the John G. Chapman painting "The Baptism of Pocahontas." These notes are somewhat elusive, except from the more established states. Those simply looking to collect the face vignettes would be better served searching the second-issue Second Charters as these are the most reasonably priced.

The Third Charter Period notes, especially those with Blue Seals, are far and away the most common National Bank Notes of this denomination, despite the fact that all were produced as the fourth note on sheets with three $10s. As usual, the Red Seals are much scarcer; as common as the Blue Seals are, notes from rare banks in elusive states bring extraordinary prices.

$20 Compound Interest Treasury Notes, Large-Size. Only one of the three types of this issue is remotely obtainable: F-191a, with the signatures of S.B. Colby and F.E. Spinner. There are about 50 of these reported. Still, even for these, recent sales results have pushed prices past the $25,000 plateau.

$20 National Gold Bank Notes, Large-Size. There are more than 30 notes known of F-1142 from the First National Gold Bank of San Francisco. Only 10 are rated as better than

Very Good. All others are at least scarce. The design characteristics follow the pattern set by the other denominations.

$20 Silver Certificates, Large-Size. The first $20 Silver Certificate issues, Series of 1878 and 1880, closely mimic their contemporaneous $10 counterparts. Robert Morris' portrait on the left side of the $10 has been moved to the right side and replaced by that of Commodore Stephen Decatur, naval officer in the War of 1812 and conqueror of the Barbary Pirates. Only one of the Series of 1878 issues (F-307) is deemed other than at least Extremely Rare, and even this note will bring a five-figure price when sold in all but the most miserable of conditions. Friedberg-309 to F-312, the other issues of the Series of 1880, are elusive in uncirculated condition, but at least a few in lower grades will usually show up at auctions every year.

The Series of 1886 Silver Certificates, by virtue of their intricate reverse design, are known as "Diamond Backs." The face of the Series of 1891 has at its center a bust of Daniel Manning, secretary of the Treasury under Grover Cleveland from 1885–1887. The 1886 series is considerably scarcer, particularly in the higher grades for which there are less than a dozen uncirculated specimens reported.

$20 Treasury or Coin Notes, Large-Size. After a celebration of Union generals on the $2, $5, and $10 Treasury Notes, an even greater American of a different calling is seen on the $20. He is John Marshall, the statesman and longest-serving U.S. Supreme Court chief justice (1801–1835) in history. Marshall's greatest enduring contribution was his opinion in the case of *Marbury v. Madison*, which had the effect of institutionalizing a basic element of our democracy: the concepts of the independent judiciary and judicial review. Unlike the lower-denomination Treasury Notes, valuations of the 1890 and 1891 series do not skew higher toward the more ornate and artistically interesting earlier issues. Friedberg-375a (1891) is a great rarity, of which there are only two pieces known, and there are just 10 for F-373 (1890). The other three issues appear with regularity, with notes at the top end of the grading range becoming appreciated for their scarcity.

$20 Gold Certificates, Large-Size. The most recent sale of one of the first $20 Gold Certificates of the Act of March 3, 1863, brought its seller more than $345,000. The note was one of only four in public hands. These, and most other Gold Certificates until those of the Series of 1907, were for bank rather than public use, so the short availability should not be surprising.

Even the next issue, the Series of 1882 with the bust of President James A. Garfield, remains relatively scarce until the last note, F-1178. There are hundreds known of this one, compared to less than 30 for any one of its companions. F-1175 is another great rarity, of which there are only two known, indicating that it probably warranted the $546,250 paid for it in late 2007.

The Gold Certificates of the Series of 1905 (F-1179–F-1180) are the famous "Technicolor Notes." Though they are nowhere near as "Technicolor" as the Rainbow Notes of the Legal Tender Series of 1869, they are the most appealing and attractive of all Gold Certificates due to the addition of a golden tint to their face. Most notes encountered are of Very Fine quality or less. One of the highest-rated uncirculated versions recently changed hands for more than $80,000, an example of the sometimes geometric rise in price when superior quality becomes an issue. The Gold Certificates from the Series of 1906 through 1922 are the same style as the Technicolor Notes but on regular paper and with gold overprints. Though these are common and easy to find in used condition, the market is now beginning to recognize the rarity of them—and of all Gold Certificates—in top quality.

$20 Federal Reserve Notes, Large-Size. These were issued in the same pattern as the other denominations of the type with the new era of modern transportation exemplified on the back by a contemporary car and locomotive at left, and an ocean liner steaming past the Statue of Liberty at right. Except for star notes, most of the many listed can be easily found.

$20 Federal Reserve Bank Notes, Large-Size. What these notes lack in appearance they make up for in scarcity. As of now, there are less than 40 pieces known of any one signature combination, and there were none made for half the Federal Reserve districts—those of Boston, New York, Cleveland, Richmond, Minneapolis, and San Francisco.

Small-Size Notes

All small-size $20 notes have Andrew Jackson on the face and the White House on the back. As we move to these and higher denominations, face value often is a more impressive component of the price than either condition or rarity.

$20 National Bank Notes, Small-Size. There is little difference even in price between these and the $10 National Bank notes issued through early 1935. As far as states are concerned, Alaska seems to take the prize.

$20 Gold Certificates, Small-Size. Some 1.5 million small-size Gold Certificates were printed for the Series of 1928-A but never were released because of the gold recall (which dictated that each citizen was allowed to retain only $100 in gold or gold certificates). Fortunately for today's collectors, not everyone paid attention, and these certificates are plentiful on today's market.

$20 Federal Reserve Bank Notes, Small-Size. Star notes for the Dallas district are the rarest of all $20 Federal Reserve Bank Notes even though 24,000 notes are reported to have been printed for each of the 12 districts. All regular issues are easy to find.

$20 Federal Reserve Notes, Small-Size. The Series of 1928-C issues, made only for Chicago and San Francisco, are the keys to the type. Commencing with the Series of 1934-C, the back was modified to include more greenery around the White House. Hawaii emergency $20 currency was issued under the Series of 1934 and 1934-A.

Anti-counterfeiting requirements led to modifications in the face and back designs beginning with the Series of 1996. These measures became more elaborate with the Series of 2004, which added green, peach, and blue background tints to both sides of the bill. This was the first time that small-size currency, except for seals and serial numbers, was printed with colors besides black and green. Other measures included color-shifting ink, an embedded security thread, a watermark, and microprinting so small that it is said to be impossible to photograph or photocopy.

LARGE-SIZE $20 NOTES

Interest-Bearing Notes of 1863

Face of F-197 and F-197a. "Victory" at left, portrait of President Lincoln at right. A mortar is shown at bottom center.

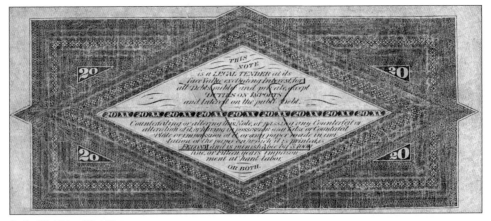

Back of F-197 and F-197a.

No.	Signatures				VG-8	F-12	VF-20
F-197	Chittenden	Spinner	Fewer than 10 known	ABN Co./ NBN Co.	$8,000	$24,500	—
F-197a	Chittenden	Spinner	Fewer than 30 known	BEP	6,000	16,000	—

Demand Notes of 1861

Face of F-11 to F-15. Liberty standing with a sword and shield. These were issued during the first year and were redeemable in gold coins on demand.

Back of F-11 to F-15.

No.	Payable at		VG-8	F-12	VF-20	EF-40
F-11	New York		$25,000	$40,000	—	—
F-11a	"For the" handwritten	Unique				
F-12	Philadelphia		25,000	40,000	$65,000	—
F-12a	"For the" handwritten	Unknown				
F-13	Boston		30,000	—	—	—
F-13a	"For the" handwritten	Unknown				
F-14	Cincinnati	Unique				
F-14a	"For the" handwritten	Unknown				
F-15	St. Louis	Unknown				

Legal Tender Notes
Series of 1862,
First Obligation

Face of F-124 and F-124a. Liberty standing with sword and shield.

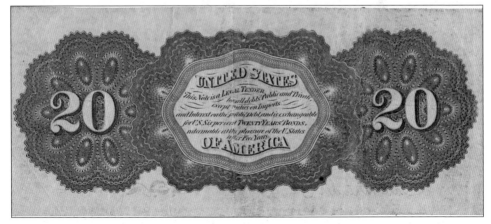

Back of F-124 and F-124a, with "First Obligation."

No.	Act	Printing Order	Signatures		Seal		VG-8	F-12	VF-20	EF-40	Unc-63
"Series" at top center											
F-124	1862	Second printed	Chittenden	Spinner	Red		$1,550	$2,500	$4,200	$6,000	—
No "Series" at top center											
F-124a	1862	First printed	Chittenden	Spinner	Red	2 reported					

Legal Tender Notes
Series of 1862 and 1863,
Second Obligation

Face of F-125 to F-126c. Same as the preceding.

Back of F-125 to F-126c.

No.	Printing Order	Act	Signatures		Seal	VG-8	F-12	VF-20	EF-40	Unc-63
National Bank Note Co. and American Bank Note Co. on lower border										
F-125		1862	Chittenden	Spinner	Red	$1,550	$2,700	$4,450	$6,400	—
F-126	First printed	1863	Chittenden	Spinner	Red, one serial no.	1,550	2,700	4,450	6,400	
American Bank Note Co. on lower border										
F-126a	Second printed	1863	Chittenden	Spinner	Red, one serial no.	1,750	3,000	4,750	6,600	—
F-126b	Fourth printed	1863	Chittenden	Spinner	Red, two serial nos. (left low, right high in field)	1,550	2,700	4,450	6,400	$11,500
F-126c	Third printed	1863	Chittenden	Spinner	Red, two serial nos. (both high in field)			About 7 known		

Legal Tender Notes
Series of 1869

Face of F-127. Profile bust of Alexander Hamilton at left, goddess Victory with helmet at right. "Rainbow Note." The star after the serial number is decorative.

Back of F-127.

No.	Signatures		Seal	VG-8	F-12	VF-20	EF-40	Unc-63
F-127	Allison	Spinner	Large red	$1,200	$2,500	$3,500	$6,250	$17,500

Legal Tender Notes
Series of 1875 to 1880

Face of F-128 to F-147.

Back of F-128 to F-147.

No.	Series	Signatures		Seal	VG-8	F-12	VF-20	EF-40	Unc-63
F-128	1875	Allison	New	Small red, rays	$800	$1,175	$1,750	$2,500	$5,800
F-129	1878	Allison	Gilfillan	Small red, rays	750	975	1,350	2,000	4,250
As above, but without "XX" and with blue serial numbers									
F-130	1880	Scofield	Gilfillan	Large brown	1,000	3,000	8,000	13,500	—
F-131	1880	Bruce	Gilfillan	Large brown	650	1,100	1,750	2,500	6,000
F-132	1880	Bruce	Wyman	Large brown	375	600	900	1,750	4,500
F-133	1880	Bruce	Wyman	Large red, plain	550	900	1,500	3,000	8,000
F-134	1880	Rosecrans	Jordan	Large red, plain	375	625	875	1,600	4,000
F-135	1880	Rosecrans	Hyatt	Large red, plain	375	600	860	1,600	2,750
F-136	1880	Rosecrans	Hyatt	Large red, spiked	350	600	800	1,400	2,900
F-137	1880	Rosecrans	Huston	Large red, spiked	350	600	800	1,400	2,900
F-138	1880	Rosecrans	Huston	Large brown	275	600	800	1,400	2,900
F-139	1880	Rosecrans	Nebeker	Large brown	750	1,500	2,500	4,500	—
F-140	1880	Rosecrans	Nebeker	Small red, scalloped	325	450	650	1,000	2,150
F-141	1880	Tillman	Morgan	Small red, scalloped	325	450	650	1,000	2,150
F-142	1880	Bruce	Roberts	Small red, scalloped	325	450	650	1,000	2,150
F-143	1880	Lyons	Roberts	Small red, scalloped	325	450	650	1,000	2,150
F-144	1880	Vernon	Treat	Small red, scalloped	325	450	650	1,000	2,150
F-145	1880	Vernon	McClung	Small red, scalloped	325	450	650	1,000	3,000
As above, but with red serial numbers									
F-146	1880	Teehee	Burke	Small red, scalloped	310	400	650	1,050	2,100
F-147	1880	Elliott	White	Small red, scalloped	275	350	575	925	2,000

Compound Interest Treasury Notes of 1864

Face of F-191 and F-191a. Design is similar to that on the Interest-Bearing Notes.

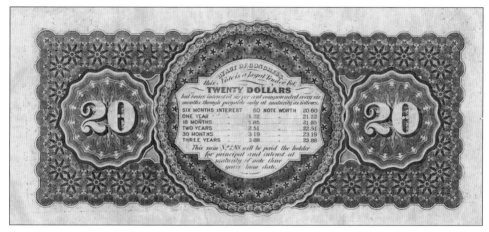

Back of F-191 and F-191a.

No.	Series		Signatures		F-12	VF-20	EF-40	Unc-63
F-191	1864	July 15, 1864	Chittenden	Spinner		Extremely rare		
F-191a	1864	Aug. 15, 1864–Oct. 16, 1865	Colby	Spinner	$2,250	$4,000	$15,000	—

National Bank Notes
Original Series
("First Charter Period")

Face of F-424 to F-429. Vignette of the Battle of Lexington-Concord at left; to right, Columbia.

Back of F-424 to F-429. Depiction of the "Baptism of Pocahontas."

No.	Signatures		Seal		VG-8	F-12	VF-20	EF-40	Unc-63
F-424	Chittenden	Spinner	Red, rays		$2,300	$2,700	$3,750	$4,500	$9,000
F-427	Colby	Spinner	Red, rays		2,300	2,700	3,750	4,500	9,000
F-428	Jeffries	Spinner	Red, rays	Unique					
F-429	Allison	Spinner	Red, rays		2,300	2,700	3,750	4,500	8,500

National Bank Notes
Series of 1875
("First Charter Period")

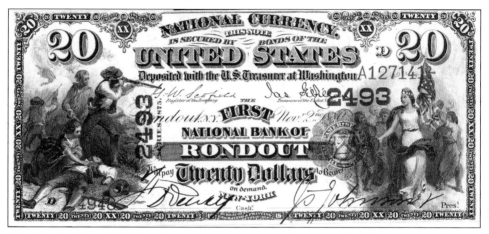

Face of F-431 to F-439. With SERIES 1875 overprinted vertically left of center; otherwise as preceding.

Back of F-431 to F-439, as preceding.

No.	Signatures		Seal		VG-8	F-12	VF-20	EF-40	Unc-63
F-431	Allison	New	Red, scalloped		$2,300	$2,700	$3,750	$4,500	$8,500
F-432	Allison	Wyman	Red, scalloped		2,300	2,700	3,750	4,500	8,500
F-433	Allison	Gilfillan	Red, scalloped		2,300	2,700	3,750	4,500	8,500
F-434	Scofield	Gilfillan	Red, scalloped		2,300	2,700	3,750	4,500	8,500
F-435	Bruce	Gilfillan	Red, scalloped		2,300	2,700	3,750	4,500	8,500
F-436	Bruce	Wyman	Red, scalloped	2 known					
F-437	Rosecrans	Huston	Red, scalloped	Rare					
F-438	Rosecrans	Nebeker	Red, scalloped	Rare					
F-439	Tillman	Morgan	Red, scalloped	Unique					

National Bank Notes
Series of 1882 Brown Back
("Second Charter Period")

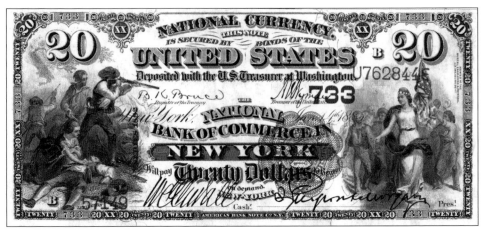

Face of F-493 to F-506.

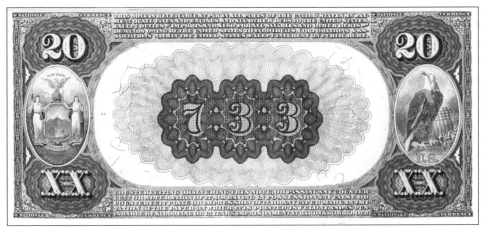

Back of F-493 to F-506. At center is the bank's charter number.

No.	Signatures			VG-8	F-12	VF-20	EF-40	Unc-63
F-493	Bruce	Gilfillan		$925	$1,100	$1,400	$1,700	$3,850
F-494	Bruce	Wyman		925	1,100	1,400	1,700	3,850
F-495	Bruce	Jordan		925	1,100	1,400	2,000	3,850
F-496	Rosecrans	Jordan		925	1,100	1,400	1,700	3,850
F-497	Rosecrans	Hyatt		925	1,100	1,400	1,700	3,850
F-498	Rosecrans	Huston		925	1,100	1,400	1,700	3,850
F-499	Rosecrans	Nebeker		925	1,100	1,400	1,700	3,850
F-500	Rosecrans	Morgan	3 known					
F-501	Tillman	Morgan		925	1,100	1,400	2,000	3,850
F-502	Tillman	Roberts		925	1,100	1,400	1,700	3,850
F-503	Bruce	Roberts		925	1,100	1,400	1,700	3,850
F-504	Lyons	Roberts		925	1,100	1,400	1,700	3,850
F-505	Lyons	Treat		1,000	1,650	2,250	2,700	—
F-506	Vernon	Treat		1,000	1,650	2,250	2,700	—

National Bank Notes
Series of 1882 Date Back
("Second Charter Period")

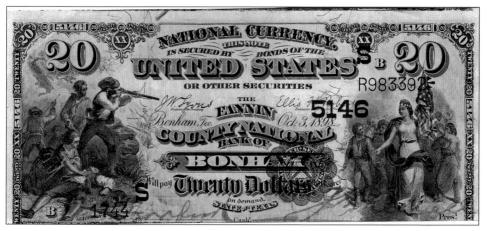

Face of F-549 to F-557. Similar to notes of the First Charter Period.

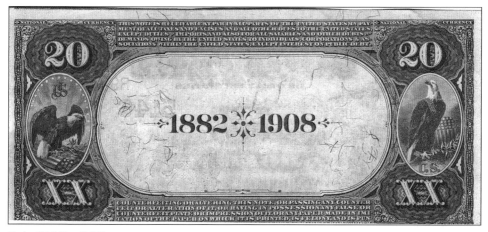

Back of F-549 to F-557.

No.	Signatures		VG-8	F-12	VF-20	EF-40	Unc-63
F-549	Rosecrans	Huston	$925	$1,100	$1,400	$2,000	$3,800
F-550	Rosecrans	Nebeker	925	1,100	1,400	2,000	3,800
F-551	Rosecrans	Morgan	2 known				
F-552	Tillman	Morgan	925	1,100	1,400	2,000	3,800
F-553	Tillman	Roberts	900	1,100	1,400	2,000	3,800
F-554	Bruce	Roberts	925	1,100	1,400	2,100	4,200
F-555	Lyons	Roberts	900	1,100	1,400	2,000	3,900
F-556	Vernon	Treat	900	1,100	1,400	2,000	3,800
F-556a	Vernon	McClung	1 known				
F-557	Napier	McClung	1,000	1,300	1,700	2,200	4,000

National Bank Notes
Series of 1882 Value Back
("Second Charter Period")

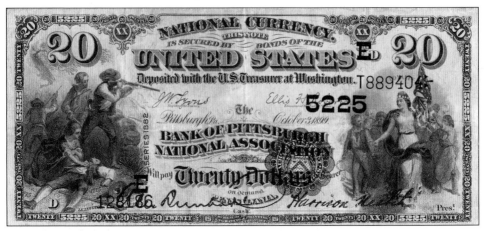

Face of F-580 to F-585.

Back of F-580 to F-585.

No.	Signatures			VG-8	F-12	VF-20	EF-40	Unc-63
F-580	Tillman	Morgan		$1,200	$1,500	$2,100	$2,750	$4,500
F-580a	Tillman	Roberts	4 known					
F-580b	Bruce	Roberts	3 known					
F-581	Lyons	Roberts		950	1,200	1,750	2,250	4,100
F-582	Lyons	Treat	Unique					
F-583	Vernon	Treat		950	1,250	1,800	2,400	4,250
F-584	Napier	McClung		950	1,200	1,800	2,400	4,250
F-584a	Parker	Burke	2 known					
F-585	Teehee	Burke	4 known					

National Bank Notes
Series of 1902 Red Seal ("Third Charter Period")

Face of F-639 to F-641. Portrait of Hugh McCulloch, Indiana banker who served two terms as the secretary of the Treasury (1865–1869 and 1884–1885).

Back of F-639 to F-641. "Columbia" and the Capitol are at left.

No.	Signatures		VG-8	F-12	VF-20	EF-40	Unc-63
F-639	Lyons	Roberts	$825	$950	$1,050	$1,750	$4,500
F-640	Lyons	Treat	825	950	1,050	1,750	4,500
F-641	Vernon	Treat	825	950	1,050	1,750	4,500

National Bank Notes
Series of 1902 Blue Seal, Date Back
("Third Charter Period")

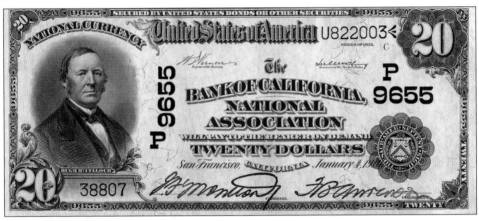

Face of F-642 to F-649a. Similar to the preceding.

Back of F-642 to F-649a. Design same as the preceding.

No.	Signatures		VG-8	F-12	VF-20	EF-40	Unc-63
F-642	Lyons	Roberts	$150	$200	$275	$385	$800
F-643	Lyons	Treat	150	200	275	385	800
F-644	Vernon	Treat	150	200	275	385	800
F-645	Vernon	McClung	150	200	275	385	800
F-646	Napier	McClung	150	275	275	385	800
F-647	Napier	Thompson	250	300	360	450	1,000
F-648	Napier	Burke	150	200	275	385	800
F-649	Parker	Burke	150	200	275	385	800
F-649a	Teehee	Burke	4 known				

National Bank Notes
Series of 1902 Blue Seal, Plain Back ("Third Charter Period")

Face of F-650 to F-663a, the same motifs as the preceding.

Back of F-650 to F-663a.

No.	Signatures		VG-8	F-12	VF-20	EF-40	Unc-63
F-650	Lyons	Roberts	$125	$145	$175	$300	$700
F-651	Lyons	Treat	125	145	175	300	700
F-652	Vernon	Treat	125	145	175	300	700
F-653	Vernon	McClung	125	145	175	300	700
F-654	Napier	McClung	125	145	175	300	700
F-665	Napier	Thompson	125	145	175	300	700
F-656	Napier	Burke	125	145	175	300	700
F-657	Parker	Burke	125	145	175	300	700
F-658	Teehee	Burke	125	145	175	300	700
F-659	Elliott	Burke	125	145	175	300	700
F-660	Elliott	White	125	145	175	300	700
F-661	Speelman	White	125	145	175	300	700
F-662	Woods	White	195	225	260	400	1,100
F-663	Woods	Tate	195	225	260	400	2,500
F-663a	Jones	Woods	—	—	—	—	—

National Gold Bank Notes

Face of F-1152 to F-1159b. Similar to the corresponding notes of the First Charter Period.

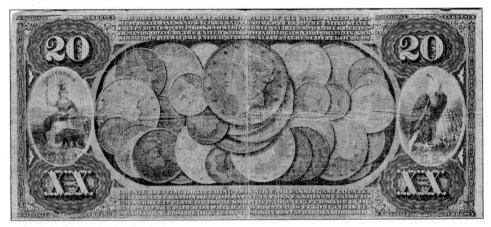

Back of F-1152 to F-1159b. An assortment of contemporary gold coins.

No.	Date	Name of Bank		Fair	VG-8	F-12	VF-20
F-1152	1870	First National Gold Bank		$5,000	$12,000	$30,000	$45,000
F-1153	1875 (Series)	First National Gold Bank		7,500	20,000	40,000	70,000
F-1154	1872	National Gold Bank of D.O. Mills and Co.		8,000	25,000	40,000	80,000
F-1155	1873	First National Gold Bank		6,000	20,000	40,000	—
F-1155a	1875	First National Gold Bank	Unique				
F-1156	1874	Farmer's National Gold Bank		10,000	30,000	50,000	—
F-1157	1875 (Series)	First National Gold Bank	2 known				
F-1158	1875	First National Gold Bank		10,000	30,000	50,000	—
F-1159	1875	Union National Gold Bank	2 known				
F-1159a	1873	First National Gold Bank	Unique				
F-1159b	1872	National Gold Bank and Trust Co.	Unknown				

Silver Certificates
Series of 1878 and 1880,
With Countersignatures

Face of F-305 to F-308. Portrait of Stephen Decatur, naval hero in the War of 1812. Standard Treasury Department signatures are above each other at the right.

Back of F-305 to F-308.

No.	Series	Countersignature	Payable At	Deposited With		VG-8	F-12
Large seal at top and large "Twenty" below							
F-305	1878	J.C. Hopper	New York	Asst. U.S. Treasurer	3 known		
F-306	1878	T. Hillhouse	New York	Asst. U.S. Treasurer	3 known		
F-306a	1878	R.M. Anthony	San Francisco	Asst. U.S. Treasurer	Unknown		
F-306b	1878	A.U. Wyman	Washington, DC	U.S. Treasurer	2 known		
F-307	1878	A.U. Wyman	Washington, DC	U.S. Treasurer		$9,000	$17,500
Face as above but with large "XX"							
F-308	1880	T. Hillhouse	New York	Asst. U.S. Treasurer		8,000	12,500

Silver Certificates
Series of 1880,
No Countersignatures

Face of F-309 to F-312. No countersignature.

Back of F-309 to F-312.

No.	Signatures		Seal	VG-8	F-12	VF-20	EF-40	Unc-63
F-309	Scofield	Gilfillan	Large brown	$2,200	$4,200	$6,000	$12,500	—
F-310	Bruce	Gilfillan	Large brown	2,200	4,200	6,000	12,500	—
F-311	Bruce	Wyman	Large brown	2,200	4,200	6,000	12,500	$42,000
As above, but with small seal at bottom, no "XX"								
F-312	Bruce	Wyman	Small red	2,800	5,000	12,500	20,000	—

Silver Certificates
Series of 1886

Face of F-313 to F-316. Portrait of the current (1885–1887) secretary of the Treasury, Daniel Manning, flanked by figures representing Agriculture and Industry.

Back of F-313 to F-316. Known as the "Diamond Back Note."

No.	Signatures		Seal	VG-8	F-12	VF-20	EF-40	Unc-63
F-313	Rosecrans	Hyatt	Large red	$1,950	$4,750	$7,000	$14,500	—
F-314	Rosecrans	Huston	Large brown	1,950	3,300	6,200	13,500	$45,000
F-315	Rosecrans	Nebeker	Large brown	1,950	4,750	7,000	14,500	45,000
As above, with small seal at lower right								
F-316	Rosecrans	Nebeker	Small red	1,950	4,000	6,200	14,000	45,000

Silver Certificates
Series of 1891

Face of F-317 to F-322. Same as the preceding.

Back of F-317 to F-322.

No.	Signatures		Seal	VG-8	F-12	VF-20	EF-40	Unc-63
F-317	Rosecrans	Nebeker	Small red	$600	$1,250	$2,000	$2,950	$7,500
F-318	Tillman	Morgan	Small red	600	1,250	2,000	2,950	7,500
F-319	Bruce	Roberts	Small red	600	1,250	2,000	2,950	7,500
F-320	Lyons	Roberts	Small red	600	1,250	2,000	2,950	7,500
As above, but with large blue "XX" at left center								
F-321	Parker	Burke	Blue	600	1,250	2,000	2,900	7,250
F-322	Teehee	Burke	Blue	600	1,250	2,000	2,900	7,250

Treasury or Coin Notes
Series of 1890

Face of F-372 to F-374. Bust of John Marshall, who served as secretary of state (1800–1801) and chief justice of the Supreme Court (1801–1835). The star at the serial number is decorative.

Back of F-372 to F-374.

No.	Signatures		Seal	VG-8	F-12	VF-20	EF-40	Unc-63
F-372	Rosecrans	Huston	Large brown	$2,000	$3,750	$6,000	$8,500	$20,000
F-373	Rosecrans	Nebeker	Large brown	4,000	8,000	—	—	—
F-374	Rosecrans	Nebeker	Small red	2,000	3,750	6,000	8,500	18,000

Treasury or Coin Notes
Series of 1891

Face of F-375 and F-375a.

Back of of F-375 and F-375a.

No.	Signatures		Seal		VG-8	F-12	VF-20	EF-40	Unc-63
F-375	Tillman	Morgan	Small red		$2,250	$3,250	$5,000	$8,000	$14,000
F-375a	Bruce	Roberts	Small red	2 known					

Gold Certificates
Act of March 3, 1863

Face of F-1166b. Eagle standing on shield draped with a flag.

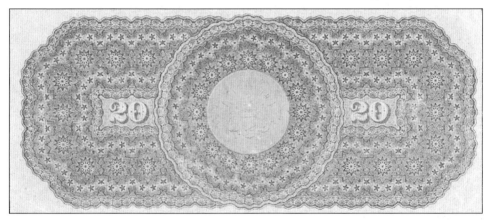

Back of F-1166b. At center is an image of a $20 gold coin, printed in yellow, but not sharply defined due to the low contrast of the ink color.

No.	Signatures		
F-1166b	Colby	Spinner	6 known, 2 of which are canceled

Gold Certificates
Series of 1882

Face of F-1174 to F-1178. Portrait of recently (1881) assassinated President James Garfield at right.

Back of F-1174 to F-1178. "Ocean Telegraph" design.

No.	Signatures		Seal	VG-8	F-12	VF-20	EF-40	Unc-63
F-1174	Bruce	Gilfillan	Brown	$2,250	$6,500	$10,000	Rare	—
With autographed countersignature by Thomas C. Acton, Asst. Treasurer, payable at New York								
F-1175	Bruce	Gilfillan	Brown	5,000	9,000	15,000	Rare	—
As no. F-1175 but with engraved countersignature								
F-1175a	Bruce	Gilfillan	Brown	4,000	6,000	10,000	Rare	—
No countersignature								
F-1176	Bruce	Wyman	Brown	2,750	5,000	7,250	$12,000	—
F-1177	Rosecrans	Huston	Large brown	2,750	5,000	7,250	12,000	—
F-1178	Lyons	Roberts	Small red	500	825	1,900	4,000	$9,500

Gold Certificates
Series of 1905

Face of F-1179 and F-1180. Bust of George Washington. "Technicolor Note."

Back of F-1179 and F-1180.

No.	Signatures		Seal	VG-8	F-12	VF-20	EF-40	Unc-63
F-1179	Lyons	Roberts	Small red	$900	$2,300	$3,500	$6,500	$17,000
F-1180	Lyons	Treat	Small red	900	2,300	3,500	6,500	17,000

Gold Certificates
Series of 1906 and 1922

Face of F-1181 to F-1187. Back is the same as the preceding.

No.	Series	Signatures		Seal	VG-8	F-12	VF-20	EF-40	Unc-63
F-1181	1906	Vernon	Treat	Gold	$200	$235	$350	$800	$2,500
F-1182	1906	Vernon	McClung	Gold	200	235	350	800	2,500
F-1183	1906	Napier	McClung	Gold	200	235	350	800	2,500
F-1184	1906	Napier	Thompson	Gold	300	375	600	1,750	4,000
F-1185	1906	Parker	Burke	Gold	200	235	350	750	2,500
F-1186	1906	Teehee	Burke	Gold	200	235	350	650	2,200
F-1187	1922	Speelman	White	Gold	200	230	300	650	2,100

Federal Reserve Notes
Series of 1914, Red Seal

Friedberg Suffix Letters on Types F-952A to F-1011C

Red Seals—*"A" suffix:* Large district letter and numeral at top right and bottom left. Small letter at top left and bottom right. *B suffix:* As above, but with small district letter and numeral added above letter at top left. As a class Red Seals are scarcer than Blue Seals.

Blue Seals—*"A" suffix:* Large district letter and numeral at top left and bottom right. *B suffix:* Large letter and numeral at top right with small district letters and numerals in the other three corners. *C suffix:* Again, a large pair of letters and numerals, but positioned both vertically, more toward the center of the note and closer to the outside edge. Also, the seals to the sides of the portrait are closer to the note's center than on the Blue Seal notes with A suffix.

Face of F-952A to F-963B. Portrait of President Grover Cleveland.

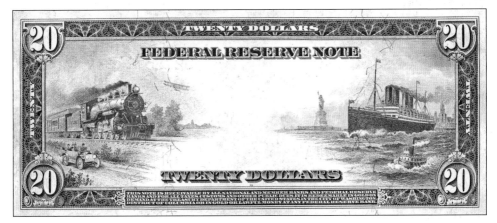

Back of F-952A to F-963B. Transportation motifs with an automobile, train, plane, tugboat, and steamship.

No.	Issuing Bank		VG-8	F-12	VF-20	EF-40	Unc-63
Signatures of Burke and McAdoo							
F-952A	Boston		$475	$950	$1,250	$2,500	$5,000
F-952B	Boston	3 known	—	—	—	2,100	—
F-953A	New York		310	525	700	1,400	4,200
F-953B	New York		310	525	700	1,400	3,400
F-954A	Philadelphia		475	950	1,500	3,200	6,000
F-954B	Philadelphia		475	950	1,500	3,200	—
F-955A	Cleveland	5 known	750	1,350	2,250	4,500	7,000
F-955B	Cleveland		475	950	1,500	2,750	—
F-956A	Richmond		550	1,200	2,000	4,000	—
F-956B	Richmond	4 known	550	1,200	2,200	—	—
F-957A	Atlanta		550	1,200	2,000	4,000	—
F-958A	Chicago		310	525	700	1,400	3,400
F-958B	Chicago		475	950	1,500	3,200	4,100
F-959A	St. Louis		310	525	700	1,400	4,400
F-959B	St. Louis		475	950	1,500	3,200	3,500
F-960A	Minneapolis		475	950	1,500	3,200	6,000
F-960B	Minneapolis		550	1,200	2,000	4,000	—
F-961A	Kansas City		475	950	1,500	3,200	6,000
F-961B	Kansas City	4 known	750	1,350	2,250	—	—
F-962	Dallas		475	950	1,500	3,200	6,000
F-963A	San Francisco		550	1,200	2,000	4,000	—
F-963B	San Francisco		550	1,200	2,000	4,000	—

Federal Reserve Notes
Series of 1914, Blue Seal

Face of F-964 to F-1011C. Back is the same as the preceding.

No.	Issuing Bank	Signatures		VG-8	F-12	VF-20	EF-40	Unc-63
F-964	Boston	Burke	McAdoo	$90	$110	$170	$450	$1,600
F-965	Boston	Burke	Glass	160	300	1,150	2,200	4,500
F-966	Boston	Burke	Houston	85	100	165	300	1,500
F-967	Boston	White	Mellon	85	100	165	300	1,450
F-968	New York	Burke	McAdoo	80	115	165	285	1,500
F-969	New York	Burke	Glass	100	145	200	400	1,600
F-970	New York	Burke	Houston	80	120	145	300	1,550
F-971A	New York	White	Mellon	80	95	170	245	600
F-971B	New York	White	Mellon	110	135	160	260	700
F-971C	New York	White	Mellon	300	550	800	1,000	—
F-972	Philadelphia	Burke	McAdoo	80	95	160	300	635
F-973	Philadelphia	Burke	Glass	120	160	265	600	1,125
F-974	Philadelphia	Burke	Houston	80	95	160	300	635
F-975	Philadelphia	White	Mellon	80	95	160	300	635
F-976	Cleveland	Burke	McAdoo	80	110	160	400	700
F-977	Cleveland	Burke	Glass	85	120	200	600	900
F-978	Cleveland	Burke	Houston	80	110	160	400	700
F-979A	Cleveland	White	Mellon	80	110	160	400	700
F-979B	Cleveland	White	Mellon	95	125	215	650	1,100
F-980	Richmond	Burke	McAdoo	75	145	165	425	800
F-981	Richmond	Burke	Glass	95	250	300	800	1,450
F-982	Richmond	Burke	Houston	75	145	165	425	800
F-983A	Richmond	White	Mellon	75	145	165	425	800
F-984	Atlanta	Burke	McAdoo	90	140	160	425	800
F-985	Atlanta	Burke	Glass	None printed				
F-986	Atlanta	Burke	Houston	85	120	145	400	700
F-987A	Atlanta	White	Mellon	85	120	145	400	700
F-988	Chicago	Burke	McAdoo	85	120	155	410	750
F-989	Chicago	Burke	Glass	95	135	175	490	925
F-990	Chicago	Burke	Houston	80	110	145	400	725
F-991A	Chicago	White	Mellon	85	120	155	410	750
F-991B	Chicago	White	Mellon	85	120	155	425	800
F-991C	Chicago	White	Mellon	200	275	525	725	850
F-992	St. Louis	Burke	McAdoo	80	100	160	400	725
F-993	St. Louis	Burke	Glass	170	250	350	750	—
F-994	St. Louis	Burke	Houston	80	100	160	400	725
F-995	St. Louis	White	Mellon	80	100	160	400	725
F-996	Minneapolis	Burke	McAdoo	85	140	160	450	800
F-997	Minneapolis	Burke	Glass	190	335	725	1,500	2,750
F-998	Minneapolis	Burke	Houston	85	145	175	500	900
F-999	Minneapolis	White	Mellon	85	140	160	450	800
F-1000	Kansas City	Burke	McAdoo	90	120	160	450	800
F-1001	Kansas City	Burke	Glass	None printed				

No.	Issuing Bank	Signatures		VG-8	F-12	VF-20	EF-40	Unc-63
F-1002	Kansas City	Burke	Houston	$85	$110	$150	$400	$750
F-1003	Kansas City	White	Mellon	95	150	175	425	775
F-1004	Dallas	Burke	McAdoo	110	125	190	425	800
F-1005	Dallas	Burke	Glass	240	335	565	850	1,500
F-1006	Dallas	Burke	Houston	90	110	175	700	1,125
F-1007	Dallas	White	Mellon	85	120	150	325	725
F-1008	San Francisco	Burke	McAdoo	85	120	150	425	1,000
F-1009	San Francisco	Burke	Glass	125	175	400	900	1,600
F-1010	San Francisco	Burke	Houston	100	135	165	500	1,200
F-1011A	San Francisco	White	Mellon	85	135	160	400	750
F-1011B	San Francisco	White	Mellon	90	150	225	475	975
F-1011C	San Francisco	White	Mellon	200	325	750	900	—

Federal Reserve Bank Notes
Series of 1915 and 1918

Face of F-822 to F-830. Bust of President Grover Cleveland.

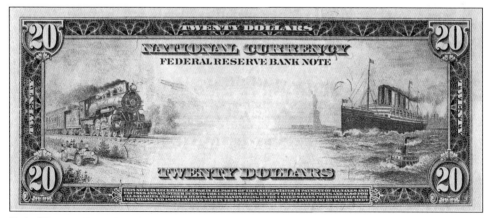

Back of F-822 to F-830. Similar to the preceding.

No.	Issuing Bank	Series	Signatures			VG-8	F-12	VF-20	EF-40	Unc-63
F-822	Atlanta	1915	Teehee	Burke						
			Bell-Cashier	Wellborn	4 known					
F-822-1	Atlanta		Same but with Bell-Secretary		4 known					
F-822a	Atlanta	1915	Teehee	Burke						
			Pike	McCord	1 known					

Chart continued on next page.

No.	Issuing Bank	Series	Signatures				VG-8	F-12	VF-20	EF-40	Unc-63
F-823	Atlanta	1918	Elliott	Burke							
			Bell	Wellborn			$1,150	$1,500	$2,000	$2,800	$8,000
F-824	Chicago	1915	Teehee	Burke							
			McLallen	McDougal			1,150	1,500	2,000	2,800	8,000
F-825	St. Louis	1918	Teehee	Burke							
			Attebery	Wells			1,150	1,500	2,000	2,800	—
F-826	Kansas City	1915	Teehee	Burke							
			Anderson	Miller			1,150	1,500	2,000	3,000	—
F-827	Kansas City	1915	Teehee	Burke							
			Cross	Miller			1,150	1,500	2,000	2,800	—
F-828	Dallas	1915	Teehee	Burke							
			Hoopes	Van Zandt			1,150	1,500	2,000	3,000	9,000
F-829	Dallas	1915	Teehee	Burke							
			Gilbert	Van Zandt	5 known						
F-830	Dallas	1915	Teehee	Burke							
			Talley	Van Zandt	3 known						

SMALL-SIZE $20 NOTES

National Bank Notes
Series of 1929, Type 1

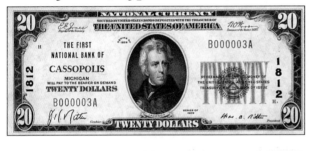

Face of F-1802-1. Portrait of President Andrew Jackson. Bank charter number in black at left and right borders.

Back of F-1802-1. The White House in Washington, DC. Back type used on all small-size $20 notes of the era.

No.		VF-20	Unc-63
F-1802-1		$75	$200

National Bank Notes
Series of 1929, Type 2

Face of F-1802-2. Same as preceding with charter numbers also in brown at lower left and upper right of portrait.

Back type used on all small-size $20 notes of the era.

No.	VF-20	Unc-63
F-1802-2	$75	$225

Gold Certificates
Series of 1928 and 1928-A, Gold Seal

Face of F-2402 to F-2403.

Back type used on all small-size $20 notes of the era.

No.	Series	Signatures		Quantity Printed	VG-8	F-12	VF-20	EF-40	Unc-63
F-2402	1928	Woods	Mellon	66,204,000	$95	$125	$175	$300	$675
F-2402★	1928	Woods	Mellon	250	500	775	1,650	7,750	
F-2403	1928-A	Woods	Mills	1,500,000	Not issued				

Federal Reserve Bank Notes
Series of 1929,
Brown Seal

Face of F-1870. Back type is the same as on all other $20 notes of the era.

No.	Issuing Bank	Quantity Printed	VG-8	F-12	VF-20	EF-40	Unc-63
F-1870A	Boston	2,568,000	$40	$45	$50	$70	$225
F-1870B	New York	1,008,000	40	45	50	70	190
F-1870C	Philadelphia	1,020,000	40	45	50	70	225
F-1870D	Cleveland	1,632,000	40	45	50	70	225
F-1870E	Richmond	960,000	45	45	50	70	375
F-1870F	Atlanta	2,028,000	40	45	50	70	375
F-1870G	Chicago	444,000	40	45	50	70	200
F-1870H	St. Louis	864,000	40	45	50	70	225
F-1870I	Minneapolis	612,000	40	45	70	125	225
F-1870J	Kansas City	468,000	40	45	50	90	325
F-1870K	Dallas	888,000	65	100	175	800	2,250
F-1870L	San Francisco		60	90	100	150	550
F-1870★	Most common districts		150	300	450	750	2,650

Federal Reserve Notes
Series of 1928 and 1928-A,
Green Seal

Face of F-2050 to F-2051. The face states that the bill is payable "in gold or lawful money." Bank location at left represented by the district number.

Back of F-2050 to F-2051.

Series of 1928—Signatures of Tate and Mellon

No.	Issuing Bank	Quantity Printed	VF-20	EF-40	Unc-63
F-2050A	Boston	3,790,880	$150	$225	$1,800
F-2050A★	Boston		375	775	2,700
F-2050B	New York	12,797,200	50	80	225
F-2050B★	New York		200	500	1,200
F-2050C	Philadelphia	3,797,200	50	90	225
F-2050C★	Philadelphia		325	600	1,700
F-2050D	Cleveland	10,626,900	50	80	200
F-2050D★	Cleveland		200	400	1,300
F-2050E	Richmond	4,119,600	60	90	250
F-2050E★	Richmond		425	825	2,500
F-2050F	Atlanta	3,842,388	65	100	275
F-2050F★	Atlanta		425	750	3,000
F-2050G	Chicago	10,891,740	45	80	200
F-2050G★	Chicago		250	600	1,500
F-2050H	St. Louis	2,523,300	50	85	225
F-2050H★	St. Louis		350	700	2,200
F-2050I	Minneapolis	2,633,100	50	90	300
F-2050I★	Minneapolis		450	775	3,000
F-2050J	Kansas City	2,584,500	50	85	200
F-2050J★	Kansas City		350	675	2,000
F-2050K	Dallas	1,568,500	60	125	450
F-2050K★	Dallas		1,250	2,250	6,000
F-2050L	San Francisco	8,404,800	50	85	250
F-2050L★	San Francisco		350	725	1,750

Series of 1928-A—Signatures of Woods and Mellon

No.	Issuing Bank	Quantity Printed	VF-20	EF-40	Unc-63
F-2051A	Boston	1,293,900	$85	$150	$525
F-2051A★	Boston		825	1,250	4,500
F-2051B	New York	1,055,800	70	135	400
F-2051B★	New York		825	1,250	4,000
F-2051C	Philadelphia	1,717,200	75	135	400
F-2051C★	Philadelphia		825	1,250	4,000
F-2051D	Cleveland	625,200	75	135	450
F-2051D★	Cleveland		825	1,250	4,000
F-2051E	Richmond	1,534,500	75	135	425
F-2051E★	Richmond		825	1,250	4,000
F-2051F	Atlanta	1,442,400	65	135	425
F-2051F★	Atlanta		825	1,250	3,750
F-2051G	Chicago	822,000	65	135	400
F-2051G★	Chicago		750	1,250	3,500
F-2061H	St. Louis	573,300	65	135	425
F-2051H★	St. Louis		750	1,350	3,750
F-2051J	Kansas City	113,900	100	160	600
F-2051J★	Kansas City		1,000	2,000	5,000
F-2051K	Dallas	1,032,000	65	135	400
F-2051K★	Dallas		775	1,250	3,750

Federal Reserve Notes
Series of 1928-B and 1928-C, Green Seal

Face of F-2052 to F-2053.

Back of F-2052 to F-2053.

Series of 1928-B—Signatures of Woods and Mellon

No.	Issuing Bank	Quantity Printed	VF-20	EF-40	Unc-63
F-2052A	Boston	7,749,636	$40	$60	$140
F-2052A★	Boston		225	350	1,250
F-2052B	New York	19,448,436	40	55	125
F-2052B★	New York		225	350	1,000
F-2052C	Philadelphia	8,095,548	40	55	125
F-2052C★	Philadelphia		225	350	1,750
F-2052D	Cleveland	11,684,196	40	55	125
F-2052D★	Cleveland		225	350	1,750
F-2052E	Richmond	4,413,900	40	55	225
F-2052E★	Richmond		300	400	1,600
F-2052F	Atlanta	2,390,240	100	250	450
F-2052F★	Atlanta		300	400	1,600
F-2052G	Chicago	17,220,276	40	55	100
F-2052G★	Chicago		200	350	950
F-2052H	St. Louis	3,834,600	40	60	150
F-2052H★	St. Louis		250	425	1,300
F-2052I	Minneapolis	3,298,920	45	65	150
F-2052I★	Minneapolis		300	700	2,500
F-2052J	Kansas City	4,941,252	40	60	125
F-2052J★	Kansas City		225	400	1,750
F-2052K	Dallas	2,406,060	40	60	200
F-2052K★	Dallas		200	350	1,750
F-2052L	San Francisco	9,689,124	40	55	160
F-2052L★	San Francisco		250	425	1,750

Note: This series comes with both light and dark green seals.

Series of 1928-C—Signatures of Woods and Mills

No.	Issuing Bank	Quantity Printed	VF-20	EF-40	Unc-63
F-2053G	Chicago	3,363,300	$500	$900	$2,250
F-2053L	San Francisco	1,420,200	825	1,300	5,000
F-2053★		Unknown	—	—	—

Federal Reserve Notes
Series of 1934 to 1934-C, Green Seal

Face of F-2054 to F-2056, now with no mention of gold in payment. District letter continued.

Back of F-2054 to F-2056.

Series of 1934—Signatures of Julian and Morgenthau

No.	Issuing Bank	Quantity Printed	VF-20	EF-40	Unc-63
F-2054A	Boston	37,673,068	$30	$45	$80
F-2054A★	Boston		85	150	550
F-2054B	New York	27,573,264	30	45	80
F-2054B★	New York		85	150	650
F-2054C	Philadelphia	53,209,968	30	45	80
F-2054C★	Philadelphia		85	150	550
F-2054D	Cleveland	48,301,416	30	45	80
F-2054D★	Cleveland		85	150	550
F-2054E	Richmond	36,259,224	30	45	80
F-2054E★	Richmond		85	150	550
F-2054F	Atlanta	41,547,660	30	45	80
F-2054F★	Atlanta		85	150	550
F-2054G	Chicago	20,777,832	30	45	80
F-2054G★	Chicago		85	150	550
F-2054H	St. Louis	21,174,552	30	45	80
F-2054H★	St. Louis		85	150	550
F-2054I	Minneapolis	16,795,116	30	45	80
F-2054I★	Minneapolis		85	150	550
F-2054J	Kansas City	28,865,304	30	45	80
F-2054J★	Kansas City		85	150	550
F-2054K	Dallas	20,852,160	30	45	80
F-2054K★	Dallas		85	150	550
F-2054L	San Francisco	32,203,956	30	45	80
F-2054L★	San Francisco		85	150	550

Series of 1934-A—Signatures of Julian and Morgenthau

No.	Issuing Bank	Quantity Printed	VF-20	EF-40	Unc-63
F-2055A	Boston	3,302,416	$30	$40	$75
F-2055A★	Boston		100	150	450
F-2055B	New York	102,555,538	25	35	65
F-2055B★	New York		75	150	450
F-2055C	Philadelphia	3,371,316	30	35	75
F-2055C★	Philadelphia		75	150	450
F-2055D	Cleveland	23,475,108	25	35	65
F-2055D★	Cleveland		75	150	450
F-2055E	Richmond	46,816,224	30	35	65
F-2055E★	Richmond		75	150	450
F-2055F	Atlanta	6,756,816	30	35	65
F-2055F★	Atlanta		75	150	450

Chart continued on next page.

No.	Issuing Bank	Quantity Printed	VF-20	EF-40	Unc-63
F-2055G	Chicago	91,141,452	$25	$35	$65
F-2055G★	Chicago		75	150	450
F-2055H	St. Louis	3,701,568	35	35	65
F-2055H★	St. Louis		75	150	450
F-2055I	Minneapolis	1,162,500	35	45	75
F-2055I★	Minneapolis		90	175	525
F-2055J	Kansas City	3,221,184	30	35	65
F-2055J★	Kansas City		75	150	450
F-2055K	Dallas	2,531,700	30	40	75
F-2055K★	Dallas		85	175	525
F-2055L	San Francisco	94,454,112	25	35	75
F-2055L★	San Francisco		75	150	450

Series of 1934-B—Signatures of Julian and Vinson

No.	Issuing Bank	Quantity Printed	VF-20	EF-40	Unc-63
F-2056A	Boston	3,904,800	$30	$40	$90
F-2056A★	Boston		150	225	800
F-2056B	New York	14,876,436	30	40	80
F-2056B★	New York		125	200	550
F-2056C	Philadelphia	3,271,452	30	40	90
F-2056C★	Philadelphia		125	200	700
F-2056D	Cleveland	2,814,600	30	40	90
F-2056D★	Cleveland		125	200	700
F-2056E	Richmond	9,451,632	30	40	100
F-2056E★	Richmond		125	200	750
F-2056F	Atlanta	6,887,640	30	40	100
F-2056F★	Atlanta		125	200	700
F-2056G	Chicago	9,084,600	30	40	80
F-2056G★	Chicago		125	200	700
F-2056H	St. Louis	5,817,300	30	40	90
F-2056H★	St. Louis		125	200	700
F-2056I	Minneapolis	2,304,800	30	45	125
F-2056I★	Minneapolis		150	200	800
F-2056J	Kansas City	3,524,244	30	40	95
F-2056J★	Kansas City		150	225	750
F-2056K	Dallas	2,807,388	30	40	95
F-2056K★	Dallas		150	225	750
F-2056L	San Francisco	5,289,540	30	40	90
F-2056L★	San Francisco		150	225	750

Federal Reserve Notes
Series of 1934 and 1934-A,
Brown Seal, Hawaii

Face of F-2304 to F-2305 with HAWAII overprinted at the left and right ends and with Treasury seal and serial numbers in brown.

Back of F-2304 to F-2305 with large HAWAII.

No.	Series	Quantity Printed	VF-20	EF-40	Unc-63
F-2304	1934	11,246,000	$175	$350	$2,625
F-2304★	1934	52,000	3,200	5,000	—
F-2305	1934-A	incl. above	125	150	900
F-2305★	1934-A	2,500	1,600	2,250	13,000

Federal Reserve Notes
Series of 1934-C and 1934-D, Green Seal

Old back with less foliage. Title as WHITE HOUSE.

New back, with more foliage. Title as THE WHITE HOUSE. Back type used from Series 1934-C (new back) to 1950-E.

Series of 1934-C—Signatures of Julian and Snyder

No.	Issuing Bank	Quantity Printed	VF-20	EF-40	Unc-63
F-2057A	Boston	7,397,352	$25	$35	$65
F-2057A★	Boston		100	145	725
F-2057B	New York	18,668,148	25	35	60
F-2057B★	New York		80	125	525
F-2057C	Philadelphia	11,590,752	25	35	60
F-2057C★	Philadelphia		80	125	525
F-2057D	Cleveland	17,912,424	25	35	60
F-2057D★	Cleveland		100	125	625
F-2057E	Richmond	22,526,568	25	35	60
F-2057E★	Richmond		100	125	625
F-2057F	Atlanta	18,858,876	25	35	60
F-2057F★	Atlanta		125	180	650
F-2057G	Chicago	26,031,660	25	35	60
F-2057G★	Chicago		80	125	525

Chart continued on next page.

No.	Issuing Bank	Quantity Printed	VF-20	EF-40	Unc-63
F-2057H	St. Louis	13,276,984	$25	$35	$60
F-2057H★	St. Louis		100	125	525
F-2057I	Minneapolis	3,490,200	30	40	90
F-2057I★	Minneapolis		100	165	625
F-2057J	Kansas City	9,675,468	25	35	65
F-2057J★	Kansas City		80	125	525
F-2057K	Dallas	10,205,364	30	40	65
F-2057K★	Dallas		100	150	650
F-2057L	San Francisco	20,580,000	25	35	65
F-2057L★	San Francisco		90	125	525

Series of 1934-D—Signatures of Clark and Snyder

No.	Issuing Bank	Quantity Printed	VF-20	EF-40	Unc-63
F-2058A	Boston	4,520,000	$25	$35	$70
F-2058A★	Boston		150	200	800
F-2058B	New York	27,894,260	25	35	70
F-2058B★	New York		100	150	500
F-2058C	Philadelphia	6,022,428	25	35	70
F-2058C★	Philadelphia		110	150	600
F-2058D	Cleveland	8,981,688	25	35	70
F-2058D★	Cleveland		110	150	750
F-2058E	Richmond	14,055,984	25	35	70
F-2058E★	Richmond		110	150	650
F-2058F	Atlanta	7,495,440	25	35	70
F-2058F★	Atlanta		150	225	825
F-2058G	Chicago	15,187,596	25	35	70
F-2058G★	Chicago		110	150	550
F-2058H	St. Louis	5,923,248	25	35	70
F-2058H★	St. Louis		130	150	600
F-2058I	Minneapolis	2,422,416	25	40	75
F-2058I★	Minneapolis		130	225	825
F-2058J	Kansas City	4,211,904	25	35	70
F-2058J★	Kansas City		130	225	825
F-2058K	Dallas	3,707,364	25	35	650
F-2058K★	Dallas		130	225	825
F-2058L	San Francisco	12,015,228	25	35	70
F-2058L★	San Francisco		125	160	600

Federal Reserve Notes
Series of 1950 to 1950-E, Green Seal

Face of F-2059 to F-2064.

Back of F-2059 to F-2064. New back.

Series of 1950—Signatures of Clark and Snyder

No.	Issuing Bank	Quantity Printed	VF-20	EF-40	Unc-63
F-2059A	Boston	23,184,000	$25	$35	$60
F-2059A★	Boston		120	175	450
F-2059B	New York	80,064,000	25	35	60
F-2059B★	New York		100	150	425
F-2059C	Philadelphia	29,520,000	25	35	60
F-2059C★	Philadelphia		90	175	400
F-2059D	Cleveland	51,120,000	25	35	70
F-2059D★	Cleveland		80	165	550
F-2059E	Richmond	67,536,000	25	35	60
F-2059E★	Richmond		85	180	400
F-2059F	Atlanta	39,312,000	25	35	70
F-2059F★	Atlanta		140	225	500
F-2059G	Chicago	70,464,000	25	35	60
F-2059G★	Chicago		75	160	550
F-2059H	St. Louis	27,352,000	25	35	70
F-2059H★	St. Louis		90	175	550
F-2059I	Minneapolis	9,216,000	30	35	95
F-2059I★	Minneapolis		140	225	550
F-2059J	Kansas City	22,752,000	25	35	70
F-2059J★	Kansas City		85	180	550
F-2059K	Dallas	22,656,000	25	35	95
F-2059K★	Dallas		100	200	575
F-2059L	San Francisco	70,272,000	25	35	70
F-2059L★	San Francisco		100	200	500

Series of 1950-A—Signatures of Priest and Humphrey

No.	Issuing Bank	Quantity Printed	VF-20	EF-40	Unc-63
F-2060A	Boston	19,656,000	$25	$30	$75
F-2060A★	Boston		80	115	225
F-2060B	New York	82,568,000	25	30	55
F-2060B★	New York		80	115	225
F-2060C	Philadelphia	16,560,000	25	30	75
F-2060C★	Philadelphia		80	115	225
F-2060D	Cleveland	50,320,000	25	30	65
F-2060D★	Cleveland		80	115	225
F-2060E	Richmond	69,544,000	25	30	65
F-2060E★	Richmond		80	115	200
F-2060F	Atlanta	27,648,000	25	30	70
F-2060F★	Atlanta		80	115	225
F-2060G	Chicago	73,720,000	25	30	65
F-2060G★	Chicago		80	115	200
F-2060H	St. Louis	22,680,000	25	30	70
F-2060H★	St. Louis		80	115	225
F-2060I	Minneapolis	5,544,000	25	30	85
F-2060I★	Minneapolis		80	115	275
F-2060J	Kansas City	22,968,000	25	30	65
F-2060J★	Kansas City		80	115	225
F-2060K	Dallas	10,728,000	25	30	70
F-2060K★	Dallas		80	115	225
F-2060L	San Francisco	85,528,000	25	30	65
F-2060L★	San Francisco		80	115	225

Series of 1950-B—Signatures of Priest and Anderson

No.	Issuing Bank	Quantity Printed	VF-20	EF-40	Unc-63
F-2061A	Boston	5,040,000		$30	$60
F-2061A★	Boston		$95	125	400
F-2061B	New York	49,960,000		25	45
F-2061B★	New York		70	100	200
F-2061C	Philadelphia	7,920,000		25	50
F-2061C★	Philadelphia		70	100	275
F-2061D	Cleveland	38,160,000		25	50
F-2061D★	Cleveland		70	100	250
F-2061E	Richmond	42,120,000		25	50
F-2061E★	Richmond		75	125	275
F-2061F	Atlanta	40,240,000		25	50
F-2061F★	Atlanta		75	100	275
F-2061G	Chicago	80,560,000		25	45
F-2061G★	Chicago		75	100	200

Chart continued on next page.

No.	Issuing Bank	Quantity Printed	VF-20	EF-40	Unc-63
F-2061H	St. Louis	19,440,000		$25	$50
F-2061H*	St. Louis		$70	100	250
F-2061I	Minneapolis	12,240,000		25	60
F-2061I*	Minneapolis		75	100	275
F-2061J	Kansas City	28,440,000		25	55
F-2061J*	Kansas City		75	100	275
F-2061K	Dallas	11,880,000		25	60
F-2061K*	Dallas		75	100	275
F-2061L	San Francisco	51,040,000		25	55
F-2061L*	San Francisco		75	100	275

Series of 1950-C—Signatures of Smith and Dillon

No.	Issuing Bank	Quantity Printed	VF-20	EF-40	Unc-63
F-2062A	Boston	7,200,000		$35	$65
F-2062A*	Boston		$60	110	300
F-2062B	New York	43,200,000		30	60
F-2062B*	New York		60	100	300
F-2062C	Philadelphia	7,560,000		30	65
F-2062C*	Philadelphia		60	100	300
F-2062D	Cleveland	28,440,000		30	65
F-2062D*	Cleveland		60	100	300
F-2062E	Richmond	37,000,000		30	60
F-2062E*	Richmond		60	100	300
F-2062F	Atlanta	19,080,000		30	60
F-2062F*	Atlanta		60	100	300
F-2062G	Chicago	29,160,000		30	60
F-2062G*	Chicago		60	100	300
F-2062H	St. Louis	12,960,000		30	60
F-2062H*	St. Louis		60	100	300
F-2062I	Minneapolis	6,480,000	25	50	75
F-2062I*	Minneapolis		60	100	300
F-2062J	Kansas City	18,360,000		35	60
F-2062J*	Kansas City		60	100	300
F-2062K	Dallas	9,000,000		30	70
F-2062K*	Dallas		75	175	425
F-2062L	San Francisco	45,360,000		30	60
F-2062L*	San Francisco		60	100	350

Series of 1950-D—Signatures of Granahan and Dillon

No.	Issuing Bank	Quantity Printed	VF-20	EF-40	Unc-63
F-2063A	Boston	9,320,000		$30	$70
F-2063A*	Boston		$60	100	200
F-2063B	New York	64,280,000		30	65
F-2063B*	New York		55	100	200
F-2063C	Philadelphia	5,400,000		30	70
F-2063C*	Philadelphia		60	100	200
F-2063D	Cleveland	23,760,000		30	70
F-2063D*	Cleveland		60	125	200
F-2063E	Richmond	30,240,000		30	70
F-2063E*	Richmond		60	125	225
F-2063F	Atlanta	22,680,000		30	70
F-2063F*	Atlanta		60	115	200
F-2063G	Chicago	67,960,000		30	65
F-2063G*	Chicago		55	100	200
F-2063H	St. Louis	6,120,000		30	70
F-2063H*	St. Louis		60	115	225
F-2063I	Minneapolis	3,240,000		30	80
F-2063I*	Minneapolis		175	225	475
F-2063J	Kansas City	8,200,000		30	70
F-2063J*	Kansas City		60	115	225
F-2063K	Dallas	6,480,000		30	70
F-2063K*	Dallas		60	115	225
F-2063L	San Francisco	69,400,000		30	70
F-2063L*	San Francisco		60	115	225

Series of 1950-E—Signatures of Granahan and Fowler

No.	Issuing Bank	Quantity Printed	VF-20	EF-40	Unc-63
F-2064B	New York	8,640,000	$50	$65	$150
F-2064B★	New York		200	300	800
F-2064G	Chicago	9,360,000	50	75	175
F-2064G★	Chicago		225	325	950
F-2064L	San Francisco	8,640,000	50	75	175
F-2064L★	San Francisco		200	300	800

Federal Reserve Notes
Series of 1963 and 1963-A, Green Seal, Motto Added

Face of F-2065 to F-2066.

Back of F-2065 to F-2082. The motto IN GOD WE TRUST is added above the White House.

Series of 1963—Signatures of Granahan and Dillon

No.	Issuing Bank	Quantity Printed	VF-20	EF-40	Unc-63
F-2065A	Boston	2,560,000		$30	$90
F-2065A★	Boston		$60	80	140
F-2065B	New York	16,640,000		30	70
F-2065B★	New York		50	70	120
F-2065D	Cleveland	7,680,000		30	80
F-2065D★	Cleveland		60	85	150
F-2065E	Richmond	4,480,000		30	80
F-2065E★	Richmond		60	80	140
F-2065F	Atlanta	10,240,000		30	85
F-2065F★	Atlanta		60	80	140
F-2065G	Chicago	2,560,000		35	80
F-2065G★	Chicago		60	90	150
F-2065H	St. Louis	3,200,000		30	80
F-2065H★	St. Louis		60	80	140
F-2065J	Kansas City	3,840,000		30	90
F-2065J★	Kansas City		60	80	140
F-2065K	Dallas	2,560,000		30	85
F-2065K★	Dallas		60	80	140
F-2065L	San Francisco	7,040,000		30	80
F-2065L★	San Francisco		60	80	140

Series of 1963-A—Signatures of Granahan and Fowler

No.	Issuing Bank	Quantity Printed	VF-20	EF-40	Unc-63
F-2066A	Boston	23,680,000		$30	$60
F-2066A★	Boston	1,280,000	$45	70	145
F-2066B	New York	93,600,000		30	60
F-2066B★	New York	3,840,000	40	60	145
F-2066C	Philadelphia	17,920,000		30	60
F-2066C★	Philadelphia	640,000	70	100	160
F-2066D	Cleveland	68,480,000		30	60
F-2066D★	Cleveland	2,560,000	45	70	145
F-2066E	Richmond	128,800,000		30	60
F-2066E★	Richmond	5,760,000	45	70	145
F-2066F	Atlanta	42,880,000		30	60
F-2066F★	Atlanta	1,920,000	45	70	145
F-2066G	Chicago	156,320,000		30	60
F-2066G★	Chicago	7,040,000	45	70	145
F-2066H	St. Louis	34,560,000		30	60
F-2066H★	St. Louis	1,920,000	45	70	145
F-2066I	Minneapolis	10,240,000		30	60
F-2066I★	Minneapolis	640,000	70	100	200
F-2066J	Kansas City	37,120,000		30	60
F-2066J★	Kansas City	1,920,000	45	70	145
F-2066K	Dallas	38,400,000		30	60
F-2066K★	Dallas	1,280,000	45	70	145
F-2066L	San Francisco	169,120,000		30	60
F-2066L★	San Francisco	8,320,000	45	70	150

Federal Reserve Notes
Series of 1969 to 1995, Green Seal

Face of F-2067 to F-2082, with modified Treasury seal. Back type is the same as on all other $20 notes of the era.

Series of 1969 (with new Treasury seal)—Signatures of Elston and Kennedy

No.	Issuing Bank	Quantity Printed	VF-20	EF-40	Unc-63
F-2067A	Boston	19,200,000		$30	$55
F-2067A★	Boston	1,280,000	$45	55	150
F-2067B	New York	106,400,000		30	55
F-2067B★	New York	5,106,000	30	40	110
F-2067C	Philadelphia	10,880,000		30	55
F-2067C★	Philadelphia	1,280,000	45	55	150
F-2067D	Cleveland	60,160,000		30	55
F-2067D★	Cleveland	2,560,000	45	55	150
F-2067E	Richmond	66,560,000		30	55
F-2067E★	Richmond	2,560,000	40	50	125
F-2067F	Atlanta	36,480,000		30	55
F-2067F★	Atlanta	1,280,000	45	55	150
F-2067G	Chicago	107,680,000		30	55
F-2067G★	Chicago	3,200,000	45	55	110
F-2067H	St. Louis	19,200,000		30	55
F-2067H★	St. Louis	640,000	45	55	125
F-2067I	Minneapolis	12,160,000		30	55
F-2067I★	Minneapolis	640,000	45	55	140
F-2067J	Kansas City	39,040,000		30	55
F-2067J★	Kansas City	1,280,000	45	55	125
F-2067K	Dallas	25,600,000		30	55
F-2067K★	Dallas	640,000	50	60	150
F-2067L	San Francisco	103,840,000		30	55
F-2067L★	San Francisco	5,120,000	45	55	125

Series of 1969-A—Signatures of Kabis and Connally

No.	Issuing Bank	Quantity Printed	VF-20	EF-40	Unc-63
F-2068A	Boston	13,440,000	$25	$35	$70
F-2068B	New York	69,760,000		35	65
F-2068B★	New York	2,460,000	50	60	125
F-2068C	Philadelphia	13,440,000		35	70
F-2068D	Cleveland	29,440,000		35	70
F-2068D★	Cleveland	640,000	55	65	150
F-2068E	Richmond	42,400,000		35	70
F-2068E★	Richmond	1,920,000	50	60	140
F-2068F	Atlanta	13,440,000		35	70
F-2068G	Chicago	81,640,000		35	65
F-2068G★	Chicago	1,920,000	50	60	125
F-2068H	St. Louis	14,080,000		35	70
F-2068H★	St. Louis	640,000	55	65	140
F-2068I	Minneapolis	7,040,000		35	80
F-2068J	Kansas City	16,040,000		35	70
F-2068K	Dallas	14,720,000		35	70
F-2068K★	Dallas	640,000	55	65	125
F-2068L	San Francisco	50,560,000		35	75
F-2068L★	San Francisco	1,280,000	65	75	125

Series of 1969-B—Signatures of Banuelos and Connally

No.	Issuing Bank	Quantity Printed	VF-20	EF-40	Unc-63
F-2069B	New York	39,200,000	$40	$55	$200
F-2069B★	New York	480,000	90	175	500
F-2069D	Cleveland	6,400,000	40	55	225
F-2069E	Richmond	27,520,000	40	55	225
F-2069F	Atlanta	14,080,000	40	55	200
F-2069F★	Atlanta	640,000	150	275	600
F-2069G	Chicago	14,240,000	40	55	200
F-2069G★	Chicago	1,112,000	125	325	600
F-2069H	St. Louis	5,120,000	45	55	275
F-2069I	Minneapolis	2,560,000	50	60	325
F-2069J	Kansas City	3,840,000	45	55	250
F-2069J★	Kansas City	640,000	125	250	575
F-2069K	Dallas	12,160,000	45	55	225
F-2069L	San Francisco	26,000,000	40	55	200
F-2069L★	San Francisco	640,000	110	250	575

Series of 1969-C—Signatures of Banuelos and Shultz

No.	Issuing Bank	Quantity Printed	VF-20	EF-40	Unc-63
F-2070A	Boston	17,280,000		$25	$55
F-2070A★	Boston	640,000	$45	60	125
F-2070B	New York	135,200,000		25	50
F-2070B★	New York	1,640,000	40	50	100
F-2070C	Philadelphia	40,960,000		25	50
F-2070C★	Philadelphia	640,000	40	50	135
F-2070D	Cleveland	57,760,000		25	65
F-2070D★	Cleveland	480,000	50	60	150
F-2070E	Richmond	80,160,000		25	60
F-2070E★	Richmond	1,920,000	40	50	100
F-2070F	Atlanta	35,840,000		25	60
F-2070F★	Atlanta	640,000	40	60	135
F-2070G	Chicago	78,720,000		25	50
F-2070G★	Chicago	640,000	40	50	125
F-2070H	St. Louis	33,920,000		25	60
F-2070H★	St. Louis	640,000	50	70	160
F-2070I	Minneapolis	14,080,000		25	65
F-2070I★	Minneapolis	640,000	50	60	135
F-2070J	Kansas City	32,000,000		25	60
F-2070J★	Kansas City	640,000	50	70	160
F-2070K	Dallas	31,360,000		25	60
F-2070K★	Dallas	1,920,000	45	55	130
F-2070L	San Francisco	82,080,000		25	60
F-2070L★	San Francisco	1,120,000	45	55	130

Series of 1974—Signatures of Neff and Simon

No.	Issuing Bank	Quantity Printed	VF-20	EF-40	Unc-63
F-2071A	Boston	56,960,000		$25	$55
F-2071A★	Boston	768,000	$40	50	110
F-2071B	New York	296,640,000		25	45
F-2071B★	New York	7,616,000	35	40	75
F-2071C	Philadelphia	59,680,000		25	55
F-2071C★	Philadelphia	1,760,000	35	45	110
F-2071D	Cleveland	148,000,000		25	60
F-2071D★	Cleveland	3,296,000	40	50	110
F-2071E	Richmond	149,920,000		25	60
F-2071E★	Richmond	3,040,000	40	50	110
F-2071F	Atlanta	53,280,000		25	60
F-2071F★	Atlanta	480,000	50	60	125
F-2071G	Chicago	249,920,000		25	45
F-2071G★	Chicago	4,608,000	35	40	85
F-2071H	St. Louis	73,120,000		25	60
F-2071H★	St. Louis	1,120,000	40	50	110
F-2071I	Minneapolis	39,040,000		25	55
F-2071I★	Minneapolis	1,280,000	50	60	115
F-2071J	Kansas City	74,400,000		25	55
F-2071J★	Kansas City	736,000	50	60	110
F-2071K	Dallas	68,640,000		25	60
F-2071K★	Dallas	608,000	50	60	110
F-2071L	San Francisco	128,800,000		25	55
F-2071L★	San Francisco	4,320,000	45	55	110

Series of 1977—Signatures of Morton and Blumenthal

No.	Issuing Bank	Quantity Printed	VF-20	EF-40	Unc-63
F-2072A	Boston	94,720,000		$25	$50
F-2072A★	Boston	2,688,000	$35	50	90
F-2072B	New York	569,600,000		25	50
F-2072B★	New York	12,416,000	25	40	90
F-2072C	Philadelphia	117,760,000		25	50
F-2072C★	Philadelphia	117,760,000	25	40	90
F-2072D	Cleveland	189,440,000		25	50
F-2072D★	Cleveland	5,632,000	35	50	90
F-2072E	Richmond	257,280,000		25	50
F-2072E★	Richmond	6,272,000	35	50	90
F-2072F	Atlanta	70,400,000		25	50
F-2072F★	Atlanta	2,698,000	35	50	90
F-2072G	Chicago	358,400,000		25	50
F-2072G★	Chicago	7,552,000	35	50	90
F-2072H	St. Louis	98,560,000		25	50
F-2072H★	St. Louis	1,792,000	35	50	90
F-2072I	Minneapolis	15,360,000		25	60
F-2072I★	Minneapolis	512,000	50	65	120
F-2072J	Kansas City	148,480,000		25	50
F-2072J★	Kansas City	4,864,000	35	50	90
F-2072K	Dallas	163,840,000		25	50
F-2072K★	Dallas	6,656,000	25	45	90
F-2072L	San Francisco	263,680,000		25	50
F-2072L★	San Francisco	6,528,000	35	50	90

Series of 1981—Signatures of Buchanan and Regan

No.	Issuing Bank	Quantity Printed	VF-20	EF-40	Unc-63
F-2073A	Boston	191,360,000	$25	$35	$65
F-2073A★	Boston	1,024,000	45	75	150
F-2073B	New York	559,360,000	25	35	65
F-2073B★	New York	5,312,000	30	60	110
F-2073C	Philadelphia	146,560,000	25	35	65
F-2073C★	Philadelphia	1,280,000	45	70	150
F-2073D	Cleveland	146,560,000	25	35	65
F-2073D★	Cleveland	1,280,000	45	70	150
F-2073E	Richmond	296,320,000	25	35	65

No.	Issuing Bank	Quantity Printed	VF-20	EF-40	Unc-63
F-2073E★	Richmond	1,280,000	$45	$70	$150
F-2073F	Atlanta	93,440,000	25	35	65
F-2073F★	Atlanta	3,200,000	45	70	150
F-2073G	Chicago	361,600,000	25	35	65
F-2073G★	Chicago	2,688,000	30	40	125
F-2073H	St. Louis	76,160,000	25	35	65
F-2073H★	St. Louis	1,536,000	45	70	150
F-2073I	Minneapolis	23,040,000	25	35	75
F-2073I★	Minneapolis	256,000	65	95	200
F-2073J	Kansas City	147,840,000	25	35	65
F-2073J★	Kansas City	1,280,000	45	70	150
F-2073K	Dallas	95,360,000	25	35	65
F-2073K★	Dallas	896,000	60	70	175
F-2073L	San Francisco	404,480,000	25	35	65
F-2073L★	San Francisco	1,424,000	45	70	140

Series of 1981-A—Signatures of Ortega and Regan

No.	Issuing Bank	Quantity Printed	VF-20	EF-40	Unc-63
F-2074A	Boston	156,800,000		$25	$50
F-2074B	New York	352,000,000		25	40
F-2074C	Philadelphia	57,600,000		25	50
F-2074D	Cleveland	160,000,000		25	50
F-2074D★	Cleveland	3,840,000	$35	55	95
F-2074E	Richmond	214,400,000		25	50
F-2074F	Atlanta	140,800,000		25	50
F-2074F★	Atlanta	3,200,000	35	55	100
F-2074G	Chicago	211,200,000		25	50
F-2074H	St. Louis	73,600,000		25	50
F-2074I	Minneapolis	19,200,000		25	50
F-2074J	Kansas City	86,400,000		25	50
F-2074K	Dallas	99,200,000		25	50
F-2074L	San Francisco	457,600,000		25	40
F-2074L★	San Francisco	6,400,000	35	55	115

Series of 1985—Signatures of Ortega and Baker

No.	Issuing Bank	Quantity Printed	Unc-63	No.	Issuing Bank	Quantity Printed	Unc-63
F-2075A	Boston	416,000,000	$40	F-2075G	Chicago	729,600,000	$40
F-2075A★	Boston	3,200,000	80	F-2075G★	Chicago	5,760,000	75
F-2075B	New York	1,728,000,000	40	F-2073H	St. Louis	203,400,000	40
F-2075B★	New York	5,760,000	75	F-2075I	Minneapolis	112,000,000	50
F-2075C	Philadelphia	224,000,000	40	F-2075J	Kansas City	204,800,000	40
F-2075C★	Philadelphia	6,400,000	80	F-2075J★	Kansas City	3,200,000	80
F-2075D	Cleveland	585,600,000	40	F-2075K	Dallas	192,000,000	40
F-2075D★	Cleveland	6,400,000	80	F-2075K★	Dallas	3,200,000	80
F-2075E	Richmond	864,000,000	40	F-2075L	San Francisco	1,129,600,000	40
F-2075E★	Richmond	6,400,000	80	F-2075L★	San Francisco	3,200,000	80
F-2075F	Atlanta	313,600,000	40				

Series of 1988

None printed.

Series of 1988-A—Signatures of Villalpando and Brady

No.	Issuing Bank	Quantity Printed	Unc-63	No.	Issuing Bank	Quantity Printed	Unc-63
F-2076A	Boston	313,600,000	$55	F-2076G	Chicago	563,200,000	$50
F-2076B	New York	979,200,000	50	F-2076G★	Chicago	3,200,000	95
F-2076B★	New York	6,560,000	100	F-2076H	St. Louis	108,800,000	55
F-2076C	Philadelphia	96,000,000	55	F-2076I	Minneapolis	25,600,000	55
F-2076C★	Philadelphia	3,200,000	120	F-2076J	Kansas City	137,200,000	55
F-2076D	Cleveland	307,200,000	55	F-2076K	Dallas	51,200,000	55
F-2076E	Richmond	281,600,000	60	F-2076K★	Dallas	3,200,000	100
F-2076F	Atlanta	288,000,000	55	F-2076L	San Francisco	729,600,000	55
F-2076F★	Atlanta	3,200,000	100				

Series of 1990—Signatures of Villalpando and Brady
Printed in Washington, DC
Security thread and micro-size printing introduced

No.	Issuing Bank	Quantity Printed	VF-20	Unc-63	No.	Issuing Bank	Quantity Printed	VF-20	Unc-63
F-2077A	Boston	345,600,000		$35	F-2077F	Atlanta	460,800,000		$35
F-2077A★	Boston	3,200,000	$30	75	F-2077G	Chicago	652,800,000		35
F-2077B	New York	1,446,400,000		30	F-2077H	St. Louis	172,800,000		35
F-2077B★	New York	16,640,000	30	75	F-2077H★	St. Louis	3,200,000	$35	85
F-2077C	Philadelphia	96,000,000		35	F-2077I	Minneapolis	70,400,000		40
F-2077D	Cleveland	281,600,000		35	F-2077J	Kansas City	83,200,000		35
F-2077D★	Cleveland	3,200,000	30	75	F-2077K	Dallas	25,600,000		40
F-2077E	Richmond	307,200,000		35	F-2077L	San Francisco	416,000,000		35
F-2077E★	Richmond	3,200,000	30	75					

Series of 1990—Signatures of Villalpando and Brady
Printed at the Western Facility (Fort Worth, Texas)

No.	Issuing Bank	Quantity Printed	VF-20	Unc-63	No.	Issuing Bank	Quantity Printed	VF-20	Unc-63
F-2078F★	Atlanta	1,280,000	$35	$75	F-2078I★	Minneapolis	5,120,000	$35	$80
F-2078G★	Chicago	13,400,000	35	75	F-2078L	San Francisco	incl. above		35

Note: Notes printed in Fort Worth may be identified by a small "FW" on the right front side next to the plate check letter-number.

Series of 1993—Signatures of Withrow and Bentsen
Printed in Washington, DC

No.	Issuing Bank	Quantity Printed	VF-20	Unc-63	No.	Issuing Bank	Quantity Printed	VF-20	Unc-63
F-2079A	Boston	288,000,000	$22.50	$45	F-2079D★	Cleveland	1,920,000	$30.00	$55
F-2079A★	Boston	2,560,000	30.00	55	F-2079E	Richmond	656,000,000	22.50	45
F-2079B	New York	640,000,000	22.50	45	F-2079E★	Richmond	8,960,000	30.00	55
F-2079B★	New York	4,920,000	27.50	50	F-2079F	Atlanta	300,800,000	22.50	45
F-2079C	Philadelphia	147,200,000	22.50	45	F-2079H	St. Louis	19,200,000	22.50	45
F-2079D	Cleveland	329,600,000	22.50	45					

Series of 1993—Signatures of Withrow and Bentsen
Printed at the Western Facility (Fort Worth, Texas)

No.	Issuing Bank	Quantity Printed	VF-20	Unc-63	No.	Issuing Bank	Quantity Printed	VF-20	Unc-63
F-2080F	Atlanta	51,200,000	$22.50	$45	F-2080J	Kansas City	102,400,000	$22.50	$45
F-2080F★	Atlanta	3,200,000	30.00	65	F-2080L	Dallas	185,600,000	22.50	45
F-2080G	Chicago	390,400,000	22.50	40	F-2080L★	San Francisco	806,400,000	22.50	45
F-2080H	St. Louis	166,400,000	22.50	40					

Series of 1995—Signatures of Withrow and Rubin
Printed in Washington, DC

No.	Issuing Bank	Quantity Printed	VF-20	Unc-63	No.	Issuing Bank	Quantity Printed	VF-20	Unc-63
F-2081B	New York	403,200,000		$40	F-2081D	Cleveland	140,800,000		$40
F-2081B★	New York	5,760,000	$25.00	55	F-2081D★	Cleveland	640,000	$27.50	70
F-2081C	Philadelphia	70,400,000		40	F-2081E	Richmond	166,400,000		40

Series of 1995—Signatures of Withrow and Rubin
Printed at the Western Facility (Fort Worth, Texas)

No.	Issuing Bank	Quantity Printed	VF-20	Unc-63	No.	Issuing Bank	Quantity Printed	VF-20	Unc-63
F-2082F	Atlanta	307,200,000		$40	F-2082I	Minneapolis	44,800,000		$50
F-2082F★	Atlanta	3,200,000	$27.50	65	F-2082J	Kansas City	230,400,000		40
F-2082G	Chicago	492,800,000		40	F-2082K	Dallas	249,600,000		40
F-2082H	St. Louis	140,800,000		40	F-2082L	San Francisco	614,400,000		40

Federal Reserve Notes
Series of 1996 to 2001,
Green Seal, Security Features

Face of F-2083 to F-2088, the type of Series 1996 to 2001. Jackson's portrait is modified, as are other aspects, and security features have been added.

Back of F-2083 to F-2088. The White House motif has been revised and other features have been changed. Back type used from Series 1996 to 2001.

Series of 1996—Signatures of Withrow and Rubin
Printed in Washington, DC

No.	Issuing Bank	Quantity Printed	Unc-63	No.	Issuing Bank	Quantity Printed	Unc-63
F-2083A	Boston	883,200,000	$32.50	F-2083C★	Philadelphia	3,200,000	$45.00
F-2083A★	Boston	10,880,000	45.00	F-2083D	Cleveland	364,000,000	32.50
F-2083B	New York	896,000,000	32.50	F-2083D★	Cleveland	6,400,000	45.00
F-2083B★	New York	3,200,000	45.00	F-2083E	Richmond	483,200,000	32.50
F-2083C	Philadelphia	506,400,000	32.50	F-2083F	Atlanta	925,600,000	32.50

Series of 1996—Signatures of Withrow and Rubin
Printed at the Western Facility (Fort Worth, Texas)

No.	Issuing Bank	Quantity Printed	Unc-63	No.	Issuing Bank	Quantity Printed	Unc-63
F-2084E★	Richmond	3,200,000	$35.00	F-2084H★	St. Louis	640,000	$150
F-2084F	Atlanta	925,600,000	30.00	F-2084I	Minneapolis	112,800,000	30
F-2084F★	Atlanta	3,200,000	35.00	F-2084J	Kansas City	276,800,000	30
F-2084G	Chicago	1,151,200,000	30.00	F-2084K	Dallas	276,800,000	30
F-2084G★	Chicago	12,800,000	32.50	F-2084L	San Francisco	457,600,000	30
F-2084H	St. Louis	257,600,000	30.00	F-2084L★	San Francisco	7,040,000	40

Series of 1999—Signatures of Withrow and Summers
Printed in Washington, DC

No.	Issuing Bank	Quantity Printed	Unc-63	No.	Issuing Bank	Quantity Printed	Unc-63
F-2085B	Boston	57,600,000	$30	F-2085C	Philadelphia	192,000,000	$30
F-2085A★	Boston	1,920,000	55	F-2085D	Cleveland	268,800,000	30
F-2085B	New York	608,000,000	30	F-2085D★	Cleveland	5,760,000	55
F-2085B★	New York	1,920,000	45	F-2085E	Richmond	492,800,000	30

Series of 1999—Signatures of Withrow and Summers
Printed at the Western Facility (Fort Worth, Texas)

No.	Issuing Bank	Quantity Printed	Unc-63	No.	Issuing Bank	Quantity Printed	Unc-63
F-2086B★	New York	3,200,000	$50	F-2086H	St. Louis	102,400,000	$30
F-2086D	Cleveland	12,800,000	30	F-2086I	Minneapolis	25,600,000	35
F-2086F	Atlanta	409,600,000	30	F-2086J	Kansas City	70,400,000	30
F-2086G	Chicago	704,000,000	30	F-2086L	San Francisco	32,000,000	30
F-2086G★	Chicago	7,040,000	50	F-2086L★	San Francisco	3,200,000	50

Series of 2001—Signatures of Marin and O'Neill
Printed in Washington, DC

No.	Issuing Bank	Quantity Printed	Unc-63	No.	Issuing Bank	Quantity Printed	Unc-63
F-2087B	New York	403,200,000	$30	F-2087D	Cleveland	83,200,000	$30
F-2087B★	New York	320,000	125	F-2087E	Richmond	140,800,000	30

Series of 2001—Signatures of Marin and O'Neill
Printed at the Western Facility (Fort Worth, Texas)

No.	Issuing Bank	Quantity Printed	Unc-63	No.	Issuing Bank	Quantity Printed	Unc-63
F-2088B	New York	249,600,000	$30	F-2088I	Minneapolis	57,600,000	$30
F-2088E	Richmond	153,600,000	30	F-2088J	Kansas City	112,000,000	30
F-2088F	Atlanta	313,600,000	30	F-2088J★	Kansas City	3,200,000	50
F-2088G	Chicago	224,000,000	30	F-2088K	Dallas	166,400,000	45
F-2088G★	Chicago	3,200,000	50	F-2088L	San Francisco	384,000,000	30
F-2088H	St. Louis	44,800,000	30	F-2088L★	San Francisco	3,200,000	50

Federal Reserve Notes
Series of 2004 to Date,
Green Seal, Additional Features

Face of F-2089 to date. Similar to the preceding, but with color and other security features added and with an additional seal to the lower right of the portrait.

Back of F-2089 to date. Similar to the preceding, but with tiny yellow "20" numbers and other security features added.

Series of 2004 (color added)—Signatures of Marin and Snow
Printed in Washington, DC

No.	Issuing Bank	Unc-63	No.	Issuing Bank	Unc-63
F-2089A	Boston	$30	F-2089C★	Philadelphia	$50
F-2089A★	Boston	75	F-2089D	Cleveland	30
F-2089B	New York	30	F-2089E	Richmond	30
F-2089B★	New York	110	F-2089E★	Richmond	65
F-2089C	Philadelphia	30			

Series of 2004—Signatures of Marin and Snow
Printed at the Western Facility (Fort Worth, Texas)

No.	Issuing Bank	Unc-63	No.	Issuing Bank	Unc-63
F-2090D	Cleveland	$30	F-2090I	Minneapolis	$35
F-2090E	Richmond	30	F-2090J	Kansas City	35
F-2090F	Atlanta	40	F-2090J★	Kansas City	50
F-2090F★	Atlanta	50	F-2090K	Dallas	30
F-2090G	Chicago	30	F-2090K★	Dallas	50
F-2090G★	Chicago	50	F-2090L	San Francisco	30
F-2090H	St. Louis	30	F-2090L★	San Francisco	50

Series of 2004-A—Signatures of Cabral and Snow
Printed in Washington, DC

No.	Issuing Bank	Unc-63	No.	Issuing Bank	Unc-63
F-2091A	Boston	$27.50	F-2091E★	Richmond	$45.00
F-2091A★	Boston	45.00	F-2091F	Atlanta	27.50
F-2091B	New York	27.50	F-2091F★	Atlanta	45.00
F-2091B★	New York	45.00	F-2091G	Chicago	27.50
F-2091C	Philadelphia	27.50	F-2091I	Minneapolis	27.50
F-2091D	Cleveland	27.50	F-2091J	Kansas City	27.50
F-2091E	Richmond	27.50			

Series of 2004-A—Signatures of Cabral and Snow
Printed at the Western Facility (Fort Worth, Texas)

No.	Issuing Bank	Unc-63	No.	Issuing Bank	Unc-63
F-2092F	Atlanta	$27.50	F-2092K	Dallas	$27.50
F-2092H	St. Louis	27.50	F-2092K★	Dallas	50.00
F-2092I	Minneapolis	27.50	F-2092L	San Francisco	27.50
F-2092J	Kansas City	27.50			

Series of 2006—Signatures of Cabral and Paulson
Printed in Washington, DC

No.	Issuing Bank	Unc-63	No.	Issuing Bank	Unc-63
F-2093A	Boston	$27.50	F-2093G★	Chicago	$45.00
F-2093B	New York	27.50	F-2093H	St. Louis	27.50
F-2093C	Philadelphia	27.50	F-2093I	Minneapolis	27.50
F-2093D	Cleveland	27.50	F-2093J	Kansas City	27.50
F-2093E	Richmond	27.50	F-2093K	Dallas	27.50
F-2093F	Atlanta	27.50	F-2093K★	Dallas	45.00
F-2093F★	Atlanta	45.00	F-2093L	San Francisco	27.50
F-2093G	Chicago	27.50	F-2093L★	San Francisco	45.00

Series of 2006—Signatures of Cabral and Paulson
Printed at the Western Facility (Fort Worth, Texas)

No.	Issuing Bank	Unc-63	No.	Issuing Bank	Unc-63
F-2094A★	Boston	$45.00	F-2094H	St. Louis	$27.50
F-2094D	Cleveland	27.50	F-2094I	Minneapolis	27.50
F-2094F	Atlanta	27.50	F-2094J	Kansas City	27.50
F-2094G	Chicago	27.50	F-2094K	Dallas	27.50
F-2094G★	Chicago	45.00	F-2094L	San Francisco	27.50

COLLECTING $50 NOTES

From here forward, we enter the rarified air of the most serious, sophisticated, and wealthy collectors. Even today, the $50 bill is not one we use frequently in standard trade, so imagine the scarcity and unfamiliarity of these notes when they were first made in the 1860s.

Large-Size Notes

$50 Interest-Bearing Notes, Large-Size. Considering that these were used more by institutions than individuals, it is not surprising that there are more $50 issues than of the $10 or $20. There were six different types, and although all are too rare to publish a catalog price, some recent transactions include $60,375 for F-203 and $172,500 for F-207 (sales in 2005), and $138,000 for F-212 and $80,500 for F-212d (2007).

$50 Legal Tender Notes (United States Notes), Large-Size. Alexander Hamilton, found on the $20 Legal Tender notes of the Series of 1869 to 1880, was earlier seen on the three known $50 issues of 1862 and 1863. The first and rarest is F-148. This is the only one with the First Obligation and, with two dozen known, also is the most common. Fewer than a dozen of each are known for F-150 and F-150a. An extremely fine specimen of F-150 sold for $299,000 at auction in January 2008.

The Series of 1869 "Rainbow Notes" break a trend in that they are the only denomination of that series of Legal Tender Notes not to have their face design carried over to the Series of 1874 to 1880. They bear the portrait of the silver-tongued "Great Compromiser" between North and South, Speaker of the House, senator, secretary of state, and frequent presidential candidate, Henry Clay of Kentucky. These are scarce and highly sought after today. There is only one uncirculated specimen known, and it has not been on the market since 1998.

The Series of 1874 through 1880 have at their right side one of the more unusual depictions of Liberty, here dressed as Columbia (see the preceding page). There are the usual variations in the color and placement of the seal among the 13 notes of this type. Rarest are F-158 and F-163, with eight and five known, respectively (all but one of the five F-163 notes in the highest grades).

$50 National Bank Notes, Large-Size. National Bank Notes of the $50 denomination follow precisely the pattern of their predecessors. Valuations for $50 notes of the First Charter period become stratospheric; expect to pay a five figure sum even for a "common" note, unless—perhaps—it falls apart in your hands. The face of the First and Second Charter notes show Washington Crossing the Delaware on the left and kneeling in prayer at right. The Second Charter Brown Backs and Date Backs are easier to find, but all are still scarce. The Value Back (FIFTY DOLLARS) is very rare; it was issued for only two banks, one in New Orleans and the other in Dayton, Ohio. With the discovery of a note in 2001, there are now five known altogether.

The Series of 1902 $50 Red Seals are three to four times more valuable than the two Blue Seal issues. The portrait is of John Sherman, who was both secretary of state and of the Treasury. He also was also the brother of Union General William Tecumseh Sherman. John Sherman's enduring accomplishment was the Sherman Anti-Trust Act, and his presumably endearing personality resulted in the nickname "The Ohio Icicle."

$50 National Gold Bank Notes, Large-Size. This is the most unobtainable note in the series. Although records indicate that nine banks issued $50 National Gold Bank notes, they are only known from three (F-1160, F-1160a, F-1161). Notes of the latter two numbers are unique, and there are only four known of F-1160.

$50 Compound Interest Treasury Notes, Large-Size. If you find a specimen of F-192a, do not buy it without having it authenticated by an expert. Every known specimen has been proven counterfeit. There are about a dozen of F-192b in private hands, but caution should be exercised with this note, as well. When last sold in January 2008, a better than Very Fine example brought a price of $69,000.

$50 Silver Certificates, Large-Size. The face design is fairly constant for this denomination. All notes have a half-length bust of Edward Everett, who at various times was a congressman, governor of Massachusetts, ambassador to Britain, president of Harvard, secretary of state, and U.S. senator. Despite these many accomplishments, he is mostly forgotten as the "other speaker" at Gettysburg in 1863. The Series of 1879 and 1880 are similar in style to the $10 and $20 denominations. All are scarce. The two most common are F-328 and F-329 with just over two dozen known of each. The Series of 1891, especially the last issue, is seen somewhat more often, excepting the six known examples of F-330.

$50 Treasury or Coin Notes, Large-Size. Treasury Notes of the $50 denomination, with the bust of Lincoln's secretary of state, William H. Seward, exist only for the Series of 1891 and in only one signature combination. Whenever one of the 21 notes recorded is offered for sale, a five- or six-figure price is virtually guaranteed.

$50 Gold Certificates, Large-Size. More than half of the known Series of 1882 Gold Certificates are rare; there are not more than 20 listed for any of them. Only the later five (F-1193–F-1197) are regularly seen, very rarely in uncirculated quality. The Series of 1913 and 1992 notes are collectible, but prices escalate dramatically as they progress upward on the grading scale.

$50 Federal Reserve Notes, Large-Size. The Red Seal issues are five to six times more expensive than the Blue Seals. For the most part, the recorded population is considerably smaller than for $20 notes of the same type—and substantially more expensive.

$50 Federal Reserve Bank Notes, Large-Size. The key to the series, these were issued only for the St. Louis bank, and there are 50 serial numbers recorded today. Nonetheless, it is not unusual to see them offered for sale several times a year.

Small-Size Notes

All have the portrait of Ulysses S. Grant on the face and the U.S. Capitol on the back.

$50 National Bank Notes, Small-Size. These are similar to all other small-size National Bank Notes but, given the high face value, a province only of the most serious collectors. As with other denominations, there are rare states, towns, and banks. A majority of states did not issue the Type 2 variety.

$50 Gold Certificates, Small-Size. Sixty million fewer of these notes were printed than for the $20 Gold Certificate, but there is an ample supply to fill any needs.

$50 Federal Reserve Bank Notes, Small-Size. These were not printed for the Boston, Philadelphia, Richmond, Atlanta, and St. Louis districts. The face value is a substantial percentage of the selling price when these are offered in the lower grades.

$50 Federal Reserve Notes, Small-Size. These were mostly static in design from the Series 1928 to the Series of 1996, when they were redesigned as part of the Bureau of Engraving and Printing's anti-counterfeiting program. No notes were printed for the Series of 1999.

The face and back designs were modified again, commencing with the Series of 2004. Our current notes have Grant's portrait removed from its frame and background colors of blue and red, along with small yellow "50"s added to both sides of the bill. Also now standard is a watermark, color-shifting green-copper ink, an embedded security thread, and microprinting. We should probably expect similar, once-a-decade changes from now on.

LARGE-SIZE $50 NOTES

Interest-Bearing Notes of March 2, 1861, 6%, 2 Years

Face of F-202a. This is a very early Interest-Bearing Note, authorization of March 2, 1861. The inked date is August 9, 1861. At right is the inked signature of F.E. Spinner, treasurer of the United States. At first Spinner personally autographed such notes; clerks were later trained to imitate his signature. These were mainly bought as investments by banks and did not circulate.

Back of F-202a.

No.	Act	Signatures		Seal	
F-202a	March 2, 1861	Chittenden	Spinner	No Treasury seal	2 known

Interest-Bearing Notes of July 17, 1861, 7.3%, 3 Years

Face of F-207. Large eagle at center. American Bank Note Co., New York, imprint.

Back of F-207.

No.	Act	Signatures		Seal	
F-207	July 17, 1861	Chittenden	Spinner	Red	1 known

Interest-Bearing Notes of March 3, 1863, 5%, 1 Year

Face of F-198. Justice with Shield, and Loyalty (a.k.a. Liberty) to right; portrait of Alexander Hamilton. COMPOUND INTEREST TREASURY NOTE overprinted with bronzing powder. "Engraved and Printed at the Treasury Department" imprint.

Back of F-198.

No.	Act	Signatures		Seal	
F-198	March 3, 1863	Chittenden	Spinner	Red	Extremely rare

Interest-Bearing Notes of March 3, 1863, 5%, 2 Years

Face of F-203. Overprint date of April 22, 1864, in green panel below "Washington," the date of commencement of the interest on this particular note. Other overprint dates exist. The vignettes are of allegorical figures representing Caduceus, Justice with Shield, and Loyalty. American Bank Note Company, New York, imprint.

Back of F-203.

No.	Act	Signatures		Seal	
F-203	March 3, 1863	Chittenden	Spinner	Red	7 known

Interest-Bearing Notes of June 30, 1864, 7.3%, 3 Years

Face of F-212. Large eagle at center. Dated August 15, 1864. Treasury Department imprint. This eagle, when inverted, has the appearance of a jackass. It was also used on the $10 Legal Tender Note, Series of 1869 to 1880, and on the Fractional Currency Shield.

Back of F-212.

No.	Act	Signatures		Seal	
F-212	June 30, 1864	Colby	Spinner	Red	7 known

Interest-Bearing Notes of March 3, 1865, 7.3%, 3 Years

Face of F-212d. Large eagle at center, design similar to the preceding. Dated June 15, 1865. Treasury Department imprint.

Back of F-212d.

No.	Act	Signatures		Seal	
F-212d	March 3, 1865	Colby	Spinner	Red	8 known

Legal Tender Notes
Series of 1862,
First Obligation

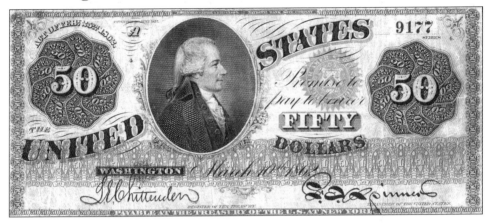

Face of F-148. Bust of Alexander Hamilton. National Bank Note Company.

Back of F-148 with "First Obligation" at the center. National Bank Note Company.

No.	Act	Signatures		Seal	VG-8	F-12	VF-20	EF-40	Unc-63
F-148	1862	Chittenden	Spinner	Red	$12,500	$27,500	$40,000	$55,000	—

Legal Tender Notes
Series of 1863,
Second Obligation

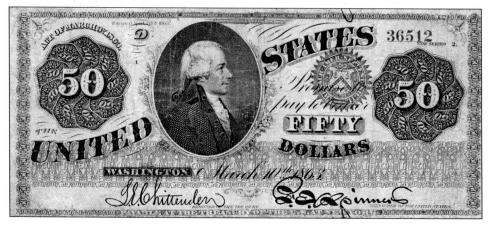

Face of F-150 and F-150a. Design as preceding, with bust of Alexander Hamilton.

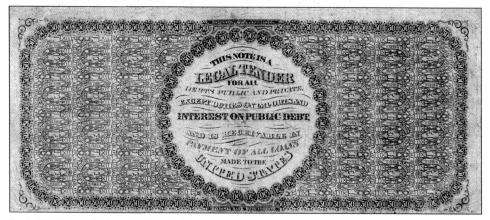

Back of F-150 and F-150a with "Second Obligation" at the center. National Bank Note Company.

No.	Act	Signatures		Seal	VG-8	F-12	VF-20	EF-40	Unc-63
National Bank Note Co. printed on top border									
F-150	1863	Chittenden	Spinner	Red	$7,500	$13,500	$30,000	—	—
National Bank Note Co. and American Bank Note Co. printed on top border									
F-150a	1863	Chittenden	Spinner	Red	8,000	15,500	32,250	—	—

Legal Tender Notes
Series of 1869

Face of F-151. "Rainbow Note." At left, "Return of Peace," a goddess holding a statuette. At right is a bust of Henry Clay. Blue-tinted paper. The star after the serial number is decorative.

Back of F-151. American Bank Note Company.

No.	Signatures		Seal	VG-8	F-12	VF-20	EF-40	Unc-63
F-151	Allison	Spinner	Large red	$9,500	$21,000	$30,000	$50,000	—

Legal Tender Notes
Series of 1874 to 1880

Face of F-152 to F-154. Bust of Benjamin Franklin at left, Liberty at right.

Back of F-152 to F-164.

Face of F-155 to F-164, similar to the preceding but without the large L's to each side of the center.

No.	Series	Signatures		Seal		VG-8	F-12	VF-20	EF-40	Unc-63
F-152	1874	Spinner	Allison	Small red, rays		$3,500	$6,000	$9,750	$16,000	$57,500
F-153	1875	Wyman	Allison	Small red, rays	3 known					
F-154	1878	Gilfillan	Allison	Small red, rays		3,750	6,500	10,000	20,000	60,000

No.	Series	Signatures		Seal		VG-8	F-12	VF-20	EF-40	Unc-63
Face as above but without the "L's"										
F-155	1880	Gilfillan	Bruce	Large brown		$3,750	$7,250	$11,000	$24,000	—
F-156	1880	Wyman	Bruce	Large brown		3,500	6,500	11,000	24,000	$36,500
F-157	1880	Jordan	Rosecrans	Large red, plain		3,750	6,850	11,000	18,500	32,500
F-158	1880	Hyatt	Rosecrans	Large red, plain		4,000	8,500	11,000	17,500	62,500
F-159	1880	Hyatt	Rosecrans	Large red, spiked		3,350	6,500	8,000	12,000	32,500
F-160	1880	Huston	Rosecrans	Large red, spiked		3,750	6,650	8,500	13,000	—
F-161	1880	Huston	Rosecrans	Large brown		3,200	4,250	6,500	12,500	15,000
F-162	1880	Tillman	Morgan	Small red, scalloped		3,000	3,900	6,100	13,000	21,250
F-163	1880	Bruce	Roberts	Small red, scalloped	5 known					
F-164	1880	Lyons	Roberts	Small red, scalloped		2,150	3,300	5,125	8,000	20,000

Compound Interest Treasury Notes of 1863 and 1864

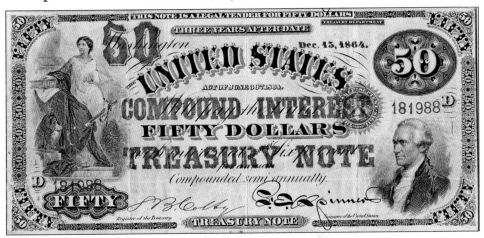

Face of F-192 to F-192b. *Justice with Shield, and Loyalty; portrait of Alexander Hamilton. Red overprinted date December 15, 1864 (other dates exist). Treasury Department imprint.*

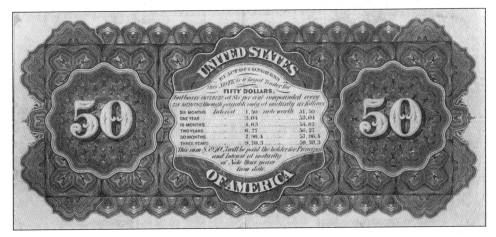

Back of F-192 to F-192b.

No.	Series	Overprint Date	Signatures			VG-8	F-12	VF-20	EF-40
F-192	1863	June 10, 1864	Chittenden	Spinner	2 known				
F-192a	1864	July 15, 1864	Chittenden	Spinner	Unknown				
F-192b	1864	Aug. 15, 1864–Sep. 1, 1864	Colby	Spinner		$17,000	$35,000	$45,000	$60,000

National Bank Notes
Original Series ("First Charter Period")

Designs of the face and back are identical to those of the Series of 1875, below.

No.	Signatures		Seal		VG-8	F-12	VF-20	EF-40
F-440	Chittenden	Spinner	Red, rays		$14,500	$17,000	$21,500	$35,000
F-442	Colby	Spinner	Red, rays		14,500	17,000	21,500	35,000
F-443	Allison	Spinner	Red, rays	3 known				

National Bank Notes
Series of 1875 ("First Charter Period")

Face of F-444 to F-451. "Washington Crossing the Delaware" at left; at right, "Prayer for Peace."

Back of F-444 to F-451. "The Embarkation of the Pilgrims."

No.	Signatures		Seal		VG-8	F-12	VF-20	EF-40
F-444	Allison	New	Red, scalloped		$14,750	$17,000	$22,500	$35,000
F-444a	Allison	Wyman	Red, scalloped	4 known				
F-445	Allison	Gilfillan	Red, scalloped	5 known				
F-446	Scofield	Gilfillan	Red, scalloped		14,750	17,000	22,500	35,000
F-447	Bruce	Gilfillan	Red, scalloped		14,750	17,000	22,500	35,000
F-448	Bruce	Wyman	Red, scalloped		14,750	17,000	22,500	35,000
F-449	Rosecrans	Huston	Red, scalloped		14,750	17,000	22,500	35,000
F-450	Rosecrans	Nebeker	Red, scalloped		14,750	17,000	22,500	35,000
F-451	Tillman	Morgan	Red, scalloped		14,750	17,000	22,500	35,000

National Bank Notes
Series of 1882 Brown Back
("Second Charter Period")

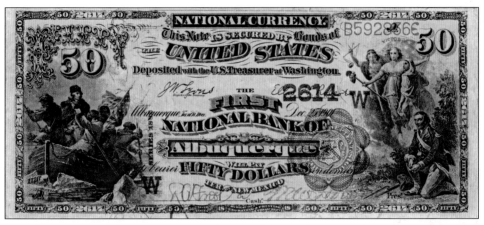

Face of F-507 to F-518a. Vignettes same as on the $50 notes of the First Charter Period.

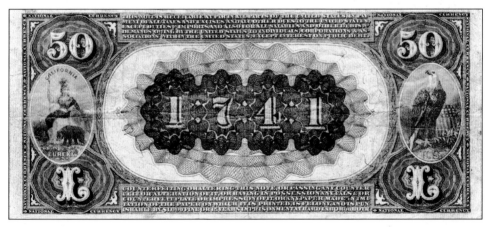

Back of F-507 to F-518a. At center is the bank's charter number.

No.	Signatures			VG-8	F-12	VF-20	EF-40	Unc-63
F-507	Bruce	Gilfillan		$4,750	$5,500	$6,750	$8,500	$16,000
F-508	Bruce	Wyman		4,750	5,500	6,750	8,500	16,000
F-509	Bruce	Jordan	6 known					
F-510	Rosecrans	Jordan		4,750	5,500	6,750	8,500	16,000
F-511	Rosecrans	Hyatt		4,750	5,500	6,750	8,500	16,000
F-512	Rosecrans	Huston		4,750	5,500	6,750	8,500	16,000
F-513	Rosecrans	Nebeker		4,750	5,500	6,750	8,500	16,000
F-514	Rosecrans	Morgan		4,750	5,500	6,750	8,500	16,000
F-515	Tillman	Morgan		4,750	5,500	6,750	8,500	16,000
F-516	Tillman	Roberts	4 known					
F-517	Bruce	Roberts		4,750	5,500	6,750	8,500	16,000
F-518	Lyons	Roberts		4,750	5,500	6,750	8,500	16,000
F-518a	Vernon	Treat	2 known					

National Bank Notes
Series of 1882 Date Back
("Second Charter Period")

Face of F-558 to F-565. Design same as the preceding.

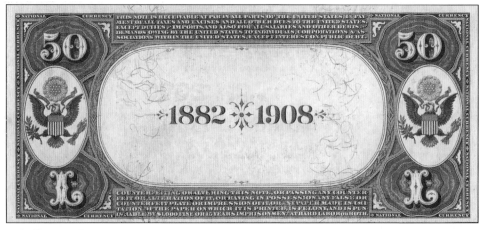

Back of F-558 to F-565.

No.	Signatures		VG-8	F-12	VF-20	EF-40	Unc-63
F-558	Rosecrans	Huston	$5,250	$6,250	$7,000	$8,125	$15,000
F-559	Rosecrans	Nebeker	5,250	6,250	7,000	8,125	15,000
F-560	Tillman	Morgan	5,250	6,250	7,000	8,125	15,000
F-561	Tillman	Roberts	5,250	6,250	7,000	8,125	15,000
F-562	Bruce	Roberts	5,250	6,250	7,000	8,125	15,000
F-563	Lyons	Roberts	5,000	6,000	6,750	8,000	15,000
F-564	Vernon	Treat	5,250	6,250	7,000	8,125	15,000
F-565	Napier	McClung	5,250	6,250	7,000	8,125	15,000

National Bank Notes
Series of 1882 Value Back
("Second Charter Period")

Face of F-586, similar to the preceding.

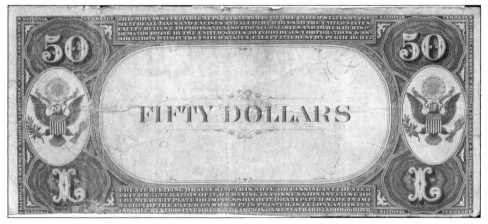

Back of F-586. Only two banks issued this type.

No.	Signatures		
F-586	Lyons	Roberts	7 known

National Bank Notes
Series of 1902 Red Seal
("Third Charter Period")

Designs similar to the following, without the date 1902–1908 on the back.

No.	Signatures		VG-8	F-12	VF-20	EF-40	Unc-63
F-664	Lyons	Roberts	$4,000	$6,500	$7,000	$9,500	$16,000
F-665	Lyons	Treat	5,000	6,750	8,000	10,500	16,750
F-666	Vernon	Treat	5,000	6,750	8,000	10,500	16,750

National Bank Notes
Series of 1902 Blue Seal, Date Back
("Third Charter Period")

Face of F-667 to F-674a. Bust of John Sherman, secretary of the Treasury from 1877 to 1881 and secretary of state from 1897 to 1898.

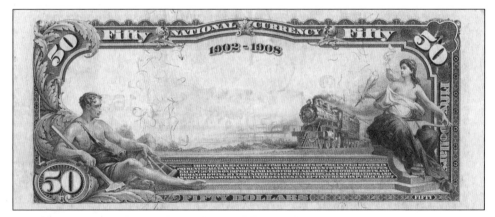

Back of F-667 to F-674a. Vignette titled "Mechanics and Navigation."

No.	Signatures		VG-8	F-12	VF-20	EF-40	Unc-63
F-667	Lyons	Roberts	$850	$1,000	$1,450	$2,650	$5,250
F-668	Lyons	Treat	850	1,000	1,450	2,650	5,250
F-669	Vernon	Treat	850	1,000	1,450	2,650	5,250
F-670	Vernon	McClung	850	1,000	1,450	2,650	5,250
F-671	Napier	McClung	850	1,000	1,450	2,650	5,250
F-672	Napier	Thompson	850	1,000	1,450	2,650	5,250
F-673	Napier	Burke	850	1,000	1,450	2,650	5,250
F-674	Parker	Burke	850	1,000	1,450	2,650	5,250
F-674a	Teehee	Burke	850	1,000	1,450	2,650	5,250

National Bank Notes
Series of 1902 Blue Seal, Plain Back
("Third Charter Period")

The face and back of this note (not shown) are similar to those of the previous type.

No.	Signatures			VG-8	F-12	VF-20	EF-40	Unc-63
F-675	Lyons	Roberts		$900	$1,300	$1,600	$2,400	$5,000
F-676	Lyons	Treat		900	1,300	1,600	2,400	5,000
F-677	Vernon	Treat		900	1,300	1,600	2,400	5,000
F-678	Vernon	McClung		900	1,300	1,600	2,400	5,000
F-679	Napier	McClung		900	1,300	1,600	2,400	5,000
F-679a	Napier	Thompson		1,400	1,850	2,250	3,400	5,625
F-680	Napier	Burke	7 known	1,400	1,850	2,250	3,400	5,625
F-681	Parker	Burke		900	1,300	1,600	2,400	5,000
F-682	Teehee	Burke		900	1,300	1,600	2,400	5,000
F-683	Elliott	Burke		900	1,300	1,600	2,400	5,000
F-684	Elliott	White		900	1,300	1,600	2,400	5,000
F-685	Speelman	White		900	1,300	1,600	2,400	5,000
F-685a	Woods	White	2 known					

Gold Certificates
Series of 1882

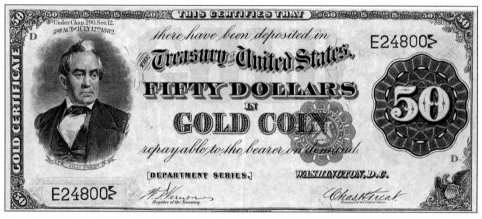

Face of F-1188 to F-1197. Earliest issues F-1188 to F-1189a have countersignatures. Portrait of Silas Wright, New York state senator and governor.

Back of F-1188 to F-1197.

No.	Signatures		Seal		VG-8	F-12	VF-20	EF-40	Unc-63
F-1188	Bruce	Gilfillan	Brown	7 known					
With autographed countersignature by Thomas C. Acton, Asst. Treasurer, payable at New York									
F-1189	Bruce	Gilfillan	Brown		—	—	—	—	—
As no. F-1189 but with engraved countersignature									
F-1189a	Bruce	Gilfillan	Brown		$14,000	$18,000	$35,000	Rare	—

Chart continued on next page.

No.	Signatures		Seal		VG-8	F-12	VF-20	EF-40	Unc-63
No countersignature									
F-1190	Bruce	Wyman	Brown	5 known	$20,000	$25,000	—	—	—
F-1191	Rosecrans	Hyatt	Large red	4 known					
F-1192	Rosecrans	Huston	Large brown		14,000	18,500	$40,000	—	—
F-1192a	Rosecrans	Huston	Small red	Unique					
F-1193	Lyons	Roberts	Small red		925	1,600	2,825	$5,750	$25,000
F-1194	Lyons	Treat	Small red		975	1,675	2,900	11,000	Rare
F-1195	Vernon	Treat	Small red		975	1,675	2,900	11,000	30,000
F-1196	Vernon	McClung	Small red		975	1,675	3,100	11,000	Rare
F-1197	Napier	McClung	Small red		925	1,600	2,825	5,750	20,000

National Gold Bank Notes

Face of F-1160 to F-1161f. Same design as on the $50 National Bank Notes of the First Charter Period.

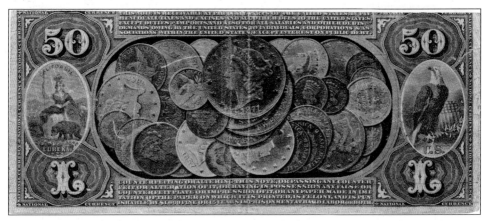

Back of F-1160 to F-1161f. A montage of contemporary gold coins.

No.	Date	Name of Bank	City	
F-1160	1870	First National Gold Bank	San Francisco	4 known
F-1160a	1875 (Series)	First National Gold Bank	San Francisco	Unique
F-1161	1874	Farmer's National Gold Bank	San Jose	Unique
F-1161a	1872	National Gold Bank and Trust Company	San Francisco	Unknown
F-1161b	1872	National Gold Bank of D.O. Mills and Co.	Sacramento	Unknown
F-1161c	1873	First National Gold Bank	Stockton	Unknown
F-1161d	1873	First National Gold Bank	Santa Barbara	Unknown
F-1161e	1874	First National Gold Bank	Petaluma	Unknown
F-1161f	1873	Union National Gold Bank	Oakland	Unknown

Silver Certificates
Series of 1878,
With Countersignatures

The face and back of the type of F-323 to F-324c (not shown) are similar to those of the following type.

No.	Countersignature	Payable At	
F-323	W.G. White or J.C. Hopper	New York	Unknown
F-324	T. Hillhouse	New York	2 known
F-324a	R.M. Anthony	San Francisco	Unique
F-324b	A.U. Wyman	Washington, DC	Unknown
F-324c	A.U. Wyman	Washington, DC	3 known

Note: All notes have signatures of Scofield and Gilfillan and large red seal. All have engraved countersignatures except for notes F-323 and 324b, which are autographed.

Silver Certificates
Series of 1880,
No Countersignatures

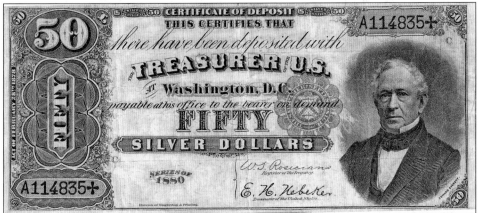

Face of F-325 to F-329. Bust of Edward Everett, orator and secretary of state from 1852 to 1855. F-328 and F-329 lack the large L (Roman numeral for 50) at bottom center.

Back of F-325 to F-329.

See next page for chart.

No.	Signatures		Seal	VG-8	F-12	VF-20	EF-40	Unc-63
F-325	Scofield	Gilfillan	Large brown, rays	Unique				
F-326	Bruce	Gilfillan	Large brown, rays	$20,000	$25,000	$40,000	$62,500	Rare
F-327	Bruce	Wyman	Large brown, rays	17,500	22,500	35,000	97,500	Rare
As above with large seal in center, no "L" or "Fifty"								
F-328	Rosecrans	Huston	Large brown, spikes	8,250	16,000	32,500	50,000	$85,000
As above, with small seal at right center								
F-329	Rosecrans	Nebeker	Small red	8,250	16,000	30,000	52,500	90,000

Silver Certificates
Series of 1891

Face of F-330 to F-335. Similar to the preceding.

Back of F-330 to F-335.

No.	Signatures		Seal	VG-8	F-12	VF-20	EF-40	Unc-63
F-330	Rosecrans	Nebeker	Small red	$7,500	$15,000	$20,000	$25,000	—
F-331	Tillman	Morgan	Small red	2,000	3,000	4,000	11,500	$35,000
F-332	Bruce	Roberts	Small red	1,750	2,750	4,000	10,000	—
F-333	Lyons	Roberts	Small red	1,750	2,750	4,000	10,500	30,000
F-334	Vernon	Treat	Small red	1,900	3,000	5,000	7,500	24,000
F-335	Parker	Burke	Blue	1,650	2,400	4,500	7,000	16,000

Treasury or Coin Notes
Series of 1891

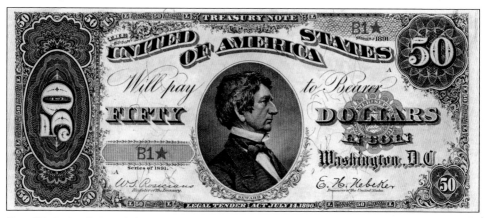

Face of F-376. Profile bust of William Seward, secretary of state from 1860 to 1869.

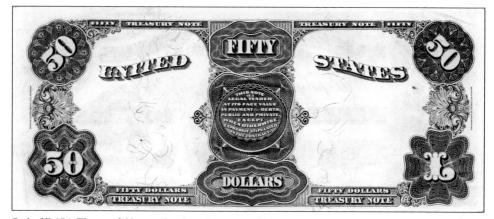

Back of F-376. The open fields were thought to deter counterfeiting.

No.	Signatures		Seal	VG-8	F-12	VF-20	EF-40	Unc-63
F-376	Rosecrans	Nebeker	Small red	$14,500	$38,500	$50,000	—	—

Gold Certificates
Series of 1913 and 1922

Face of F-1198 to F-1200a. Bust of President U.S. Grant.

Back of F-1198 to F-1200a.

No.	Series	Signatures		Seal	VG-8	F-12	VF-20	EF-40	Unc-63
F-1198	1913	Parker	Burke	Gold	$675	$850	$1,450	$2,500	$7,750
F-1199	1913	Teehee	Burke	Gold	575	700	1,100	2,300	7,500
F-1200	1922	Speelman	White	Gold	550	650	950	1,650	7,250
F-1200a	1922	Speelman	White	Gold, small serial nos.	650	725	1,150	1,875	7,750

Federal Reserve Notes
Series of 1914, Red Seal

Designs are identical to the following, except that the seal and serial numbers are red.

Friedberg Suffix Letters on Types F-1012A to F-1071

Red Seals—*"A" suffix:* Large district letter and numeral at top right and bottom left. Small letter at top left and bottom right. *B suffix:* As above, but with small district letter and numeral added above letter at top left. As a class Red Seals are scarcer than Blue Seals.

Blue Seals—*"A" suffix:* Large district letter and numeral at top left and bottom right. *B suffix:* Large letter and numeral at top right with small district letters and numerals in the other three corners.

No.	Issuing Bank	VG-8	F-12	VF-20	EF-40	Unc-63
Signatures of Burke and McAdoo						
F-1012A	Boston	$2,250	$3,500	$13,750	$22,000	—
F-1012B	Boston	2,100	2,875	6,500	13,000	—
F-1013A	New York	1,400	2,375	4,000	6,250	—
F-1013B	New York	1,400	2,375	4,000	6,250	$12,000
F-1014A	Philadelphia	1,400	2,375	4,000	6,250	12,000
F-1014B	Philadelphia	1,400	2,375	4,000	6,250	—
F-1015A	Cleveland	2,100	2,875	6,500	13,000	14,000
F-1015B	Cleveland	1,400	2,625	4,250	6,750	14,000
F-1016A	Richmond	1,450	2,625	4,250	6,750	—
F-1016B	Richmond	1,400	2,375	4,000	6,250	—
F-1017A	Atlanta	1,450	2,350	4,000	6,250	—
F-1018A	Chicago	2,100	2,875	6,500	13,000	—
F-1018B	Chicago	1,400	2,350	4,000	6,250	—
F-1019A	St. Louis	1,400	2,350	4,000	6,250	—
F-1019B	St. Louis	1,400	2,350	4,000	6,250	15,000
F-1020A	Minneapolis	2,100	3,250	4,250	6,750	—
F-1020B	Minneapolis	1,400	2,350	4,000	6,250	—
F-1021A	Kansas City	3,500	6,500	13,000	21,000	—
F-1021B	Kansas City	3,500	6,500	13,000	21,000	—
F-1022	Dallas	1,400	2,350	4,000	6,250	—
F-1023A	San Francisco	2,000	3,250	6,000	8,000	—
F-1023B	San Francisco	1,400	2,350	4,000	6,250	15,000

Federal Reserve Notes
Series of 1914, Blue Seal

Face of F-1024 to F-1071. Portrait of President U.S. Grant.

Back of F-1024 to F-1071. Female figure representing Panama on land between the Atlantic and Pacific Oceans.

See next page for chart.

No.	Issuing Bank	Signatures			VG-8	F-12	VF-20	EF-40	Unc-63
F-1024	Boston	Burke	McAdoo		$225	$300	$500	$1,100	$2,950
F-1025	Boston	Burke	Glass		225	300	500	1,200	2,500
F-1026	Boston	Burke	Houston		550	850	1,500	2,675	9,000
F-1027	Boston	White	Mellon		—	—	—	—	—
F-1028	New York	Burke	McAdoo		225	275	500	950	2,600
F-1029	New York	Burke	Glass		325	375	600	1,300	3,300
F-1030	New York	Burke	Houston		225	335	550	850	2,000
F-1031A	New York	White	Mellon		225	335	525	850	2,000
F-1031B	New York	White	Mellon		325	400	650	1,500	—
F-1032	Philadelphia	Burke	McAdoo		225	300	500	925	2,100
F-1033	Philadelphia	Burke	Glass		325	400	750	3,000	8,500
F-1034	Philadelphia	Burke	Houston		225	275	475	925	2,200
F-1035	Philadelphia	White	Mellon		225	275	475	1,100	2,200
F-1036	Cleveland	Burke	McAdoo		225	275	475	925	2,200
F-1037	Cleveland	Burke	Glass		325	400	875	2,500	5,500
F-1038	Cleveland	Burke	Houston		250	325	625	1,450	2,425
F-1039A	Cleveland	White	Mellon		225	300	500	900	2,750
F-1039B	Cleveland	White	Mellon		225	275	475	900	2,700
F-1040	Richmond	Burke	McAdoo		225	275	475	900	2,700
F-1041	Richmond	Burke	Glass		425	550	1,125	3,000	8,500
F-1042	Richmond	Burke	Houston		225	275	500	1,000	3,100
F-1043	Richmond	White	Mellon		225	275	500	1,000	3,250
F-1044	Atlanta	Burke	McAdoo		275	360	550	1,000	2,500
F-1045	Atlanta	Burke	Glass		1,875	3,625	6,500	16,250	—
F-1046	Atlanta	Burke	Houston		225	315	525	850	2,275
F-1047	Atlanta	White	Mellon		250	425	550	1,000	2,700
F-1048	Chicago	Burke	McAdoo		225	300	525	850	2,600
F-1049	Chicago	Burke	Glass		250	325	525	950	2,325
F-1050	Chicago	Burke	Houston		275	360	525	900	2,200
F-1051	Chicago	White	Mellon		225	300	500	1,100	2,100
F-1052	St. Louis	Burke	McAdoo		275	300	600	925	2,350
F-1053	St. Louis	Burke	Glass		375	425	700	1,125	2,700
F-1054	St. Louis	Burke	Houston		225	300	500	950	2,200
F-1055	St. Louis	White	Mellon	None reported					
F-1056	Minneapolis	Burke	McAdoo		300	375	600	975	2,850
F-1057	Minneapolis	Burke	Glass	None printed					
F-1058	Minneapolis	Burke	Houston		500	800	1,600	3,750	10,000
F-1059	Minneapolis	White	Mellon		1,750	3,250	6,250	—	—
F-1060	Kansas City	Burke	McAdoo		275	360	500	2,000	4,000
F-1061	Kansas City	Burke	Glass	None printed					
F-1062	Kansas City	Burke	Houston	None printed					
F-1063	Kansas City	White	Mellon	2 known					
F-1064	Dallas	Burke	McAdoo		325	400	675	1,600	3,000
F-1065	Dallas	Burke	Glass	None reported					
F-1066	Dallas	Burke	Houston	3 known					
F-1067	Dallas	White	Mellon	None reported					
F-1068	San Francisco	Burke	McAdoo		225	300	600	850	2,375
F-1069	San Francisco	Burke	Glass	None printed					
F-1070	San Francisco	Burke	Houston		225	325	500	1,100	4,000
F-1071	San Francisco	White	Mellon		225	325	500	1,100	4,000

Federal Reserve Bank Notes
Series of 1918

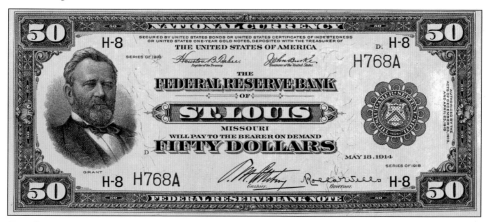

Face of F-831. Bust of President U.S. Grant. Issued only by the St. Louis bank.

Back of F-831. Female figure representing Panama on land between the Atlantic and Pacific Oceans.

No.	Issuing Bank	Series	Treasury Signatures	Bank Signatures	VG-8	F-12	VF-20	EF-40	Unc-63
F-831	St. Louis	1918	Teehee Burke	Attebery Wells	$3,750	$9,000	$12,000	$17,500	$33,000

SMALL-SIZE $50 NOTES
National Bank Notes
Series of 1929,
Type 1

Face of F-1803-1. Portrait of President U.S. Grant.

Back of F-1803-1. The United States Capitol in Washington, DC.

No.	VG-8	F-12	VF-20	EF-40	Unc-63
F-1803-1	$200	$250	$350	$475	$550

National Bank Notes
Series of 1929,
Type 2

Face of F-1803-2. As preceding with bank charter number also in brown at lower left and upper right of portrait. Back is same as preceding type.

No.	VG-8	F-12	VF-20	EF-40	Unc-63
F-1803-2	$225	$300	$400	$500	$700

Gold Certificates
Series of 1928,
Gold Seal

Face of F-2404. Portrait of President U.S. Grant.

Back of F-2404.

No.	Signatures		VG-8	F-12	VF-20	EF-40	Unc-63
F-2404	Woods	Mellon	$295	$325	$450	$1,000	$2,750
F-2404★	Woods	Mellon	1,950	2,750	4,250	9,500	14,000

Federal Reserve Bank Notes
Series of 1929,
Brown Seal

Face of F-1880. Similar to the National Bank Note. Back is same as preceding type.

No.	Issuing Bank	Quantity Printed	VG-8	F-12	VF-20	EF-40	Unc-63
F-1880B	New York	636,000	$80	$90	$115	$150	$350
F-1880D	Cleveland	684,000	80	90	115	135	350
F-1880G	Chicago	300,000	80	90	115	135	350
F-1880I	Minneapolis	132,000	85	95	125	150	400
F-1880J	Kansas City	276,000	80	90	115	140	350
F-1880K	Dallas	168,000	190	275	475	1,000	3,500
F-1880L	San Francisco	576,000	95	110	160	225	350
F-1880★	Most common districts		350	450	650	1,000	3,100

Federal Reserve Notes
Series of 1928 and 1928-A, Green Seal

Face of F-2100 to F-2101.

Back of F-2100 to F-2101.

Series of 1928—Signatures of Woods and Mellon

No.	Issuing Bank	Quantity Printed	VG-8	F-12	VF-20	EF-40	Unc-63
F-2100A	Boston	265,200	$125	$170	$250	$500	$2,750
F-2100A★	Boston		1,250	2,250	4,500	6,000	15,000
F-2100B	New York	1,351,800	80	100	175	250	825
F-2100B★	New York		150	225	475	575	1,900
F-2100C	Philadelphia	997,056	90	120	190	300	800
F-2100C★	Philadelphia		150	350	550	825	2,600
F-2100D	Cleveland	1,161,900	80	100	190	300	625
F-2100D★	Cleveland		150	350	550	825	2,500
F-2100E	Richmond	539,400	80	100	190	275	650
F-2100E★	Richmond		150	350	550	825	2,550
F-2100F	Atlanta	538,800	90	110	200	325	675
F-2100F★	Atlanta		150	350	550	850	2,550
F-2100G	Chicago	1,348,620	75	100	160	250	525
F-2100G★	Chicago		110	175	425	750	1,775
F-2100H	St. Louis	627,300	80	100	160	275	650
F-2100H★	St. Louis		150	350	525	750	2,200
F-2100I	Minneapolis	106,200	125	200	275	500	1,775
F-2100I★	Minneapolis		500	1,300	2,750	4,500	8,000
F-2100J	Kansas City	252,600	80	125	200	300	1,200
F-2100J★	Kansas City		275	525	650	1,300	2,600
F-2100K	Dallas	109,920	115	175	225	400	1,850
F-2100K★	Dallas		575	875	1,500	3,000	8,000
F-2100L	San Francisco	447,600	80	110	200	275	650
F-2100L★	San Francisco		200	300	525	750	2,525

Series of 1928-A—Signatures of Woods and Mellon

No.	Issuing Bank	Quantity Printed	VG-8	F-12	VF-20	EF-40	Unc-63
F-2101A	Boston	1,834,989	$65	$70	$90	$125	$375
F-2101B	New York	3,392,328	65	70	90	125	375
F-2101C	Philadelphia	3,078,944	65	70	90	125	375
F-2101D	Cleveland	2,453,364	65	70	90	125	375
F-2101E	Richmond	1,516,500	65	70	90	125	375
F-2101F	Atlanta	338,400	80	90	110	140	475
F-2101G	Chicago	5,263,956	65	70	90	125	375
F-2101H	St. Louis	880,500	65	70	85	125	375
F-2101I	Minneapolis	780,240	65	70	85	125	375
F-2101J	Kansas City	791,604	65	70	85	125	375
F-2101K	Dallas	701,496	65	70	85	125	375
F-2101L	San Francisco	1,522,620	65	70	85	125	375
F-2101★	Several Chicago stars known		900	1,000	4,750	10,000	12,500

Federal Reserve Notes
Series of 1934 to 1934-D, Green Seal

Face of F-2102 to F-2106, now with no mention of gold in payment.

Back of F-2102 to F-2106.

Series of 1934—Signatures of Julian and Morgenthau

No.	Issuing Bank	Quantity Printed	VG-8	F-12	VF-20	EF-40	Unc-63
F-2102A	Boston	2,729,400		$55	$65	$100	$235
F-2102A★	Boston		$90	100	150	190	800
F-2102B	New York	17,894,676		55	65	90	235
F-2102B★	New York		90	100	150	190	800
F-2102C	Philadelphia	5,833,200		55	65	90	235
F-2102C★	Philadelphia		90	125	150	190	800
F-2102D	Cleveland	8,817,720		55	65	90	235
F-2102D★	Cleveland		90	100	150	190	800
F-2102E	Richmond	4,826,628		55	65	90	235
F-2102E★	Richmond		90	125	150	225	800
F-2102F	Atlanta	3,069,348		55	65	90	235
F-2102F★	Atlanta		90	100	150	190	800
F-2102G	Chicago	8,675,940		55	65	90	235
F-2102G★	Chicago		90	100	150	190	800
F-2102H	St. Louis	1,497,144		55	65	90	235
F-2102H★	St. Louis		90	100	160	225	950
F-2102I	Minneapolis	539,700		60	70	100	275
F-2102I★	Minneapolis		110	130	200	300	1,000
F-2102J	Kansas City	1,133,520		60	70	100	235
F-2102J★	Kansas City		90	100	150	190	800
F-2102K	Dallas	1,194,876		55	65	90	235
F-2102K★	Dallas		90	100	200	300	1,000
F-2102L	San Francisco	8,101,200		55	65	90	235
F-2102L★	San Francisco		90	100	150	190	800

Note: The two shades of green seal also exist in this series. The lighter variety is slightly scarcer, with star notes much more scarce.

Series of 1934-A—Signatures of Julian and Morgenthau

No.	Issuing Bank	Quantity Printed	VG-8	F-12	VF-20	EF-40	Unc-63
F-2103A	Boston	406,200	$55	$80	$90	$115	$425
F-2103A★	Boston		125	175	375	575	1,500
F-2103B	New York	4,710,648	55	70	80	100	275
F-2103B★	New York		90	120	150	200	950
F-2103D	Cleveland	864,168	55	70	80	100	300
F-2103D★	Cleveland		150	225	425	650	1,300
F-2103E	Richmond	2,235,372	55	65	80	100	300
F-2103E★	Richmond		150	225	425	650	1,175
F-2103F	Atlanta	416,100	55	65	80	100	375
F-2103F★	Atlanta		150	225	400	625	1,250
F-2103G	Chicago	1,014,600	55	65	80	100	300
F-2103G★	Chicago		125	200	375	550	1,150

Chart continued on next page.

No.	Issuing Bank	Quantity Printed	VG-8	F-12	VF-20	EF-40	Unc-63
F-2103H	St. Louis	361,944	$55	$80	$95	$115	$375
F-2103H★	St. Louis		150	225	400	650	1,300
F-2103I	Minneapolis	93,300	55	80	95	115	500
F-2103I★	Minneapolis		150	225	400	650	1,300
F-2103J	Kansas City	189,300	55	80	95	115	500
F-2103J★	Kansas City		150	225	400	650	1,300
F-2103K	Dallas	266,700	55	80	95	115	375
F-2103K★	Dallas		150	225	400	650	1,300
F-2103L	San Francisco	162,000	55	80	95	115	375
F-2103L★	San Francisco		150	225	400	650	1,300

Series of 1934-B—Signatures of Julian and Vinson

No.	Issuing Bank	Quantity Printed	VF-20	EF-40	Unc-63
F-2104C	Philadelphia	509,100	$80	$140	$350
F-2104C★	Philadelphia		1,150	1,250	4,000
F-2104D	Cleveland	359,100	80	140	350
F-2104D★	Cleveland		950	1,250	4,000
F-2104E	Richmond	596,700	85	140	350
F-2104E★	Richmond		1,250	1,375	4,000
F-2104F	Atlanta	416,720	85	145	400
F-2104G	Chicago	306,000	80	140	400
F-2104H	St. Louis	306,000	85	145	400
F-2104I	Minneapolis	120,000	145	225	500
F-2104J	Kansas City	221,340	85	150	450
F-2104J★	Kansas City	2,500	950	1,250	4,000
F-2104K	Dallas	120,108	120	200	500
F-2104L	San Francisco	441,000	85	145	350

Series of 1934-C—Signatures of Julian and Snyder

No.	Issuing Bank	Quantity Printed	F-12	VF-20	EF-40	Unc-63
F-2105A	Boston	117,600	$90	$110	$145	$325
F-2105B	New York	1,556,400	75	90	115	250
F-2105B★	New York		225	400	650	1,500
F-2105C	Philadelphia	107,283	90	110	145	325
F-2105C★	Philadelphia		400	600	900	1,950
F-2105D	Cleveland	374,400	75	90	115	250
F-2105D★	Cleveland		225	400	700	1,500
F-2105E	Richmond	1,821,960	75	90	115	250
F-2105E★	Richmond		225	400	700	1,500
F-2105F	Atlanta	107,640	100	125	200	900
F-2105G	Chicago	294,432	75	90	115	250
F-2105G★	Chicago		225	400	650	1,500
F-2105H	St. Louis	535,200	75	90	115	250
F-2105H★	St. Louis		225	400	900	1,500
F-2105I	Minneapolis	118,800	90	110	145	325
F-2105I★	Minneapolis		250	425	700	1,500
F-2105J	Kansas City	303,600	75	90	115	250
F-2105K	Dallas	429,900	75	90	115	250
F-2105K★	Dallas		250	425	700	1,500

Series of 1934-D—Signatures of Clark and Snyder

No.	Issuing Bank	Quantity Printed	F-12	VF-20	EF-40	Unc-63
F-2106A	Boston	279,600	$85	$125	$145	$325
F-2106A★	Boston		600	1,000	1,400	3,500
F-2106B	New York	898,776	75	90	115	250
F-2106B★	New York		550	900	1,300	3,000
F-2106C	Philadelphia	699,000	75	90	115	250
F-2106C★	Philadelphia		600	1,000	1,400	3,250
F-2106E	Richmond	156,000	90	130	145	325
F-2106E★	Richmond		650	1,150	2,000	3,500
F-2106F	Atlanta	216,000	85	125	145	325
F-2106F★	Atlanta		600	1,000	1,400	3,500
F-2106G	Chicago	494,016	75	90	115	250
F-2106G★	Chicago		600	1,000	1,400	3,000
F-2106I	Minneapolis		375	600	—	—
F-2106K	Dallas	103,200	80	100	125	375

Federal Reserve Notes
Series of 1950 to 1950-E, Green Seal

Face of F-2107 to F-2112. Obligation at upper left in three lines instead of four, WASHINGTON moved to above Treasury seal. Back design is same as that used on all $50 notes through the 1950s.

Series of 1950—Signatures of Clark and Snyder

No.	Issuing Bank	Quantity Printed	VF-20	EF-40	Unc-63
F-2107A	Boston	1,248,000	$75	$120	$225
F-2107A★	Boston		175	325	1,000
F-2107B	New York	10,236,000	75	110	200
F-2107B★	New York		150	275	675
F-2107C	Philadelphia	2,352,000	75	110	200
F-2107C★	Philadelphia		250	450	1,200
F-2107D	Cleveland	6,180,000	75	110	200
F-2107D★	Cleveland		150	275	675
F-2107E	Richmond	5,064,000	75	110	200
F-2107E★	Richmond		175	350	775
F-2107F	Atlanta	1,812,000	75	110	200
F-2107F★	Atlanta		175	350	775
F-2107G	Chicago	4,212,000	75	110	200
F-2107G★	Chicago		150	275	675
F-2107H	St. Louis	892,000	75	110	200
F-2107H★	St. Louis		175	350	825
F-2107I	Minneapolis	384,000	95	150	475
F-2107I★	Minneapolis		550	1,000	3,500
F-2107J	Kansas City	696,000	75	110	200
F-2107J★	Kansas City		350	700	2,000
F-2107K	Dallas	1,100,000	75	110	200
F-2107K★	Dallas		150	275	675
F-2107L	San Francisco	3,996,000	75	110	200
F-2107L★	San Francisco		150	275	675

Series of 1950-A—Signatures of Priest and Humphrey

No.	Issuing Bank	Quantity Printed	VF-20	EF-40	Unc-63
F-2108A	Boston	720,000	$75	$125	$175
F-2108A★	Boston		115	200	425
F-2108B	New York	6,495,000	75	100	165
F-2108B★	New York		115	200	425
F-2108C	Philadelphia	1,728,000	75	100	165
F-2108C★	Philadelphia		115	200	425
F-2108D	Cleveland	1,872,000	75	100	165
F-2108D★	Cleveland		115	200	425
F-2108E	Richmond	2,016,000	75	100	165
F-2108E★	Richmond		115	200	425
F-2108F	Atlanta	288,000	90	125	225
F-2108F★	Atlanta		115	200	525
F-2108G	Chicago	2,016,000	75	100	165
F-2108G★	Chicago		115	200	425
F-2108H	St. Louis	576,000	85	110	200
F-2108H★	St. Louis		115	200	425
F-2108J	Kansas City	144,000	100	140	250
F-2108J★	Kansas City		115	200	425
F-2108K	Dallas	864,000	75	100	165
F-2108K★	Dallas		115	200	425
F-2108L	San Francisco	576,000	85	110	200
F-2108L★	San Francisco		115	200	425

Series of 1950-B—Signatures of Priest and Anderson

No.	Issuing Bank	Quantity Printed	VF-20	EF-40	Unc-63
F-2109A	Boston	864,000	$60	$95	$150
F-2109A★	Boston		100	140	400
F-2109B	New York	8,352,000	55	75	115
F-2109B★	New York		75	120	250
F-2109C	Philadelphia	2,592,000	60	80	125
F-2109C★	Philadelphia		100	140	400
F-2109D	Cleveland	1,728,000	60	80	125
F-2109D★	Cleveland		100	140	400
F-2109E	Richmond	1,584,000	60	80	125
F-2109E★	Richmond		110	175	500
F-2109G	Chicago	4,320,000	55	75	115
F-2109G★	Chicago		100	140	400
F-2109H	St. Louis	576,000	75	100	200
F-2109H★	St. Louis		110	175	500
F-2109J	Kansas City	1,008,000	65	85	175
F-2109J★	Kansas City		110	175	500
F-2109K	Dallas	1,008,000	65	85	175
F-2109K★	Dallas		110	175	500
F-2109L	San Francisco	1,872,000	60	80	125
F-2109L★	San Francisco		110	175	500

Series of 1950-C—Signatures of Smith and Dillon

No.	Issuing Bank	Quantity Printed	VF-20	EF-40	Unc-63
F-2110A	Boston	720,000	$60	$75	$120
F-2110A★	Boston		140	200	550
F-2110B	New York	5,328,000	60	75	120
F-2110B★	New York		125	180	500
F-2110C	Philadelphia	1,296,000	60	75	120
F-2110C★	Philadelphia		140	200	550
F-2110D	Cleveland	1,296,000	60	75	120
F-2110D★	Cleveland		125	180	500
F-2110E	Richmond	1,296,000	60	75	120
F-2110E★	Richmond		140	200	550
F-2110G	Chicago	1,728,000	60	75	120
F-2110G★	Chicago		125	180	500
F-2110H	St. Louis	576,000	60	75	120
F-2110H★	St. Louis		125	180	500
F-2110I	Minneapolis	144,000	70	100	250
F-2110I★	Minneapolis		225	400	1,250
F-2110J	Kansas City	432,000	70	100	250
F-2110J★	Kansas City		140	200	550
F-2110K	Dallas	720,000	60	75	120
F-2110K★	Dallas		140	200	550
F-2110L	San Francisco	1,152,000	60	75	120
F-2110L★	San Francisco		125	200	550

Series of 1950-D—Signatures of Granahan and Dillon

No.	Issuing Bank	Quantity Printed	VF-20	EF-40	Unc-63
F-2111A	Boston	1,728,000	$65	$90	$200
F-2111A★	Boston		100	160	550
F-2111B	New York	7,200,000	60	80	130
F-2111B★	New York		100	160	450
F-2111C	Philadelphia	2,736,000	60	80	130
F-2111C★	Philadelphia		100	160	450
F-2111D	Cleveland	28,125,000	60	80	110
F-2111D★	Cleveland		100	160	400
F-2111E	Richmond	2,616,000	60	80	110
F-2111E★	Richmond		100	160	450
F-2111F	Atlanta	576,000	60	80	110
F-2111F★	Atlanta		125	225	500
F-2111G	Chicago	4,176,000	60	80	110
F-2111G★	Chicago		100	160	400
F-2111H	St. Louis	1,440,000	60	80	130
F-2111H★	St. Louis		100	160	400
F-2111I	Minneapolis	288,000	75	110	200
F-2111I★	Minneapolis		150	225	900
F-2111J	Kansas City	720,000	60	80	130
F-2111J★	Kansas City		100	160	400
F-2111K	Dallas	1,296,000	75	100	275
F-2111K★	Dallas		150	225	850
F-2111L	San Francisco	2,160,000	70	110	200
F-2111L★	San Francisco		100	160	400

Series of 1950-E—Signatures of Granahan and Fowler

No.	Issuing Bank	Quantity Printed	VF-20	EF-40	Unc-63
F-2112B	New York	3,024,000	$125	$150	$275
F-2112B★	New York		325	450	1,200
F-2112G	Chicago	1,008,000	130	175	450
F-2112G★	Chicago		550	875	2,100
F-2112L	San Francisco	1,296,000	125	165	350
F-2112L★	San Francisco		375	575	1,250

Federal Reserve Notes
Series of 1963-A,
Green Seal, Motto Added

Face of F-2113 to F-2125. The Treasury seal was modernized commencing with F-2114.

Back of F-2113 to F-2125. The motto IN GOD WE TRUST is added.

No.	Issuing Bank	Quantity Printed	VF-20	EF-40	Unc-63
Signatures of Granahan and Fowler					
F-2113A	Boston	1,536,000		$90	$125
F-2113A★	Boston	320,000	$125	165	325
F-2113B	New York	11,008,000		80	110
F-2113B★	New York	1,408,000	90	125	225
F-2113C	Philadelphia	3,328,000		85	145
F-2113C★	Philadelphia	704,000	100	145	300
F-2113D	Cleveland	3,584,000		80	110
F-2113D★	Cleveland	256,000	100	160	300
F-2113E	Richmond	3,072,000		85	145
F-2113E★	Richmond	704,000	100	145	300
F-2113F	Atlanta	768,000		90	200
F-2113F★	Atlanta	384,000	110	175	300
F-2113G	Chicago	6,912,000		80	140
F-2113G★	Chicago	768,000	90	125	225
F-2113H	St. Louis	512,000		90	165
F-2113H★	St. Louis	128,000	100	160	325
F-2113I	Minneapolis	512,000		85	210
F-2113I★	Minneapolis	128,000	110	175	450
F-2113J	Kansas City	512,000		90	165
F-2113J★	Kansas City	64,000	100	160	325
F-2113K	Dallas	1,536,000		85	140
F-2113K★	Dallas	128,000	125	180	500
F-2113L	San Francisco	4,352,000		80	120
F-2113L★	San Francisco	704,000	100	150	275

Federal Reserve Notes
Series of 1969 to 1993, Green Seal

Series of 1969 (with new Treasury seal)—Signatures of Elston and Kennedy

No.	Issuing Bank	Quantity Printed	VF-20	EF-40	Unc-63
F-2114A	Boston	2,048,000		$75	$175
F-2114B	New York	12,032,000		60	125
F-2114B★	New York	384,000	$75	100	225
F-2114C	Philadelphia	3,584,000		65	150
F-2114C★	Philadelphia	128,000	75	100	225
F-2114D	Cleveland	3,584,000		65	125
F-2114D★	Cleveland	192,000	85	125	250
F-2114E	Richmond	2,560,000		65	150
F-2114E★	Richmond	64,000	120	145	375
F-2114F	Atlanta	256,000		80	200
F-2114G	Chicago	9,728,000		60	125
F-2114G★	Chicago	256,000	75	100	225
F-2114H	St. Louis	256,000		80	200
F-2114I	Minneapolis	512,000		75	175
F-2114J	Kansas City	1,280,000		65	150
F-2114J★	Kansas City	64,000	140	165	450
F-2114K	Dallas	1,536,000		65	150
F-2114K★	Dallas	64,000	140	165	450
F-2114L	San Francisco	6,912,000		60	125
F-2114L★	San Francisco	256,000	120	145	275

Series of 1969-A—Signatures of Kabis and Connally

No.	Issuing Bank	Quantity Printed	VF-20	Unc-63	No.	Issuing Bank	Quantity Printed	VF-20	Unc-63
F-2115A	Boston	1,536,000		$135	F-2115G	Chicago	3,584,000		$115
F-2115A★	Boston	128,000		225	F-2115G★	Chicago	192,000		225
F-2115B	New York	9,728,000		115	F-2115H	St. Louis	256,000		175
F-2115B★	New York	704,000		225	F-2115I	Minneapolis	512,000		150
F-2115C	Philadelphia	2,560,000		115	F-2115J	Kansas City	256,000		175
F-2115D	Cleveland	2,816,000		115	F-2115K	Dallas	1,024,000		115
F-2115E	Richmond	2,304,000		115	F-2115K★	Dallas	64,000	$100	500
F-2115E★	Richmond	64,000	$100	500	F-2115L	San Francisco	5,120,000		115
F-2115F	Atlanta	256,000		175	F-2115L★	San Francisco	256,000	80	300
F-2115F★	Atlanta	64,000	110	500					

Series of 1969-B—Signatures of Banuelos and Connally

No.	Issuing Bank	Quantity Printed	VF-20	Unc-63	No.	Issuing Bank	Quantity Printed	VF-20	Unc-63
F-2116A	Boston	1,024,000	$250	$1,100	F-2116F	Atlanta	512,000	$350	$1,250
F-2116B	New York	2,560,000	225	900	F-2116G	Chicago	1,024,000	250	1,100
F-2116C	Philadelphia	2,048,000	225	900	F-2116K	Dallas	1,024,000	250	1,100
F★2116E	Richmond	1,536,000	250	1,100	F-2116K★	Dallas	128,000	850	2,250

Series of 1969-C—Signatures of Banuelos and Shultz

No.	Issuing Bank	Quantity Printed	Unc-63	No.	Issuing Bank	Quantity Printed	Unc-63
F-2117A	Boston	1,792,000	$110	F-2117G	Chicago	6,784,000	$90
F-2117A★	Boston	64,000	375	F-2117G★	Chicago	576,000	200
F-2117B	New York	7,040,000	90	F-2117H	St. Louis	2,688,000	100
F-2117B★	New York	192,000	275	F-2117H★	St. Louis	64,000	375
F-2117C	Philadelphia	3,584,000	100	F-2117I	Minneapolis	256,000	145
F-2117C★	Philadelphia	256,000	275	F-2117I★	Minneapolis	64,000	375
F-2117D	Cleveland	5,120,000	100	F-2117J	Kansas City	1,280,000	125
F-2117D★	Cleveland	192,000	250	F-2117J★	Kansas City	128,000	325
F-2117E	Richmond	2,304,000	100	F-2117K	Dallas	3,456,000	125
F-2117E★	Richmond	64,000	375	F-2117K★	Dallas	64,000	375
F-2117F	Atlanta	256,000	125	F-2117L	San Francisco	4,608,000	100
F-2117F★	Atlanta	64,000	300	F-2117L★	San Francisco	256,000	325

Series of 1974—Signatures of Neff and Simon

No.	Issuing Bank	Quantity Printed	Unc-63	No.	Issuing Bank	Quantity Printed	Unc-63
F-2118A	Boston	3,840,000	$125	F-2118G	Chicago	30,720,000	$80
F-2118A★	Boston	256,000	225	F-2118G★	Chicago	1,536,000	175
F-2118B	New York	38,400,000	100	F-2118H	St. Louis	1,920,000	165
F-2118B★	New York	768,000	175	F-2118H★	St. Louis	128,000	300
F-2118C	Philadelphia	7,040,000	125	F-2118I	Minneapolis	3,200,000	150
F-2118C★	Philadelphia	192,000	275	F-2118I★	Minneapolis	192,000	325
F-2118D	Cleveland	21,200,000	100	F-2118J	Kansas City	4,480,000	125
F-2118D★	Cleveland	640,000	200	F-2118J★	Kansas City	192,000	325
F-2118E	Richmond	14,080,000	125	F-2118K	Dallas	8,320,000	150
F-2118E★	Richmond	576,000	200	F-2118K★	Dallas	128,000	325
F-2118F	Atlanta	1,280,000	125	F-2118L	San Francisco	7,378,000	150
F-2118F★	Atlanta	640,000	250	F-2118L★	San Francisco	64,000	400

Series of 1977—Signatures of Morton and Blumenthal

No.	Issuing Bank	Quantity Printed	Unc-63	No.	Issuing Bank	Quantity Printed	Unc-63
F-2119A	Boston	16,400,000	$100	F-2119G	Chicago	47,360,000	$80
F-2119A★	Boston	1,088,000	200	F-2119G★	Chicago	2,304,000	200
F-2119B	New York	49,920,000	80	F-2119H	St. Louis	3,840,000	125
F-2119B★	New York	2,112,000	165	F-2119H★	St. Louis	512,000	225
F-2119C	Philadelphia	5,120,000	80	F-2119I	Minneapolis	3,840,000	115
F-2119C★	Philadelphia	128,000	250	F-2119I★	Minneapolis	128,000	275
F-2119D	Cleveland	23,040,000	80	F-2119J	Kansas City	7,680,000	110
F-2119D★	Cleveland	1,024,000	200	F-2119J★	Kansas City	256,000	250
F-2119E	Richmond	19,200,000	80	F-2119K	Dallas	14,080,000	125
F-2119E★	Richmond	896,000	200	F-2119K★	Dallas	576,000	225
F-2119F	Atlanta	2,560,000	80	F-2119L	San Francisco	19,200,000	80
F-2119F★	Atlanta	128,000	200	F-2119L★	San Francisco	768,000	200

Series of 1981—Signatures of Buchanan and Regan

No.	Issuing Bank	Quantity Printed	Unc-63	No.	Issuing Bank	Quantity Printed	Unc-63
F-2120A	Boston	18,560,000	$135	F-2120G★	Chicago	128,000	$275
F-2120B	New York	78,080,000	135	F-2120H	St. Louis	4,480,000	160
F-2120B★	New York	768,000	250	F-2120I	Minneapolis	5,760,000	150
F-2120C	Philadelphia	1,280,000	135	F-2120I★	Minneapolis	128,000	325
F-2120D	Cleveland	28,160,000	135	F-2120J	Kansas City	18,560,000	135
F-2120D★	Cleveland	256,000	275	F-2120J★	Kansas City	128,000	300
F-2120E	Richmond	25,600,000	150	F-2120K	Dallas	19,840,000	135
F-2120F	Atlanta	4,480,000	160	F-2120L	San Francisco	35,200,000	135
F-2120F★	Atlanta	768,000	250	F-2120L★	San Francisco	256,000	250
F-2120G	Chicago	67,200,000	135				

Series of 1981-A—Signatures of Ortega and Regan

No.	Issuing Bank	Quantity Printed	Unc-63	No.	Issuing Bank	Quantity Printed	Unc-63
F-2121A	Boston	9,600,000	$135	F-2121G	Chicago	28,800,000	$115
F-2121B	New York	28,800,000	115	F-2121H	St. Louis	3,200,000	140★
F-2121B★	New York	3,200,000	250	F-2121I	Minneapolis	3,200,000	140
F-2121D	Cleveland	12,800,000	125	F-2121J	Kansas City	6,400,000	130
F-2121E	Richmond	12,800,000	125	F-2121K	Dallas	6,400,000	130
F-2121E★	Richmond	704,000	400	F-2121L	San Francisco	22,400,000	120
F-2121F	Atlanta	3,200,000	150	F-2121L★	San Francisco	640,000	250

Series of 1985—Signatures of Ortega and Baker

No.	Issuing Bank	Quantity Printed	Unc-63	No.	Issuing Bank	Quantity Printed	Unc-63
F-2122A	Boston	51,200,000	$90	F-2122F	Atlanta	9,600,000	$90
F-2122A★	Boston	64,000	375	F-2122G	Chicago	112,000,000	90
F-2122B	New York	182,400,000	90	F-2122G★	Chicago	1,280,000	250
F-2122B★	New York	1,408,000	225	F-2122H	St. Louis	6,400,000	90
F-2122C	Philadelphia	3,200,000	90	F-2122I	Minneapolis	12,800,000	90
F-2122D	Cleveland	57,600,000	90	F-2122J	Kansas City	9,600,000	90
F-2122D★	Cleveland	64,000	375	F-2122K	Dallas	25,600,000	90
F-2122E	Richmond	54,400,000	90	F-2122L	San Francisco	57,600,000	90

Series of 1988—Signatures of Ortega and Brady

No.	Issuing Bank	Quantity Printed	Unc-63	No.	Issuing Bank	Quantity Printed	Unc-63
F-2123A	Boston	9,600,000	$125	F-2123E	Richmond	12,800,000	$125
F-2123B	New York	214,400,000	100	F-2123G	Chicago	80,000,000	100
F-2123B★	New York	1,408,000	250	F-2123J	Kansas City	6,400,000	125
F-2123D	Cleveland	32,000,000	125	F-2123L	San Francisco	12,800,000	125

Series of 1988-A

None printed.

Series of 1990—Signatures of Villalpando and Brady

No.	Issuing Bank	Quantity Printed	Unc-63	No.	Issuing Bank	Quantity Printed	Unc-63
F-2124A	Boston	28,800,000	$85	F-2124G★	Chicago	1,032,000	$110
F-2124B	New York	232,000,000	85	F-2124H	St. Louis	16,000,000	85
F-2124B★	New York	3,116,000	125	F-2124I	Minneapolis	22,400,000	85
F-2124C	Philadelphia	41,600,000	85	F-2124J	Kansas City	35,200,000	85
F-2124C★	Philadelphia	1,280,000	125	F-2124J★	Kansas City	640,000	150
F-2124D	Cleveland	92,800,000	85	F-2124K	Dallas	16,000,000	85
F-2124E	Richmond	76,800,000	85	F-2124L	San Francisco	119,200,000	85
F-2124G	Chicago	108,800,000	85				

Series of 1993—Signatures of Withrow and Bentsen

No.	Issuing Bank	Quantity Printed	Unc-63	No.	Issuing Bank	Quantity Printed	Unc-63
F-2125A	Boston	41,600,000	$85	F-2125G	Chicago	144,000,000	$85
F-2125B	New York	544,000,000	85	F-2125G★	Chicago	1,280,000	100
F-2125B★	New York	4,224,000	100	F-2125H	St. Louis	3,200,000	85
F-2125D	Cleveland	60,800,000	85	F-2125J	Kansas City	12,800,000	85
F-2125D★	Cleveland	1,280,000	125	F-2125K	Dallas	9,600,000	85
F-2125E	Richmond	35,200,000	85				

Federal Reserve Notes
Series of 1996 to 2001,
Green Seal, Security Features

Face of F-2126 to F-2127. Grant's portrait is modified as are other aspects, and security features have been added.

Back of F-2126 to F-2127. The Capitol motif has been revised and certain other features modified.

Series of 1996—Signatures of Withrow and Rubin
Printed in Washington, DC

No.	Issuing Bank	Quantity Printed	Unc-63	No.	Issuing Bank	Quantity Printed	Unc-63
F-2126A	Boston	54,400,000	$75	F-2126G★	Chicago	1,280,000	$100
F-2126B	New York	560,800,000	70	F-2126H	St. Louis	28,800,000	70
F-2126B★	New York	5,120,000	100	F-2126I	Minneapolis	35,200,000	70
F-2126C	Philadelphia	76,800,000	70	F-2126J	Kansas City	57,600,000	70
F-2126D	Cleveland	119,200,000	70	F-2126J★	Kansas City	1,920,000	100
F-2126E	Richmond	106,400,000	70	F-2126K	Dallas	92,800,000	70
F-2126F	Atlanta	119,200,000	70	F-2126L	San Francisco	219,200,000	70
F-2126G	Chicago	241,600,000	70	F-2126L★	San Francisco	3,200,000	100

Series of 1999—Signatures of Withrow and Summers
None printed.

Series of 2001—Signatures of Marin and O'Neill
Printed in Washington, DC

No.	Issuing Bank	Quantity Printed	Unc-63	No.	Issuing Bank	Quantity Printed	Unc-63
F-2127A	Boston	6,400,000	$70	F-2127F	Atlanta	22,800,000	$70
F-2127B	New York	54,400,000	70	F-2127G	Chicago	35,200,000	70
F-2127B★	New York	320,000	300	F-2127H	St. Louis	3,200,000	80
F-2127C	Philadelphia	19,200,000	70	F-2127I	Minneapolis	3,200,000	80
F-2127D	Cleveland	16,000,000	70	F-2127J	Kansas City	3,200,000	80
F-2127E	Richmond	32,000,000	70	F-2127K	Dallas	6,400,000	70
F-2127E★	Richmond	64,000	175	F-2127L	San Francisco	32,000,000	70

Federal Reserve Notes
Series of 2004 to Date,
Green Seal, Additional Features

Face of F-2128 to date, similar in style to the preceding, but with color and other security features added with a star to the lower right of the portrait.

Back of F-2128 to date, similar in style to the preceding, but with the background of the Capitol revised and now with tiny yellow "50" numbers and other security features added.

See next page for chart.

Series of 2004 (color added)—Signatures of Marin and Snow

Printed at the Western Facility (Fort Worth, Texas)

No.	Issuing Bank	Quantity Printed	Unc-63	No.	Issuing Bank	Quantity Printed	Unc-63
F-2128A	Boston	9,600,000	$65	F-2128G★	Chicago	3,200,000	$90
F-2128B	New York	41,600,000	65	F-2128H	St. Louis	9,600,000	65
F-2128C	Philadelphia	22,400,000	65	F-2128I	Minneapolis	12,800,000	65
F-2128D	Cleveland	32,000,000	65	F-2128J	Kansas City	22,400,000	65
F-2128E	Richmond	32,000,000	65	F-2128K	Dallas	32,000,000	65
F-2128E★	Richmond	800,000	150	F-2128K★	Dallas	3,200,000	110
F-2128F	Atlanta	44,800,000	65	F-2128L	San Francisco	51,200,000	65
F-2128G	Chicago	115,200,000	65				

Series of 2004-A—Signatures of Cabral and Snow

Printed at the Western Facility (Fort Worth, Texas)

No.	Issuing Bank	Unc-63	No.	Issuing Bank	Unc-63
F-2129A	Boston	$65	F-2129F	Atlanta	$65
F-2129B	New York	65	F-2129G	Chicago	65
F-2129B★	New York	500	F-2129J	Kansas City	65
F-2129E	Richmond	65	F-2129L	San Francisco	65
F-2129E★	Richmond	80			

Series of 2006—Signatures of Cabral and Paulson

Printed at the Western Facility (Fort Worth, Texas)

No.	Issuing Bank	Unc-63	No.	Issuing Bank	Unc-63
F-2130A	Boston	Current	F-2130G	Chicago	Current
F-2130A★	Boston	Current	F-2130G★	Chicago	Current
F-2130B	New York	Current	F-2130H	St. Louis	Current
F-2130C	Philadelphia	Current	F-2130I	Minneapolis	Current
F-2130D	Cleveland	Current	F-2130J	Kansas City	Current
F-2130E	Richmond	Current	F-2130K	Dallas	Current
F-2130F	Atlanta	Current	F-2130L	San Francisco	Current

COLLECTING $100 NOTES

Hundred-dollar notes are probably the one denomination of American currency more popular outside the United States than within it. It has been reported to Congress that two-thirds of all $100 notes outstanding are held abroad; it has been the currency of choice in many countries suffering economic and political upheaval. Only recently, with the success of the Euro and €200 and €500 notes (roughly $300 and $750 as this book went to press) competing against a declining and less-respected dollar, has a rival been found to the greenback as the world's reserve currency.

Large-Size Notes

$100 Interest-Bearing Notes, Large-Size. There were four issues of this denomination, two of them unknown, the other two extremely rare.

$100 Legal Tender Notes (United States Notes), Large-Size. This series mirrors the $50 issues' pattern. The first type, F-165–F-167b, is also the first to feature the American eagle. Were this design used on a lower denomination, it would be the equal of any note in popularity among collectors. As it is, there is probably a sufficient supply for those who can afford to collect them, with 22 known for No. F-167a and about a dozen each for F-165 and F-165a. When F-167a was last sold in uncirculated quality, it went for $184,000.

The Series of 1869 Legal Tender Notes existing today number over two dozen and are offered at auctions usually a couple of times a year. The series from 1875, 1878, and 1880 continue the same basic face design with variations similar to those of the lower denominations. There are only two known of F-175. The most common is F-181, of which we can find more than 40.

$100 Compound Interest Treasury Notes, Large-Size. There are three varieties of this type. Two are known of the first (F-193), which last sold for $74,750 in 2006. Friedberg-193a is unique and sold for $126,500 in 2005, while F-193b is the "common" variety—there are a dozen of those and you can expect to pay in the mid to high five-figure range for one.

$100 National Bank Notes, Large-Size. During the First Charter Period, these were usually printed at the bottom of a sheet with three $50 notes, and infrequently on a two-subject sheet as $50-$100 or $100-$100. This makes them even more scarce than the $50 issues. The vignette on the back, Trumbull's "The Signing of the Declaration of Independence," is found today on the $2 Federal Reserve Note.

The $100 Series of 1882 Second Charter Period Brown Backs was printed as the lower half of a two-subject sheet with the $50 on top, so the two denominations are of equivalent rarity. The Date Backs are the most common of the Second Charter issues, and even these are scarce. The $100 Value Back was issued by the same two banks in New Orleans and Dayton (Ohio) that issued the $50 Value Back, and is a great rarity.

The Third Charter Period Red Seal notes also were from the bottom half of a two-subject sheet with a $50 on top, so there is little difference between the two except for their face value. Although their prices are similar, Date Backs were issued by at least 240 more banks than were Plain Backs. These are more scarce than the corresponding $50 notes.

$100 National Gold Bank Notes, Large-Size. Notes are unknown from three of the nine banks said to have issued them, and notes from two banks are unique. These two, undoubtedly, are six-figure notes today.

$100 Silver Certificates, Large-Size. Early issues of the $100 Silver Certificate are all extremely rare at a minimum. The older 1880 issues, from F-340–F-342 and those of 1891 (F-343–F-344), while not common by any means, are found with regularity in the upper levels of the auction world.

$100 Treasury or Coin Notes, Large-Size. The Treasury Note or Coin Note of 1890 is the "Watermelon Note," one of the most famous and eagerly sought-after issues of them all. On the face is Civil War hero David G. Farragut, the U.S. Navy's first admiral. There are 34 recorded of this issue, against a dozen of Series of 1891, yet the Watermelon's popularity brings the price of the two issues within reach of each other.

$100 Gold Certificates, Large-Size. Gold Certificates issued under the Act of 1863 are extreme rarities today. Varieties include issues bearing the dates 1863, 1870, 1871, and 1875. The Series of 1882 and 1922 Gold Certificates were made with the usual different Treasury seals and signature combinations. The last issue, F-1215, is by far the one most frequently offered for sale. The vast majority of these were redeemed in compliance with Roosevelt's gold recall.

$100 Federal Reserve Notes, Large-Size. The profile bust of Benjamin Franklin on these issues has captured the fancy of many collectors for its attractiveness compared to the portrait we are used to. Blue Seals, especially, are available (for a price!) to those wishing to see for themselves. There are now more than 1,000 serial numbers recorded for the various banks and signature combinations.

Small-Size Notes

All have the portrait of Benjamin Franklin on the face and Philadelphia's Independence Hall on the back.

$100 National Bank Notes, Small-Size. These are similar to the other denominations except for the fact that banks in fewer than 18 states issued notes of the Type 2 variety. In low condition, Type 1 notes are eminently affordable.

$100 Gold Certificates, Small-Size. Small-size Gold Certificates were printed for the Series of 1928 and 1934, though the last was never meant to be released to the public. It was printed (along with similar $1,000, $10,000, and $100,000 notes) for Federal Reserve banks and was to be used only to facilitate internal transactions. Instead of green, it had an orange-gold back similar to the large size Gold Certificates. The Series of 1928 notes with Woods-Mellon signatures are still easy to find.

$100 Federal Reserve Bank Notes, Small-Size. No notes were printed for the Boston, Philadelphia, Atlanta, St. Louis, or San Francisco districts. Star notes for Minneapolis and Dallas are rare.

$100 Legal Tender Notes, Small-Size. These were issued for the Series of 1966 and 1966-A to comply with the 1878 statutory requirement (since eliminated by Congress) that the face value of this category of notes outstanding be $346,681,016. Many were kept in a room at the Treasury to comply with the law, but a sufficient quantity is still available for collectors.

$100 Federal Reserve Notes, Small-Size. Today, these are the highest-denomination bills produced. It is now thought that having notes of higher denominations in circulation would encourage illicit cash transactions.

The $100 note was the first to undergo security design revisions. The evolution of the note we see today began with the Series of 1990, when a plastic security strip was added to the paper and microprinting was put in the frame around the portrait. Then, in 1996, Franklin's portrait was enlarged and other security modifications were made, including the addition of a watermark, additional microprinting, and color-shifting ink. The Bureau of Engraving and Printing has announced that this will be the next note to be redesigned.

LARGE-SIZE $100 NOTES

Interest-Bearing Notes of March 3, 1863, 5%, 1 Year

Face of F-199. *"The Guardian" at lower left, Washington at center, Justice with shield at lower right. Overprinted with issue date, March 25, 1864.*

Back of F-199.

No.	Signatures		Seal	
F-199	Chittenden	Spinner	Red	3 known

Interest-Bearing Notes of March 3, 1863, 5%, 2 Years

Face of F-204. Vignette of a farmer and mechanic at lower left, Treasury Building at top center, and soldiers firing a cannon at lower right. Issued without and with attached coupons.

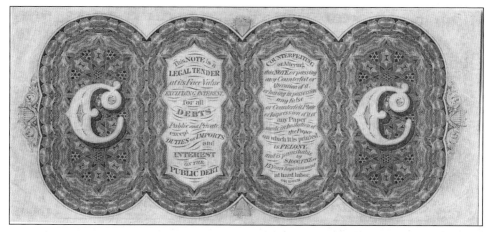

Back of F-204.

No.	Signatures		Seal	
F-204	Chittenden	Spinner	Red	2 known

Interest-Bearing Notes of June 30, 1864, 7.3%, 3 Years

Face of F-212a. Portrait of General Winfield Scott. Printed date of August 15, 1864.

Back of F-212a.

No.	Signatures		Seal	
F-212a	Colby	Spinner	Red	3 known

Interest-Bearing Notes of March 3, 1865, 7.3%, 3 Years

Face of F-212e. Portrait of General Winfield Scott, known as "Old Fuss and Feathers."

Back of F-212e.

No.	Signatures		Seal	
F-212e	Colby	Spinner	Red	3 known

Legal Tender Notes
Series of 1862,
First Obligation

Face of F-165 and F-165a.

Back of F-165 and F-165a with First Obligation.

No.	Signatures		Seal	VG-8	F-12	VF-20	EF-40	Unc-63
American Bank Note Co. monogram in upper left								
F-165	Chittenden	Spinner	Red	$15,000	$26,250	$42,500	$65,000	—
As above, no ABNCO monogram								
F-165a	Chittenden	Spinner	Red	15,000	26,250	42,500	65,000	—

Legal Tender Notes
Series of 1862 and 1863,
Second Obligation

Face of F-167 to F-167b.

Back of F-167 to F-167b.

No.	Signatures		Seal		VG-8	F-12	VF-20	EF-40	Unc-63
National Bank Note Co. and American Bank Note Co. printed at top									
F-167	Chittenden	Spinner	Red, one serial no.	2 known					
As above, without NBNCO and ABNCO									
F-167a	Chittenden	Spinner	Red, two serial nos.		$15,000	$26,250	$42,500	$65,000	—
F-167b	Chittenden	Spinner	Red, one serial no.	2 known					

Legal Tender Notes
Series of 1869

Face of F-168. Portrait of Lincoln at left, small vignette of woman's head at bottom center, allegory of "Reconstruction" at right. The star at the serial number is decorative.

Back of F-168.

No.	Signatures		Seal	VG-8	F-12	VF-20	EF-40	Unc-63
F-168	Allison	Spinner	Large red	$10,000	$20,000	$30,000	$55,000	$125,000

Legal Tender Notes
Series of 1875 to 1880

Face of F-169 to F-182. Vignettes similar to the preceding. With UNITED STATES NOTE at bottom border. The light pink floral design above UNITED STATES is on F-169 to F-171. Black ink is on F-172 to F-182.

Back of F-169 to F-182. There are minor differences in the imprints of manufacture.

No.	Series	Signatures		Seal		VG-8	F-12	VF-20	EF-40	Unc-63
F-169	1875	Allison	New	Small red, rays (Series A)		$8,500	$20,000	$33,500	$47,500	$65,000
F-170	1875	Allison	Wyman	Small red, rays		9,500	19,500	33,000	45,000	65,000
F-171	1878	Allison	Gilfillan	Small red, rays		8,000	16,500	32,500	42,500	—
Face as above but with black floral design at top										
F-172	1880	Bruce	Gilfillan	Large brown		6,750	12,500	25,000	37,500	90,000
F-173	1880	Bruce	Wyman	Large brown		6,750	16,500	26,250	42,500	75,000
F-174	1880	Rosecrans	Jordan	Large red, plain		6,750	13,000	26,250	35,000	70,000
F-175	1880	Rosecrans	Hyatt	Large red, plain	Very rare					
F-176	1880	Rosecrans	Hyatt	Large red, spiked		6,500	13,000	26,250	47,500	65,000
F-177	1880	Rosecrans	Huston	Large red, spiked		6,500	11,250	23,500	40,000	65,000
F-178	1880	Rosecrans	Huston	Large brown		6,500	11,250	23,500	42,500	65,000
F-179	1880	Tillman	Morgan	Small red, scalloped		8,500	13,000	22,500	32,500	75,000
F-180	1880	Bruce	Roberts	Small red, scalloped		8,500	12,500	21,500	30,000	50,000
F-181	1880	Lyons	Roberts	Small red, scalloped		5,625	7,500	13,500	27,500	40,000
F-182	1880	Napier	McClung	Small red, scalloped	Unknown					

Compound Interest Treasury Notes of 1863 and 1864

Face of F-193 to F-193b. Vignette of "The Guardian" at left, George Washington standing at center, and Justice seated at right. The overprint date refers to the date from which calculation of interest started.

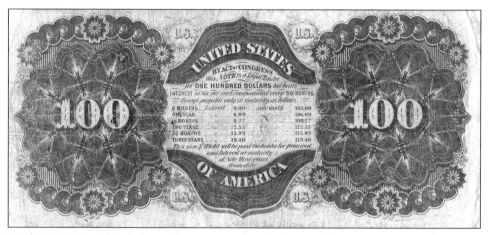

Back of F-193 to F-193b.

No.	Act	Overprint Date	Signatures		Seal	VG-8	F-12	VF-20
F-193	1863	June 10, 1864	Chittenden	Spinner	Red			2 known
F-193a	1864	July 15, 1864	Chittenden	Spinner	Red			1 known
F-193b	1864	Aug. 15, 1864–Sep. 1, 1865	Colby	Spinner	Red	$500,000	—	—

National Bank Notes
Original Series
("First Charter Period")

Face of F-452 to F-455. The "Battle of Lake Erie" vignette is to the left; at right is a winged Liberty seated with fasces.

Back of F-452 to F-455. "Signing of the Declaration of Independence," by John Trumbull.

No.	Series	Signatures		Seal		VG-8	F-12	VF-20
F-452	Original	Chittenden	Spinner	Red, rays	Rare			
F-454	Original	Colby	Spinner	Red, rays		$17,500	$24,000	$30,000
F-455	Original	Allison	Spinner	Red, rays	Rare			

National Bank Notes
Series of 1875
("First Charter Period")

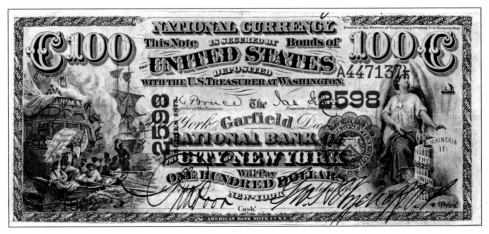

Face of F-456 to F-463. With SERIES 1875 overprint.

Back of F-456 to F-463.

No.	Series	Signatures		Seal		VG-8	F-12	VF-20
F-456	1875	Allison	New	Red, scalloped		$17,500	$24,000	$30,000
F-457	1875	Allison	Wyman	Red, scalloped		17,500	24,000	30,000
F-458	1875	Allison	Gilfillan	Red, scalloped	Rare			
F-459	1875	Scofield	Gilfillan	Red, scalloped		17,500	24,000	30,000
F-460	1875	Bruce	Gilfillan	Red, scalloped		17,500	24,000	30,000
F-461	1875	Bruce	Wyman	Red, scalloped		17,500	24,000	30,000
F-462	1875	Rosecrans	Huston	Red, scalloped	Rare			
F-462a	1875	Rosecrans	Nebeker	Red, scalloped	Rare			
F-463	1875	Tillman	Morgan	Red, scalloped	Rare			

National Bank Notes
Series of 1882 Brown Back
("Second Charter Period")

Face of F-519 to F-531. Similar to the preceding.

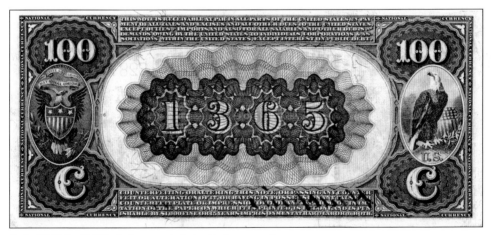

Back of F-519 to F-531. At the center is the bank's charter number.

No.	Signatures		VG-8	F-12	VF-20	EF-40	Unc-63
F-519	Bruce	Gilfillan	$6,000	$7,525	$8,750	$10,000	$20,000
F-520	Bruce	Wyman	6,000	7,525	8,750	10,000	20,000
F-521	Bruce	Jordan	6,000	7,525	8,750	10,000	20,000
F-522	Rosecrans	Jordan	6,000	7,525	8,750	10,000	20,000
F-523	Rosecrans	Hyatt	6,000	7,525	8,750	10,000	20,000
F-524	Rosecrans	Huston	6,000	7,525	8,750	10,000	20,000
F-525	Rosecrans	Nebeker	6,000	7,525	8,750	10,000	20,000
F-526	Rosecrans	Morgan	6,000	7,525	8,750	10,000	20,000
F-527	Tillman	Morgan	6,000	7,525	8,750	10,000	20,000
F-528	Tillman	Roberts	6,000	7,525	8,750	10,000	20,000
F-529	Bruce	Roberts	6,000	7,525	8,750	10,000	20,000
F-530	Lyons	Roberts	6,000	7,525	8,750	10,000	20,000
F-531	Vernon	Treat	6,000	7,525	8,750	10,000	20,000

National Bank Notes
Series of 1882 Date Back
("Second Charter Period")

Face of F-566 to F-572a. Similar to the preceding.

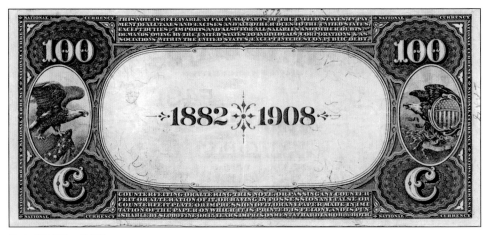

Back of F-566 to F-572a.

No.	Signatures		VG-8	F-12	VF-20	EF-40	Unc-63
F-566	Rosecrans	Huston	$6,500	$7,500	$8,500	$11,000	$16,000
F-567	Rosecrans	Nebeker	6,500	7,500	8,500	11,000	16,000
F-568	Tillman	Morgan	6,500	7,500	8,500	11,000	16,000
F-569	Tillman	Roberts	6,500	7,500	8,500	11,000	16,000
F-570	Bruce	Roberts	6,500	7,500	8,500	11,000	16,000
F-571	Lyons	Roberts	6,500	7,500	8,500	11,000	16,000
F-572	Vernon	Treat	6,500	7,500	8,500		
F-572a	Napier	McClung	7,000	8,500	8,500	11,000	17,500

National Bank Notes
Series of 1882 Value Back
("Second Charter Period")

Face of F-586a. Similar to the preceding.

Back of F-586a. Just two banks issued this type.

No.	Signatures		
F-586a	Lyons	Roberts	Very rare

National Bank Notes
Series of 1902 Red Seal
("Third Charter Period")

Face of F-686 to F-688. Portrait of John J. Knox, comptroller of the currency from 1871 to 1884.

Back of F-686 to F-688. Allegorical male figures flanking a shield and eagle. Washington Monument and the Treasury Building in the background.

No.	Signatures		VG-8	F-12	VF-20	EF-40	Unc-63
F-686	Lyons	Roberts	$7,500	$9,000	$10,500	$14,000	$17,500
F-687	Lyons	Treat	7,750	9,250	11,000	14,500	18,000
F-688	Vernon	Treat	7,750	9,250	11,000	14,500	18,000

National Bank Notes
Series of 1902 Blue Seal, Date Back
("Third Charter Period")

Designs same as the preceding type, but dates 1902 and 1908 have been added to top of reverse.

No.	Signatures		VG-8	F-12	VF-20	EF-40	Unc-63
F-689	Lyons	Roberts	$1,750	$2,300	$2,750	$3,625	$7,000
F-690	Lyons	Treat	1,750	2,300	2,750	3,625	7,000
F-691	Vernon	Treat	1,750	2,300	2,750	3,625	7,000
F-692	Vernon	McClung	1,750	2,300	2,750	3,625	7,000
F-693	Napier	McClung	1,750	2,300	2,750	3,625	7,000
F-694	Napier	Thompson	1,950	2,875	3,600	4,125	7,500
F-695	Napier	Burke	1,750	2,300	2,750	3,625	7,000
F-696	Parker	Burke	1,750	2,300	2,750	3,625	7,000
F-697	Teehee	Burke	1,750	2,300	2,750	3,625	7,000

National Bank Notes
Series of 1902 Blue Seal, Plain Back
("Third Charter Period")

Face of F-698 to F-707a.

Back of F-698 to F-707a.

See next page for chart.

No.	Signatures		VG-8	F-12	VF-20	EF-40	Unc-63
F-698	Lyons	Roberts	$1,700	$2,250	$2,850	$3,500	$7,150
F-699	Lyons	Treat	1,700	2,250	2,850	3,500	7,150
F-700	Vernon	Treat	1,700	2,250	2,850	3,500	7,150
F-701	Vernon	McClung	1,700	2,250	2,850	3,500	7,150
F-702	Napier	McClung	1,700	2,250	2,850	3,500	7,150
F-702a	Napier	Thompson	1,700	2,250	2,850	3,500	7,150
F-702b	Napier	Burke	1,700	2,250	2,850	3,500	7,150
F-703	Parker	Burke	1,700	2,250	2,850	3,500	7,150
F-704	Teehee	Burke	1,700	2,250	2,850	3,500	7,150
F-705	Elliott	Burke	1,700	2,250	2,850	3,500	7,150
F-706	Elliott	White	1,700	2,250	2,850	3,500	7,150
F-707	Speelman	White	1,700	2,250	2,850	3,500	7,150
F-707a	Woods	White	Rare				

National Gold Bank Notes

Face of F-1162 to F-1166IV. Similar to the $100 National Bank Notes of the First Charter Period.

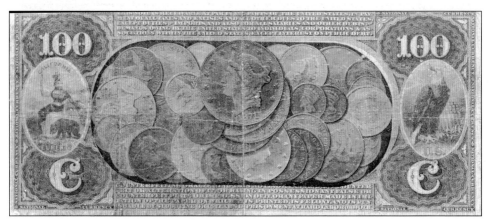

Back of F-1162 to F-1166IV. Montage of contemporary gold coins.

No.	Date	Name of Bank City		
F-1162	1870	First National Gold Bank	San Francisco	3 known
F-1163	1875 (Series)	First National Gold Bank	San Francisco	2 known
F-1164	1873	First National Gold Bank	Santa Barbara	Unique
F-1165	1874	First National Gold Bank	Petaluma	2 known
F-1166	1875	Union National Gold Bank	Oakland	Unique
F-1166I	1872	National Gold Bank and Trust Company	San Francisco	Unknown
F-1166II	1872	National Gold Bank of D.O. Mills and Co.	Sacramento	Unknown
F-1166III	1873	First National Gold Bank	Stockton	Rare
F-1166IV	1874	Farmer's National Gold Bank	San Jose	Unknown

Silver Certificates
Series of 1878, With Countersignatures

Face of F-336 to F-337b. James Madison at left. Each with countersignatures in addition to the Treasury signatures. These are engraved, except for F-337 and F-337a, which are signed by hand.

Back of F-336 to F-337b. Earlier issues are on blue-tinted paper.

No.	Countersignature	Payable At	
F-336	W.G. White	New York	Unique
F-336a	J.C. Hopper or T. Hillhouse	New York	Unknown
F-337★	R.M. Anthony	San Francisco	Unique
F-337a★	A.U. Wyman	Washington, DC	Unique
F-337b	A.U. Wyman	Washington, DC	4 known

Silver Certificates
Series of 1880,
No Countersignatures

Face of F-338 to F-342. Same as preceding, but no countersignatures. F-338 to F-340 have a large "C" overprint.

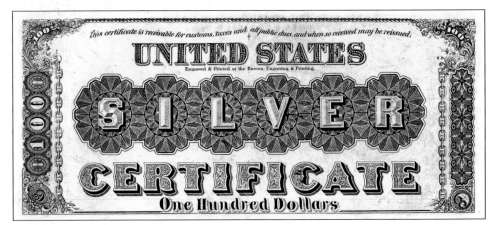

Back of F-338 to F-342.

No.	Signatures		Seal		VG-8	F-12	VF-20
F-338	Scofield	Gilfillan	Large brown, rays	Unknown			
F-339	Bruce	Gilfillan	Large brown, rays	4 known			
F-340	Bruce	Wyman	Large brown, rays		$8,250	$22,500	$42,500
As above, with large "C" below. No countersignature							
F-341	Rosecrans	Huston	Large brown, spikes		7,750	24,000	40,000
As above, with large seal in center, no "C" or "100"							
F-342	Rosecrans	Nebeker	Small red		7,750	24,000	40,000

Silver Certificates
Series of 1891

Face of F-343 and F-344. Facing bust of James Monroe.

Back of F-343 and F-344.

No.	Signatures		Seal	VG-8	F-12	VF-20	EF-40	Unc-63
F-343	Rosecrans	Nebeker	Small red	$7,000	$13,000	$24,500	$52,500	—
F-344	Tillman	Morgan	Small red	7,000	13,000	24,500	52,500	—

Treasury or Coin Notes
Series of 1890

Face of F-377. Bust of Admiral David Farragut.

Back of F-377. The famous "Watermelon Note," so called because of the design of the zeroes.

No.	Signatures		Seal	VG-8	F-12	VF-20	EF-40	Unc-63
F-377	Rosecrans	Huston	Large brown	$20,000	$50,000	$100,000	$170,000	—

Treasury or Coin Notes
Series of 1891

Face of F-378. Similar to the preceding

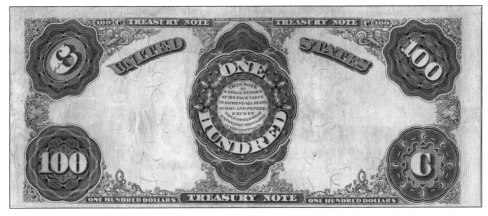

Back of F-378.

No.	Signatures		Seal	VG-8	F-12	VF-20	EF-40	Unc-63
F-378	Rosecrans	Nebeker	Small red	$20,000	$65,000	$127,500	$150,000	—

Gold Certificates, *Act of March 3, 1863*

Face of note F-1166c is similar to the $20 F-1166b. These were issued circa 1865 to 1869. Back has "One Hundred Dollars" in a rectangular panel.

No.	Signatures		Seal					
F-1166c	Colby	Spinner	Red					3 known

Gold Certificates, *Series of 1870 and 1875*

Face with bust of Senator Thomas Hart Benton of Missouri at left, denomination in two ornate disks at right. A more ornate version of F-1201 to F-1213. Issued under the Act of March 3, 1863. The back is blank.

No.	Series	Signatures		Seal				
F-1166h	1870	Allison	Two Treasury clerks	Red				Unknown
F-1166m	1875	Allison	New	Red				3 known

Gold Certificates
Series of 1882

Face of F-1201 to F-1215. Bust of Thomas Hart Benton at left.

Back of F-1201 to F-1215. Eagle perched on fasces.

No.	Series	Signatures		Seal		VG-8	F-12	VF-20	EF-40	Unc-63
F-1201	1882	Bruce	Gilfillan	Brown	10 known					
With countersignature by Thomas C. Acton, Asst. Treasurer, payable at New York										
F-1202	1882	Bruce	Gilfillan	Brown	2 known					
As above, but without Acton countersignature										
F-1203	1882	Bruce	Wyman	Brown	3 known					
F-1204	1882	Rosecrans	Hyatt	Large red	4 known					
F-1205	1882	Rosecrans	Huston	Large brown	8 known					
F-1206	1882	Lyons	Roberts	Small red		$850	$2,300	$3,600	$5,500	$11,000
F-1207	1882	Lyons	Treat	Small red		1,975	3,750	6,000	9,250	20,000
F-1208	1882	Vernon	Treat	Small red		1,150	2,300	3,600	7,750	16,500
F-1209	1882	Vernon	McClung	Small red		725	1,250	2,150	3,850	14,000
F-1210	1882	Napier	McClung	Small red		875	1,325	3,000	4,750	15,000
F-1211	1882	Napier	Thompson	Small red		675	1,200	2,150	4,500	14,500
F-1212	1882	Napier	Burke	Small red		675	1,200	2,150	4,500	14,500
F-1213	1882	Parker	Burke	Small red		675	1,200	2,150	4,750	15,000
F-1214	1882	Teehee	Burke	Small red		625	950	1,750	3,600	11,500
F-1215	1922	Speelman	White	Small red		600	900	1,375	3,300	7,500

Federal Reserve Notes
Series of 1914, Red Seal
Friedberg Suffix Letters on Types F-1072A to F-1083B

Red Seals—*"A" suffix:* Large district letter and numeral at top right and bottom left. Small letter at top left and bottom right. *B suffix:* As above, but with small district letter and numeral added above letter at top left. As a class Red Seals are scarcer than Blue Seals.

Face of F-1072A to F-1083B. Portrait of Franklin.

Back of F-1072A to F-1083B. "Labor, Plenty, America, Peace, and Commerce," by Kenyon Cox.

No.	Issuing Bank	VG-8	F-12	VF-20	EF-40	Unc-63
Signatures of Burke and McAdoo						
F-1072A	Boston	$1,700	$2,750	$5,000	$7,000	$30,000
F-1072B	Boston	1,600	2,500	4,850	7,000	—
F-1073A	New York	1,600	2,500	4,850	7,000	30,000
F-1073B	New York	1,900	2,875	5,500	8,500	—
F-1074A	Philadelphia	1,500	2,700	4,850	7,000	32,500
F-1074B	Philadelphia	1,800	2,750	4,850	7,000	—
F-1075A	Cleveland	1,350	3,250	5,500	8,500	—
F-1075B	Cleveland	1,600	2,500	5,250	7,500	—
F-1076A	Richmond	1,600	2,600	5,500	10,000	—
F-1076B	Richmond	1,600	2,600	5,250	10,000	—
F-1077A	Atlanta	1,600	2,500	6,000	11,000	—
F-1077B	Atlanta 2 known					
F-1078A	Chicago	2,000	3,000	5,550	8,000	—
F-1078B	Chicago	2,200	3,000	5,650	9,500	—
F-1079A	St. Louis	2,100	3,200	6,000	9,750	—
F-1079B	St. Louis	2,100	3,200	6,000	9,750	—

Chart continued on next page.

No.	Issuing Bank		VG-8	F-12	VF-20	EF-40	Unc-63
F-1080A	Minneapolis	3 known					
F-1080B	Minneapolis		$2,625	$6,800	$9,750	$16,500	—
F-1081A	Kansas City		2,100	3,200	5,250	9,500	—
F-1081B	Kansas City		2,750	4,000	5,750	9,500	—
F-1082A	Dallas		3,500	6,500	12,500	22,500	—
F-1082B	Dallas		3,500	6,500	12,500	22,500	—
F-1083A	San Francisco		2,100	3,000	5,550	9,750	—
F-1083B	San Francisco		2,100	3,000	5,550	8,000	$30,000

Federal Reserve Notes
Series of 1914, Blue Seal

Face of F-1084 to F-1131. Signatures of White and Mellon. Design similar to the preceding. Back same as preceding.

No.	Issuing Bank	Signatures			VG-8	F-12	VF-20	EF-40	Unc-63
F-1084	Boston	Burke	McAdoo		$475	$650	$800	$1,575	$3,600
F-1085	Boston	Burke	Glass		475	625	900	1,800	3,750
F-1086	Boston	Burke	Houston	None printed					
F-1087	Boston	White	Mellon		475	775	900	1,450	3,500
F-1088	New York	Burke	McAdoo		475	625	800	1,350	3,350
F-1089	New York	Burke	Glass		475	675	800	1,350	3,350
F-1090	New York	Burke	Houston		475	675	800	1,350	3,350
F-1091	New York	White	Mellon		475	675	800	1,350	3,350
F-1092	Philadelphia	Burke	McAdoo		475	675	900	1,450	3,500
F-1093	Philadelphia	Burke	Glass	None printed					
F-1094	Philadelphia	Burke	Houston	None printed					
F-1095	Philadelphia	White	Mellon		900	1,100	1,625	2,350	4,250
F-1096	Cleveland	Burke	McAdoo		875	1,000	1,500	1,800	3,750
F-1097	Cleveland	Burke	Glass		875	1,000	1,500	1,800	3,750
F-1098	Cleveland	Burke	Houston		475	625	800	1,650	3,425
F-1099	Cleveland	White	Mellon		500	750	800	1,675	3,650
F-1100	Richmond	Burke	McAdoo		475	675	800	1,475	3,375
F-1101	Richmond	Burke	Glass		475	650	800	1,475	3,200
F-1102	Richmond	Burke	Houston		800	1,100	1,350	1,600	4,500
F-1103	Richmond	White	Mellon	None printed					
F-1104	Atlanta	Burke	McAdoo		475	625	800	1,475	3,250
F-1105	Atlanta	Burke	Glass	None printed					
F-1106	Atlanta	Burke	Houston		825	925	1,500	2,000	4,425
F-1107	Atlanta	White	Mellon		575	700	1,350	1,850	3,700
F-1108	Chicago	Burke	McAdoo		475	625	800	1,450	3,425
F-1109	Chicago	Burke	Glass	None printed					
F-1110	Chicago	Burke	Houston		475	625	800	1,425	3,425
F-1111	Chicago	White	Mellon	None printed					

No.	Issuing Bank	Signatures			VG-8	F-12	VF-20	EF-40	Unc-63
F-1112	St. Louis	Burke	McAdoo		$550	$650	$800	$1,600	$3,700
F-1113	St. Louis	Burke	Glass	None printed					
F-1114	St. Louis	Burke	Houston	None printed					
F-1115	St. Louis	White	Mellon	None printed					
F-1116	Minneapolis	Burke	McAdoo		475	625	800	1,475	3,700
F-1117	Minneapolis	Burke	Glass		475	625	800	1,475	3,750
F-1118	Minneapolis	Burke	Houston		525	700	1,325	1,900	4,200
F-1119	Minneapolis	White	Mellon		550	750	1,150	1,900	4,000
F-1120	Kansas City	Burke	McAdoo		525	700	800	1,575	3,750
F-1121	Kansas City	Burke	Glass	None printed					
F-1122	Kansas City	Burke	Houston	None printed					
F-1123	Kansas City	White	Mellon		575	725	875	1,550	3,750
F-1124	Dallas	Burke	McAdoo		475	675	800	1,550	3,300
F-1125	Dallas	Burke	Glass	None printed					
F-1126	Dallas	Burke	Houston	None printed					
F-1127	Dallas	White	Mellon		1,100	1,650	3,750	5,500	12,000
F-1128	San Francisco	Burke	McAdoo		475	625	800	1,550	3,300
F-1129	San Francisco	Burke	Glass	None printed					
F-1130	San Francisco	Burke	Houston		475	625	800	1,550	3,600
F-1131	San Francisco	White	Mellon		475	625	800	1,700	3,850

Note: A large number of F-1092 notes are suspected of being extremely high-quality counterfeits made in the 1930s—caution is advised.

SMALL-SIZE $100 NOTES

National Bank Notes
Series of 1929, Type 1

Face of F-1804-1. Portrait of Benjamin Franklin. Brown Treasury seal at right.

Back of F-1804-1. Independence Hall in Philadelphia.

No.	VF-20	EF-40	Unc-63
F-1804-1	$400	$525	$800

National Bank Notes
Series of 1929, Type 2

Face of F-1804-2. Same design as preceding with bank charter number also in brown at lower left and upper right of portrait.

No.		VF-20	EF-40	Unc-63
F-1804-2		$500	$600	$1,200

Gold Certificates
Series of 1928 and 1934, Gold Seal

Face of F-2405 to F-2406. Gold Treasury seal and serial numbers. Payable in gold.

Back of F-2405 to F-2406.

No.	Series	Signatures		Quantity Printed		VF-20	EF-40	Unc-63
F-2405	1928	Woods	Mellon	3,240,000		$925	$1,750	$4,000
F-2405★	1928	Woods	Mellon			4,500	12,500	—
F-2406	1934	Julian	Morgenthau	120,000	Not issued			

Federal Reserve Bank Notes
Series of 1929,
Brown Seal

Face of F-1890. Similar to the National Bank Notes of the period. Back design is same as that used on all $100 notes of the era.

No.	Issuing Bank	Quantity Printed	VF-20	EF-40	Unc-63
F-1890B	New York	480,000	$165	$225	$375
F-1890D	Cleveland	276,000	165	225	375
F-1890E	Richmond	142,000	165	200	375
F-1890G	Chicago	384,000	165	200	375
F-1890I	Minneapolis	144,000	165	200	375
F-1890J	Kansas City	96,000	165	200	375
F-1890K	Dallas	36,000	300	525	1,250
F-1890★	Most common districts		700	825	1,250

Legal Tender Notes
Series of 1966 and 1966-A,
Red Seal

Face of F-1550 to F-1551. Issued mainly for accounting purposes to comply with the law that there must be a fixed value ($346,681,016) of Legal Tender Notes in circulation. All held by the Treasury were destroyed by 1996.

The back with IN GOD WE TRUST added.

No.	Series	Signatures		Quantity Printed	VF-20	EF-40	Unc-63
F-1550	1966	Granahan	Fowler	768,000	$175	$200	$400
F-1550★	1966	Granahan	Fowler	128,000	400	600	1,700
F-1551	1966A	Elston	Kennedy	512,000	250	300	850

Federal Reserve Notes
Series of 1928 and 1928-A, Green Seal

Series of 1928—Signatures of Woods and Mellon

Face of F-2150. Bank represented by district number. The face printing notes that the bill is payable "in gold or lawful money."

Back used on all $100 notes through Series 1950-E.

No.	Issuing Bank	Quantity Printed	VF-20	EF-40	Unc-63
F-2150A	Boston	376,000	$185	$250	$550
F-2150A★	Boston		1,250	2,250	4,000
F-2150B	New York	755,400	185	250	475
F-2150B★	New York		650	1,000	1,925
F-2150C	Philadelphia	389,100	185	250	550
F-2150C★	Philadelphia		650	1,000	2,100
F-2150D	Cleveland	542,400	185	250	550
F-2150D★	Cleveland		650	1,000	2,200
F-2150E	Richmond	364,416	185	250	550
F-2150E★	Richmond		750	1,100	2,200
F-2150F	Atlanta	357,000	185	250	550
F-2150F★	Atlanta		750	1,100	2,200
F-2150G	Chicago	783,300	185	250	475
F-2150G★	Chicago		750	1,000	1,925
F-2150H	St. Louis	187,200	185	250	550
F-2150H★	St. Louis		750	1,000	2,200
F-2150I	Minneapolis	102,000	185	250	550
F-2150I★	Minneapolis		1,600	2,750	4,250
F-2150J	Kansas City	234,612	185	250	525
F-2150J★	Kansas City		4,000	6,000	—
F-2150K	Dallas	80,140	200	275	2,750
F-2150K★	Dallas		1,500	2,400	4,000
F-2150L	San Francisco	486,000	185	250	475
F-2150L★	San Francisco		1,500	2,400	4,000

Series of 1928-A—Signatures of Woods and Mellon

Face of F-2151. Bank now represented by a district letter. Back same as used on all $100 notes through Series 1950-E.

No.	Issuing Bank	Quantity Printed	VF-20	EF-40	Unc-63
F-2151A	Boston	980,400	$165	$190	$300
F-2151B	New York	2,938,176	160	175	275
F-2151B★	New York		3,000	6,000	9,500
F-2151C	Philadelphia	1,496,844	160	190	300
F-2151D	Cleveland	992,436	160	190	300
F-2151E	Richmond	621,364	170	225	375
F-2151F	Atlanta	371,400	175	225	375
F-2151G	Chicago	4,010,424	160	185	280
F-2151H	St. Louis	749,544	165	190	300
F-2151H★	St. Louis	24,000	3,000	6,000	9,500
F-2151I	Minneapolis	503,040	170	225	375
F-2151J	Kansas City	681,804	160	185	280
F-2151K	Dallas	594,456	160	185	280
F-2151L	San Francisco	1,228,032	160	190	300

Federal Reserve Notes
Series of 1934 to 1934-D, Green Seal

Face of F-2152 to F-2156. With no mention of gold in payment. Back same as used on all $100 notes through Series 1950-E.

Series of 1934—Signatures of Julian and Morgenthau

No.	Issuing Bank	Quantity Printed	VF-20	EF-40	Unc-63
F-2152A	Boston	3,710,000	$150	$175	$275
F-2152A★	Boston		200	450	975
F-2152B	New York	3,086,000	150	175	275
F-2152B★	New York		200	450	975
F-2152C	Philadelphia	2,776,800	150	175	275
F-2152C★	Philadelphia		200	450	975
F-2152D	Cleveland	3,447,108	150	175	275
F-2152D★	Cleveland		200	450	975
F-2152E	Richmond	4,317,600	150	175	275
F-2152E★	Richmond		200	450	975
F-2152F	Atlanta	3,264,420	150	175	275
F-2152F★	Atlanta		200	450	975
F-2152G	Chicago	7,075,000	150	175	275
F-2152G★	Chicago		200	450	975
F-2152H	St. Louis	2,106,192	150	175	275
F-2152H★	St. Louis		200	450	975
F-2152I	Minneapolis	852,600	150	175	275

Note: The two shades of green seals also exist in this series. Notes with the darker green seal are worth approximately 10% more.

Chart continued on next page.

No.	Issuing Bank	Quantity Printed	VF-20	EF-40	Unc-63
F-2152I*	Minneapolis		$200	$450	$975
F-2152J	Kansas City	1,932,900	150	175	275
F-2152J*	Kansas City		200	450	975
F-2152K	Dallas	1,506,516	150	175	275
F-2152K*	Dallas		200	450	975
F-2152L	San Francisco	6,521,940	150	175	275
F-2152L*	San Francisco		200	450	975

Note: The two shades of green seals also exist in this series. Notes with the darker green seal are worth approximately 10% more.

Series of 1934-A—Signatures of Julian and Morgenthau

No.	Issuing Bank	Quantity Printed	VF-20	EF-40	Unc-63
F-2153A	Boston	102,000	$135	$175	$250
F-2153A*	Boston		265	350	775
F-2153B	New York	15,278,892	135	175	250
F-2153B*	New York		265	350	775
F-2153C	Philadelphia	588,000	135	175	250
F-2153C*	Philadelphia		265	350	775
F-2153D	Cleveland	645,300	135	175	250
F-2153E	Richmond	770,000	135	175	250
F-2153F	Atlanta	589,886	135	175	250
F-2153G	Chicago	3,328,800	135	175	250
F-2153G*	Chicago		250	325	725
F-2153H	St. Louis	434,208	135	175	250
F-2153I	Minneapolis	153,000	135	175	250
F-2153I*	Minneapolis		265	350	775
F-2153J	Kansas City	455,000	135	175	250
F-2153J*	Kansas City		265	350	775
F-2153K	Dallas	226,164	135	175	250
F-2153L	San Francisco	1,130,400	135	175	250
F-2153L*	San Francisco		265	350	775

Series of 1934-B—Signatures of Julian and Vinson

No.	Issuing Bank	Quantity Printed	VF-20	EF-40	Unc-63
F-2154A	Boston	41,400	$150	$180	$325
F-2154C	Philadelphia	39,600	150	180	325
F-2154D	Cleveland	61,200	150	180	325
F-2154E	Richmond	977,400	150	180	325
F-2154E*	Richmond		775	1,375	3,250
F-2154F	Atlanta	645,000	150	180	325
F-2154F*	Atlanta		1,725	2,750	7,500
F-2154G	Chicago	396,000	150	180	325
F-2154H	St. Louis	676,200	150	180	325
F-2154H*	St. Louis		775	1,375	3,250
F-2154I	Minneapolis	377,000	150	180	325
F-2154I*	Minneapolis		775	1,375	3,250
F-2154J	Kansas City	364,500	150	180	325
F-2154J*	Kansas City		775	1,250	3,250
F-2154K	Dallas	392,700	150	180	325
F-2154K*	Dallas		775	1,375	3,250

Series of 1934-C—Signatures of Julian and Snyder

No.	Issuing Bank	Quantity Printed	VF-20	EF-40	Unc-63
F-2155A	Boston	13,800	$160	$225	$300
F-2155B	New York	1,556,400	150	175	250
F-2155C	Philadelphia	13,200	160	225	300
F-2155D	Cleveland	1,473,200	150	175	250
F-2155D*	Cleveland		850	1,625	3,375
F-2155E	Richmond		150	175	250
F-2155E*	Richmond		850	1,625	3,375
F-2155F	Atlanta	493,900	150	175	250
F-2155F*	Atlanta		850	1,625	3,375
F-2155G	Chicago	612,000	150	175	250
F-2155G*	Chicago		850	1,625	3,375
F-2155H	St. Louis	957,000	150	175	250
F-2155H*	St. Louis		850	1,625	3,375
F-2155I	Minneapolis	392,904	150	175	250
F-2155I*	Minneapolis		850	1,625	3,375
F-2155J	Kansas City	401,100	150	175	250
F-2155K	Dallas	280,700	150	175	250
F-2155K*	Dallas		1,250	2,200	4,000
F-2155L	San Francisco	432,600	150	175	250
F-2155L*	San Francisco		850	1,625	3,375

Series of 1934-D—Signatures of Clark and Snyder

No.	Issuing Bank	Quantity Printed		VF-20	EF-40	Unc-63
F-2156B	New York	156	Rare			
F-2156C	Philadelphia	308,400		$250	$350	$450
F-2156C★	Philadelphia			1,800	3,000	5,000
F-2156F	Atlanta	260,400		250	350	450
F-2156F★	Atlanta			1,625	2,900	4,900
F-2156G	Chicago	78,000		250	400	500
F-2156G★	Chicago			1,625	2,900	4,900
F-2156H	St. Louis	166,800		250	375	475
F-2156K	Dallas	66,000		350	450	625

Federal Reserve Notes
Series of 1950 to 1950-E, Green Seal

Face of F-2157 to F-2162. Obligation at upper left in three lines instead of four, WASHINGTON moved to above Treasury seal. Back same as the preceding.

Series of 1950—Signatures of Clark and Snyder

No.	Issuing Bank	Quantity Printed	VF-20	EF-40	Unc-63
F-2157A	Boston	768,000		$150	$325
F-2157A★	Boston		$225	300	950
F-2157B	New York	3,908,000		150	275
F-2157B★	New York		225	300	950
F-2157C	Philadelphia	1,332,000		150	275
F-2157C★	Philadelphia		225	300	950
F-2157D	Cleveland	1,632,000		150	275
F-2157E	Richmond	4,076,000		150	275
F-2157E★	Richmond		225	300	950
F-2157F	Atlanta	1,824,000		150	275
F-2157G	Chicago	4,428,000		150	275
F-2157G★	Chicago		225	300	950
F-2157H	St. Louis	1,284,000		150	275
F-2157H★	St. Louis		225	300	950
F-2157I	Minneapolis	564,000		150	425
F-2157J	Kansas City	864,000		150	275
F-2157J★	Kansas City		225	300	975
F-2157K	Dallas	1,216,000		150	275
F-2157L	San Francisco	2,524,000		150	275
F-2157L★	San Francisco		225	300	975

Series of 1950-A—Signatures of Priest and Humphrey

No.	Issuing Bank	Quantity Printed	EF-40	Unc-63	No.	Issuing Bank	Quantity Printed	EF-40	Unc-63
F-2158A	Boston	1,008,000	$125	$250	F-2158G	Chicago	864,000	$125	$250
F-2158A★	Boston		250	600	F-2158G★	Chicago		250	600
F-2158B	New York	2,880,000	125	250	F-2158H	St. Louis	432,000	125	250
F-2158B★	New York		250	600	F-2158H★	St. Louis		250	600
F-2158C	Philadelphia	576,000	125	250	F-2158I	Minneapolis	144,000	125	250
F-2158C★	Philadelphia		250	600	F-2158J	Kansas City	288,000	125	250
F-2158D	Cleveland	288,000	125	250	F-2158J★	Kansas City		250	600
F-2158D★	Cleveland		250	600	F-2158K	Dallas	432,000	125	250
F-2158E	Richmond	2,160,000	125	250	F-2158K★	Dallas		400	900
F-2158E★	Richmond		250	600	F-2158L	San Francisco	720,000	125	250
F-2158F	Atlanta	288,000	125	250	F-2158L★	San Francisco		250	600

Series of 1950-B—Signatures of Priest and Anderson

No.	Issuing Bank	Quantity Printed	EF-40	Unc-63	No.	Issuing Bank	Quantity Printed	EF-40	Unc-63
F-2159A	Boston	720,000	$125	$200	F-2159G★	Chicago		$250	$550
F-2159B	New York	6,636,000	125	200	F-2159H	St. Louis	1,152,000	125	200
F-2159B★	New York		250	550	F-2159H★	St. Louis		250	550
F-2159C	Philadelphia	720,000	125	200	F-2159I	Minneapolis	288,000	125	200
F-2159C★	Philadelphia		250	550	F-2159I★	Minneapolis		250	625
F-2159D	Cleveland	432,000	125	200	F-2159J	Kansas City	720,000	125	200
F-2159D★	Cleveland		250	550	F-2159J★	Kansas City		250	550
F-2159E	Richmond	1,008,000	125	200	F-2159K	Dallas	1,728,000	125	200
F-2159F	Atlanta	576,000	125	200	F-2159K★	Dallas		250	625
F-2159F★	Atlanta		250	550	F-2159L	San Francisco	2,880,000	125	200
F-2159G	Chicago	2,592,000	125	200	F-2159L★	San Francisco		250	625

Series of 1950-C—Signatures of Smith and Dillon

No.	Issuing Bank	Quantity Printed	EF-40	Unc-63	No.	Issuing Bank	Quantity Printed	EF-40	Unc-63
F-2160A	Boston	864,000	$125	$225	F-2160G	Chicago	1,584,000	$125	$225
F-2160A★	Boston		275	550	F-2160G★	Chicago		250	550
F-2160B	New York	2,448,000	125	200	F-2160H	St. Louis	720,000	125	225
F-2160B★	New York		275	550	F-2160H★	St. Louis		275	550
F-2160C	Philadelphia	576,000	125	225	F-2160I	Minneapolis	288,000	125	225
F-2160C★	Philadelphia		275	550	F-2160I★	Minneapolis		275	550
F-2160D	Cleveland	576,000	125	225	F-2160J	Kansas City	432,000	125	225
F-2160D★	Cleveland		375	725	F-2160K	Dallas	720,000	125	225
F-2160E	Richmond	1,440,000	125	225	F-2160K★	Dallas		275	550
F-2160E★	Richmond		250	550	F-2160L	San Francisco	2,160,000	125	200
F-2160F	Atlanta	1,296,000	125	225	F-2160L★	San Francisco		275	550
F-2160F★	Atlanta		250	550					

Series of 1950-D—Signatures of Granahan and Dillon

No.	Issuing Bank	Quantity Printed	EF-40	Unc-63	No.	Issuing Bank	Quantity Printed	EF-40	Unc-63
F-2161A	Boston	1,872,000	$125	$200	F-2161G	Chicago	4,608,000	$125	$200
F-2161A★	Boston		325	600	F-2161G★	Chicago		250	475
F-2161B	New York	7,632,000	125	200	F-2161H	St. Louis	1,440,000	125	200
F-2161B★	New York		250	475	F-2161H★	St. Louis		250	475
F-2161C	Philadelphia	1,872,000	125	200	F-2161I	Minneapolis	432,000	125	200
F-2161C★	Philadelphia		325	600	F-2161I★	Minneapolis		250	475
F-2161D	Cleveland	1,584,000	125	200	F-2161J	Kansas City	864,000	125	200
F-2161D★	Cleveland		250	475	F-2161J★	Kansas City		250	475
F-2161E	Richmond	2,880,000	125	200	F-2161K	Dallas	1,728,000	125	200
F-2161E★	Richmond		250	500	F-2161K★	Dallas		250	475
F-2161F	Atlanta	1,872,000	125	200	F-2161L	San Francisco	3,312,000	125	200
F-2161F★	Atlanta		250	475	F-2161L★	San Francisco		250	475

Series of 1950-E—Signatures of Granahan and Fowler

No.	Issuing Bank	Quantity Printed	EF-40	Unc-63	No.	Issuing Bank	Quantity Printed	EF-40	Unc-63
F-2162B	New York	3,024,000	$225	$450	F-2162G★	Chicago		$1,250	$3,000
F-2162B★	New York		925	1,900	F-2162L	San Francisco	2,736,000	225	450
F-2162G	Chicago	576,000	275	600	F-2162L★	San Francisco		1,250	3,000

Federal Reserve Notes
Series of 1963-A,
Green Seal, Motto Added

Face of F-2163 to F-2174. Shown is the modernized seal beginning with the Series of 1969.

Back of F-2163 to F-2174. The motto IN GOD WE TRUST is added.

No.	Issuing Bank	Quantity Printed	EF-40	Unc-63	No.	Issuing Bank	Quantity Printed	EF-40	Unc-63
Signatures of Granahan and Fowler									
F-2163A	Boston	1,536,000		$200	F-2163G	Chicago	4,352,000		$200
F-2163A★	Boston	128,000		300	F-2163G★	Chicago	512,000		300
F-2163B	New York	12,544,000		200	F-2163H	St. Louis	1,536,000		200
F-2163B★	New York	1,536,000		300	F-2163H★	St. Louis	256,000		300
F-2163C	Philadelphia	1,792,000		200	F-2163I	Minneapolis	512,000		200
F-2163C★	Philadelphia	192,000		300	F-2163I★	Minneapolis	128,000		300
F-2163D	Cleveland	2,304,000		200	F-2163J	Kansas City	1,024,000		200
F-2163D★	Cleveland	192,000		300	F-2163J★	Kansas City	128,000		300
F-2163E	Richmond	2,816,000		200	F-2163K	Dallas	1,536,000		200
F-2163E★	Richmond	192,000		300	F-2163K★	Dallas	192,000		300
F-2163F	Atlanta	1,280,000		200	F-2163L	San Francisco	6,400,000		200
F-2163F★	Atlanta	128,000		300	F-2163L★	San Francisco	832,000		300

Federal Reserve Notes
Series of 1969 to 1993,
Green Seal

Series of 1969 (with new Treasury seal)—Signatures of Elston and Kennedy

No.	Issuing Bank	Quantity Printed	EF-40	Unc-63	No.	Issuing Bank	Quantity Printed	EF-40	Unc-63
F-2164A	Boston	2,048,000		$200	F-2164G	Chicago	5,888,000		$200
F-2164A★	Boston	128,000	$225	425	F-2164G★	Chicago	256,000	$225	425
F-2164B	New York	11,520,000		200	F-2164H	St. Louis	1,280,000		200
F-2164B★	New York	128,000	225	425	F-2164H★	St. Louis	64,000	225	425
F-2164C	Philadelphia	2,560,000		200	F-2164I	Minneapolis	512,000		275
F-2164C★	Philadelphia	128,000	225	425	F-2164I★	Minneapolis	64,000	225	425
F-2164D	Cleveland	768,000		200	F-2164J	Kansas City	1,792,000		200
F-2164D★	Cleveland	64,000	250	475	F-2164J★	Kansas City	384,000	225	425
F-2164E	Richmond	2,560,000		200	F-2164K	Dallas	2,048,000		200
F-2164E★	Richmond	192,000	225	425	F-2164K★	Dallas	128,000	225	425
F-2164F	Atlanta	2,304,000		200	F-2164L	San Francisco	7,168,000		200
F-2164F★	Atlanta	128,000	225	425	F-2164L★	San Francisco	320,000	225	425

Series of 1969-A—Signatures of Kabis and Connally

No.	Issuing Bank	Quantity Printed	EF-40	Unc-63	No.	Issuing Bank	Quantity Printed	EF-40	Unc-63
F-2165A	Boston	1,280,000		$175	F-2165F★	Atlanta	64,000	$225	$500
F-2165A★	Boston	320,000	$225	400	F-2165G	Chicago	5,376,000		175
F-2165B	New York	11,264,000		175	F-2165G★	Chicago	320,000	225	400
F-2165B★	New York	640,000	225	400	F-2165H	St. Louis	1,024,000		175
F-2165C	Philadelphia	2,048,000		175	F-2165H★	St. Louis	64,000	225	500
F-2165C★	Philadelphia	448,000	225	400	F-2165I	Minneapolis	1,024,000		175
F-2165D	Cleveland	1,280,000		175	F-2165J	Kansas City	512,000	225	400
F-2165D★	Cleveland	192,000	225	400	F-2165K	Dallas	3,328,000		175
F-2165E	Richmond	2,304,000		175	F-2165K★	Dallas	128,000	225	400
F-2165E★	Richmond	192,000	225	400	F-2165L	San Francisco	4,352,000		175
F-2165F	Atlanta	2,304,000		175	F-2165L★	San Francisco	640,000	225	400

Series of 1969-B

None printed.

Series of 1969-C—Signatures of Banuelos and Shultz

No.	Issuing Bank	Quantity Printed	EF-40	Unc-63	No.	Issuing Bank	Quantity Printed	EF-40	Unc-63
F-2166A	Boston	2,048,000		$200	F-2166G	Chicago	6,016,000		$200
F-2166A★	Boston	64,000	$165	400	F-2166G★	Chicago	320,000	$165	375
F-2166B	New York	15,616,000		200	F-2166H	St. Louis	5,376,000		200
F-2166B★	New York	256,000	165	375	F-2166H★	St. Louis	64,000	165	375
F-2166C	Philadelphia	2,816,000		200	F-2166I	Minneapolis	512,000		250
F-2166C★	Philadelphia	64,000	165	400	F-2166I★	Minneapolis	64,000	165	400
F-2166D	Cleveland	3,456,000		200	F-2166J	Kansas City	4,736,000		200
F-2166D★	Cleveland	64,000	165	400	F-2166J★	Kansas City	192,000	165	375
F-2166E	Richmond	7,296,000		200	F-2166K	Dallas	2,944,000		200
F-2166E★	Richmond	128,000	165	375	F-2166K★	Dallas	64,000	165	400
F-2166F	Atlanta	2,432,000		200	F-2166L	San Francisco	10,240,000		200
F-2166F★	Atlanta	64,000	165	400	F-2166L★	San Francisco	512,000	165	400

Series of 1974—Signatures of Neff and Simon

No.	Issuing Bank	Quantity Printed	EF-40	Unc-63	No.	Issuing Bank	Quantity Printed	EF-40	Unc-63
F-2167A	Boston	11,520,000		$175	F-2167G	Chicago	26,880,000		$175
F-2167A★	Boston	320,000	$180	350	F-2167G★	Chicago	1,216,000	$180	350
F-2167B	New York	62,720,000		175	F-2167H	St. Louis	5,760,000		175
F-2167B★	New York	1,728,000	180	350	F-2167H★	St. Louis	192,000	180	400
F-2167C	Philadelphia	7,680,000		175	F-2167I	Minneapolis	4,480,000		175
F-2167C★	Philadelphia	192,000	180	350	F-2167I★	Minneapolis	256,000	175	400
F-2167D	Cleveland	8,320,000		175	F-2167J	Kansas City	5,760,000		175
F-2167D★	Cleveland	256,000	180	400	F-2167J★	Kansas City	448,000	175	400
F-2167E	Richmond	11,520,000		175	F-2167K	Dallas	10,240,000		175
F-2167E★	Richmond	256,000	180	400	F-2167K★	Dallas	192,000	175	400
F-2167F	Atlanta	4,480,000		175	F-2167L	San Francisco	29,440,000		175
F-2167F★	Atlanta	128,000	180	400	F-2167L★	San Francisco	896,000	175	400

Series of 1977—Signatures of Morton and Blumenthal

No.	Issuing Bank	Quantity Printed	Unc-63	No.	Issuing Bank	Quantity Printed	Unc-63
F-2168A	Boston	19,200,000	$175	F-2168G	Chicago	39,680,000	$175
F-2168A★	Boston	320,000	250	F-2168G★	Chicago	960,000	250
F-2168B	New York	166,400,000	175	F-2168H	St. Louis	15,360,000	175
F-2168B★	New York	1,664,000	250	F-2168H★	St. Louis	448,000	250
F-2168C	Philadelphia	5,195,000	175	F-2168I	Minneapolis	5,195,000	175
F-2168C★	Philadelphia	128,000	250	F-2168I★	Minneapolis	192,000	250
F-2168D	Cleveland	16,640,000	175	F-2168J	Kansas City	38,400,000	175
F-2168D★	Cleveland	192,000	250	F-2168J★	Kansas City	640,000	250
F-2168E	Richmond	24,320,000	175	F-2168K	Dallas	38,400,000	175
F-2168E★	Richmond	384,000	250	F-2168K★	Dallas	640,000	250
F-2168F	Atlanta	3,840,000	175	F-2168L	San Francisco	39,680,000	175
F-2168F★	Atlanta	64,000	300	F-2168L★	San Francisco	576,000	250

Series of 1981—Signatures of Buchanan and Regan

No.	Issuing Bank	Quantity Printed	EF-40	Unc-63	No.	Issuing Bank	Quantity Printed	EF-40	Unc-63
F-2169A	Boston	8,960,000		$200	F-2169G	Chicago	33,280,000		$175
F-2169B	New York	105,600,000		175	F-2169H	St. Louis	5,760,000		175
F-2169C	Philadelphia	12,800,000		175	F-2169I	Minneapolis	3,200,000		175
F-2169D	Cleveland	5,760,000		175	F-2169J	Kansas City	23,680,000		175
F-2169E	Richmond	23,680,000		175	F-2169K	Dallas	23,680,000		175
F-2169E★	Richmond	640,000	$750	1,350	F-2169L	San Francisco	24,960,000		175
F-2169F	Atlanta	6,400,000		175					

Series of 1981-A—Signatures of Ortega and Regan

No.	Issuing Bank	Quantity Printed	EF-40	Unc-63	No.	Issuing Bank	Quantity Printed	EF-40	Unc-63
F-2170A	Boston	16,000,000		$175	F-2170G	Chicago	22,400,000		$175
F-2170B	New York	64,000,000		150	F-2170H	St. Louis	12,800,000		175
F-2170C	Philadelphia	3,200,000		175	F-2170I	Minneapolis	3,200,000		175
F-2170D	Cleveland	6,400,000		175	F-2170K	Dallas	3,200,000		175
F-2170E	Richmond	12,800,000		175	F-2170L	San Francisco	19,200,000		175
F-2170F	Atlanta	12,800,000		175	F-2170L★	San Francisco	640,000	$400	750

Series of 1985—Signatures of Ortega and Baker

No.	Issuing Bank	Quantity Printed	EF-40	Unc-63	No.	Issuing Bank	Quantity Printed	EF-40	Unc-63
F-2171A	Boston	32,000,000		$175	F-2171G	Chicago	64,000,000		$175
F-2171B	New York	259,200,000		175	F-2171H	St. Louis	12,800,000		175
F-2171B★	New York		$135	275	F-2171I	Minneapolis	12,800,000		175
F-2171C	Philadelphia	19,200,000		175	F-2171J	Kansas City	12,800,000		175
F-2171D	Cleveland	28,800,000		175	F-2171J★	Kansas City	1,280,000	$135	275
F-2171D★	Cleveland	1,280,000	150	325	F-2171K	Dallas	48,000,000		175
F-2171E	Richmond	54,400,000		175	F-2171K★	Dallas	3,200,000	135	275
F-2171F	Atlanta	16,000,000		175	F-2171L	San Francisco	38,400,000		175

Series of 1988—Signatures of Ortega and Brady

No.	Issuing Bank	Quantity Printed	EF-40	Unc-63	No.	Issuing Bank	Quantity Printed	EF-40	Unc-63
F-2172A	Boston	9,600,000		$175	F-2172E	Richmond	19,200,000		$175
F-2172B	New York	448,000,000		175	F-2172G	Chicago	51,200,000		175
F-2172B★	New York	4,480,000	$175	450	F-2172H	St. Louis	9,600,000		175
F-2172C	Philadelphia	9,600,000		175	F-2172J	Kansas City	9,600,000		175
F-2172D	Cleveland	35,200,000		175	F-2172L	San Francisco	10,200,000		175

Series of 1988-A

None printed.

Series of 1990—Signatures of Villalpando and Brady

No.	Issuing Bank	Quantity Printed	EF-40	Unc-63	No.	Issuing Bank	Quantity Printed	EF-40	Unc-63
F-2173A	Boston	76,800,000		$150	F-2173G★	Chicago	640,000		$200
F-2173B	New York	595,200,000		150	F-2173H	St. Louis	121,600,000		150
F-2173B★	New York	1,880,000		200	F-2173I	Minneapolis	48,000,000		150
F-2173C	Philadelphia	112,000,000		150	F-2173J	Kansas City	76,800,000		150
F-2173C★	Philadelphia	1,280,000	$125	200	F-2173J★	Kansas City	3,200,000	$125	200
F-2173D	Cleveland	115,200,000		150	F-2173K	Dallas	165,400,000		150
F-2173E	Richmond	108,800,000		150	F-2173K★	Dallas	1,920,000	125	200
F-2173F	Atlanta	64,000,000		150	F-2173L	San Francisco	147,200,000		150
F-2173G	Chicago	134,400,000		150	F-2173L★	San Francisco	3,200,000	125	200

Series of 1993—Signatures of Withrow and Bentsen

No.	Issuing Bank	Quantity Printed	EF-40	Unc-63	No.	Issuing Bank	Quantity Printed	EF-40	Unc-63
F-2174A	Boston	83,200,000		$150	F-2174F	Atlanta	150,400,000		$150
F-2174B	New York	288,000,000		150	F-2174G	Chicago	44,800,000		150
F-2174B★	New York	2,560,000	$125	190	F-2174H	St. Louis	16,000,000		150
F-2174C	Philadelphia	41,600,000		150	F-2174H★	St. Louis	640,000	$125	190
F-2174C★	Philadelphia	1,280,000	125	190	F-2174I	Minneapolis	9,600,000		150
F-2174D	Cleveland	9,600,000		150	F-2174J	Kansas City	9,600,000		150
F-2174D★	Cleveland	1,024,000		150	F-2174K	Dallas	51,200,000		150
F-2174E	Richmond	64,000,000	125	190	F-2174L	San Francisco	19,200,000		150

Federal Reserve Notes
Series of 1996 to 2006, Green Seal, Security Features

Face of F-2175 to F-2181. Franklin's portrait is modified, and security features have been added.

Back of F-2175 to F-2181. The Independence Hall motif is retained, but with added security features.

Series of 1996—Signatures of Withrow and Rubin
Printed in Washington, DC

No.	Issuing Bank	Quantity Printed	Unc-63	No.	Issuing Bank	Quantity Printed	Unc-63
F-2175A	Boston	125,600,000	$130	F-2175F★	Atlanta	2,560,000	$165
F-2175A★	Boston	2,560,000	165	F-2175G	Chicago	244,800,000	130
F-2175B	New York	2,325,600,000	130	F-2175G★	Chicago	1,920,000	165
F-2175B★	New York	17,920,000	165	F-2175H	St. Louis	112,800,000	130
F-2175C	Philadelphia	86,400,000	130	F-2175I	Minneapolis	32,000,000	130
F-2175D	Cleveland	176,800,000	130	F-2175J	Kansas City	83,200,000	130
F-2175D★	Cleveland	160,000	425	F-2175K	Dallas	144,800,000	130
F-2175E	Richmond	276,800,000	130	F-2175K★	Dallas	1,920,000	165
F-2175E★	Richmond	3,200,000	165	F-2175L	San Francisco	406,400,000	130
F-2175F	Atlanta	222,400,000	130	F-2175L★	San Francisco	2,560,000	165

Series of 1999—Signatures of Withrow and Summers
Printed in Washington, DC

No.	Issuing Bank	Quantity Printed	Unc-63	No.	Issuing Bank	Quantity Printed	Unc-63
F-2176A	Boston	48,000,000	$125	F-2176F	Atlanta	16,000,000	$125
F-2176A★	Boston	3,520,000	160	F-2176G	Chicago	52,400,000	125
F-2176B	New York	172,800,000	125	F-2176H	St. Louis	22,400,000	125
F-2176B★	New York	3,840,000	165	F-2176I	Minneapolis	70,400,000	125
F-2176C	Philadelphia	3,200,000	125	F-2176J	Kansas City	25,600,000	125
F-2176D	Cleveland	19,200,000	125	F-2176K	Dallas	19,200,000	125
F-2176E	Richmond	60,800,000	125				

Series of 2001—Signatures of Marin and O'Neill
Printed in Washington, DC

No.	Issuing Bank	Quantity Printed	Unc-63	No.	Issuing Bank	Quantity Printed	Unc-63
F-2177A	Boston	32,000,000	$125	F-2177F	Atlanta	99,200,000	$125
F-2177B	New York	579,200,000	125	F-2177F★	Atlanta	1,600,000	125
F-2177B★	New York	320,000	250	F-2177G	Chicago	57,600,000	125
F-2177C	Philadelphia	32,000,000	125	F-2177H	St. Louis	25,600,000	125
F-2177D	Cleveland	19,200,000	125	F-2177I	Minneapolis	9,600,000	125
F-2177D★	Cleveland	1,920,000	125	F-2177J	Kansas City	22,400,000	125
F-2177E	Richmond	64,000,000	125	F-2177K	Dallas	60,800,000	125
F-2177E★	Richmond	1,920,000	125	F-2177L	San Francisco	147,200,000	125

Series of 2003—Signatures of Marin and Snow
Printed in Washington, DC

No.	Issuing Bank	Unc-63	No.	Issuing Bank	Unc-63	No.	Issuing Bank	Unc-63
F-2178A	Boston	$125	F-2178B★	New York	$250	F-2178D	Cleveland	$125
F-2178B	New York	125	F-2178C	Philadelphia	125	F-2178E	Richmond	125

No.	Issuing Bank	Unc-63	No.	Issuing Bank	Unc-63	No.	Issuing Bank	Unc-63
F-2178E★	Richmond	$250	F-2178H	St. Louis	$125	F-2178K★	Dallas	$250
F-2178F	Atlanta	125	F-2178I	Minneapolis	125	F-2178L	San Francisco	125
F-2178F★	Atlanta	250	F-2178J	Kansas City	125			
F-2178G	Chicago	125	F-2178K	Dallas	125			

Series of 2003-A—Signatures of Cabral and Snow
Printed in Washington, DC

No.	Issuing Bank	Unc-63	No.	Issuing Bank	Unc-63	No.	Issuing Bank	Unc-63
F-2179A	Boston	$125	F-2179F	Atlanta	$125	F-2179J	Kansas City	$125
F-2179B	New York	125	F-2179G	Chicago	125	F-2179K	Dallas	125
F-2179B★	New York	175	F-2179G★	Chicago	175	F-2179L	San Francisco	125
F-2179C	Philadelphia	125	F-2179H	St. Louis	125	F-2179L★	San Francisco	175
F-2179D	Cleveland	125	F-2179H★	St. Louis	175			
F-2179E	Richmond	125	F-2179I	Minneapolis	125			

Series of 2006—Signatures of Cabral and Paulson
Printed in Washington, DC

No.	Issuing Bank	Unc-63	No.	Issuing Bank	Unc-63	No.	Issuing Bank	Unc-63
F-2180A	Boston	Current	F-2180E★	Richmond	Current	F-2180J	Kansas City	Current
F-2180B	New York	Current	F-2180F	Atlanta	Current	F-2180K	Dallas	Current
F-2180B★	New York	Current	F-2180F★	Atlanta	Current	F-2180L	San Francisco	Current
F-2180C	Philadelphia	Current	F-2180G	Chicago	Current	F-2180L★	San Francisco	Current
F-2180D	Cleveland	Current	F-2180H	St. Louis	Current			
F-2180E	Richmond	Current	F-2180I	Minneapolis	Current			

Series of 2006—Signatures of Cabral and Paulson
Printed at the Western Facility (Fort Worth, Texas)

No.	Issuing Bank	Unc-63	No.	Issuing Bank	Unc-63	No.	Issuing Bank	Unc-63
F-2181B	New York	Current	F-2181K	Dallas	Current	F-2181L	San Francisco	Current
F-2181J	Kansas City	Current	F-2181K★	Dallas	Current	F-2181L★	San Francisco	Current

Federal Reserve Notes
Series of 2009 to Date, Green Seal, Additional Features

Face of F-2182 to date. Security features, including microprinting and color-shifting ink, have been added.

Back of F-2182 to date. Security features, including microprinting and color-shifting ink, have been added.

Series of 2009 (color added)—Signatures of Geithner and Rios
Printed in Washington, DC

No.	
F-2182	Now in production. Districts unknown as of press time. Scheduled for release Feb. 10, 2011.

Series of 2009—Signatures of Geithner and Rios
Printed at the Western Facility (Fort Worth, Texas)

No.	
F-2183	Now in production. Districts unknown as of press time. Scheduled for release Feb. 10, 2011.

COLLECTING $500 NOTES

A recent Congressional report contained the estimate that some 286,000 notes of the $500 denomination, with a total face value of $143,889,500, are still outstanding. The only large-size notes that may be considered collectible are the later Gold Certificates (F-1216 to F-1217) and the Federal Reserve Notes, Series of 1918. For these, you can expect to pay a five-figure sum.

Small-size notes of this denomination, on the other hand, are surprisingly affordable, and in sufficient supply in the dealer pipeline that they can be found without difficulty. In less than Extremely Fine condition, it is even possible to see them for less than twice their face value.

LARGE-SIZE $500 NOTES

Interest-Bearing Notes of March 2, 1861, 60 Days

No.	Signatures		Seal	
F-195d	Chittenden	Spinner	No Treasury seal	1 Proof known

Interest-Bearing Notes of March 2, 1861, 6%, 2 Years

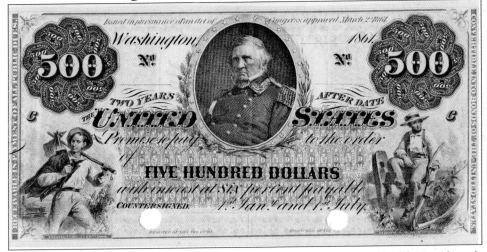

Face of F-202c with man carrying bindle stick at left, portrait of General Winfield Scott at center, and farmer with a scythe to the left. Green security overprint at center.

Back of F-202c printed in brown with vertical center inscriptions, small "500" numbers at left and right. Vertical D in disk at center. The illustration is of a proof. *See next page for chart.*

No.	Signatures		Seal	
F-202c	Chittenden	Spinner	No Treasury seal	Unknown

Interest-Bearing Notes of July 17, 1861, 7.3%, 3 Years

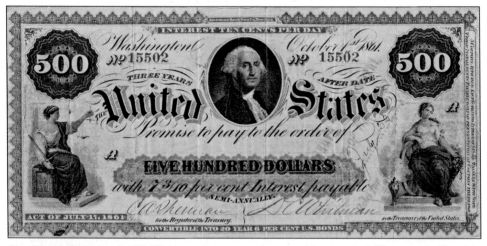

Face of F-209. Justice seated at left, Washington in center, seated woman with wagon wheel ("Transportation") at right.

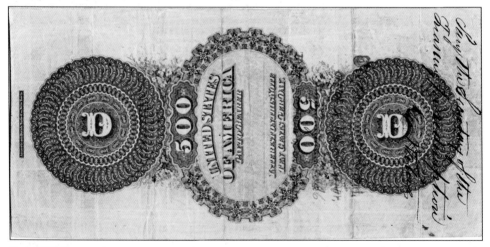

Back of F-209.

No.		
F-209	2005 Heritage Auction, sold for $299,000	2 known

Interest-Bearing Notes of March 3, 1863, 5%, 1 Year

Vignettes similar to those used on Compound Interest Treasury Notes.

No.	Signatures		Seal	
F-200	Chittenden	Spinner	Red	Unknown

Interest-Bearing Notes of March 3, 1863, 5%, 2 Years

Face with Liberty standing at left, hand on top of fasces, American flag in rear. Eagle at center. Back with 500 twice in large numerals, inscriptions, and ornamental vignettes. Proof impressions exist.

No.	Signatures		Seal	
F-205	Chittenden	Spinner	Red	Unknown

Interest-Bearing Notes of June 30, 1864, 7.3%, 3 Years

Similar to design below (F-212f).

No.	Date Imprint	Signatures		Seal	
F-212b	August 15, 1864–March 3, 1865	Colby	Spinner	Red	Unknown

Interest-Bearing Notes of March 3, 1865, 7.3%, 3 Years

Face of F-212f. Mortar at lower left, Alexander Hamilton at center, three-quarter portrait of Washington at lower right.

Back of F-212f.

No.	Signatures		Seal	
F-212f	Colby	Spinner	Red	1 known (punch-canceled)

Legal Tender Notes
Series of 1862,
First Obligation

Face of F-183a. Half-length bust of Secretary of the Treasury Albert Gallatin at center.

Back of F-183a.

No.	Act	Signatures		Seal	
F-183a	1862	Chittenden	Spinner	Red	1 known

Legal Tender Notes
Series of 1862 and 1863, Second Obligation

Back of F-183b to F-183d. Front is same as the preceding.

No.	Act	Signatures		Seal	
F-183b	1862	Chittenden	Spinner	Red	Unknown
F-183c	1863	Chittenden	Spinner	Red, one serial no.	4 known
F-183d	1863	Chittenden	Spinner	Red, two serial nos.	1 known

Legal Tender Notes
Series of 1869

Face of F-184. Justice seated at left. Bust of John Quincy Adams to the right.

No.	Signatures		Seal	
F-184	Allison	Spinner	Large red	4 known

Legal Tender Notes
Series of 1874 to 1880

Face of F-185a to F-185n. At left, Victory standing with wreath; at center, large 500; at right, bust of General Joseph King Mansfield.

Back of F-185a to F-185n.

No.	Series	Signatures		Seal	
F-185a	1874	Allison	Spinner	Small red, rays	5 known
F-185b	1875	Allison	New	Small red, rays	1 known
F-185c	1875	Allison	Wyman	Small red, rays	1 known
F-185d	1878	Allison	Gilfillan	Small red, rays	6 known
F-185e	1880	Scofield	Gilfillan	Large brown	Unknown
F-185f	1880	Bruce	Wyman	Large brown	2 known
F-185g	1880	Rosecrans	Jordan	Large red, plain	Unknown
F-185h	1880	Rosecrans	Hyatt	Large red, plain	Unknown
F-185i	1880	Rosecrans	Huston	Large red, spiked	3 known
F-185j	1880	Rosecrans	Nebeker	Small red, scalloped	2 known
F-185k	1880	Tillman	Morgan	Small red, scalloped	6 known
F-185l	1880	Bruce	Roberts	Small red, scalloped	5 known
F-185m	1880	Lyons	Roberts	Small red, scalloped	5 known
F-185n	1880	Napier	McClung	Small red, scalloped	Unknown

National Bank Notes
Original Series ("First Charter Period")

Designs similar to the following.

No.	Signatures		Seal	
F-464	Colby	Spinner	Red	Extremely rare

National Bank Notes
Series of 1875 ("First Charter Period")

Face of F-464a. At left, a vignette titled "Civilization." At right is "The Arrival of the Sirius, 1838."

Back of F-464a. The "Surrender of General Burgoyne to General Gates."

No.	Signatures		Seal	
F-464a	Scofield	Gilfillan	Red	Unique

Compound Interest Treasury Notes of 1863 and 1864

Notes F-194 to F-194b show the ship *New Ironsides* and the vignette "The Standard Bearer." None known. Proof impressions exist.

No.	Act	Overprint Date	Signatures		Seal	
F-194	1863	June 10, 1864	Chittenden	Spinner	Red	Unknown
F-194a	1864	July 15, 1864	Chittenden	Spinner	Red	Unknown
F-194b	1864	Aug 15, 1864–Oct 1, 1865	Colby	Spinner	Red	Unknown

National Gold Bank Notes

Face design is the same as that of F-464. Back with montage of contemporary gold coins, printed in brown. None known.

No.	Series	Payable At	
F-1166a	Original	First National Gold Bank of San Francisco	Unknown
F-1166a	Original	National Gold Bank and Trust Co. of San Francisco	Unknown
F-1166a	Original	National Gold Bank of D.O. Mills & Co., Sacramento	Unknown

Silver Certificates, *Series of 1878, With Countersignatures*

Face of F-345a has the portrait of abolitionist Senator Charles Sumner of Massachusetts.

No.	Countersignature	Payable At	
F-345a	A.U. Wyman	Washington, DC	1 known

Silver Certificates, *Series of 1880, No Countersignatures*

Face of F-345b to F-345d. As preceding, without countersignatures.

Back of F-345b to F-345d.

No.	Signatures		Seal	
F-345b	Scofield	Gilfillan	Large brown	Unknown
F-345c	Bruce	Gilfillan	Large brown	5 known
F-345d	Bruce	Wyman	Large brown	2 known

Gold Certificates, *Act of March 3, 1863*

Face design unknown. Back with D to each side and FIVE / HUNDRED in circle at center, ornate vignettes surrounding. None known.

No.	Signatures		Seal	
F-1166d	Colby	Spinner	None	Unknown

Gold Certificates, *Series of 1870 and 1875*

Face with bust of Abraham Lincoln at left. Back is blank.

No.	Series	Signatures		Seal	
F-1166i	1870	Allison	Two Treasury clerks	Red	1 known
F-1166n	1875	Allison	New	Red	Unknown

Gold Certificates, *Series of 1882 and 1922*

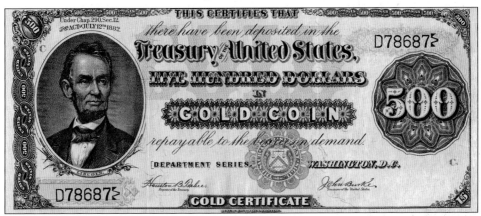

Face of F-1215a to F-1217. Bust of Lincoln at left.

Back of F-1215a to F-1217. Large D at left. Eagle perched on flag.

No.	Series	Signatures		Seal		VG-8	F-12	VF-20	EF-40
F-1215a	1882	Bruce	Gilfillan	Brown	1 known	2006 auction, sold for $276,000			
With countersignature by Thomas C. Acton, Asst. Treasurer, payable at New York									
F-1215b	1882	Bruce	Gilfillan	Brown	Unknown				
As above, but without Acton countersignature									
F-1215c	1882	Bruce	Wyman	Brown	1 known				
F-1215d	1882	Rosecrans	Hyatt	Large red	1 known				

Chart continued on next page.

No.	Series	Signatures		Seal	VG-8	F-12	VF-20	EF-40
F-1216	1882	Lyons	Roberts	Small red	$5,625	$10,500	$22,250	$45,000
F-1216a	1882	Parker	Burke	Small red	5,625	10,750	21,000	42,500
F-1216b	1882	Teehee	Burke	Small red	5,750	10,500	22,250	40,000
F-1217	1922	Speelman	White	Small red	5,750	10,750	22,500	65,000

Federal Reserve Notes
Series of 1918, Blue Seal

Face of F-1132 to F-1132b-J. Bust of Chief Justice James Marshall.

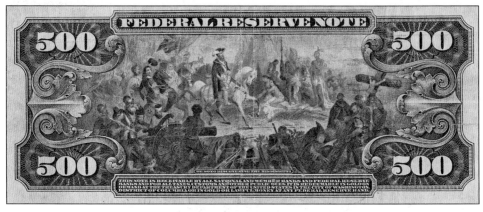

Back of F-1132 to F-1132b-J. "George Washington Resigning His Commission."

No.	Issuing Bank	Signatures			VG-8	F-12	VF-20	EF-40	Unc-63
F-1132A	Boston	Burke	Glass	4 known	$8,500	$13,000	$22,500	$33,250	—
F-1132B	New York	Burke	Glass		5,000	8,000	20,000	32,500	—
F-1132C	Philadelphia	Burke	Glass	4 known	8,500	19,000	22,500	45,000	—
F-1132D	Cleveland	Burke	Glass		5,000	9,500	20,000	30,000	—
F-1132E	Richmond	Burke	Glass	Unknown					
F-1132F	Atlanta	Burke	Glass		5,000	8,500	20,000	30,000	—
F-1132G	Chicago	Burke	Glass		5,000	8,500	20,000	24,000	—
F-1132H	St. Louis	Burke	Glass	5 known	5,000	9,500	22,500	32,250	
F-1132I	Minneapolis	Burke	Glass	Unique					
F-1132J	Kansas City	Burke	Glass		5,000	12,000	20,000	26,000	—
F-1132K	Dallas	Burke	Glass	4 known	8,500	15,500	22,500	36,000	—
F-1132L	San Francisco	Burke	Glass		5,000	9,500	20,000	32,500	—
F-1132a-L	San Francisco	Burke	Houston	2 known					—
F-1132b-B	New York	White	Mellon		8,500	16,000	30,000	40,000	
F-1132b-F	Atlanta	White	Mellon	Unknown					
F-1132b-J	Kansas City	White	Mellon	Unknown					

SMALL-SIZE $500 NOTES
Gold Certificates, *Series of 1928, Gold Seal*

Note F-2407 has the same designs as Federal Reserve Notes F-2200 through F-2204.

No.	Signatures		Quantity Printed	VG-8	F-12	VF-20	EF-40	Unc-63
F-2407	Woods	Mellon	420,000	$2,750	$4,675	$7,125	$14,500	$40,000

Federal Reserve Notes, *Series of 1928, Green Seal*

Note F-2200 has the same designs as the following type.

No.	Issuing Bank	Quantity Printed		EF-40	Unc-63
F-2200A	Boston	69,120		$10,500	$32,500
F-2200A★	Boston		Unknown		
F-2200B	New York	299,400		1,500	3,000
F-2200B★	New York		Unknown		
F-2200C	Philadelphia	135,120		1,500	3,000
F-2200C★	Philadelphia			17,500	—
F-2200D	Cleveland	166,440		1,500	3,000
F-2200D★	San Francisco		Unknown		
F-2200E	Richmond	84,720		1,600	3,000
F-2200E★	Richmond		Unknown		
F-2200F	Atlanta	69,360		1,600	3,000
F-2200F★	Atlanta		Unknown		
F-2200G	Chicago	573,600		1,500	3,000
F-2200G★	Chicago			Rare	35,000
F-2200H	St Louis	66,180		1,500	3,000
F-2200H★	St Louis		Unknown		
F-2200I	Minneapolis	34,680		1,700	3,750
F-2200I★	Minneapolis		Unknown		
F-2200J	Kansas City	510,720		1,500	3,000
F-2200J★	Kansas City		Unknown		
F-2200K	Dallas	70,560		1,600	6,000
F-2200K★	Dallas		Unknown		
F-2200L	San Francisco	64,080		1,600	3,000
F-2200L★	San Francisco		Unknown		

Federal Reserve Notes
Series of 1934 to 1934-C, Green Seal

Series of 1934—Signatures of Julian and Morgenthau

Face of F-2201. Bust of William McKinley. Face printing states (since rescinded) that the bill is payable "in gold or lawful money."

Back of F-2201.

See next page for chart.

No.	Issuing Bank	Quantity Printed	EF-40	Unc-63	No.	Issuing Bank	Quantity Printed	EF-40	Unc-63
F-2201A	Boston	56,628	$1,100	$1,950	F-2201G★	Chicago		$3,500	$7,250
F-2201B	New York	288,000	1,100	1,800	F-2201H	St Louis	24,000	1,225	2,300
F-2201B★	New York		3,750	7,500	F-2201H★	St Louis		4,250	8,000
F-2201C	Philadelphia	31,200	1,100	1,950	F-2201I	Minneapolis	24,000	1,225	2,300
F-2201C★	Philadelphia		3,750	7,500	F-2201I★	Minneapolis		5,000	—
F-2201D	Cleveland	39,000	1,100	1,950	F-2201J	Kansas City	40,800	1,100	1,950
F-2201D★	Cleveland		3,750	7,500	F-2201J★	Kansas City		4,500	—
F-2201E	Richmond	40,800	1,100	1,800	F-2201K	Dallas	31,200	1,200	2,100
F-2201E★	Richmond		3,750	7,500	F-2201K★	Dallas		4,750	—
F-2201F	Atlanta	46,200	1,100	1,800	F-2201L	San Francisco	83,400	1,100	1,850
F-2201F★	Atlanta		3,750	7,500	F-2201L★	San Francisco		3,750	8,500
F-2201G	Chicago	212,400	1,000	1,800					

Series of 1934-A—Signatures of Julian and Morgenthau

Face of F-2202. Same as preceding but with no mention of gold in payment.

Back of F-2202.

No.	Issuing Bank	Quantity Printed	EF-40	Unc-63	No.	Issuing Bank	Quantity Printed	EF-40	Unc-63
F-2202B	New York	276,000	$1,100	$2,000	F-2202H	St Louis	57,600	$1,100	$2,000
F-2202B★	New York		6,000	9,000	F-2202I	Minneapolis	14,400	1,400	2,500
F-2202C	Philadelphia	45,300	1,100	2,000	F-2202J	Kansas City	55,200	1,100	2,000
F-2202D	Cleveland	28,800	1,100	2,000	F-2202J★	Kansas City		6,000	9,000
F-2202E	Richmond	36,000	1,100	2,000	F-2202K	Dallas	34,800	1,100	2,000
F-2202F	Atlanta	included above	1,100	2,000	F-2202L	San Francisco	93,000	1,100	2,000
F-2202G	Chicago	214,800	1,100	2,000	F-2202L★	San Francisco		6,000	9,000
F-2202G★	Chicago		6,000	9,000					

Series of 1934-B—Signatures of Julian and Vinson

Samples were printed, but none were issued.

No.	Issuing Bank	Quantity Printed	
F-2203F	Atlanta	2,472	None issued

Series of 1934-C—Signatures of Julian and Snyder

Samples were printed, but none were issued.

No.	Issuing Bank	Quantity Printed	
F-2204A	Boston	1,440	None issued
F-2204B	New York	204	None issued

COLLECTING $1,000 NOTES

As with the $500 denomination, it is possible to collect the later, large-size Gold Certificates and the Series of 1918 Federal Reserve Notes, both of which appear at important auction sales more frequently than one might think. The most famous $1,000 note is the "Grand Watermelon" (F-379a–b), so called for the same reason as the $100 Watermelon note.

Current government estimates are that there are still 167,701 individual $1,000 notes in existence. Most of these are certainly of the small-size variety. Federal Reserve Notes are much easier to find than the Series of 1928 Gold Certificates and, once again, the premium over face value is not exorbitant in lower conditions. See the $100 notes chapter for an explanation of the Gold Certificates of 1934.

LARGE-SIZE $1,000 NOTES

Interest-Bearing Notes

Face of note F-201 has standing figure of Justice at left, eagle with shield at top center, and standing Liberty with fasces and flag at right. None known. Back design unknown.

No.	
F-201	Unknown

Face of F-202d and F-206, with portrait of Washington to the left, standing figure of Victory at center, and view of the Treasury Building at right. Proof illustrated.

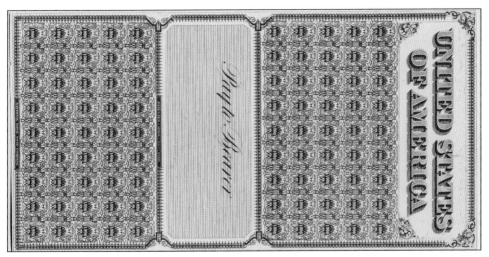

Back of F-202d and F-206 with vertical inscriptions. UNITED STATES OF AMERICA at top, Pay to Bearer at center. Small "1000" numbers at each side of center. Proof illustrated.

No.	
F-202d	1 Proof known
F-206	Unknown

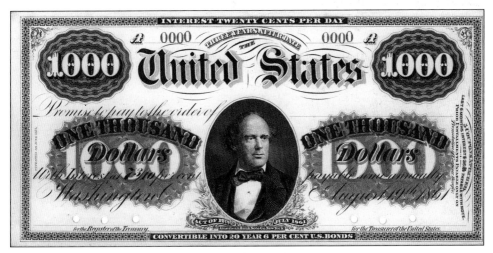

Face of F-210 to F-212g. Bust of Salmon P. Chase. Proof illustrated.

Entry continued on next page.

Back of F-210 to F-212g. Proof impression illustrated.

No.		
F-210		Unknown
F-212c	Probably issued	Unknown
F-212g		3 known

Legal Tender Notes
Series of 1862,
First Obligation

Face of F-186a with facing bust of Robert Morris, superintendent of finance from 1781 to 1784.

No.	Act	Signatures		Seal	
F-186a	1862	Chittenden	Spinner	Red	Unknown

Legal Tender Notes
Series of 1862 and 1863, Second Obligation

Face of F-186b to F-186e, with portrait of Robert Morris.

Back of F-186b to F-186e.

No.	Act	Signatures		Seal	
F-186b	1862	Chittenden	Spinner	Red	Unknown
American Bank Note Co. at right, National Bank Note Co. at left					
F-186c	1863	Chittenden	Spinner	Red, one serial no.	Unique
American Bank Note Co. at right only					
F-186d	1863	Chittenden	Spinner	Red, one serial no.	3 known
F-186e	1863	Chittenden	Spinner	Red, two serial nos.	Unique

Legal Tender Notes
Series of 1869

Face of F-186f. At left, Christopher Columbus with globe; at center, DeWitt Clinton.

Back of F-186f.

No.	Act	Signatures		Seal	
F-186f	1869	Allison	Spinner	Large red	2 known

Legal Tender Notes
Series of 1878 and 1880

Face of F-187a to F-187l. Similar to preceding.

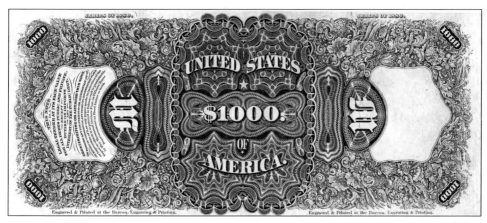

Back of F-187a to F-187l.

No.	Series	Signatures		Seal	
F-187a	1878	Allison	Gilfillan	Small red, rays	Extremely rare
F-187b	1880	Bruce	Wyman	Large brown	Extremely rare
F-187c	1880	Rosecrans	Jordan	Large red, plain	Extremely rare
F-187d	1880	Rosecrans	Hyatt	Large red, spiked	Extremely rare
F-187e	1880	Rosecrans	Huston	Large red, spiked	Extremely rare
F-187f	1880	Rosecrans	Nebeker	Large brown	Extremely rare
F-187g	1880	Tillman	Morgan	Small red, scalloped	Extremely rare
F-187h	1880	Tillman	Roberts	Small red, scalloped	Extremely rare
F-187i	1880	Bruce	Roberts	Small red, scalloped	Extremely rare
F-187j	1880	Lyons	Roberts	Small red, scalloped	Extremely rare
F-187k	1880	Vernon	Trent	Small red, scalloped	Extremely rare
F-187l	1880	Napier	McClung	Small red, scalloped	Extremely rare

Compound Interest Treasury Notes of June 30, 1864

Vignettes similar to those used for the One-Year Interest-Bearing Note.

No.	Overprint Date	Signatures		Seal	
F-195	July 15, 1864	Chittenden	Spinner	Red	Unknown
F-195a	Aug. 15, 1864–Sep. 15, 1865	Colby	Spinner	Red	Unknown

National Bank Notes
Original Series and Series of 1875
("First Charter Period")

Face of F-465. Vignette of "General Scott's Entrance Into Mexico City" at left, U.S. Capitol at right. Back of this type shows "Washington Resigning His Commission."

No.	
F-465	Unknown, although 21 pieces are still outstanding

Silver Certificates
Series of 1878 and 1880

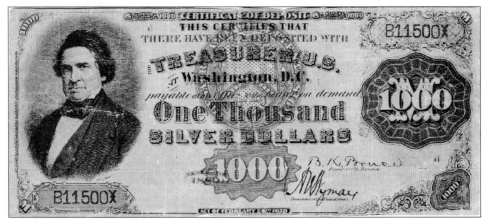

Face of F-346a to F-346d. Half-length portrait of William L. Marcy.

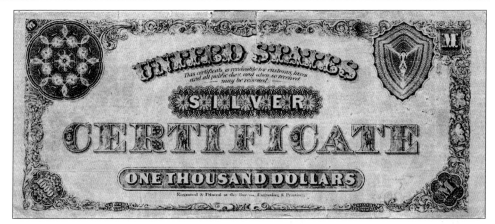

Back of F-346a to F-346d.

No.	Series	Signatures		Seal	
F-346a	1878	Scofield	Gilfillan	Large red, rays (countersigned)	Unknown
F-346b	1880	Scofield	Gilfillan	Large brown	Unknown
F-346c	1880	Bruce	Gilfillan	Large brown	Unknown
F-346d	1880	Bruce	Wyman	Large brown	5 known

Silver Certificates
Series of 1891

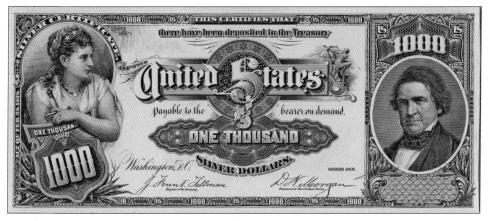

Face of F-346e. At left is a woman with hand resting on shield; at right, William L. Marcy. Back has "1000" in large numerals at center with ornamental vignettes at sides. Proof illustrated.

No.	Signatures		Seal	
F-346e	Tillman	Morgan	Small red	2 known

Treasury or Coin Notes
Series of 1890

Face of F-379a and F-379b. Bust of General George Meade.

Back of F-379a and F-379b. The famous "Grand Watermelon."

No.	Signatures		Seal	
F-379a	Rosecrans	Huston	Large brown	Extremely rare; an AU was the first note to sell in auction for over $1 million
F-379b	Rosecrans	Nebeker	Small red	2 known

Treasury or Coin Notes
Series of 1891

Face of F-379c and F-379d. Design same as the preceding.

Back of F-379c and F-379d.

No.	Signatures		Seal	
F-379c	Tillman	Morgan	Small red	Unique; reportedly sold privately for over $2 million
F-379d	Rosecrans	Nebeker	Small red	Unique

Gold Certificates
Act of March 3, 1863

Face of F-1166e has eagle standing on draped shield. Back with denomination and inscriptions.

No.	Signatures		Seal	
F-1166e	Colby	Spinner	None	1 known

Gold Certificates
Series of 1870 and 1875

Face of F-1166j has portrait of Alexander Hamilton at left. Back is blank.

No.	Series	Signatures		Seal	
F-1166j	1870	Allison	Two Treasury clerks	Red	1 known
F-1166o	1875	Allison	New	Red	Unknown

Gold Certificates
Series of 1882

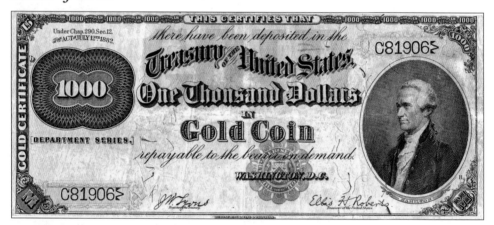

Face of F-1218 to F-1218g. Bust of Alexander Hamilton.

Back of F-1218 to F-1218g.

No.	Signatures		Seal	
With countersignature by Thomas C. Acton, Asst. Treasurer, payable at New York				
F-1218	Bruce	Gilfillan	Brown	Unknown
F-1218a	Bruce	Gilfillan	Brown	Extremely rare
As above, but without Acton countersignature				
F-1218b	Bruce	Wyman	Brown	Unique
F-1218c	Rosecrans	Hyatt	Large red	Unique
F-1218d	Rosecrans	Huston	Large brown	Extremely rare; an AU was the second note to be sold at auction for over $1 million
F-1218e	Rosecrans	Nebeker	Small red	Extremely rare
F-1218f	Lyons	Roberts	Small red	Rare
F-1218g	Lyons	Treat	Small red	Rare

Gold Certificates
Series of 1907 and 1922

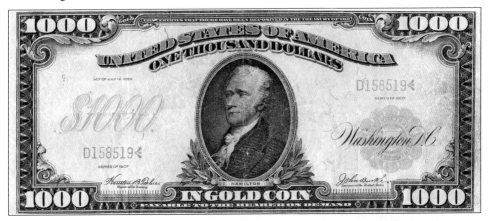

Face of F-1219 to F-1220. Bust of Alexander Hamilton.

Back of F-1219 to F-1220. Great Seal of the United States.

No.	Series	Signatures		Seal		VG-8	F-12	VF-20	EF-40	Unc-63
F-1219	1907	Vernon	Treat	Gold	Rare					
F-1219a	1907	Vernon	McClung	Gold	Unknown					
F-1219b	1907	Napier	McClung	Gold	Unique					
F-1219c	1907	Napier	Burke	Gold	Extremely rare					
F-1219d	1907	Parker	Burke	Gold		$10,500	$22,000	$37,500	—	—
F-1219e	1907	Teehee	Burke	Gold		10,500	17,500	32,500	—	—
F-1220	1922	Speelman	White	Gold		10,500	20,000	36,000	$55,000	—

Federal Reserve Notes
Series of 1918,
Blue Seal

Face of F-1133A to F-1133b-L. Bust of Alexander Hamilton.

Back of F-1133A to F-1133b-L. Eagle perched on flag.

No.	Issuing Bank	Signatures			VG-8	F-12	VF-20	EF-40	Unc-63
F-1133A	Boston	Burke	Glass		$8,000	$12,000	$22,500	$35,000	$50,000
F-1133B	New York	Burke	Glass		7,000	11,000	20,000	24,000	40,000
F-1133C	Philadelphia	Burke	Glass		7,000	11,000	20,000	24,000	40,000
F-1133D	Cleveland	Burke	Glass		7,000	11,000	20,000	24,000	40,000
F-1133E	Richmond	Burke	Glass	Unknown					
F-1133F	Atlanta	Burke	Glass		7,000	10,000	21,000	—	—
F-1133G	Chicago	Burke	Glass		7,000	9,500	20,000	24,000	40,000
F-1133H	St. Louis	Burke	Glass		7,500	13,000	22,500	—	—
F-1133I	Minneapolis	Burke	Glass	2 known					
F-1133J	Kansas City	Burke	Glass		8,750	16,000	25,000	45,000	55,000
F-1133K	Dallas	Burke	Glass		8,750	16,000	25,000	40,000	
F-1133L	San Francisco	Burke	Glass		7,000	9,500	13,500	27,500	45,000
F-1133a-B	New York	Burke	Houston		8,500	15,000	24,000	40,000	—
F-1133b-F	Atlanta	White	Mellon		8,500	15,000	24,000	40,000	—
F-1133b-J	Kansas City	White	Mellon	Unknown					
F-1133b-L	San Francisco	White	Mellon		8,500	15,000	26,000	40,000	50,000

SMALL-SIZE $1,000 NOTES

Gold Certificates
Series of 1928, Gold Seal

Face of F-2408. Portrait of Grover Cleveland.

Back of F-2408. Back type used on all issued small-size $1,000 notes. Printed in green.

No.	Signatures		Quantity Printed	VG-8	F-12	VF-20	EF-40	Unc-63
F-2408	Woods	Mellon	28,800	$5,000	$8,500	$11,000	$20,000	$45,000

Gold Certificates
Series of 1934, Gold Seal

Designs as preceding, except that the back is printed in gold. None were released.

No.	Signatures		Quantity Printed	
F-2409	Julian	Morgenthau	84,000	For government use only

Federal Reserve Notes
Series of 1928,
Green Seal

Face of F-2210. Bust of Grover Cleveland. The obligation (since rescinded) states that the bill is payable "in gold or lawful money."

Back of F-2210.

No.	Issuing Bank	Quantity Printed		VF-20	EF-40	Unc-63
F-2210A	Boston	58,320		$5,750	$25,000	$52,000
F-2210A★	Boston		Unknown			
F-2210B	New York	139,200		2,150	2,625	4,000
F-2210B★	New York			32,500	60,000	—
F-2210C	Philadelphia	96,708		2,150	2,775	4,250
F-2210C★	Philadelphia			32,500	60,000	—
F-2210D	Cleveland	79,680		2,150	2,625	4,250
F-2210D★	Cleveland			32,500	60,000	—
F-2210E	Richmond	66,840		2,150	2,625	4,250
F-2210E★	Richmond			32,500	60,000	—
F-2210F	Atlanta	47,400		2,150	2,875	5,000
F-2210F★	Atlanta		Unknown			
F-2210G	Chicago	355,800		2,150	2,625	4,250
F-2210G★	Chicago			32,500	60,000	—
F-2210H	St. Louis	60,000		2,150	3,375	4,750
F-2210H★	St. Louis			32,500	60,000	—
F-2210I	Minneapolis	26,640		2,500	3,125	6,000
F-2210I★	Minneapolis			32,500	60,000	—
F-2210J	Kansas City	62,172		2,150	2,625	4,250
F-2210J★	Kansas City		Unknown			
F-2210K	Dallas	42,960		2,450	3,500	6,000
F-2210K★	Dallas		Unknown			
F-2210L	San Francisco	67,920		2,300	2,800	4,750
F-2210L★	San Francisco		Unknown			

Federal Reserve Notes
Series of 1934 to 1934-C, Green Seal

Face of F-2211 to F-2213. As preceding but with no mention of gold in payment. Back type is as preceding.

Series of 1934—Signatures of Julian and Morgenthau

No.	Issuing Bank	Quantity Printed	VF-20	EF-40	Unc-63
F-2211A	Boston	46,200	$2,125	$2,400	$4,000
F-2211A★	Boston		8,600	12,000	—
F-2211B	New York	322,784	2,025	2,275	3,250
F-2211B★	New York		14,500	18,500	—
F-2211C	Philadelphia	33,000	2,125	2,400	3,250
F-2211C★	Philadelphia		4,850	7,250	16,500
F-2211D	Cleveland	35,400	2,125	2,400	3,250
F-2211D★	Cleveland		4,850	6,600	16,500
F-2211E	Richmond	19,560	2,125	2,400	3,500
F-2211E★	Richmond		18,500	—	—
F-2211F	Atlanta	67,800	2,125	2,400	3,500
F-2211F★	Atlanta		6,750	8,650	—
F-2211G	Chicago	167,040	2,025	2,275	3,250
F-2211G★	Chicago		4,850	6,600	16,500
F-2211H	St. Louis	22,400	2,125	2,400	3,500
F-2211H★	St. Louis		7,750	—	—
F-2211I	Minneapolis	12,000	2,250	2,650	5,000
F-2211I★	Minneapolis		11,500	—	—
F-2211J	Kansas City	51,840	2,125	2,400	3,500
F-2211J★	Kansas City		9,000	12,500	—
F-2211K	Dallas	46,800	2,150	2,400	4,600
F-2211K★	Dallas		9,500	12,500	25,000
F-2211L	San Francisco	90,600	2,125	2,400	3,500
F-2211L★	San Francisco		4,375	6,500	16,500

Series of 1934-A—Signatures of Julian and Morgenthau

No.	Issuing Bank	Quantity Printed	VF-20	EF-40	Unc-63
F-2212A	Boston	30,000	$2,100	$2,400	$3,500
F-2212B	New York	174,348	2,100	2,400	3,500
F-2212B★	New York		13,000	16,000	Rare
F-2212C	Philadelphia	78,000	2,100	2,400	3,500
F-2212D	Cleveland	28,800	2,100	2,400	3,500
F-2212E	Richmond	16,800	2,450	2,800	3,500
F-2212F	Atlanta	80,964	2,100	2,400	3,500
F-2212F★	Atlanta	Unknown			
F-2212G	Chicago	134,400	2,100	2,400	3,500
F-2212G★	Chicago		8,500	12,500	Rare
F-2212H	St. Louis	39,600	2,100	2,400	3,500
F-2212I	Minneapolis	4,800	2,575	3,525	7,000
F-2212J	Kansas City	21,600	2,100	2,400	3,500
F-2212L	San Francisco	36,600	2,100	2,400	3,500

Series of 1934-C—Signatures of Julian and Snyder

No.	Issuing Bank	Quantity Printed			
F-2213A	Boston	1,200			Unknown to collectors
F-2213B	New York	168			Unknown to collectors

COLLECTING $5,000 NOTES

Large-size $5,000 notes are not collectible. There are so few known of all types combined that they only merit academic discussion. Treasury records indicate that 342 small-size notes are still outstanding, but far fewer than that are known. In terms of availability, there are less of these than there are of the $10,000 denomination.

Production of these notes (and all denominations $500 and higher) ended in 1946. Today, any notes turned into a bank are supposed to be returned to the Federal Reserve and withdrawn from circulation.

LARGE-SIZE $5,000 NOTES

Interest-Bearing Notes

No.	
F-202	Unknown
F-211	Unknown

Legal Tender Notes, *Series of 1878*

Face of F-188. Bust of James Madison. Specimen illustrated.

Back of F-188. Eagle perched on shield. U.S. Capitol in the distance. Specimen illustrated.

No.	Signatures		Seal
F-188	Scofield	Gilfillan	Large brown

Gold Certificates
Act of March 3, 1863

Face with eagle standing on draped shield. Back with denomination and inscriptions.

No.	Signatures		Seal	
F-1166f	Colby	Spinner	None	Unique

Gold Certificates
Series of 1870 and 1875

Face with portrait of James Madison to the left. Denomination on back.

No.	
F-1166k	Unknown

Gold Certificates
Series of 1882 and 1888

Face with bust of James Madison. Gold overprint. Back with small perched eagle at right.

No.	Series	Signatures		Seal	
F-1221	1882	Bruce	Gilfillan	Brown	Unknown
With countersignature by Thomas C. Acton, Asst. Treasurer, payable at New York					
F-1221a	1882	Bruce	Gilfillan	Brown	Unknown
As above, but without Acton countersignature					
F-1221b	1882	Bruce	Wyman	Brown	Unknown
F-1221c	1882	Rosecrans	Hyatt	Large red	Unknown
F-1221d	1882	Rosecrans	Nebeker	Small red	Unknown
F-1221e	1882	Lyons	Roberts	Small red	Unknown
F-1221f	1882	Vernon	Treat	Small red	Unknown
F-1221g	1882	Vernon	McClung	Small red	Unknown
F-1221h	1882	Napier	McClung	Small red	Unknown
F-1221i	1882	Parker	Burke	Small red	Unknown
F-1221j	1882	Teehee	Burke	Small red	2 known
F-1222	1888	Rosecrans	Hyatt	Large red	All redeemed, none outstanding
F-1222a	1888	Rosecrans	Nebeker	Small red	All redeemed, none outstanding
F-1222b	1888	Lyons	Roberts	Small red	All redeemed, none outstanding

Federal Reserve Notes
Series of 1918, Blue Seal

Face of F-1134. Bust of James Madison.

Back of F-1134. *"Washington Resigning His Commission."*

No.	Issuing Bank	Signatures		
F-1134	New York	Burke	Glass	2 known
F-1134	Cleveland	Burke	Glass	1 known
F-1134	Chicago	Burke	Glass	1 known
F-1134	San Francisco	Burke	Glass	1 known

SMALL-SIZE $5,000 NOTES

Gold Certificates, *Series of 1928, Gold Seal*

Design is identical to that of the Federal Reserve Notes that follow, but with "Gold Certificate" wording and use of gold seal and serial numbers.

No.	Signatures		Design No.	Quantity Printed	
F-2410	Woods	Mellon	234	24,000	Rare

Federal Reserve Notes, *Series of 1928, Green Seal*

Face of F-2220. *Bust of James Madison. Printing states that bill is payable "in gold or lawful money."*

Back of F-2220.

No.	Issuing Bank	Quantity Printed		VF-20	EF-40	Unc-63
F-2220A	Boston	1,320		$65,000	$90,000	$125,000
F-2220B	New York	2,640	Unknown			
F-2220D	Cleveland	3,000	Unknown			
F-2220E	Richmond	3,984		65,000	90,000	125,000
F-2220F	Atlanta	1,440		65,000	90,000	125,000
F-2220G	Chicago	3,480		65,000	90,000	125,000
F-2220J	Kansas City	720		95,000	—	—
F-2220K	Dallas	360	Unknown			
F-2220L	San Francisco	1,300	Unknown			

Federal Reserve Notes
Series of 1934 to 1934-B, Green Seal

Face of F-2221 to F-2223. No mention of payment in gold.

Back of F-2221 to F-2223. Back type used on all small-size $1,000 notes.

Series of 1934—Signatures of Julian and Morgenthau

No.	Issuing Bank	Quantity Printed	VF-20	EF-40	Unc-63
F-2221A	Boston	9,480	$50,000	$67,500	$85,000
F-2221B	New York	11,520	50,000	67,500	82,500
F-2221C	Philadelphia	3,000	50,000	67,500	85,000
F-2221D	Cleveland	1,680	50,000	67,500	90,000
F-2221E	Richmond	2,400	50,000	67,500	90,000
F-2221F	Atlanta	3,600	50,000	67,500	85,000
F-2221G	Chicago	6,600	50,000	67,500	85,000
F-2221H	St. Louis	2,400	50,000	67,500	85,000
F-2221J	Kansas City	2,400	50,000	67,500	85,000
F-2221K	Dallas	2,400	52,500	72,500	91,500
F-2221L	San Francisco	6,000	50,000	67,500	85,000

Series of 1934-A—Signatures of Julian and Morgenthau

No.	Issuing Bank	Quantity Printed	
F-2222H	St. Louis	1,440	Unknown

Series of 1934-B—Signatures of Julian and Vinson

Although Bureau of Engraving and Printing records indicate that F-2223-A and F-2223-B exist, none are known.

No.	Issuing Bank	Quantity Printed	
F-2223A	Boston	1,200	Unknown
F-2223B	New York	12	Unknown

Under Chap. 290, Sec. 12,
OF THE ACT OF JULY 12TH 1882.

JACKSON

K310715

TEN-THOUSAND-DOLLAR NOTES

COLLECTING $10,000 NOTES

There are fewer than a dozen large-size notes of this denomination known of all types combined. Of the 61,000 small-size Federal Reserve Notes printed, there are now 200 outstanding. Half of these were on an ostentatiously kitschy public display for years, framed in a Gulliver-esque horseshoe at Binion's Horseshoe Casino in Las Vegas. These notes came onto the market after the display was removed in a cost-cutting measure in the early 2000s. They were dispersed in a manner that likely assures they will be traded, probably at escalating prices, for many years to come.

LARGE-SIZE $10,000 NOTES

Legal Tender Notes
Series of 1878

Face of F-189 has portrait of Andrew Jackson at left. Back with perched eagle, flag draped from pole, seascape at right. Some 4,000 were printed, but none are known.

No.	Series	Signatures		Seal	
F-189	1878	Scofield	Gilfillan	Large brown	Unknown

Gold Certificates
Act of March 3, 1863

Face design unknown. Back with 10,000 near each of four corners, X at center, with ornate vignettes.

No.	
F-1166g	Unknown

Gold Certificates
Series of 1870 and 1875

Face with portrait of Andrew Jackson to the left. Back is plain.

No.	Series	Signatures		Seal	
F-1166l	1870	Allison	Two Treasury clerks	Red	Unknown
F-1166q	1875	Allison	New	Red	1 known

Gold Certificates
Series of 1882

Face of F-1223 to F-1223g. Bust of Andrew Jackson.

Back of F-1223 to F-1223g. Small perched eagle at right.

No.	Signatures		Seal	
F-1223	Bruce	Gilfillan	Brown	Unknown
With countersignature by Thomas C. Acton, Asst. Treasurer, payable at New York				
F-1223a	Bruce	Gilfillan	Brown	Unknown
As above, but without Acton countersignature				
F-1223b	Bruce	Wyman	Brown	Unknown
F-1223c	Rosecrans	Hyatt	Large red	Unknown
F-1223d	Rosecrans	Nebeker	Small red	Unknown
F-1223e	Lyons	Roberts	Small red	Unknown
F-1223f	Vernon	Treat	Small red	2 known
F-1223g	Teehee	Burke	Small red	All redeemed, none outstanding

Gold Certificates
Series of 1888 and 1900

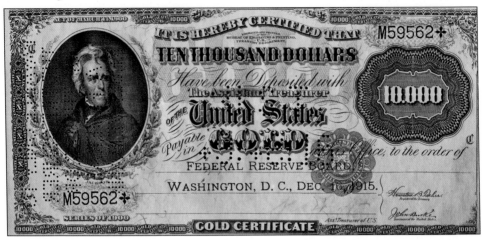

Face of F-1224 to F-1225. Type used on all notes of Series of 1882 through 1900, although imprints vary. Back is plain.

No.	Series	Signatures		Seal	
F-1224	1888	Rosecrans	Hyatt	Large red	All redeemed, none outstanding
F-1224a	1888	Rosecrans	Nebeker	Small red	All redeemed, none outstanding
F-1224b	1888	Lyons	Roberts	Small red	All redeemed, none outstanding
F-1225	1900				All known notes are canceled—not redeemable

Federal Reserve Notes
Series of 1918, Blue Seal

Face of F-1135-B to F-1135-L. Bust of Salmon P. Chase. Back with "Embarkation of the Pilgrims."

No.	Issuing Bank	Signatures		
F-1135B	New York	Burke	Glass	2 known
F-1135D	Cleveland	Burke	Glass	1 known
F-1135L	San Francisco	Burke	Glass	2 known

SMALL-SIZE $10,000 NOTES

Gold Certificates
Series of 1928, Gold Seal

The design of F-2411 is identical to that of the Federal Reserve Notes to follow, except for "Gold Certificate" wording and use of gold seal and serial number. Salmon P. Chase at center. Back with 10,000 five times, TEN THOUSAND DOLLARS at center, inscriptions, and vignettes. Back printed in green.

No.	Signatures		Quantity Printed	
F-2411	Woods	Mellon	48,000	Unknown

Gold Certificates
Series of 1934, Gold Seal

Designs are as preceding, except that the back is printed in gold. None were released.

No.	Signatures		Quantity Printed	
F-2412	Julian	Morgenthau	36,000	—

Federal Reserve Notes
Series of 1928, Green Seal

Face of F-2230. Bust of Salmon P. Chase. The face notes that the bill is payable "in gold or lawful money."

Back of F-2230.

No.	Issuing Bank	Quantity Printed		VF-20	EF-40	Unc-63
F-2230A	Boston	1,320	Unknown			
F-2230B	New York	4,680	Unknown			
F-2230D	Cleveland	960		$115,000	$135,000	$250,000
F-2230E	Richmond	3,024		115,000	130,000	200,000
F-2230F	Atlanta	1,440	Unknown			
F-2230G	Chicago	1,800	Unknown			
F-2230H	St. Louis	480	Unknown			
F-2230I	Minneapolis	480	Unknown			
F-2230J	Kansas City	480	Unknown			
F-2230K	Dallas	360	Unknown			
F-2230L	San Francisco	1,824	Unknown			

Federal Reserve Notes
Series of 1934 to 1934-C, Green Seal

Face of F-2231 to F-2233. No mention of gold in payment. Back is same as the preceding.

Back of F-2231 to F-2233.

Series of 1934—Signatures of Julian and Morgenthau

No.	Issuing Bank	Quantity Printed		VF-20	EF-40	Unc-63
F-2231A	Boston	9,720		$70,000	$82,250	$95,000
F-2231B	New York	11,520		60,000	70,000	85,000
F-2231C	Philadelphia	6,000		65,000	75,000	—
F-2231D	Cleveland	1,480	Unknown			
F-2231E	Richmond	1,200		65,000	82,250	—
F-2231F	Atlanta	2,400		65,000	82,250	—
F-2231G	Chicago	3,840		65,000	82,250	85,000
F-2231H	St. Louis	2,040		65,000	82,250	—
F-2231J	Kansas City	1,200		65,000	82,250	—
F-2231K	Dallas	1,200		65,000	82,250	85,000
F-2231L	San Francisco	3,600		65,000	82,250	—

Series of 1934-A—Signatures of Julian and Morgenthau

No.	Issuing Bank	Quantity Printed
F-2232G	Chicago	1,560

Series of 1934-B—Signatures of Julian and Vinson

No.	Issuing Bank	Quantity Printed
F-2233B	New York	24

SPECIAL $100,000 NOTES

Gold Certificates
Series of 1934—Signatures of Julian and Morgenthau

Small-size notes of the $100,000 denomination were made to facilitate internal transactions with the government. Woodrow Wilson is on the face. The back is printed in orange and has 100,000 five times and ONE HUNDRED THOUSAND / DOLLARS in large letters. Of the 42,000 printed, several are preserved by the Treasury Department and are occasionally displayed.

CERTIFICATION. IDENTIFICATION.
PRESERVATION.

Note Types Eligible for PMG Grading

US Large and Small Sizes

Military Payment Certificates

Cut and Uncut Sheets, up to 12 subjects

Fractional

Obsolete

Confederate

Colonial

Canada

World Notes

Scrip

Collectors prefer PMG for grading and encapsulation.

Your notes deserve the best. As part of our commitment to providing the industry's most accurate and consistent currency grading, PMG has developed a holder that combines the qualities most important to collectors.

Protection. The PMG holder is composed of the highest-quality inert materials with no openings or perforations, to protect your notes from environmental hazards and contaminants.

Attribution. PMG-graded notes are clearly identified by the distinguished PMG label, featuring full attributions, pedigree information and graders' comments when applicable.

Longevity. The holder's durable, heavy-gauge material is ideal for long-term storage, providing superior protection even for notes printed on the thinnest papers, such as Obsolete and Confederate banknotes.

Your treasured notes belong in the industry's most innovative holder. **To have your notes graded and encapsulated by our trusted experts, visit www.PMGnotes.com or call 877-PMG-5570.**

PMG COLLECTORS SOCIETY

PAPER MONEY GUARANTY

P.O. Box 4755 | Sarasota, FL 34230 | **877-PMG-5570** (764-5570) | www.PMGnotes.com

An Independent Member of the Certified Collectibles Group

Fractional Currency

COLLECTING FRACTIONAL CURRENCY

Many a beginning collector is staggered to find it's possible to collect U.S. paper money with a spendable value of as low as three cents! Not only is it possible, it is both relatively easy and inexpensive to complete a type set of all 23 types of the 3-, 5-, 10-, 15- (yes, 15!), 25-, and 50-cent notes printed as currency by the United States from 1862 to 1876.

As we have already seen with many of the large-size notes in earlier parts of this book, we owe the presence of Fractional Currency—commonly known at the time as "shinplasters"—to the chaos caused by the Civil War. It is essentially an emergency currency. By 1862, the financial implications of the Civil War were being felt. The federal government was issuing huge amounts of paper to finance the war and refusing to redeem any of it in coins. Major banks, therefore, had no choice but go along or be wiped out of their holdings. In December 1861, the banks also suspended payments in coin. The immediate result was a massive hoarding of gold and silver coins in circulation; combine that with the fact that copper was needed for the war, and the result was a total lack of the small change necessary for day-to-day commerce.

Merchants and banks, of course, still had business to do, and there soon arose an abundance of creative alternatives. Among them were the barter system, nearly worthless promissory notes, equally good-for-nothing private bank notes, privately issued merchant tokens that had more advertising appeal than commercial effectiveness, postage stamps, and, as we shall see later, encased postage stamps. (The stamp idea had some legs, so much so that soon there were not enough stamps available for their intended use of mailing letters!)

That was when General Francis Elias Spinner, appointed by Lincoln as U.S. treasurer, pasted a few stamps onto a piece of paper in his office, signed his name to it (thinking it would then be more counterfeit-proof), and liked what he saw. He proposed that Congress authorize the printing of small notes that looked like stamps. The president signed the Postage Currency Act on July 17, 1862. The first issue was properly called "Postage Currency," not Fractional Currency, and made its appearance a few months later on August 21. It was issued in 5-, 10-, 25- and 50-cent denominations until May 27, 1863.

Counterfeiting was a constant problem with these issues, necessitating relatively frequent changes in design. The next four issues fell under the Act of March 3, 1863, and are true Fractional Currency. As the designs became more elaborate, there also were experiments with different kinds of paper, and seals and signatures were added. However, it was a Sisyphean task to stay ahead of the counterfeiters.

The second issue lasted from October 10, 1863, to February 23, 1867, and consisted of the same denominations but in slightly larger quantities than the first issue. All second-issue notes have the bust of George Washington in a bronze oval frame that was applied after printing. The design is the same for each denomination, but the backs are each printed in a different color.

The third issue, from December 5, 1864, to August 16, 1869, was the largest in number of pieces, face value, and number of denominations printed. The three-cent note is unique to the third issue. It was issued as a complement to the nickel three-cent coin, first issued in 1865, and the three-cent silver coins it replaced. Spencer M. Clark, superintendent of the National Currency Bureau, put his own bust on the five-cent note instead of that of the explorer William Clark. This resulted in the still-standing law that no living person can appear on U.S. coins or currency. One of the 50-cent notes of this issue has Spinner's bust.

The fourth issue was from July 14, 1869, to February 16, 1875, and includes the only 15-cent denomination in U.S. government monetary history. The other denominations were 10, 20, and 50 cents. This is probably the most appealing of the five issues from an artistic standpoint, with a variety of well-executed busts and embellishments to the notes themselves.

There were only three notes in the fifth issue of February 26, 1874, to February 15, 1876, the only issue that managed to defy the counterfeiters. The 50-cent piece has been a favorite of collectors for years. The face has a facing bust of William H. Crawford. Crawford was an accomplished American politician in the first half of the nineteenth century. He was a senator from Georgia (1807–1813), ambassador to France (1813–1815), secretary of war (1815–1816) and Treasury (1816–1825), and a candidate for president in 1824. Making note of these great accomplishments, you will have only one thought when you look at him on the currency: his similarity to the great American comedian Bob Hope.

The Civil War ended in 1865, another decade passed, and there again was sufficient coin in circulation that the emergency currency was no longer needed. It had served its purpose. On January 14, 1874, the Specie Resumption Act (repeated in the Act of April 17, 1876) allowed for coins in storage to be exchanged for Fractional Currency and provided for the currency's retirement by redemption into silver coin. By this time, the currency was popular and redemption was slow, so it took a supplemental act—that of July 22, 1876, authorizing the issue of $10 million in silver coin—and other provisions to encourage redemption. Spinner's stamp experiment in his office 14 years earlier resulted in an issue of paper totaling 1,819,223,300 pieces with a face value of $368,724,079.45. The balance not redeemed is still on the Treasury's books—and in the collections of many paper money and stamp enthusiasts today.

As much as for Fractional Currency, if not more, Francis E. Spinner should be recognized by history for being the first U.S. government official to hire women. He did so at first because they could not be drafted into the army, but then he continued, defending his female employees and paying them well, long after the war's end.

First Issue, Postage Currency
August 21, 1862, to May 27, 1863

Denominations of 5¢, 10¢, 25¢, and 50¢. The designs copied contemporary postage stamps. Early issues had perforated edges; later ones, straight. Face designs: 5¢ (a 5¢ stamp), 10¢ (10¢ stamp), 25¢ (five 5¢ stamps), and 50¢ (five 10¢ stamps). Printed by the National Bank Note Company (faces) and the American Bank Note Company (backs) in New York City. *Sizes:* 5¢ and 10¢: 65 mm wide x 45 mm high • 25¢ and 50¢: 78 x 48 mm

Face of F-1228 to F-1231. Engraving of 5¢ stamp with bust of Thomas Jefferson.

Back of F-1228 to F-1231.

No.	Denomination	Variety	VG-8	F-12	VF-20	EF-40	Unc-63
F-1228	5 cents	Perforated edges; monogram (ABCO) of American Bank Note Co. on back	$40	$65	$85	$115	$350
F-1229	5 cents	Perforated edges; no monogram	45	70	95	135	425
F-1230	5 cents	Straight edges; with monogram	30	40	50	70	125
F-1231	5 cents	Straight edges; no monogram	40	60	80	110	400

Face of F-1240 to F-1243. Engraving of
10¢ stamp with bust of George Washington.

Back of F-1240 to F-1243.

No.	Denomination	Variety	VG-8	F-12	VF-20	EF-40	Unc-63
F-1240	10 cents	Perforated edges; monogram (ABCO) of American Bank Note Co. on back	$40	$65	$90	$125	$275
F-1241	10 cents	Perforated edges; no monogram	45	75	100	140	375
F-1242	10 cents	Straight edges; with monogram	25	30	40	60	100
F-1243	10 cents	Straight edges; no monogram	40	55	80	120	400

Face of F-1279 to F-1282. Five 5¢
stamps with bust of Thomas Jefferson.

Back of F-1279 to F-1282.

No.	Denomination	Variety	VG-8	F-12	VF-20	EF-40	Unc-63
F-1279	25 cents	Perforated edges; monogram (ABCO) of American Bank Note Co. on back	$40	$65	$85	$145	$400
F-1280	25 cents	Perforated edges; no monogram	45	70	95	170	475
F-1281	25 cents	Straight edges; with monogram	30	40	45	65	190
F-1282	25 cents	Straight edges; no monogram	40	60	95	170	475

Face of F-1310 to F-1313. Five 10¢
stamps with bust of George Washington.

Back of F-1310 to F-1313.

No.	Denomination	Variety	VG-8	F-12	VF-20	EF-40	Unc-63
F-1310	50 cents	Perforated edges; monogram (ABCO) of American Bank Note Co. on back	$40	$60	$80	$125	$400
F-1310a	50 cents	Same, but 14 perforations each 20 mm instead of 12		Rare	—	2,500	3,750
F-1311	50 cents	Perforated edges; no monogram	50	70	100	175	600
F-1312	50 cents	Plain edges; monogram	35	45	55	75	215
F-1313	50 cents	Plain edges; no monogram	40	70	125	200	800

Second Issue, Fractional Currency
October 20, 1863, to February 23, 1867

Denominations of 5¢, 10¢, 25¢, and 50¢. All with same vignette and portrait of Washington within an overprinted bronze oval. Produced by the National Currency Bureau in the Treasury Building in Washington, DC, under the supervision of Spencer M. Clark, including impressions on special membrane paper using heavy hydrostatic presses. *Size:* 66 x 48 mm

Face of F-1232 to F-1235. Head of George Washington in bronze-colored oval frame.

Back of F-1232 to F-1235.

No.	Denomination	Variety	VG-8	F-12	VF-20	EF-40	Unc-63
F-1232	5 cents	No figures on corners of back	$25	$30	$40	$55	$100
F-1233	5 cents	With surcharge figures "18-63" on corners of back	25	30	45	60	125
F-1234	5 cents	With surcharge figures "18-63" and "S"	25	30	60	70	200
F-1235	5 cents	With surcharge figures "18-63" and "R-1"; fiber paper	45	85	125	200	600

Face of F-1244 to F-1249. Head of George Washington in bronze-colored oval frame.

Back of F-1244 to F-1249.

No.	Denomination	Variety	VG-8	F-12	VF-20	EF-40	Unc-63
F-1244	10 cents	Without small surcharged figures on corners of back	$25	$30	$40	$55	$100
F-1245	10 cents	With surcharge "18-63"	25	30	40	60	120
F-1246	10 cents	With surcharge "18-63" and "S"	30	40	50	75	200
F-1247	10 cents	With surcharge "18-63" and "I"	50	70	90	120	425
F-1248	10 cents	With surcharge "0-63"	900	1,100	1,750	2,300	4,800
F-1249	10 cents	With surcharge "18-63" and "T-1"; fiber paper	35	70	95	135	600

Face of F-1283 to F-1290. Head of George Washington in bronze-colored oval frame.

Back of F-1283 to F-1290.

No.	Denomination	Variety	VG-8	F-12	VF-20	EF-40	Unc-63
F-1283	25 cents	No small surcharged figures on corners of back	$30	$40	$50	$70	$250
F-1284	25 cents	Surcharge "18-63"	30	45	60	80	280
F-1285	25 cents	Surcharge "18-63" and "A"	30	50	70	85	280
F-1286	25 cents	Surcharge "18-63" and "S"	30	40	50	70	250
F-1288	25 cents	Surcharge "18-63" and "2"	30	45	60	80	280
F-1289	25 cents	Surcharge "18-63" and "T-1"; fiber paper	45	60	75	160	600
F-1290	25 cents	Surcharge "18-63" and "T-2"; fiber paper	45	60	85	150	525

Face of F-1314 to F-1322. Head of George Washington in bronze-colored oval frame.

Back of F-1314 to F-1322.

No.	Denomination	Variety	VG-8	F-12	VF-20	EF-40	Unc-63
F-1314	50 cents	No surcharge figures on corners of back	Only known as a specimen				
F-1316	50 cents	Surcharge "18-63"	$30	$50	$65	$80	$300
F-1317	50 cents	Surcharge "18-63" and "A"	30	50	65	80	300
F-1318	50 cents	Surcharge "18-63" and "1"	30	50	65	80	300
F-1320	50 cents	Surcharge "18-63" and "0-1"; fiber paper	40	60	85	120	475
F-1321	50 cents	Surcharge "18-63" and "R-2"; fiber paper	45	65	160	275	675
F-1322	50 cents	Surcharge "18-63" and "T-1"; fiber paper	45	70	95	110	425

Third Issue, Fractional Currency
December 5, 1864, to August 16, 1869

Denominations of 3¢, 5¢, 10¢, 25¢, and 50¢. The 3¢ was made for just a short time, as the law of March 3, 1865, authorizing the nickel three-cent coin, prohibited any further issue of Fractional Currency of this value. Spencer M. Clark, superintendent of the Currency Bureau, had his own portrait placed on the 5¢ note, although most people thought it was the explorer William Clark. This is said to have been the reason for the enactment of legislation prohibiting the portrayal of living people on American financial instruments. Three designs were made of the 50¢.

Sizes: 3¢: 67 x 42 mm (shortest in the series) • 5¢: 67 x 48 mm • 10¢: 84 x 48 mm • 25¢: 98 x 48 mm • 50¢: 115 (widest in the series) x 49 mm

Face of F-1226 and F-1227.
Bust of George Washington.

Back of F-1226 and F-1227.

No.	Denomination	Variety	VG-8	F-12	VF-20	EF-40	Unc-63
F-1226	3 cents	Light background behind portrait	$40	$50	$60	$70	$140
F-1227	3 cents	Dark background behind portrait	40	55	75	110	350

Face of F-1236 to F-1239. Bust of
Spencer M. Clark, superintendent
of the National Currency Bureau.

Back of F-1236 to F-1239.

No.	Denomination	Variety	VG-8	F-12	VF-20	EF-40	Unc-63
F-1236	5 cents	Red back	$35	$60	$85	$110	$275
F-1237	5 cents	Red back with design letter "a" at extreme left on face	45	70	100	135	400
F-1238	5 cents	Green back	25	35	45	65	125
F-1239	5 cents	Green back with design letter "a" at extreme left on face	25	40	50	75	180

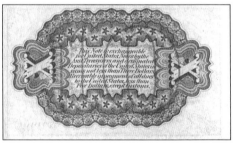

Face of F-1251 to F-1256. Bust of George Washington.

Back of F-1251 to F-1256.

No.	Denomination	Variety	VG-8	F-12	VF-20	EF-40	Unc-63
F-1251	10 cents	Red back	$35	$50	$70	$95	$195
F-1252	10 cents	Red back with design numeral "1" on face	40	60	85	110	250
F-1253	10 cents	Red back with autographed signatures of Colby and Spinner	55	80	125	180	350
F-1254	10 cents	Red back with autographed signatures of Jeffries and Spinner	70	100	195	295	700
F-1255	10 cents	Green back	25	30	35	45	125
F-1255a	10 cents	Green back with autographed signatures of Colby and Spinner			2 known		
F-1256	10 cents	Green back with design numeral "1" on face	25	35	45	55	140

Face of F-1291 to F-1300. Bust of Treasury
Secretary (1864–1865) William P. Fessenden.

Back of F-1291 to F-1300.

No.	Denomination	Variety	VG-8	F-12	VF-20	EF-40	Unc-63
F-1291	25 cents	Red back	$35	$55	$75	$100	$400
F-1292	25 cents	Red back with small design letter "a" on face	40	65	85	115	375
F-1294	25 cents	Green back	25	30	40	60	300
F-1295	25 cents	Green back with small design letter "a" on face	25	35	45	65	200
F-1296	25 cents	Green back with large design letter "a" on face, 7 mm to the lower right of the normal location	1,000	1,450	2,400	2,750	6,000
F-1297	25 cents	Green back with surcharge "M-2-6-5"; fiber paper	50	65	85	115	425
F-1298	25 cents	Same as above but with design letter "a" on face	55	75	100	175	600
F-1299	25 cents	Green back with surcharge "M-2-6-5"; the two ornamental designs on face surcharged in heavy solid bronze, and not merely outlined as on previous issues; fiber paper	200	350	700	1,250	3,500
F-1300	25 cents	Same as above but with design letter "a" on face	600	875	1,850	2,750	5,750

Face of F-1324 to F-1342. Bust of U.S. Treasurer (1861–1875) F.E. Spinner.

Back of F-1324 to F-1342.

No.	Denomination	Variety	VG-8	F-12	VF-20	EF-40	Unc-63
Red back and surcharge "A-2-6-5"							
F-1324	50 cents	No design figures on face	$75	$125	$150	$175	$425
F-1325	50 cents	Figures "1" and "a" on face	100	125	175	350	1,000
F-1326	50 cents	Figure "1" only on face	75	100	120	150	450
F-1327	50 cents	Figure "a" only on face	75	100	125	170	500
F-1328	50 cents	Autographed signatures of Colby and Spinner	85	135	140	190	500
F-1329	50 cents	Autographed signatures of Allison and Spinner	95	100	150	200	750
F-1330	50 cents	Autographed signatures of Allison and New	900	1,300	1,950	2,700	5,000
Green back, no surcharge							
F-1331	50 cents	No design figures on face	45	75	90	110	400
F-1332	50 cents	Figures "1" and "a" on face	90	110	125	150	625
F-1333	50 cents	Figure "1" only on face	45	85	100	125	400
F-1334	50 cents	Figure "a" only on face	45	85	100	125	400
Green back and surcharge "A-2-6-5"							
F-1335	50 cents	Without design figures on face	75	100	125	150	400
F-1336	50 cents	Figures "1" and "a" on face	325	600	1,000	1,750	4,000
F-1337	50 cents	Figure "1" only on face	90	110	135	150	650
F-1338	50 cents	Figure "a" only on face	90	110	140	170	800
F-1339	50 cents	Green back; no surcharges and design figures	45	75	90	120	400
F-1340	50 cents	Green back; figures "1" and "a" on face	110	170	225	290	1,000
F-1341	50 cents	Green back; figure "1" only on face	60	80	100	145	500
F-1342	50 cents	Green back; figure "a" only on face	60	80	120	160	550

Face of F-1343 to F-1373a. Justice seated with arm on shield.

Back of F-1343 to F-1373a.

No.	Denomination	Variety	VG-8	F-12	VF-20	EF-40	Unc-63
Red back, no surcharge							
F-1343	50 cents	No design figures on face	$80	$95	$120	$170	$500
F-1344	50 cents	Design figures "1" and "a" on face	350	500	1,100	1,600	3,800
F-1345	50 cents	Design figure "1" only on face	85	110	135	200	600
F-1346	50 cents	Design figure "a" only on face	85	110	135	200	600
Red back and surcharge "A-2-6-5"							
F-1347	50 cents	No design figures on face	80	95	120	170	500
F-1348	50 cents	Design figures "1" and "a" on face	400	900	1,600	2,000	4,000
F-1349	50 cents	Design figure "1" only on face	80	110	145	225	750
F-1350	50 cents	Design figure "a" only on face	80	110	145	225	950
Red back and surcharge "S-2-6-4"; printed signatures							
F-1351	50 cents	No design figures on face; fiber paper	2,500	4,500	8,500	12,000	22,000
F-1352	50 cents	Design figures "1" and "a" on face; fiber paper			3 known		
F-1353	50 cents	Design figure "1" only on face; fiber paper	3,000	5,500	12,500	16,000	24,000
F-1354	50 cents	Design figure "a" only on face; fiber paper	3,250	5,500	13,000	17,000	26,000
Red back; autographed signatures of Colby and Spinner							
F-1355	50 cents	No surcharges and design figures	85	110	160	225	525
F-1356	50 cents	Surcharge "A-2-6-5" on back	85	125	225	275	600
F-1357	50 cents	Surcharge "S-2-6-4"; fiber paper	200	300	450	900	2,500
Green back; no surcharge							
F-1358	50 cents	No design figures on face	45	75	90	110	700
F-1359	50 cents	Design figures "1" and "a" on face	500	1,000	1,450	2,000	4,750
F-1360	50 cents	Design figure "1" only on face	50	80	110	135	500
F-1361	50 cents	Design figure "a" only on face	50	80	110	140	600
Green back and surcharge "A-2-6-5" compactly spaced							
F-1362	50 cents	No design figures on face	45	75	90	110	400
F-1363	50 cents	Design figures "1" and "a" on face	125	250	350	450	1,100
F-1364	50 cents	Design figure "1" only on face	50	80	110	135	500
F-1365	50 cents	Design figure "a" only on face	50	80	110	140	525
Green back and surcharge "A-2-6-5" widely spaced							
F-1366	50 cents	No design figures on face	45	75	130	225	500
F-1367	50 cents	Design figures "1" and "a" on face	450	900	1,400	2,000	6,000
F-1368	50 cents	Design figure "1" only on face	55	100	140	350	750
F-1369	50 cents	Design figure "a" only on face	65	130	200	450	1,650
Green back with surcharge "A-2-6-5"; fiber paper							
F-1370	50 cents	No design figures on face	80	100	170	300	1,000
F-1371	50 cents	Design figures "1" and "a" on face	450	600	1,500	2,000	5,000
F-1372	50 cents	Design figure "1" only on face	90	120	200	350	1,000
F-1373	50 cents	Design figure "a" only on face	100	135	220	400	1,200
F-1373a	50 cents	Green back with surcharge "S-2-6-4"; fiber paper; printed signatures; no design figure or letter	7,500	10,000	15,000	23,000	—

Fourth Issue, Fractional Currency

July 14, 1869, to February 16, 1875

Denominations of 10¢, 15¢, 25¢, and 50¢. This series included the only 15¢ denomination. Three designs were made of the 50¢ note, each of a different size. Some Fourth Issue bills were printed on paper with blue tinting, also used on certain National Bank and Legal Tender notes of the era. Most printing was done by the American Bank Note Company and National Bank Note Company in New York. *Sizes:* 10¢: 80 x 47 mm • 15¢: 90 x 48 mm • 25¢: 97 x 47 mm • 50¢ Lincoln: 106 x 47 mm, Stanton 103 x 47 mm, Dexter 96 x 55 mm (tallest in the series)

Face of F-1257 to F-1261. Bust of Liberty.   Back of F-1257 to F-1261.

No.	Denomination	Variety	VG-8	F-12	VF-20	EF-40	Unc-63
F-1257	10 cents	Large red seal; watermarked paper with pink silk fibers	$25	$35	$45	$60	$175
F-1258	10 cents	Large red seal; unwatermarked paper with pink silk fibers	25	35	45	60	175
F-1259	10 cents	Large red seal; paper with violet silk fibers and blue right end on face	25	35	45	60	175
F-1261	10 cents	Smaller red seal; paper with violet silk fibers and blue right end on face	25	35	45	60	175

Face of F-1267 to F-1271. Bust of
Columbia in oval frame above fasces.

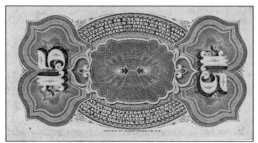

Back of F-1267 to F-1271.

No.	Denomination	Variety	VG-8	F-12	VF-20	EF-40	Unc-63
F-1267	15 cents	Large red seal; watermarked paper with pink silk fibers	$55	$80	$95	$120	$250
F-1268	15 cents	Large red seal; unwatermarked paper with pink silk fibers	300	500	800	1,000	—
F-1269	15 cents	Large red seal; paper with violet fibers and blue right end on face	55	80	95	120	250
F-1271	15 cents	Smaller red seal; paper with violet fibers and blue right end on face	55	80	95	120	275

Face of F-1301 to F-1307. Bust of George Washington.

Back of F-1301 to F-1307.

No.	Denomination	Variety	VG-8	F-12	VF-20	EF-40	Unc-63
F-1301	25 cents	Large red seal; watermarked paper with pink silk fibers	$25	$30	$45	$65	$140
F-1302	25 cents	Large red seal; unwatermarked paper with pink silk fibers	25	30	45	65	200
F-1303	25 cents	Large red seal; paper with violet fibers and blue right end on face	25	35	50	75	200
F-1307	25 cents	Smaller red seal; paper with violet fibers and blue right end on face	25	30	45	65	170

Face of F-1374. Bust of Abraham Lincoln.

Back of F-1374.

No.	Denomination	Variety	VG-8	F-12	VF-20	EF-40	Unc-63
F-1374	50 cents	Large seal; watermarked paper with pink silk fibers	$50	$100	$145	$250	$750

Face of F-1376. Bust of Secretary of War Edwin M. Stanton.

Back of F-1376.

No.	Denomination	Variety	VG-8	F-12	VF-20	EF-40	Unc-63
F-1376	50 cents	Small red seal; paper with violet fibers and blue right end on face	$35	$50	$70	$110	$400

Face of F-1379. Bust of War and Treasury
Secretary (1800–1801) Samuel Dexter.

Back of F-1379.

No.	Denomination	Variety	VG-8	F-12	VF-20	EF-40	Unc-63
F-1379	50 cents	Green seal; paper with light violet fibers and blue right end on face	$35	$50	$65	$95	$400

Fifth Issue, Fractional Currency

February 26, 1874, to February 15, 1876

Denominations of 10¢, 25¢, and 50¢. The backs of the two lower denominations were printed by the Columbian Bank Note Company in Washington, DC, and the backs of the 50¢ notes by Joseph R. Carpenter in Philadelphia. The faces were by the Bureau of Engraving and Printing. Many pieces were sold by banks to dealers, as the collecting of such bills had become popular. *Sizes:* 10¢: 84 x 53 mm • 25¢: 91 x 53 mm • 50¢: 112 x 53 mm

Face of F-1264 to F-1266. Bust of Treasury Secretary (1849–1850) William M. Meredith.

Back of F-1264 to F-1266.

No.	Denomination	Variety	VG-8	F-12	VF-20	EF-40	Unc-63
F-1264	10 cents	Green seal	$30	$40	$60	$75	$200
F-1265	10 cents	Red seal with long, thin key	22	28	35	45	85
F-1266	10 cents	Red seal with short, thick key	22	28	35	45	85

Face of F-1308 and F-1309. Bust of Treasury Secretary (1845–1849) Robert J. Walker.

Back of F-1308 and F-1309.

No.	Denomination	Variety	VG-8	F-12	VF-20	EF-40	Unc-63
F-1308	25 cents	With long, thin key in Treasury seal (5 mm)	$22	$28	$35	$45	$80
F-1309	25 cents	With short, thick key in Treasury seal (4 mm)	22	28	35	45	80

*Face of F-1380 and F-1381. Bust of War and Treasury
Secretary (1815–1825) William H. Crawford.*

Back of F-1380 and F-1381.

No.	Denomination	Variety	VG-8	F-12	VF-20	EF-40	Unc-63
F-1380	50 cents	Red seal; paper on face a light pink color with silk fibers	$26	$36	$45	$60	$145
F-1381	50 cents	Red seal; white paper with silk fibers and blue right end on face	26	36	45	60	145

FRACTIONAL CURRENCY SHIELDS

To aid in the identification of counterfeits and to provide bills for display to banks and others
interested, the Treasury Department created Fractional Currency Shields. These consisted of the
outline of a shield below an eagle and stars. Thirty-nine pieces of the first three issues of Fractional Currency—20 faces and 19 backs—were pasted by hand. These were sold for $4.50 each,
beginning in 1867. Purchasers mounted many of them under glass in a wooden frame with a gilt
inner strip, and backed by thin wooden slats.

No records of issue numbers have been found, but the figure was certainly in the high hundreds. Most of these have water stains along the bottom from slight flooding in the Treasury
Department basement, where they were stored.

No.	Denomination	Variety	
F-1382	Fractional Currency Shield	With gray background	$4,500
F-1383	Fractional Currency Shield	With pink background	10,000
F-1383a	Fractional Currency Shield	With green background	13,000

SPECIMENS

Specimen impressions of Fractional Currency bills, face or back designs, printed on one side, in either wide-margin or narrow-margin versions, were very popular with stamp collectors as well as numismatists, and large quantities were sold through dealers in these fields. For information refer to *Paper Money of the United States* by Arthur L. and Ira S. Friedberg.

Postage Currency and Fractional Currency notes tended to become dirty and tattered quickly and could not be counted easily. The public referred to them derisively as "stamps."

It is a curious sidelight on the collecting of United States paper money that in the 1860s and 1870s the acquisition of regular and specimen Fractional Currency notes was a passion for many, and all dealers with storefront shops maintained good stocks of it.

After the War of 1812 commenced in June 1812, the United States Treasury raised funds by issuing interest-bearing obligations. These were sold by subscription to investors and banks. These were issued in five series from 1812 to 1815, in denominations ranging from $3 to $1,000. All bore interest at the rate of one-half cent per day per $100 of face value, except for certain low denominations of 1815. Today, all these notes range from scarce to rare. Some numismatists collect them in conjunction with the later federal currency issued in quantity beginning in 1861.

FIRST ISSUE

Originally suggested in 1810 by then secretary of the Treasury Albert Gallatin, Treasury Notes as a resource for raising government revenue were first authorized by Congress on June 30, 1812. A total of $15,000,000 in denominations of $100 and $1,000 was authorized and by December 1812 was fully subscribed by the banks. The notes bore interest at 5.4% or one-half cent a day per $100.

Subsequent issues followed a pattern in which Congress attempted to raise funds first by floating long-term loans and then by making up the difference with Treasury Notes. Congress therefore authorized a second issue of $5,000,000 in Treasury Notes on February 25, 1813. The third issue, on March 14, 1814, authorized another $10,000,000 of Treasury Notes. Unlike the first two issues, which only authorized $100 and $1,000 notes, this issue and the next included $20 notes. The fourth issue, on December 26, 1814, authorized an additional $10,500,000 of Treasury Notes, but for the first time not all were fully subscribed ($8,318,400). Only $100 and $20 notes are believed to have been printed.

SMALL-SIZE TREASURY NOTES

With new loans and fiscal revenues far from adequate, a new monetary expedient was necessary. Specifically, the Chairman of the House Ways and Means Committee argued for a circulating currency of small denominations payable to bearer, transferable by delivery and receivable in all payments for public lands and taxes. On February 24, 1815, by which time the War of 1812 had ended, Congress authorized 25,000,000 of these small-denomination Treasury Notes. Only $4,969,400 of $100 notes bearing interest at 5.4% and $3,392,994 of $3, $5, $10, $20, and $50 denominations were actually issued (although a total of $9,070,386 in these notes was reissued). The last bore no interest by circulating as money.

All Treasury Notes were made by Murray, Draper, Fairman, and Co. and are one-sided. The first two issues were signed by Timothy Matlock and Charles Biddle, while the last three were signed by Earnest Fox and Samuel Clarke. The last issue was alternately signed by F.W. McGeary and C.A. Colville. Some were countersigned by William White (first two issues), T.D.T. Tucker (last two issues), or Joseph Nourse (the register on the last issue only).

The small-denomination Treasury Notes of $3 to $50 were used to purchase goods and services by individuals, pay customs duties by merchants, and act as cash reserves for banks, thus preventing them from being discounted. As a result, they are considered by some to be the first circulating currency issued by the United States government after the Revolutionary War period.

All these series are extremely rare in any form, and nearly all of the few known are specimens, proofs, or remainders, with most canceled in some way. Fully signed, dated and numbered, and uncanceled notes are virtually nonexistent.

Act of June 30, 1812

One-year notes of this issue bore interest at 5.4%. One hundred notes are outstanding. ·

Note TN-1. Spread eagle at upper left, facing right. Shield and cannon at lower center.

No.	Denomination		Quantity Issued		VF-20	Unc-63
TN-1	One thousand dollars	Unsigned remainder	2,000	3 known	$25,000	$40,000

Note TN-2. Eagle on branch at upper right. Shield and cannon at lower center.

No.	Denomination		Quantity Issued		VF-20	Unc-63
TN-2	One hundred dollars	Unsigned remainder	15,000	5 known	$17,500	$30,000

Act of February 25, 1813

One-year notes of this issue bore interest at 5.4%. Nine hundred notes are outstanding.

No.	Denomination	Quantity Issued	
TN-3	One thousand dollars	4,000	No notes known
TN-4	One hundred dollars	5,000	No notes known

Act of March 4, 1814

One-year notes bore interest at 5.4%. Of this issue, 43,160 notes are outstanding.

No.	Denomination		Quantity Issued		VF-20	Unc-63
TN-5	One thousand dollars		6,000 est.		No notes known	
TN-6	One hundred dollars	Remainder signed by Edward Fox and Samuel Clarke; dated 1/15/15	24,000 est.	3 known	$20,000	$30,000
TN-7	Twenty dollars		8,000 est.		No notes known	

Act of December 26, 1814

One-year notes bore interest at 5.4%. Of this issue, 41,030 notes are outstanding.

Note TN-8 to TN-8p. Eagle on branch at upper right corner. Shield and cannon below center.

No.	Denomination			VF-20	Unc-63
TN-8	One hundred dollars	Unsigned, numbered, dated 2/11/15	1 known	$20,000	$25,000
TN-8a	One hundred dollars	Signed undated remainder (all known are canceled)	3 known	15,000	20,000
TN-8p	One hundred dollars	Proof, hole canceled	2 known	15,000	20,000

Note TN-9 to TN-9p. Spread eagle on shield at upper left; 20 surrounded by cornucopia in lower center.

No.	Denomination			VF-20	Unc-63
TN-9	Twenty dollars	Unsigned remainder	1 known	$10,000	$15,000
TN-9a	Twenty dollars	Signed undated remainder		8,000	12,500
TN-9p	Twenty dollars	Proof, hole canceled	4 known	8,000	12,500

Act of February 24, 1815

$100 notes bore interest at 5.4%. Unknown outstanding for $100; 2,061 for "small notes."

Note TN-10 to TN-10p. Eagle on branch at upper right; shield at lower center.

No.	Denomination		Quantity Issued		VF-20	Unc-63
TN-10	One hundred dollars	Unsigned remainder	49,694	3 known	$8,000	$12,500
TN-10a	One hundred dollars	Signed undated remainder		Unconfirmed		
TN-10p	One hundred dollars	Proof, hole canceled		4 known	8,000	12,500

Note TN-11 to TN-11p. Spread eagle on branch at upper right. Signed by F.W. McGeary and C.C. Biddle; countersigned by Joseph Nourse.

No.	Denomination			VF-20	Unc-63
TN-11	Fifty dollars	Unsigned remainder	Unconfirmed		
TN-11a	Fifty dollars	Singly signed remainder	4 known	$10,000	$12,500
TN-11b	Fifty dollars	Fully signed and hole canceled		6,000	9,000
TN-11p	Fifty dollars	Proof, hole canceled	3 known	8,500	12,500

Note TN-12 to TN-13a. Spread eagle on branch at upper left.

No.	Denomination			VF-20	Unc-63
TN-12	Twenty dollars	Unsigned remainder		$6,500	$10,000
TN-12a	Twenty dollars	Double signature remainder	Unconfirmed		
TN-12p	Twenty dollars	Proof, hole canceled	3 known	7,000	10,000
TN-13	Ten dollars	Unsigned remainder	Unconfirmed		
TN-13a	Ten dollars	Double signature remainder		8,500	12,500

Note TN-14 to TN-15p. Spread eagle with shield on branch at upper left. Signed by Samuel Clarke and Edward Fox.

No.	Denomination			VF-20	Unc-63
TN-14	Ten dollars	Unsigned remainder		$6,500	$8,500
TN-14a	Ten dollars	Double signature remainder		5,500	8,000
TN-14b	Ten dollars	Fully signed	1 known	—	—
TN-14p	Ten dollars	Proof, hole canceled	3 known	6,500	11,000
TN-15	Five dollars	Unsigned remainder		5,000	7,500
TN-15a	Five dollars	Double signature remainder		8,000	11,500
TN-15p	Five dollars	Proof, hole canceled	4 known	6,500	11,000

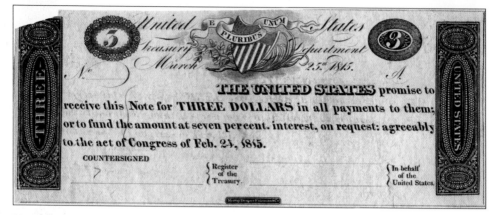

Note TN-16 to TN-16b. Shield with motto in upper center.

No.	Denomination			VF-20	Unc-63
TN-16	Three dollars	Unsigned remainder		$7,000	$12,000
TN-16a	Three dollars	Double signature remainder	4 known	8,000	12,500
TN-16b	Three dollars	Fully signed	1 known	—	—

NOVEL FORM OF MONEY
BORN OF NECESSITY

Among the entrepreneurs with an eye to profiting from the extreme shortage of coins in the summer of 1862 was John Gault of Boston, who in the same year moved to New York City. Born in Baltimore in 1831, he had moved with his family to Boston circa 1840. In 1850 he headed for California, one year too late to be a Forty-Niner, but in time to be a part of the action. He remained there until 1855, although he did not make his "pile," as the term went. Few others did either.

In 1855 he came back to Boston, and went to work in a machine shop. Possessing an inventive turn of mind, he developed several gadgets and improvements, including an illuminated coal-hole cover, an improved lockstitch device for the sewing machine (then the most popular type of appliance in the American market), and a sharpener for erasers. By that time he had a business in Boston at 5 Water Street. It was there that he worked on military improvements and crafted three different variations of artillery shrapnel rounds. Some time early in 1862 he moved to New York City, in time to become engaged in the encased-postage-stamp enterprise.

Recognizing that stamps glued to paper or cardboard would soon become discolored or damaged, and that those in envelopes would be clumsy to inspect and also might become damaged, he felt that "encased" postage stamps would serve a need. Basically the unit consisted of a multiple-part arrangement displayed in an encasement made of brass.

The back part could be blank or bear simply the name of Gault, or it could be sold as an advertising medium. Within the frame was a small piece of cardboard padding, then a regular postage stamp with its corners folded down, then a thin sheet of clear mica, then a top frame to fit around the back frame, in the manner that might be used to make a brass button. The result was a colorful and attractive token, about the size of a quarter dollar, with a clear view of a particular postage stamp, usable in circulation at that value. Businesses warmed to the idea of advertising, and most encased postage stamps bore commercial messages, such as for Ayer's Sarsaparilla, Brown's Bronchial Troches, or perhaps the name of a hotel or the business of a hat manufacturer—there were over two dozen variations.

The original time of Gault's production is not known, but it commenced after his patent no. 1627 was granted on August 2, 1862, and certainly lasted through spring 1863, at which time Postage Currency notes issued by the Treasury Department flooded circulation. The encased postage stamps were made by the Scovill Manufacturing Company of Waterbury, Connecticut, long established as a maker of buttons, tokens (including in the Hard Times era), and other small metal goods.

In 1863 millions of privately issued copper tokens were also available, these containing less than one cent's worth of metal, and thus yielding a nice profit to those who made them and those who used them for advertisements. Probably, these pieces, called Civil War tokens today, lessened the demand for Gault's product. The situation remains something of a mystery, for the leading advertisers on encased postage stamps did not advertise on Civil War tokens. Whatever the reasons, by the summer of 1863 there were so many tokens and Postal Currency notes in circulation, plus a flood of privately printed scrip notes, that the encased postage stamps no longer filled a critical need. It is likely that existing encased postage stamps circulated occasionally for a year or two afterward, as some in existence today show extensive wear in the form of dents on the cases or cracks or breaks in the mica. The glory period of encased postage was probably less than a year.

THE PANORAMA OF
ENCASED POSTAGE STAMPS

During this time 31 different merchants signed up to advertise on encased postage stamps. Today, the collecting of encased postage stamps is a vital specialty in American numismatics. As a class all varieties are scarce or rare, with the consequence that if interest were to become very widespread there simply would not be enough to go around, even of certain issues that are viewed as plentiful within the series.

Postage-stamp denominations used included these:

1¢ blue. Franklin portrait. August 17, 1861. Scott-63.

3¢ rose. Washington portrait. 1861. S-65.

5¢ red-brown. Jefferson portrait. January 2, 1862. S-75.

10¢ yellow-green. Washington portrait. August 20, 1861. S-68.

12¢ black. Washington portrait. After August 20, 1861. S-69. This is a very scarce denomination today.

24¢ red-lilac. Washington portrait. January 7, 1862. S-70. Also very scarce.

30¢ orange. Franklin portrait. August 20, 1861. S-71. Seldom seen in the marketplace.

90¢ blue. Washington portrait. After November 1861. S-72. The rarest of all encased postage denominations.

Occasionally a two-cent stamp with the Jackson portrait is offered on the market as an encased postage stamp, as it may be, but no *originals* are believed to have been issued by Gault. The position of a stamp within an encasement can vary. While most are oriented vertically, many are tilted one way or the other, or are off center, in some rare instances with a few edge perforations visible.

Detail of a Plain Frame (on HB-151, Hunt & Nash 5¢) and a Ribbed Frame (HB-152) as used on encased postage stamps. Ribbed Frame varieties are only a small fraction of the population of encasements in existence today.

Some varieties of stamps were issued with the back brass panel partially tinned (sometimes called "silvered"), with areas of brass showing through. Most encased postage stamps have plain tabs on the front of the case—the projections extending from left to right. A few varieties have *ribbed* frames with ridges. Plain Frame and Ribbed Frame are often capitalized in numismatic usage.

Around the back border there is raised beading on all varieties except Brown's Bronchial Troches and Hunt & Nash (which have a plain inner rim) and J. Gault. The Gault encasement is unique with its circle of recessed dots and recessed (incuse) lettering.

Various deceptions exist among stamps in numismatic hands today, including fabrications of supposed rarities and new varieties made by the opening of cases and substituting of a more valuable high-denomination stamp for a lower one, or the insertion of stamps not used originally in the series, or of varieties of denominations made after 1863. An extensive discussion of such impostures is given in the *Standard Catalogue of Encased Postage Stamps* by Michael Hodder and Q. David Bowers (Bowers and Merena Galleries, 1989). A detailed description of the issuers of encased postage stamps may also be found in the Hodder-Bowers book.

The encased postage stamps are arranged by HB (Hodder-Bowers) numbers and cross-referenced to EP (Friedberg) numbers, both systems being in popular use today.

GRADING ENCASED POSTAGE STAMPS

Grading encased postage stamps presents some problems unique to the series. Each encasement was composed of several separate items, including the stamp and its backing, the mica facing, and the two-part case containing the other two components.

Each item was, and is, subject to its own types of change over time, through wear or simple aging. Accordingly, grading encased postage stamps must take into account the conditions of the major constituents of each piece: the stamp, the mica, and the case. Stamps can be bright or faded, intact or torn, wrinkled or smooth, water stained or not, and so on. Similarly, the mica can be clear or crazed, cracked or sound, laminated or not, and so on. Probably, most stamps were issued with the mica either clear or with only tiny laminations, as occur in nature. In its turn, the case may be dark or bright; have full, most, or only partial tinning; be dented, bent, or both; and so on.

Any description of an encased postage stamp should accurately convey to the potential collector the individual conditions of each of the three major components just described. Finally, summing up the conditions of the stamp, mica, and case, an overall adjectival grade can be assigned to the specimen, which represents the overall "eye appeal" and condition of the piece. In the descriptions that follow, varieties are valued under three grade columns. While these grades are an approximate guide, specific descriptions of an encasement are always desirable as a supplement.

Low Grades, Damaged, and Impaired: Encased postage stamps with pieces of the mica broken out, parts of the stamp missing, the stamp severely faded, or a bent, damaged, or obviously tampered-with frame are worth fractions of the prices listed for VF-20. If the case is well preserved and it can be viewed from the back, it will be more valuable than if the case is damaged. Encasements with severe problems have relatively little added value if they enclose a damaged high-denomination stamp.

Very Fine-20: Mica intact, but may have laminations, flaking, or small cracks, but with a clear view of the stamp. Stamp bright or only slightly faded. Brass case may be slightly oxidized or dark, but will have no major problems. This is a typical nice-quality encasement, attractive and without major problems except for mica.

Extremely Fine-40: Mica intact with no more than minor flaking or lamination. Stamp bright. A prime grade for the specialist, a reasonable objective for the advanced collector.

MARKET VALUES

The prime determinant of market value is the rarity of the encased postage stamp as a basic type. Accordingly, examples from such issuers as B.F. Miles, Sands' Ale, and Arthur M. Claflin will elevate the temperature in an auction room. This reflects that the preponderance of numismatists desire just one of each issuer. High-denomination stamps also add significant value, such as the 12¢, with importance increasing through the 24¢, 30¢, and in particular the 90¢. Of less importance value-wise are rare frame or lettering varieties of otherwise plentiful issues, although these varieties do have their own audience.

Values are given in two grades: VF-20 and EF-40, as described. The prices of the more elusive issues are apt to vary widely at auction and private sale, and it is not unusual to see a Very Fine example priced at $2,000 in one place and $3,000 or even $4,000 in another. Pedigree and eye appeal are factors as well.

Aerated Bread Company

Denomination	No.		VF-20	EF-40
1¢	1, EP-1		$4,750	$7,000
5¢	2, EP-59a	Unique	—	—

Ayer's Cathartic Pills

Denomination	No.		VF-20	EF-40
1¢	3, EP-2	Short arrows	$250	$350
	4	Long arrows Unique	—	—
3¢	5, EP-32	Short arrows	200	300
	6, EP-32a	Long arrows	375	550
5¢	7, EP-60	Short arrows	800	1,200
	8, EP-60a	Long arrows	800	1,500
	9, EP-96	Short arrows	500	800
	10, EP-96a	Long arrows	1,100	1,900
12¢	11, EP-135	Short arrows	1,300	2,000

Denomination	No.			VF-20	EF-40
	12, EP-135a	Long arrows		$2,200	—
24¢	13, EP-159b	Short arrows		2,700	$3,500
	14	Long arrows		—	—
30¢	15, EP-172b	Long arrows		2,200	3,000
	16	Short arrows	Unique	—	—

"Take Ayer's Pills"

Denomination	No.			VF-20	EF-40
1¢	17, EP-3			$325	$500
3¢	18, EP-33			300	400
5¢	19, EP-61	Plain frame		900	1,600
	20, EP-62	Ribbed frame		3,200	4,400
10¢	21, EP-97	Plain frame		600	1,200
	22, EP-97a	Ribbed frame	Unique	—	4,888
12¢	23, EP-136			1,400	2,000
24¢	24, EP-159c		Unique	—	—
30¢	25			—	—
90¢	26, EP-183a			—	—

Ayer's Sarsaparilla

Denomination	No.			VF-20	EF-40
1¢	27, EP-4	Small AYER's, plain frame		$750	$1,200
	28, EP-4a	Medium AYER's, plain frame		300	400
3¢	29, EP-34	Small AYER's, plain frame		325	425
	30, EP-34a	Medium AYER's, plain frame		300	400
	31, EP-35	Same, ribbed frame		1,600	2,300
	32, EP-34b	Large AYER's, plain frame		350	450
5¢	33, EP-63	Medium AYER's, plain frame		375	475
	34, EP-63a	Large AYER's, plain frame		1,800	2,200
10¢	35, EP-98	Small AYER's, plain frame		1,500	2,000
	36, EP-98a	Medium AYER's, plain frame		450	625
	37, EP-99	Same, ribbed frame		1,400	1,900
	38, EP-98B	Large AYER's, plain frame		900	1,400
12¢	39, EP-137a	Small AYER's, plain frame		2,750	3,500
	40, EP-137	Medium AYER's, plain frame		4,000	6,500
	41	Large AYER's, plain frame	Unique	—	—
30¢	42, EP-173	Medium AYER's, plain frame	Unique	—	—
90¢	43, EP-183B	Medium AYER's, plain frame		12,000	14,000

J. Bailey & Company

Denomination	No.	VF-20	EF-40	Denomination	No.	VF-20	EF-40
1¢	44, EP-5	$1,200	$1,800	10¢	47, EP-100	$750	$1,800
3¢	45, EP-36	1,400	2,000	12¢	48, EP-138	—	—
5¢	46, EP-64	750	1,800				

Joseph L. Bates

Denomination	No.		VF-20	EF-40
1¢	49, EP-6a	FANCYGOODS as one word	$650	$800
	50, EP-6	FANCY GOODS	900	1,400
3¢	51, EP-37a	FANCYGOODS as one word	—	—
	52, EP-37	FANCY GOODS	1,000	1,500
5¢	53, EP-66a	FANCYGOODS as one word, plain frame	—	—
	54, EP-65	FANCY GOODS, plain frame	1,000	1,500
	55, EP-66	FANCY GOODS, ribbed frame	1,800	2,750
10¢	56, EP-102a	FANCYGOODS as one word, plain frame	1,000	1,500
	57, EP-102	FANCY GOODS, ribbed frame	800	1,200
	58, EP-101	FANCY GOODS, plain frame	1,200	1,700
12¢	59, EP-139		3,000	4,000
24¢	60, EP-160a	Unique	—	—
90¢	61	Unique	—	—

Brown's Bronchial Troches

Denomination	No.	VF-20	EF-40	Denomination	No.	VF-20	EF-40
1¢	62, EP-7	$1,400	$1,650	10¢	65, EP-103	$500	$700
3¢	63, EP-38	375	550	12¢	66, EP-140	2,500	3,200
5¢	64, EP-67	350	500				

F. Buhl and Company

Denomination	No.	VF-20	EF-40	Denomination	No.	VF-20	EF-40
1¢	67, EP-8	$1,500	$2,250	10¢	70, EP-104	$1,200	$1,600
3¢	68, EP-38A	—	—	12¢	71, EP-141	—	—
5¢	69, EP-68	1,400	1,800	24¢	72, EP-162	—	—

Burnett's Cocoaine Kalliston

Denomination	No.	VF-20	EF-40	Denomination	No.	VF-20	EF-40
1¢	73, EP-9	$500	$750	12¢	77, EP-142	$2,600	$3,500
3¢	74, EP-39	425	550	24¢	78, EP-163	—	—
5¢	75, EP-69	425	550	30¢	79, EP-175	—	—
10¢	76, EP-105	425	550	90¢	80, EP-184	—	—

Burnett's Standard Cooking Extracts

Denomination	No.		VF-20	EF-40	Denomination	No.		VF-20	EF-40
1¢	81, EP-10		$550	$650	12¢	86, EP-143		$1,300	$1,600
3¢	82, EP-40		375	550	24¢	87, EP-164		2,300	3,000
5¢	83, EP-70		475	700	30¢	88, EP-176		2,500	3,200
10¢	84, EP-106	Plain frame	500	850	90¢	89, EP-184a	Unique	—	—
	85, EP-107	Ribbed frame	—	—					

Arthur M. Claflin

Denomination	No.	VF-20	EF-40	Denomination	No.	VF-20	EF-40
1¢	89a, EP-11	—	—	10¢	92, EP-108a	—	—
3¢	90, EP-40a	—	—	12¢	93, EP-144	—	—
5¢	91, EP-71	—	—				

H.A. Cook

Denomination	No.	VF-20	EF-40	Denomination	No.	VF-20	EF-40
5¢	94, EP-72	$2,500	$3,500	10¢	95, EP-108	$2,800	$4,000

Dougan the Hatter

Denomination	No.	VF-20	EF-40	Denomination	No.	VF-20	EF-40
1¢	96, EP-12	$1,500	$2,100	5¢	98, EP-73	$2,500	$3,800
3¢	97, EP-41	2,500	3,800	10¢	99, EP-109	3,000	4,000

Drake's Plantation Bitters

Denomination	No.		VF-20	EF-40	Denomination	No.	VF-20	EF-40
1¢	100, EP-13		$350	$500	12¢	106, EP-145	$1,400	$2,100
3¢	101, EP-42		350	500	24¢	107, EP-165	2,500	3,200
5¢	102, EP-74	Plain frame	400	600	30¢	108, EP-177	2,400	3,000
	103, EP-75	Ribbed frame	—	—	90¢	109, EP-185	7,500	8,599
10¢	104, EP-110	Plain frame	600	950				
	105, EP-110	Ribbed frame	—	—				

Ellis, McAlpin & Company

Denomination	No.	VF-20	EF-40	Denomination	No.	VF-20	EF-40
1¢	110, EP-13a	—	—	10¢	113, EP-112	$700	$900
3¢	111, EP-43	—	—	12¢	114, EP-146	2,700	3,400
5¢	112, EP-76	$1,000	$1,400	24¢	115, EP-166	1,300	1,700

G.G. Evans

Denomination	No.	VF-20	EF-40	Denomination	No.	VF-20	EF-40
1¢	116, EP-14	$1,250	$1,600	5¢	118, EP-76a	$4,000	$6,000
3¢	117, EP-44	1,250	1,600	10¢	119, EP-113	—	—

Gage Brothers & Drake (Tremont House)

Denomination	No.		VF-20	EF-40	Denomination	No.		VF-20	EF-40
1¢	120, EP-15		$900	$1,200	10¢	123, EP-114	Plain frame	$600	$800
3¢	121, EP-45		650	900		124, EP-119	Ribbed frame	—	—
5¢	122, EP-77		600	800	12¢	125, EP-147		—	—

John Gault

Denomination	No.		VF-20	EF-40	Denomination	No.		VF-20	EF-40
1¢	126, EP-16	Plain frame	$550	$700	12¢	135, EP-148	Plain frame	$700	$850
	127, EP-17	Ribbed frame	—	—		136, EP-149	Ribbed frame	—	—
2¢	128, EP-31	Plain frame (not a circulation issue)	—	—	24¢	137, EP-167	Plain frame	1,300	1,750
						138, EP-168	Ribbed frame	2,200	2,600
3¢	129, EP-46	Plain frame	450	600	30¢	139, EP-178	Plain frame	3,000	3,600
	130, EP-47	Ribbed frame	—	—		140, EP-179	Ribbed frame	3,300	3,800
5¢	131, EP-78	Plain frame	325	450	90¢	141, EP-186	Plain frame	7,500	8,000
	132, EP-79	Ribbed frame	450	600		142	Ribbed frame	—	—
10¢	133, EP-116	Plain frame	325	450					
	134, EP-117	Ribbed frame	400	550					

L.C. Hopkins & Co.

Denomination	No.	VF-20	EF-40	Denomination	No.	VF-20	EF-40
1¢	143, EP-17a	—	—	5¢	145, EP-80	$3,750	$5,000
3¢	144, EP-48	$3,750	$5,000	10¢	146, EP-117a	—	—

Hunt & Nash (Irving House)

Denomination	No.		VF-20	EF-40	Denomination	No.		VF-20	EF-40
1¢	147, EP-18	Plain frame	—	—	12¢	155, EP-150	Plain frame	$2,200	$3,000
	148	Ribbed frame	—	—		156, EP-156	Ribbed frame	2,400	3,200
3¢	149, EP-49	Plain frame	$700	$950	24¢	157, EP-169	Plain frame	2,400	3,000
	150, EP-49a	Ribbed frame	—	—		158, EP-170	Ribbed frame	—	—
5¢	151, EP-81	Plain frame	1,200	2,700	30¢	159, EP-180		—	—
	152, EP-82	Ribbed frame	500	700					
10¢	153, EP-118	Plain frame	1,100	1,500					
	154, EP-119	Ribbed frame	475	650					

Kirkpatrick & Gault

Denomination	No.	VF-20	EF-40	Denomination	No.	VF-20	EF-40
1¢	160, EP-19	$1,600	$2,300	12¢	164, EP-152	$1,000	$1,300
3¢	161, EP-50	—	—	24¢	165, EP-171	750	1,200
5¢	162, EP-83	600	850	30¢	166, EP-181	2,300	3,000
10¢	163, EP-120	650	900	90¢	167, EP-187	7,000	8,000

Lord & Taylor

Denomination	No.	VF-20	EF-40	Denomination	No.	VF-20	EF-40
1¢	168, EP-20	$2,750	$3,500	12¢	172, EP-153	$2,100	$2,600
3¢	169, EP-51	900	1,400	24¢	173, EP-172	2,200	2,700
5¢	170, EP-84	800	1,100	30¢	174, EP-182	3,200	4,000
10¢	171, EP-121	850	1,200	90¢	175, EP-188	—	—

Mendum's Family Wine Emporium

Denomination	No.		VF-20	EF-40	Denomination	No.		VF-20	EF-40
1¢	176, EP-21		$775	$1,100	10¢	179, EP-122	Plain frame	$600	$800
3¢	177, EP-52		—	—		180, EP-123	Ribbed frame	1,600	2,300
5¢	178, EP-85		850	1,250	12¢	181, EP-154		2,200	2,750

B.F. Miles

Denomination	No.	VF-20	EF-40	Denomination	No.	VF-20	EF-40
1¢	182, EP-22	—	—	5¢	183, EP-86	—	—

John W. Norris

Denomination	No.	VF-20	EF-40	Denomination	No.	VF-20	EF-40
1¢	184, EP-23	$950	$4,000	5¢	186, EP-87	$2,000	$2,750
3¢	185, EP-52a	2,200	3,000	10¢	187, EP-124	3,500	5,000

North American Life Insurance Company

Denomination	No.		VF-20	EF-40
1¢	188, EP-24	Straight inscription; plain frame	$450	$550
	189, EP-24a	Curved inscription; plain frame	650	800
3¢	190, EP-53	Straight inscription; plain frame	550	650
	191, EP-53a	Curved inscription; plain frame	—	—
5¢	192, EP-88	Straight inscription; plain frame	—	—
	193, EP-88b	Curved inscription; plain frame	Unique	—	—
	194, EP-88a	Straight inscription; ribbed frame	—	—
10¢	195, EP-125	Straight inscription; plain frame	1,000	1,450
	196, EP-125a	Curved inscription; plain frame	1,200	1,750
	197, EP-125b	Straight inscription; ribbed frame	—	—
	198, EP-126	Curved inscription; ribbed frame	1,600	2,300
12¢	199, EP-155	Straight inscription; plain frame	2,300	2,600
	200, EP-155a	Curved inscription; plain frame	—	—

Pearce, Tolle & Holton

Denomination	No.	VF-20	EF-40	Denomination	No.	VF-20	EF-40
1¢	201, EP-246	—	—	10¢	204, EP-127	—	—
3¢	202, EP-54	$2,100	$2,750	12¢	205, EP-156	—	—
5¢	203, EP-89	2,400	3,000	24¢	206, EP-172a	—	—

Sands' Ale

Denomination	No.	VF-20	EF-40	Denomination	No.	VF-20	EF-40
5¢	207, EP-90	$15,000	$18,500	12¢	209, EP-156a	—	—
10¢	208, EP-128	17,000	19,500	30¢	210, EP-183	—	—

Schapker & Bussing

Denomination	No.	VF-20	EF-40	Denomination	No.		VF-20	EF-40
1¢	211, EP-25	$1,300	$1,600	10¢	214, EP-129		$850	$975
3¢	212, EP-55	1,100	1,300	12¢	215, EP-157	Unique	—	—
5¢	213, EP-91	650	950					

John Shillito & Co.

Denomination	No.	VF-20	EF-40	Denomination	No.	VF-20	EF-40
1¢	216, EP-26	$1,700	$2,000	10¢	219, EP-130	$500	$625
3¢	217, EP-56	600	900	12¢	220, EP-158	—	—
5¢	218, EP-92	450	600				

S. Steinfeld

Denomination	No.	VF-20	EF-40	Denomination	No.	VF-20	EF-40
1¢	221, EP-27	$1,700	$3,300	10¢	223, EP-131	—	—
5¢	222, EP-93	—	—	12¢	224, EP-159	—	—

N.G. Taylor & Co.

Denomination	No.	VF-20	EF-40	Denomination	No.	VF-20	EF-40
1¢	225, EP-28	$1,700	$2,800	10¢	228, EP-132	—	—
3¢	226, EP-57	1,500	2,600	12¢	229, EP-159a	—	—
5¢	227, EP-93a	—	—				

Weir & Larminie

Denomination	No.	VF-20	EF-40	Denomination	No.	VF-20	EF-40
1¢	230, EP-29	$3,250	$4,000	5¢	232, EP-94	—	—
3¢	231, EP-58	—	—	10¢	233, EP-133	$2,750	$3,500

White the Hatter

Denomination	No.	VF-20	EF-40	Denomination	No.	VF-20	EF-40
1¢	234, EP-30	$2,500	$3,250	5¢	236, EP-95	$3,000	$4,000
3¢	235, EP-59	2,700	3,500	10¢	237, EP-134	—	—

COLLECTING ERROR NOTES

Although errors have occurred in all sizes and types of U.S. currency since the nation first started printing paper money, error note collecting has historically been a very limited pursuit. In the past 30 years, however, errors have grown into a widely collected part of the hobby.

Error notes can be inexpensive or very costly, depending on what you collect. A double denomination (the "king of errors" in the banknote field) is the rarest of the rare—for example, a 1934-D note with a $5 face and a $10 back is worth $12,500 in Very Fine or $20,000 in Uncirculated condition. Other errors can be easily obtained for $10 to $15 over face value.

Mistakes on large-size notes are mostly very rare. Errors have also been found on National Bank Notes but are extremely rare.

These images depict just a few examples of different types of paper money errors.

Gutters or Creases

The value of such an error will depend on size and severity: for a minor crease, the note will be worth about $15 more than face value in Very Fine condition, or $25 over face value in Uncirculated. A larger or more severe crease increases the value to $25 over face value in Very Fine, or $100+ in Uncirculated.

Offset Transfers

Face on Back

A note that exhibits the face design on the back will bring prices according to how bold the transfer is. A partial or faint image will bring $25 over face value in Very Fine or $50 in Uncirculated. If the transfer is complete and strong, collectors will pay $200 and $500 over face value in Very Fine and Uncirculated.

Back on Face

A complete and dark view of the back design on the note's face will increase its value by $150 to $200, in grades ranging from Very Fine to Uncirculated.

Ink Smears

A minor ink smear increases a note's worth by $20 over face in Very Fine, or $50 in Uncirculated.

Shifts or Misaligned Overprints

While minor shifts are easily found in circulation, major displacements are more rare and thus more valuable to collectors. A shifted overprint will fetch $50 to $100 over face value, depending on the grade (Very Fine or Uncirculated). A shifted overprint appearing on a star note (a replacement for a damaged note or error caught in the production process), such as the Series 1935-E Silver Certificate pictured, is more valuable.

Mismatched Serial Numbers

These mistakes are much sought after by error note collectors. The $1 note pictured, with mismatched digits in the serial number, is worth $200 in Very Fine and $400 in Uncirculated. For the $2 note with a mismatched prefix, a collector would pay $400 in Very Fine or $800 in Uncirculated.

Inverted Serial Numbers/Seals

A note printed with upside-down serial numbers and seals is worth $250 to $750 over face value, in grades ranging from Very Fine to Uncirculated. The $20 note pictured here also exhibits selvage, or part of an adjacent note.

Inverted Face

A typical note has its face and back aligned in the same up-down position. In the Series of 1935 $1 note pictured, the face is printed upside down. This error increases its value to $400 in Very Fine or $1,650 in Uncirculated.

Seals and Serial Numbers on Back

With its seals and serial numbers printed on the back instead of the front, this $10 note would bring $150 (Very Fine) to $350 (Uncirculated) from a collector. If they were also printed upside down, the value would increase to $250 and $800, respectively.

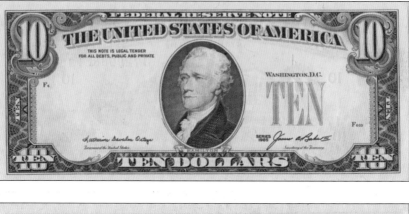

Third Printing Missing

A $5 note such as this one, with its seals and serial numbers missing, is worth $120 in Very Fine and $400 in Uncirculated.

Printed Folds

This $10 note, with its large, attractively printed-over fold, would bring $500 in Very Fine or $900 in Uncirculated.

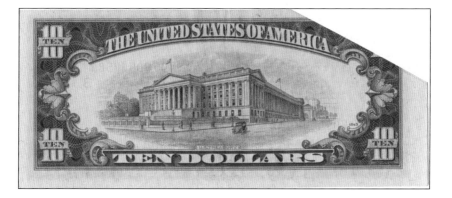

Second Printing Missing

A $1 note that is missing its second printing—that is, which bears its serial numbers and seals, but is otherwise missing the back design—is worth $300 to $750 to a collector, in Very Fine to Uncirculated condition. The dramatic and eye-catching $100 note of this type (pictured) is worth $600 in Very Fine or $1,250 in Uncirculated.

Blank Back

A note with a blank back gives a collector only half the design, while increasing its value considerably—a good example of "less is more." A $20 note made this way is worth $150 in Very Fine or $350 in Uncirculated.

Double Denomination

The most famous and desirable type of error is the "double denomination" note, with one value on the face and another on the back. These were produced in two main ways:

For small-size bills, a sheet printed on one side with $5 designs and information, but blank on the other, was then mistakenly put with one-sided $10 bills and imprinted on the other side with $10 information. A famous Series of 1934-D Silver Certificate, printed circa 1960, is of this type, with a $5 face and $10 back. Nearly a dozen of these were found by dealer Aubrey Bebee of Omaha, Nebraska. Today an example is worth about $25,000 in VF-20 grade, and $40,000 in Unc-63.

For large-size bills with more than one denomination per sheet, such an error could occur when the correct sheet was printed on the back, but upside down. A $50-$100 two-subject sheet might be printed correctly on one side, then printed on the other with the sheet misaligned so as to give the $50 note the imprint intended for the $100, and vice versa.

In March 1909, *The Numismatist* reported on a batch of misprinted notes from the First National Bank of Albuquerque, New Mexico. One of these notes was mentioned in a story that made the rounds of the American Bankers' Association Convention held in Denver the preceding autumn. A hotel cashier (who was working overtime because of the convention) counted his cash, and in turning it over counted it again, but found a $50 discrepancy. According to the story, three more days (!) were spent in counting the cash, driving the cashier to the point of distraction. Finally the bill of the $100/$50 combination was found.

Photos courtesy of Harry E. Jones, Middleburg Heights, Ohio.

APPENDIX A:
THE SIGNATURES OF
UNITED STATES CURRENCY

The following tables show the exact period of time during which each two of the various signers of our currency were in office concurrently.

| Register of the Treasury | Treasurer of the U.S. | Combined Tenure | | Length of Time | | |
		Began	Ended	Years	Months	Days
Lucius E. Chittenden	F.E. Spinner	04-17-1861	08-10-1864	3	3	23
S.B. Colby	F.E. Spinner	08-11-1864	09-21-1867	3	1	10
Noah L. Jeffries	F.E. Spinner	10-05-1867	03-15-1869	1	5	10
John Allison	F.E. Spinner	04-03-1869	06-30-1877	6	2	27
John Allison	John C. New	06-30-1875	07-01-1876	1	—	1
John Allison	A.U. Wyman	07-01-1876	06-30-1877	—	11	29
John Allison	James Gilfillan	07-01-1877	03-23-1878	—	8	22
Glenni W. Scofield	James Gilfillan	04-01-1878	05-20-1881	3	1	19
Blanche K. Bruce	James Gilfillan	05-21-1881	03-31-1883	1	10	10
Blanche K. Bruce	A.U. Wyman	04-01-1883	04-30-1885	2	—	29
Blanche K. Bruce	Conrad N. Jordan	05-01-1885	06-05-1885	—	1	4
William S. Rosecrans	Conrad N. Jordan	06-08-1885	05-23-1887	1	11	15
William S. Rosecrans	James W. Hyatt	05-24-1887	05-10-1889	1	11	16
William S. Rosecrans	J.N. Huston	05-11-1889	04-21-1891	1	11	13
William S. Rosecrans	Enos H. Nebeker	04-25-1891	05-31-1893	2	1	6
William S. Rosecrans	Daniel N. Morgan	06-01-1893	06-19-1893	—	—	18
James F. Tillman	Daniel N. Morgan	07-01-1893	06-30-1897	3	11	29
James F. Tillman	Ellis H. Roberts	07-01-1897	12-02-1897	—	5	1
Blanche K. Bruce	Ellis H. Roberts	12-03-1898	05-17-1898	—	3	14
Judson W. Lyons	Ellis H. Roberts	04-07-1898	06-30-1905	7	2	23
Judson W. Lyons	Charles H. Treat	07-01-1905	04-01-1906	—	10	—
William T. Vernon	Charles H. Treat	06-12-1906	10-30-1909	3	9	18
William T. Vernon	Lee McClung	11-01-1909	03-14-1911	1	4	13
James C. Napier	Lee McClung	08-15-1911	11-21-1912	1	4	6
James C. Napier	Carmi A. Thompson	11-22-1912	03-31-1913	—	8	9
James C. Napier	John Burke	04-01-1913	09-30-1913	—	4	29
Gabe E. Parker	John Burke	10-01-1913	12-31-1914	1	5	30
Houston B. Teehee	John Burke	03-24-1915	11-20-1919	4	2	26
William S. Elliott	John Burke	11-21-1919	01-05-1921	1	7	14
William S. Elliott	Frank White	05-02-1921	01-26-1922	—	1	22
Harley V. Speelman	Frank White	01-25-1922	09-30-1927	5	8	5
Walter O. Woods	Frank White	10-01-1927	05-01-1928	—	7	—
Walter O. Woods	H.T. Tate	05-31-1928	01-17-1929	—	7	16
Edward E. Jones	Walter O. Woods	01-22-1929	05-31-1933	4	4	9

Table continued on next page.

Secretary of the Treasury	Treasurer of the U.S.	Combined Tenure Began	Ended	Length of Time Years	Months	Days
William G. McAdoo	John Burke	04-01-1913	12-15-1918	5	8	14
Carter Glass	John Burke	12-18-1918	02-01-1920	1	1	15
D.F. Houston	John Burke	02-02-1920	01-05-1921	—	11	3
A.W. Mellon	Frank White	05-02-1921	05-01-1928	6	11	29
A.W. Mellon	H.T. Tate	04-30-1928	01-17-1929	—	8	16
A.W. Mellon	Walter O. Woods	01-18-1929	02-12-1932	3	—	25
Ogden L. Mills	Walter O. Woods	02-13-1932	03-03-1933	1	—	18
W.H. Woodin	Walter O. Woods	03-04-1933	05-31-1933	—	2	27
W.H. Woodin	W.A. Julian	06-01-1933	12-31-1933	—	7	—
Henry Morgenthau Jr.	W.A. Julian	01-01-1934	07-22-1945	11	6	22
Fred M. Vinson	W.A. Julian	07-23-1945	07-23-1946	1	—	—
John W. Snyder	W.A. Julian	01-25-1946	05-29-1949	2	10	4
John W. Snyder	Georgia Neese Clark	06-21-1949	01-20-1953	3	7	—
George M. Humphrey	Ivy Baker Priest	01-28-1953	07-28-1957	4	6	—
Robert B. Anderson	Ivy Baker Priest	07-29-1957	01-20-1961	3	5	23
C. Douglas Dillon	Elizabeth Rudel Smith	01-30-1961	04-13-1962	1	3	14
C. Douglas Dillon	Kathryn O'Hay Granahan	01-03-1963	03-01-1965	2	2	28
Henry Fowler	Kathryn O'Hay Granahan	04-01-1965	10-13-1966	1	6	13
Joseph Barr	Kathryn O'Hay Granahan*	12-23-1968	01-20-1969	—	—	28
David Kennedy	Dorothy Andrews Elston	05-08-1969	09-16-1970	1	4	8
David Kennedy	Dorothy Andrews Kabis‡	09-17-1970	02-01-1971	1	4	8
John B. Connally	Dorothy Andrews Kabis	02-08-1971	07-03-1971	—	44	25
John B. Connally	Romana Acosta Banuelos	12-17-1971	06-12-1973	—	5	26
George P. Shultz	Romana Acosta Banuelos	06-12-1972	02-14-1974	1	8	2
William E. Simon	Francine I. Neff	06-21-1974	01-19-1977	2	6	28
W. Michael Blumenthal	Azie Taylor Morton	09-12-1977	08-04-1979	1	10	24
G. William Miller	Azie Taylor Morton	08-06-1979	01-20-1981	1	5	15
Donald T. Regan	Angela Marie Buchanan	03-17-1981	07-05-1983	2	3	18
Donald T. Regan	Katherine Davalos Ortega	09-22-1983	02-03-1985	1	4	12
James A. Baker	Katherine Davalos Ortega	02-04-1985	08-18-1988	3	6	13
Nicholas F. Brady	Katherine Davalos Ortega	09-15-1988	06-30-1989	—	9	15
Nicholas F. Brady	Catalina Vasquez Villalpando	11-20-1989	01-20-1993	3	2	1
Lloyd M. Bentsen	Mary Ellen Withrow	03-01-1994	12-22-1994	—	9	22
Robert E. Rubin	Mary Ellen Withrow	10-01-1995	07-02-1999	3	9	1
Lawrence F. Summers	Mary Ellen Withrow	07-02-1999	01-20-2001	1	6	18
Paul H. O'Neill	Rosario Marin	08-16-2001	12-31-2002	1	4	15
John W. Snow	Rosario Marin	02-03-2003	06-30-2003	0	4	27
John W. Snow	Anna Escobedo Cabral	12-13-2004	06-29-2006	1	6	12
Henry M. Paulson	Anna Escobedo Cabral	07-10-2006	01-20-2009	3	0	10
Timothy F. Geithner	Rosie Rios	01-26-2009				

Although she was no longer treasurer, Kathryn Granahan's signature continued in use until Dorothy Elston was named to replace her.

‡*When Dorothy Elston married Walter Kabis on September 17, 1970, it was the first time the signature of a treasurer was changed during the term of office.*

APPENDIX B:
FRIEDBERG NUMBERS BY PAGE

APPENDIX C:
MODERN UNCUT SHEETS OF
U.S. CURRENCY OFFERED BY THE
BUREAU OF ENGRAVING AND PRINTING

Beginning in 1981, the Bureau of Engraving and Printing, a unit of the Treasury Department, joined the U.S. Mint in offering products specially made for collectors, direct to the public. The first offering consisted of sheets of $1 notes, but earlier $2 sheets from 1976 (figure 1) were offered soon thereafter, as well. Higher denominations were offered beginning with the notes of the Series of 2003 (see figures 2–4).

As seen in the following table, in some instances the sheets offered were of star notes. While in the main section of this book star notes are always more valuable than their regular-issue counterparts, with these modern sheets this is not necessarily the case. These star-note sheets represent leftovers that were not needed for their intended use as replacements. Rather than seeing them go unused and possibly destroyed, the Treasury was instead able to sell them at a profit, as collectibles.

Sheets have been offered in sizes as small as four notes and as large as 32 notes, as seen in figure 5. Current BEP issues may be purchased at the Bureau of Engraving and Printing's online store, at www.moneyfactory.gov/store/index.cfm/9.

Note: Older uncut sheets of small-size notes are not included in the table. These were usually sheets of 12 notes and were sold to the public, upon request, beginning in 1935. All sheets consisting of notes other than Federal Reserve Notes should be considered rare. Records indicate that few were printed in quantities of greater than 100.

Fr. #	Denom	Series	Federal Reserve District	Printing Facility	Fr. #	Denom	Series	Federal Reserve District	Printing Facility
1911	$1	1981	A	Washington, DC	1913	$1	1985	D	Washington, DC
1911	$1	1981	B	Washington, DC	1913	$1	1985	E	Washington, DC
1911	$1	1981	C	Washington, DC	1913	$1	1985	F	Washington, DC
1911	$1	1981	D	Washington, DC	1913	$1	1985	G	Washington, DC
1911	$1	1981	E	Washington, DC	1913	$1	1985	H	Washington, DC
1911	$1	1981	F	Washington, DC	1913	$1	1985	I	Washington, DC
1911	$1	1981	G	Washington, DC	1913	$1	1985	J	Washington, DC
1911	$1	1981	H	Washington, DC	1913	$1	1985	K	Washington, DC
1911	$1	1981	I	Washington, DC	1913	$1	1985	L	Washington, DC
1911	$1	1981	J	Washington, DC	1914	$1	1988	A	Washington, DC
1911	$1	1981	K	Washington, DC	1914	$1	1988	B	Washington, DC
1911	$1	1981	L	Washington, DC	1914	$1	1988	C	Washington, DC
1912	$1	1981A	A	Washington, DC	1914	$1	1988	D	Washington, DC
1912	$1	1981A	B	Washington, DC	1914	$1	1988	E	Washington, DC
1912	$1	1981A	C	Washington, DC	1914	$1	1988	F	Washington, DC
1912	$1	1981A	D	Washington, DC	1914	$1	1988	G	Washington, DC
1912	$1	1981A	E	Washington, DC	1914	$1	1988	H	Washington, DC
1912	$1	1981A	F	Washington, DC	1914	$1	1988	I	Washington, DC
1912	$1	1981A	G	Washington, DC	1914	$1	1988	J	Washington, DC
1912	$1	1981A	H	Washington, DC	1914	$1	1988	K	Washington, DC
1912	$1	1981A	I	Washington, DC	1914	$1	1988	L	Washington, DC
1912	$1	1981A	J	Washington, DC	1915	$1	1988A	A	Washington, DC
1912	$1	1981A	K	Washington, DC	1915	$1	1988A	B	Washington, DC
1912	$1	1981A	L	Washington, DC	1915	$1	1988A	C	Washington, DC
1913	$1	1985	A	Washington, DC	1915	$1	1988A	D	Washington, DC
1913	$1	1985	B	Washington, DC	1915	$1	1988A	E	Washington, DC
1913	$1	1985	C	Washington, DC	1915	$1	1988A	F	Washington, DC

Fr. #	Denom	Series	Federal Reserve District	Printing Facility	Fr. #	Denom	Series	Federal Reserve District	Printing Facility
1915	$1	1988A	G	Washington, DC	1935	$2	1976	C*	Washington, DC
1915	$1	1988A	H	Washington, DC	1935	$2	1976	D*	Washington, DC
1915	$1	1988A	I	Washington, DC	1935	$2	1976	E	Washington, DC
1915	$1	1988A	J	Washington, DC	1935	$2	1976	F	Washington, DC
1915	$1	1988A	K	Washington, DC	1935	$2	1976	F*	Washington, DC
1915	$1	1988A	L	Washington, DC	1935	$2	1976	G*	Washington, DC
1916	$1	1988A	K	Fort Worth, TX	1935	$2	1976	H*	Washington, DC
1918	$1	1993	D	Washington, DC	1935	$2	1976	I	Washington, DC
1918	$1	1993	E	Washington, DC	1935	$2	1976	J*	Washington, DC
1919	$1	1993	K	Fort Worth, TX	1935	$2	1976	K*	Washington, DC
1921	$1	1995	A	Washington, DC	1935	$2	1976	L*	Washington, DC
1921	$1	1995	B	Washington, DC	1936	$2	1995	F	Fort Worth, TX
1921	$1	1995	C	Washington, DC	1936	$2	1995	F*	Fort Worth, TX
1921	$1	1995	D	Washington, DC	1937	$2	2003	B	Fort Worth, TX
1921	$1	1995	E	Washington, DC	1937	$2	2003	F	Fort Worth, TX
1921	$1	1995	I	Washington, DC	1937	$2	2003	G	Fort Worth, TX
1922	$1	1995	K	Fort Worth, TX	1937	$2	2003	I	Fort Worth, TX
1924	$1	1999	A	Washington, DC	1937	$2	2003	K	Fort Worth, TX
1924	$1	1999	B	Washington, DC	1938	$2	2003A	E	Fort Worth, TX
1924	$1	1999	C	Washington, DC	1938	$2	2003A	G	Fort Worth, TX
1924	$1	1999	D	Washington, DC	1938	$2	2003A	J	Fort Worth, TX
1924	$1	1999	E*	Washington, DC	1938	$2	003A	L	Fort Worth, TX
1925	$1	1999	K	Fort Worth, TX	1984	$5	1995	A	Washington, DC
1926	$1	2001	B	Washington, DC	1985	$5	1995	F	Fort Worth, TX
1926	$1	2001	I	Washington, DC	1985	$5	1995	H	Fort Worth, TX
1926	$1	2001	K	Washington, DC	1988	$5	2001	B	Fort Worth, TX
1926	$1	2001	L	Washington, DC	1988	$5	2001	C	Fort Worth, TX
1928	$1	2003	B	Washington, DC	1989	$5	2003	G*	Washington, DC
1928	$1	2003	E	Washington, DC	1990	$5	2003A	L	Fort Worth, TX
1928	$1	2003	H	Washington, DC	1992	$5	2006	F	Fort Worth, TX
1928	$1	2003	J	Washington, DC	2032	$10	1995	F*	Fort Worth, TX
1929	$1	2003	C	Fort Worth, TX	2037	$10	2003	A*	Washington, DC
1929	$1	2003	K	Fort Worth, TX	2039	$10	2004A	B*	Fort Worth, TX
1930	$1	2003A	C	Washington, DC	2039	$10	2004A	F*	Fort Worth, TX
1930	$1	2003A	E	Washington, DC	2039	$10	2006	F	Fort Worth, TX
1930	$1	2003A	F	Washington, DC	2084	$20	1996	L*	Fort Worth, TX
1930	$1	2003A	G	Washington, DC	2089	$20	2004	A*	Washington, DC
1930	$1	2003A	L	Washington, DC	2091	$20	2004A	A*	Washington, DC
1931	$1	2003A	J	Fort Worth, TX	2093	$20	2006	B	Washington, DC
1932	$1	2006	D	Washington, DC	2128	$50	2004	G*	Fort Worth, TX
1935	$2	1976	A*	Washington, DC	2130	$50	2006	D	Fort Worth, TX
1935	$2	1976	B*	Washington, DC					

Figure 1

Figure 2

Figure 3

Figure 4

Figure 5

GLOSSARY

ace—Numismatic nickname for a $1 bill, particularly a $1 National Bank Note of the Original Series or the Series of 1875.

American Bank Note Company—Firm founded in 1858 in New York City. Provider by contract of certain federal currency and Fractional Currency notes in the 1860s through the mid-1870s. Sometimes one private firm would print the face of a note and another would print the back. In all instances, the Treasury seals were separately imprinted by the Treasury Department in Washington, DC. The ABNCo monogram appears on certain Fractional Currency and early federal notes of the 1860s.

back—The reverse side of a note, usually called the *back*, is the paper-money equivalent of *reverse* used for coins. The other side of a note is called the *face*. In Treasury records, sometimes *obverse* and *reverse* are used, but *face* and *back* are preferred by some today.

Battleship Note—Numismatic nickname for a Series of 1918 $2 Federal Reserve Bank Note with a battleship printed in green on the back.

Bison Note—Numismatic nickname for the $10 Series of 1901 Legal Tender Notes depicting such an animal. Modeled either by Pablo or by a stuffed animal; not the same bison shown on the 1913 "Buffalo" nickel.

black charter—Describes a rare variety of $5 National Bank Note issued in the 1870s, with the bank charter number printed in black (instead of the normal red overprint) as part of the printing plate.

Black Eagle Note—Numismatic nickname for the $1 Series of 1899 Silver Certificates depicting a bold eagle printed in black on the center of the face of the note. Official name of vignette: "Eagle of the Capitol."

Bureau of Engraving and Printing—Federal bureau in charge of printing paper money and certain other security items. Successor to the National Currency Bureau (see below). First housed in the Treasury Building in Washington, DC, then moved to its own building in July 1880, in the same city. Today the BEP maintains a strong outreach to numismatists, including displays at conventions and the sale of sheets and souvenirs. A branch printing facility is maintained in Fort Worth, Texas.

C note—Nickname for a $100 bill.

charter number—Beginning in 1863, thousands of National Banks were chartered by the Treasury Department and were given charter numbers which were printed on the face of each note (beginning in the early 1870s, but not on the earlier National Bank Notes of the 1860s), in addition to the serial numbers. Charters for the earlier banks were for 19 years. Charters for later banks, 1864 to the early 1920s, were for 20 years and could be extended for a further 20 years, and extended again beyond that. Later, charters were made perpetual. Sometimes when a bank changed its name or even its geographical location, the same charter number was retained.

certified note—A note graded and placed in a sealed holder by a commercial grading service.

circulation (of a National Bank)—The total face value of a given National Bank's bills in circulation in commerce (not including notes held in the bank's vault or not yet issued). From 1863 to 1900, banks could issue bills up to 90% of their paid-in capital, with appropriate bonds or other acceptable securities given as collateral. From 1900 to 1935, banks could issue up to 100% of their capital. The collateral bonds earned interest.

Coin Note—Note from $1 to $1,000 issued in the Series of 1890 and 1891, redeemable in coins (silver or gold, at the option of the Treasury Department, but in practice the bearer could make the selection). These are called Treasury Notes or Coin Notes interchangeably. The backs of the Series of 1890 issues are particularly ornate.

Columbian Bank Note Company—Firm located in Washington, DC, which undertook contract printing for the backs of certain currency in the 1870s.

Compound Interest Treasury Note—Note from $10 to $1,000 issued in the early 1860s yielding interest to the bearer. One of several distinct United States currency series (see listings under individual denominations).

Comptroller of the Currency—Treasury Department appointed official in charge of paper-money distribution, the granting of National Bank charters, and related matters.

Continental Bank Note Company—Firm founded in 1862 in New York City. Provider by contract of certain federal currency in the 1860s through the mid-1870s.

counter—Technical name for the part of a note showing the denomination in a separate vignette, such as 5, 10, 20, and so forth.

counterfeit—A bill in imitation of an original design, but printed from false plates by someone not authorized by the Treasury Department.

Date Back—Describes certain Series of 1882 National Bank Notes with the dates 1882–1908 printed prominently on the back, or certain Blue Seal Series of 1902 National Bank Notes with the dates 1902 and 1908 printed on the back (in addition to other motifs).

Demand Note—Note of a denomination from $5 to $20 issued in 1861.

denomination—The face or stated value printed on a bill, this being the amount for which the bill could be redeemed in specie or exchanged for other bills. Denominations of federal bills in use in commerce include $1, $2, $5, $10, $20, $50, $100, $500, $1,000, $10,000, and $10,000. Denominations of Fractional Currency include 3¢, 5¢, 10¢, 15¢, 25¢, and 50¢.

deuce—Nickname for a $2 bill.

Educational Note—Name for any one of the $1, $2, and $5 Series of 1896 Silver Certificates with ornately engraved designs, among the most famous of all United States currency issues.

embossing—Refers to the raised printing on a note caused when damp paper is pressed into the recesses of a printing plate.

encased postage stamp—A regular federal postage stamp of a denomination from 1¢ to 90¢, enclosed within a brass frame with clear mica face. On the back of most, embossed in raised letters in brass, is the name of an advertiser. Patented by John Gault, and popular as a money substitute in 1862 and 1863. Often collected along with Fractional Currency.

face—The front side of a note, usually called the *face*, is the paper-money equivalent of *obverse* used for coins. The other side of a note is called the *back*. In Treasury records, sometimes *obverse* and *reverse* are used, but *face* and *back* are preferred by numismatists today.

Federal Reserve Bank Note—Note from $1 to $50 (Series of 1915 and 1918, large-size) and $5 to $100 (Series of 1929, small-size). Each bears the name of a Federal Reserve Bank (bolding imprinted across the center of the face on large-size notes) and a letter designating its district.

Federal Reserve Note—Note from $1 to $10,000 issued in large-size and small-size formats, Series of 1914 to the present day (the standard imprint on all of today's notes). Each bears the name of a Federal Reserve Bank and a letter designating its district.

First Charter Note—Term used to refer to National Bank Notes of the Original Series and Series of 1875.

Fort Worth (Western Facility)—Branch currency facility of the Bureau of Engraving and Printing established in Fort Worth, Texas in the late 19th century. Bills made there are imprinted FW at the face plate number.

Fractional Currency—Federal fractional bills made in denominations of 3¢, 5¢, 10¢, 15¢, 25¢, and 50¢, issued under the Act of March 3, 1863, succeeding Postage Currency notes.

Franklin—Nickname for a small-size $100 bill, from the portrait depicted.

Gold Certificate—Note from $10 to $10,000 issued in large-size and small-size formats, redeemable in gold coins. The backs of large-size notes were printed in gold color (and in green for small-size notes).

grade—Designation assigned to signify the amount of wear or circulation a note has experienced and its condition today (see the introduction for more information). Grading can be expressed by adjectives (such as Good, Extremely Fine, and Uncirculated), or by abbreviations in combination with numbers from 1 to 70 (adapted from the coin grading system), such as EF-40 or Unc-63.

Grand Watermelon Note—Numismatic nickname for the $1,000 Series of 1890 Treasury Notes (Coin Notes), with three zeros on the back in the form, fancifully, of watermelons. Also see *Watermelon Note*.

Green Eagle Note—Numismatic nickname for a Series of 1918 $1 Federal Reserve Bank Note with an eagle printed in green on the back.

greenback—Piece of paper money of $1 face value or higher with the back printed in green. Unofficial popular term for United States paper money in general, popularized by the Legal Tender Notes of the 1860s with their green backs (though these were not the first to be printed in this color), and widely used since.

Hawaii Note—Numismatic name for certain $1 Silver Certificates and $5, $10, and $20 Federal Reserve Notes with brown seals and HAWAII overprinted on both sides, issued in Hawaii during World War II.

Indian Chief Note—Numismatic nickname for the $5 Series of 1899 Silver Certificates depicting Indian Chief Running Antelope on the face.

Interest-Bearing Note—A note from $10 to $10,000 issued in the early 1860s, yielding interest to the bearer.

Jackass Note—Numismatic nickname for the $10 Series of 1869 Legal Tender Notes showing an eagle which, if turned upside down, resembles a jackass. This eagle motif was also used on certain other denominations and on Fractional Currency Shields.

launder—Term, often used in a derogatory sense, referring to the cleaning of paper money to enhance its appearance. In fact, careful cleaning, such as to remove grease or grime, can be beneficial, but should be done only by experts.

Lazy 2, Lazy deuce—Nicknames for an Original Series or Series of 1875 National Bank Note of the $2 denomination, which has a large 2 placed horizontally in a resting or "lazy" position.

Legal Tender Note—Note from $1 to $10,000 issued in large-size and small-size formats. For a long time Legal Tender Notes were the basic mainstay of the federal paper-money system. Synonym: *United States Note*.

legal-tender status—A.k.a. *obligation*. Information given in the lettered inscriptions on the back of a note, describing its exchangeability. As an example, certain early Legal Tender Notes have this inscription: "This note is a legal tender for all debts, public and private, except duties on imports and interest on the public debt, and is receivable in payment of all loans made to the United States."

margin—The blank area at the border of a note beyond the design or printed information. The width or amount of white space on a bill can affect its value. Generally, National Bank Notes of the 1863 to 1935 era were sent to banks in the form of uncut sheets, to be cut apart at their destination. Sometimes, especially in the 19th century, such cutting was done carelessly, resulting in uneven trimming or cutting into the border or design. The margins on Original Series and Series of 1875 $5 bills were very small, as printed on the plates, and these never have wide top and bottom margins. In contrast, many Legal Tender Notes and Silver Certificates of the 19th century have wide margins all around. There are no general rules.

Martha Washington Note—Numismatic nickname for the $1 Series of 1886 and 1891 Silver Certificates depicting the first of the nation's first ladies. Synonym: *Martha Note*.

National Bank—Commercial bank incorporated under the laws of the federal government and given a federal charter number, pursuant to the National Banking Act of 1863 and its amendments. Such banks were regulated by the Comptroller of the Currency, an officer of the Treasury Department.

National Bank Note—Note bearing the imprint of a specific National Bank and its location, plus the signature of bank officers, in addition to federal signatures and information. Original Series and Series of 1875 (nickname: "First Charter") issued in denominations from $1 to $1,000, large-size. Series of 1882 (nickname: "Second Charter") issued in denominations $5 to $100. Large-size. Series of 1902 (nickname: "Third Charter"), issued in denominations $5 to $100. Large-size. Series of 1929, issued in denominations $5 to $100, Type 1 and Type 2. Small-size.

National Bank Note Company—Firm founded in 1859 in New York City; a provider by contract of certain federal currency and Fractional Currency notes in the 1860s through the mid-1870s.

National Bank Note regional letter—From about 1902 to 1924, National Bank Notes had a large capital letter printed on the face to designate the region in which it was issued. This was to help Treasury Department personnel sort the notes when they were redeemed at a later date. The letters: N (New England banks); E (East); S (South); M (Midwest); W (West); P (Pacific district).

National Currency Bureau—In 1862, with Spencer M. Clark as its first director, the National Currency Bureau began operations in the attic of the west wing of the Treasury Building in Washington, DC. In time, its facilities were expanded there, including to the basement. The bureau's operations consisted of adding Treasury seals to bills printed by private contractors; later, the printing of certain Fractional Currency; and still later, the printing of currency of all denominations. It was succeeded by the Bureau of Engraving and Printing (see above) in the 1870s.

National Gold Bank Note—A note bearing the imprint of a specific National Bank and its location, plus the signature of bank officers, in addition to federal signatures and information. Issued in the early 1870s (in denominations of $5 to $100) by National Gold Banks located in the state of California. The reverse illustrates various gold coins (the same image used on all denominations). These notes were redeemable in gold coins.

note—A piece of paper money of $1 face value or higher. Synonym: *bill*.

obligation—See *legal-tender status*.

***Paper Money* magazine**—A magazine issued six times per year by the nonprofit Society of Paper Money Collectors.

pinhole—In the 19th century it was common practice to stitch several notes together for safekeeping, for hiding within a coat's lining, or storing in a small pile. Today, when certain notes are held to the light, tiny pinholes can be seen.

Plain Back—A description of certain blue-seal Series of 1902 National Bank Notes *without* the dates 1902 and 1908 printed on the back (such notes have other motifs, however).

plate information (letters and numbers)—*National Bank Notes:* These were printed on plates with two or four subjects (and, from 1929 and later, six subjects). Although there are exceptions, generally the first note *of a given denomination* is given the plate letter A, the second note, B, and so on. Thus, if a plate had a $1-$1-$1-$2 arrangement, $1 notes would be printed with plate letters A, B, and C, sometimes with the same serial number, and other times with different serial numbers. In instances in which the same serial number was used (as in Original Series National Bank Notes), there would be three $1 notes with the same serial, differing only by plate letter A, B, or C, while the single $2 note would have the same serial as well, and plate letter A. Small-size National Bank Notes have a combination letter and number on the face, such as K124. Beginning with the Series of 1882, most (but not all) National Bank Notes bore a tiny number on the back plate. *Other Notes:* All federal notes from $1 to $10,000 bear a plate letter on the front. Small-size notes have a letter plus a number. Beginning in the late 19th century, back plates were given numbers. *Numismatic notations:* Plate information for a given note with just a plate letter on the face can be given as A, B, C, and so forth. For notes with back plate numbers, the notation can be "Plate information: A/20," as an example. For a small-size note, an example is: "C73/278."

plate information (serial numbers)—On all federal notes $1 to $10,000, a Treasury Department serial number is printed once or twice on the face. On early notes this can be a number or a number in combination with one or more letters. For small-size notes, a combination of numbers and letters is used. The same serial numbers were used on different series and varieties of notes in the same era. Accordingly, the numbering system of Series of 1886 $5 Silver Certificates was independent of numbers used on Gold Certificates or National Bank Notes, and so on. *National Bank Notes:* On a 19th-century large-size National Bank Note, one of two numbers printed on the note is the Treasury Department serial. The other (usually lower and often in the range from 1 to 10,000) is the number in a sequence for the specific bank and denomination of a given bank-note type. An example is provided by a $10 Series of 1902, Date Back note from the First National Bank of West Derry (NH).

Records show that these bills were issued with serial numbers 1 to 1570 on plates arranged $10-$10-$10-$20, meaning that each plate had three $10 notes with the same serial plus one $20 note. The total number of $10 bills made was 4,710 (three times 1,570). Today, a bill in a private collection bears plate information E/74, bank serial number 275, and Treasury Department serial number H765723.

Poker Chip Note—Nickname for the Series of 1923 $10 Legal Tender Note. The 10 denomination, given twice on the back, is surrounded with a round frame.

Porthole Note—Numismatic nickname for the $5 Series of 1923 Silver Certificate with the portrait of Abraham Lincoln in a heavy frame fancifully resembling a ship's porthole.

Postage Currency—Federal fractional bills made in denominations of 5¢, 10¢, 25¢, and 50¢, and first issued in August 1862 to help alleviate a coin shortage. These were followed by Fractional Currency notes.

Professional Currency Dealers Association—A trade group, commonly known as PCDA, composed of paper-money dealers.

proof note—A proof (not capitalized in usage) note is an impression for test or other purposes, from a complete or partially complete plate, to illustrate its appearance. Such notes usually bear no serial numbers, or else just zeroes, and may be missing other elements, such as the Treasury seal and signatures. Proof notes are usually printed on only one side, and show either the front or back, but not both. Such proof notes are highly prized today. Synonym: *Specimen note* (usually capitalized as such). Specimen Fractional Currency notes, denominations 3¢ to 50¢, are sometimes called *proof notes*.

ragpicker—Nickname used years ago, less often now, for a collector of paper money.

Rainbow Note—Nickname for a Series of 1869 Legal Tender Note so called from the colorful face.

Refunding Certificate—Interest-bearing $10 certificate, not a currency note, issued in 1879 (see listing under $10 notes).

regional letter—See *National Bank Note regional letter.*

Second Charter Note—Numismatic term for Series of 1882 National Bank Notes.

security features—Aspects of the design or printing of a note intended to deter copying and counterfeiting. In early times this consisted of minute design elements expertly engraved, as well as printing on special paper (often with silk fibers embedded) ordered by the Treasury Department. In recent years other features have included watermark designs; color-shifting ink (which changes when a note is viewed from different angles); micro-printing; and the embedment of plastic strips.

series number on face of note—On early federal currency, such as Legal Tender Notes of the early 1860s, a series number such as Series 17 was added to the face of a note. The serial numbering machines went only to 99,999, and after that number was reached the figure 100,000 was hand-set, after which the counter was reset to 1 and a new series number was added. Accordingly, in Series 17 the 100,000 note was followed by Series 18 with serial number 1.

series of notes—Describes a type or class of currency, for large-size notes usually signifying a change in authorization or design, such as Series 1875 National Bank Notes and Series 1886 Silver Certificates. For small-size notes *series* typically signifies a change in signature combinations.

sheet of notes—An uncut group of notes, as printed, usually four subjects for large-size notes of 1861 to 1929; 12 subjects (cut apart into two six-subject sheets) for early small-size notes of the late 1920s and early 1930s; later 12 subjects; and today 36 subjects.

signatures on notes, Federal Reserve Bank officials—Federal Reserve Bank Notes bear the printed signatures of two Federal Reserve Bank officials, usually the cashier and governor, in addition to two Treasury officials.

signatures on notes, National Bank Notes—National Bank Notes of 1863 to 1935 bear the printed signatures of two Treasury Department officials plus signatures of the cashier and president of the National Bank. All early notes, to the 1890s, were required to be hand-signed in ink by the bank officials. Later, rubber-stamped signatures were permitted. In a very few instances later in the large-size note era, banks paid an extra amount and had the names of officials added to the printing plate. Most 20th-century bills were hand-signed or rubber-stamped. Small-size

National Bank Notes of 1929 to 1935 bear printed signatures of bank officials. In some instances another official signed for one or another bank position, such as assistant or acting cashier and vice president, noting this with an abbreviation such as "Asst.," in front of the printed word "Cashier," or "V" before the printed word "President," and so on.

signatures on notes, Treasury officials—Most federal currency of 1861 to date includes the signatures of two Treasury Department officials. Certainly very early notes were hand-signed by the officials or designated assistants. All others, constituting the vast majority, bear printed signatures. *Register of the Treasury and treasurer:* The first combination is of Lucius E. Chittenden, register of the Treasury, and F.E. Spinner, treasurer of the United States, who were in office jointly from April 17, 1861, to August 10, 1864. The last combination printed on notes was Edward E. Jones and Walter O. Woods, who served together from January 22, 1929, to May 31, 1933. *Secretary of the Treasury and treasurer:* In time, with some overlapping of use, notes bore the imprint of these two officials, the practice in use today. The first combination printed on currency was William G. McAdoo, register, and John Burke, treasurer, in office from April 1, 1913, to December 15, 1918.

Silver Certificate—A note from $1 to $1,000 issued in large-size and small-size formats, redeemable first in silver dollars, and later in silver bullion.

Silver Dollar Note—Numismatic nickname for the $5 Series of 1886 Silver Certificates depicting five Morgan silver dollars in a row on the back (four reverses and the center coin showing the obverse of an 1886 dollar), printed in green.

Society of Paper Money Collectors—A nonprofit organization, founded in 1961, devoted to the study and appreciation of currency. Publisher of *Paper Money*, a magazine issued six times per year.

Specimen note—Same as proof note (see above). Specimen Fractional Currency note: general term for a Fractional Currency bill printed on one side only, face or back, and made for distribution to collectors, these being popular in the era in which they were made, the 1860s and 1870s. Usually capitalized, as Specimen.

stamp—Derisive nickname used by the public in the 1860s and 1870s for Fractional Currency notes.

star note—A large-size (beginning with silver certificates in 1910 and soon expanded to include all other series) or small-size note with a star next to the serial number is a replacement note, made after the first note with this number was found to be defective and then destroyed. "Star notes" form a collecting specialty, especially for small-size notes. Stars added to serial numbers before 1910 are decorative and without meaning (examples including Series of 1890 Coin or Treasury Notes).

Technicolor Note—Later numismatic nickname (employed from the 1930s to date) for the Series of 1905 large-size Gold Certificates. The face of these notes is colorful, with part of the inscription in gold ink and with gold tint to part of the paper, and *red Treasury seal* and serial numbers. Nickname derived from a patented process for color motion picture film.

Third Charter Note—Numismatic term for Series of 1902 National Bank Notes.

tinted paper—While most notes were printed on white paper, exceptions included certain issues of the late 1860s through part of the 1870s ("Rainbow Notes" in the Series of 1869 Legal Tender series, Fractional Currency, certain National Bank Notes of the era), with an area of blue tint in the paper; National Gold Bank Notes of the early 1870s, on yellow-tinted paper; and the Series of 1905 Gold Certificates.

Tombstone Note—Numismatic nickname for the $1 Series of 1886, 1891, and 1908 Silver Certificates with the portrait of the recently (1885) deceased Vice President Thomas A. Hendricks in a frame resembling the outline of a tombstone, perhaps created unintentionally.

Treasury Department—Branch of the United States government that operates the Bureau of Engraving and Printing, Federal Reserve System, Secret Service, the coinage mints, and other monetary bureaus.

Treasury Note—Same as *Coin Note* (see above).

Treasury seal—Emblem of the Treasury Department; circular, sometimes with an ornate border, and varying in size and color, as used on the face of all federal currency $1 upward from 1862 to the present, as well as the Fourth and Fifth issues of Fractional Currency. The basic motif is of a pair of scales above and a key below, with inscription surrounding. The Treasury seal style can create collectible varieties, e.g. Series of 1886 Silver Certificates with Rosecrans-Nebeker Treasury signatures exist with a large brown Treasury seal (Friedberg-220) and a small red scalloped Treasury seal (F-221).

United States Note—Same as *Legal Tender Note* (see above).

Value Back—Describes certain Series of 1882 National Bank Notes on which the denomination is printed in green on the back, spelled out, as FIVE DOLLARS, TEN DOLLARS, and so forth.

vignette—Pronounced "vinn yet." An ornamental or illustrative element of a bank note, such as a portrait, allegorical scene, or motif from history. For example, the Series of 1902 $100 National Bank Note bears a vignette of John J. Knox on its face and another of two men, a shield, and an eagle on the back.

Watermelon Note—Numismatic nickname for the $100 Series of 1890 Treasury Notes (Coin Notes) with two zeros on the back in the fanciful form, fancifully, of watermelons. Also see *Grand Watermelon Note.*

Western Facility—Branch currency facility of the Bureau of Engraving and Printing established at Fort Worth, Texas, in the late 19th century. Bills made there are imprinted FW at the face plate number.

BASIC BIBLIOGRAPHY
AND SUGGESTED READING

While there are dozens of books, past and present, on federal currency, the following are some of the basic texts used in connection with the present work. These are also recommended for addition to any numismatic library.

Bank Note Reporter, monthly magazine by F+W Publications.

Coin World's Paper Money Values, bimonthly magazine published by Amos Press, Inc.

Friedberg, Arthur L., and Ira S. Friedberg. *Paper Money of the United States.* 19th ed. Clifton, NJ: Coin & Currency Institute, 2010.

Gengerke, Martin. *U.S. Paper Money Records.* CD-ROM. 2007.

Hessler, Gene, and Carlson Chambliss. *The Comprehensive Catalog of U.S. Paper Money: All United States Federal Currency Since 1812.* 7th ed. Port Clinton, OH: BNR Press, 2006.

Huntoon, Peter. *United States Large-Size National Bank Notes.* Laramie, WY: Society of Paper Money Collectors, 1995.

Kelly, Don C. *National Bank Notes* and supplemental data CD. 5th ed. Oxford, OH: Paper Money Institute, 2006.

Paper Money, the bimonthly journal of the Society of Paper Money Collectors.

RCMS Inc. Track & Price™ computer software. http://www.currencyinventory.com.

Schwartz, John, and Scott Lindquist. *Standard Guide to Small-Size U.S. Paper Money: 1928 to Date.* 7th ed. Iola, WI: Krause, 2006.